FIRE FORCE

ATSUSHI OHKUBO

21

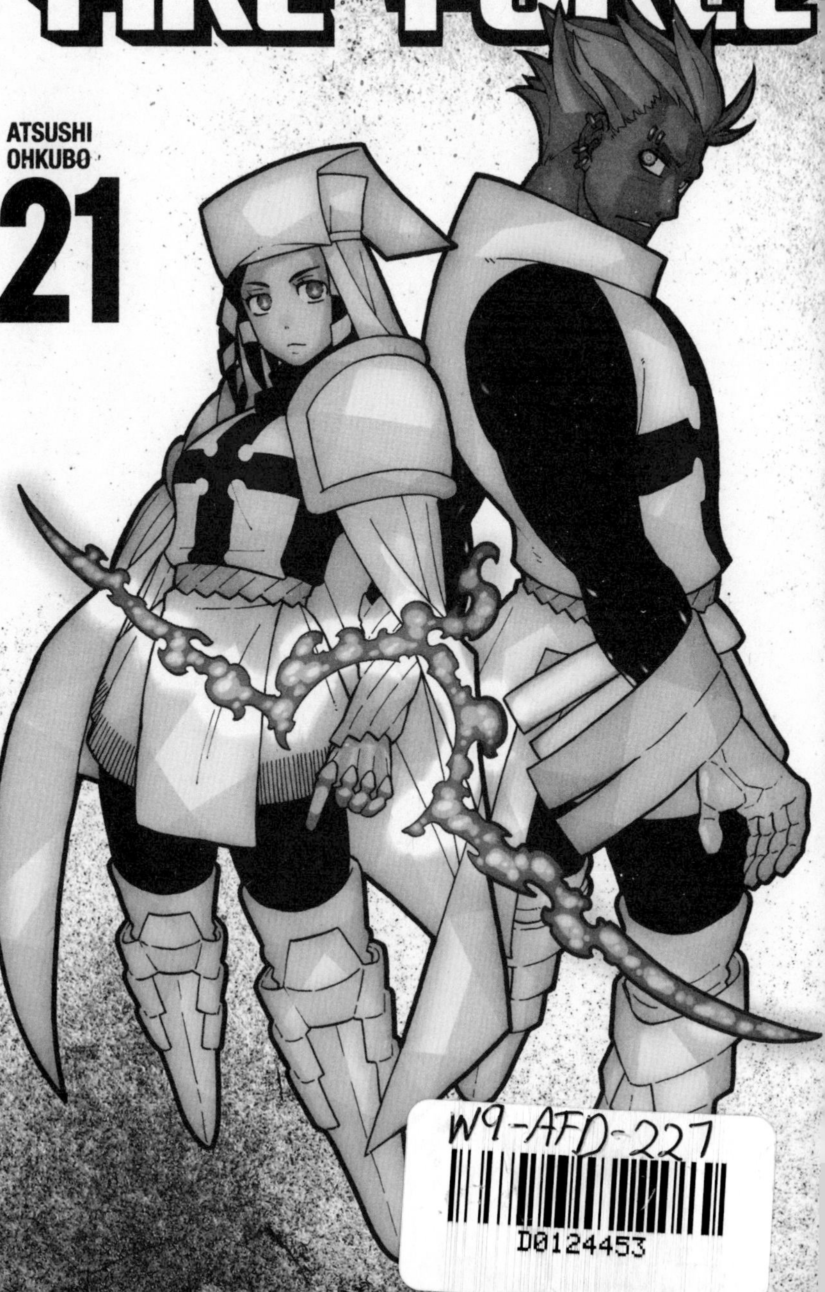

A Kodansha Comics Trade Paperback Original
Fire Force 21 copyright © 2019 Atsushi Ohkubo
English translation copyright © 2020 Atsushi Ohkubo

Published in the United States by Kodansha Comics, an imprint of Kodansha USA Publishing, LLC, New York.

Publication rights for this English edition arranged through Kodansha Ltd., Tokyo.

First published in Japan in 2019 by Kodansha Ltd., Tokyo.

ISBN 978-1-64651-041-2

Printed in the United States of America.

www.kodansha.us

9 8 7 6 5 4
Translation: Alethea Nibley & Athena Nibley
Lettering: AndWorld Design
Editing: Ryan Holmberg
Kodansha Comics edition cover design by Phil Balsman

Publisher: Kiichiro Sugawara

Director of publishing services: Ben Applegate
Associate director of operations: Stephen Pakula
Publishing services managing editor: Noelle Webster
Assistant production manager: Emi Lotto, Angela Zurlo

Jailhouse Let's

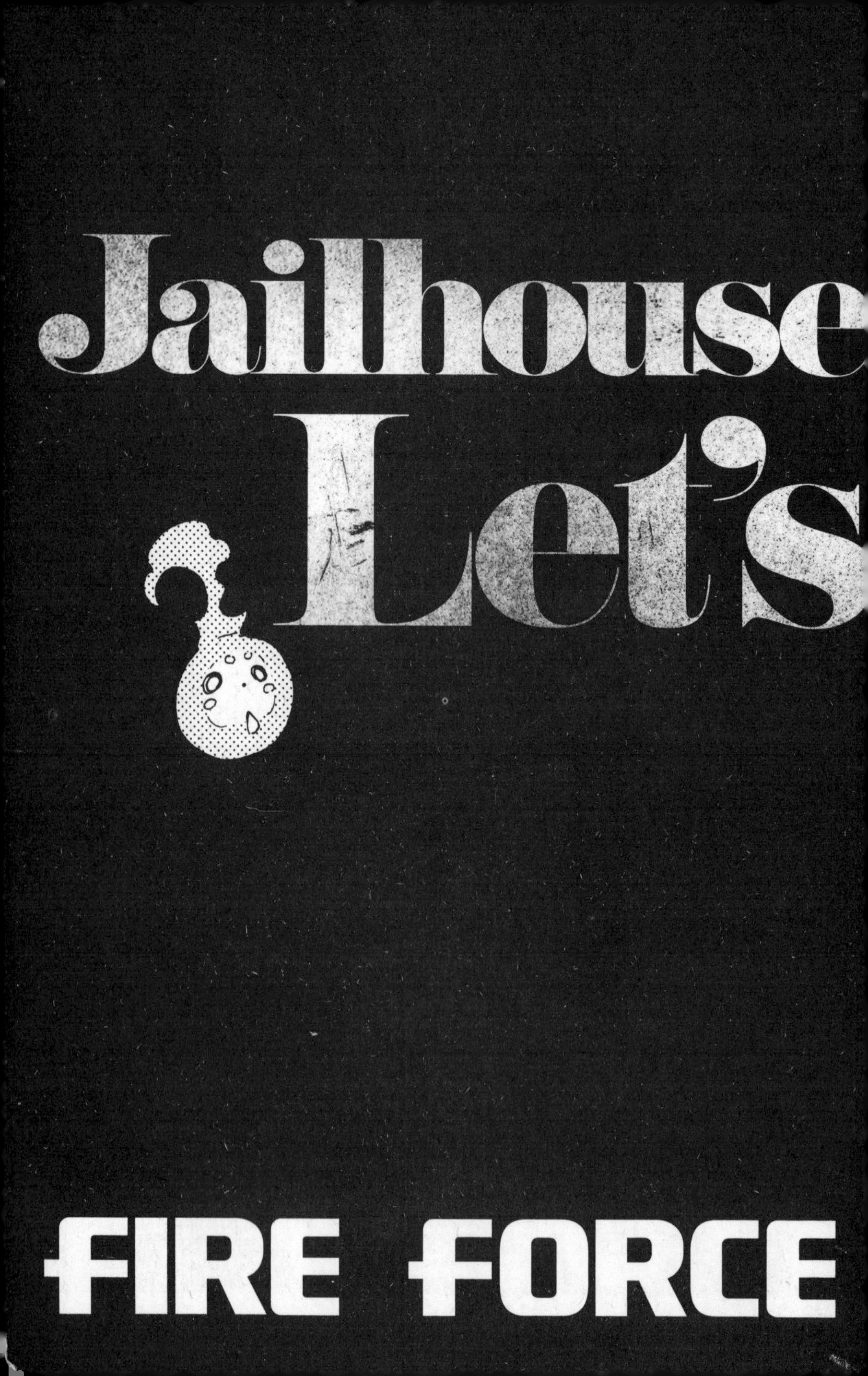

FIRE FORCE

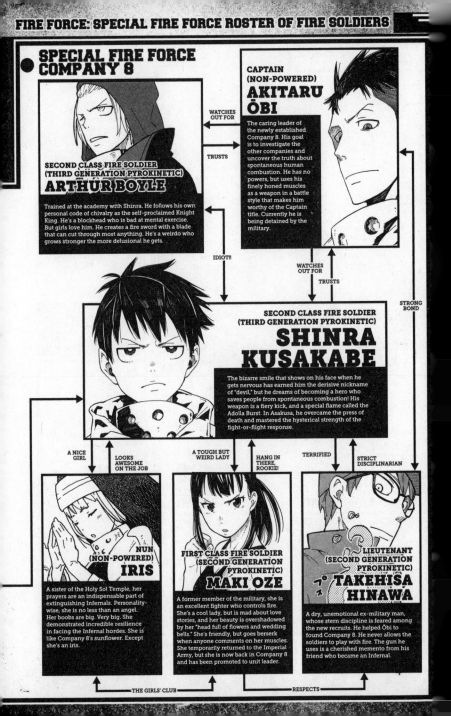

SPECIAL FIRE FORCE COMPANY 8

SECOND CLASS FIRE SOLDIER (THIRD GENERATION PYROKINETIC) ARTHUR BOYLE

Trained at the academy with Shinra. He follows his own personal code of chivalry as the self-proclaimed Knight King. He's a blockhead who is bad at mental exercise. But girls love him. He creates a fire sword with a blade that can cut through most anything. He's a weirdo who grows stronger the more delusional he gets.

CAPTAIN (NON-POWERED) AKITARU ŌBI

The caring leader of the newly established Company 8. His goal is to investigate the other companies and uncover the truth about spontaneous human combustion. He has no powers, but uses his finely honed muscles as a weapon in a battle style that makes him worthy of the Captain title. Currently he is being detained by the military.

WATCHES OUT FOR

TRUSTS

IDIOT!!

WATCHES OUT FOR

TRUSTS

STRONG BOND

SECOND CLASS FIRE SOLDIER (THIRD GENERATION PYROKINETIC) SHINRA KUSAKABE

The bizarre smile that shows on his face when he gets nervous has earned him the derisive nickname of "devil," but he dreams of becoming a hero who saves people from spontaneous combustion! His weapon is a fiery kick, and a special flame called the Adolla Burst. In Asakusa, he overcame the press of death and mastered the hysterical strength of the fight-or-flight response.

A NICE GIRL

LOOKS AWESOME ON THE JOB

A TOUGH BUT WEIRD LADY

HANG IN THERE, ROOKIE!

TERRIFIED

STRICT DISCIPLINARIAN

NUN (NON-POWERED) IRIS

A sister of the Holy Sol Temple, her prayers are an indispensable part of extinguishing Infernals. Personality-wise, she is no less than an angel. Her boobs are big. Very big. She demonstrated incredible resilience in facing the Infernal hordes. She is like Company 8's sunflower. Except she's an iris.

FIRST CLASS FIRE SOLDIER (SECOND GENERATION PYROKINETIC) MAKI OZE

A former member of the military, she is an excellent fighter who controls fire. She's a cool lady, but is mad about love stories, and her beauty is overshadowed by her "head full of flowers and wedding bells." She's friendly, but goes berserk when anyone comments on her muscles. She temporarily returned to the Imperial Army, but she is now back in Company 8 and has been promoted to unit leader.

LIEUTENANT (SECOND GENERATION PYROKINETIC) TAKEHISA HINAWA

A dry, unemotional ex-military man, whose stern discipline is feared among the new recruits. He helped Ōbi to found Company 8. He never allows the soldiers to play with fire. The gun he uses is a cherished memento from his friend who became an Infernal.

THE GIRLS' CLUB

RESPECTS

HOLY SOL TEMPLE + "EVANGELIST"

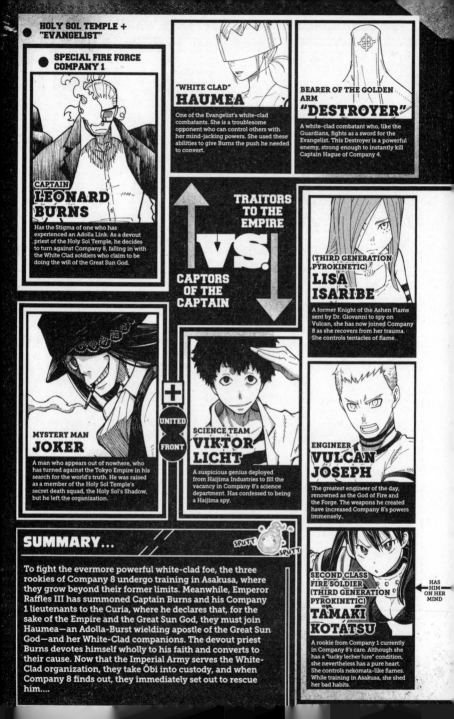

SPECIAL FIRE FORCE COMPANY 1

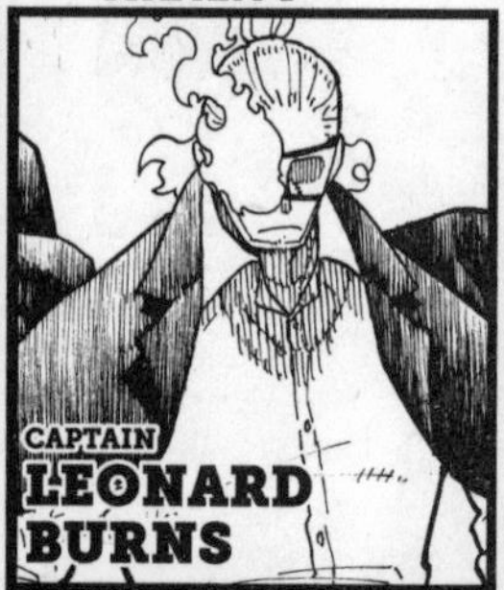

CAPTAIN
LEONARD BURNS

Has the Stigma of one who has experienced an Adolla Link. As a devout priest of the Holy Sol Temple, he decides to turn against Company 8, falling in with the White Clad soldiers who claim to be doing the will of the Great Sun God.

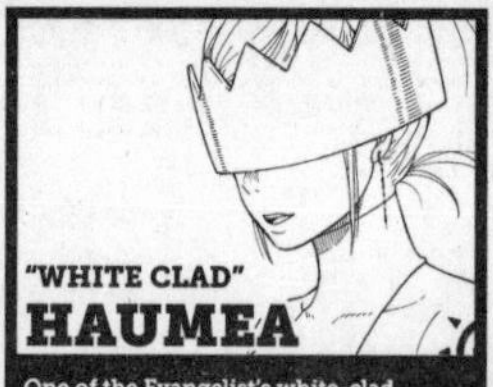

"WHITE CLAD"
HAUMEA

One of the Evangelist's white-clad combatants. She is a troublesome opponent who can control others with her mind-jacking powers. She used these abilities to give Burns the push he needed to convert.

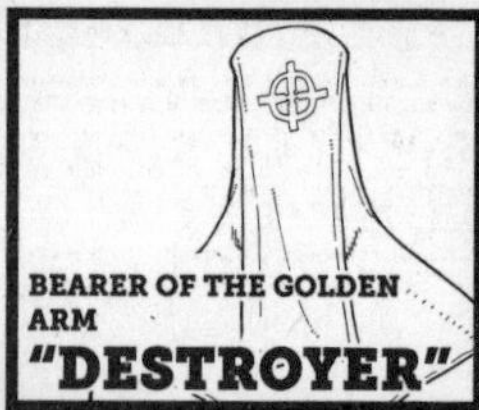

BEARER OF THE GOLDEN ARM
"DESTROYER"

A white-clad combatant who, like the Guardians, fights as a sword for the Evangelist. This Destroyer is a powerful enemy, strong enough to instantly kill Captain Hague of Company 4.

TRAITORS TO THE EMPIRE

VS.

CAPTORS OF THE CAPTAIN

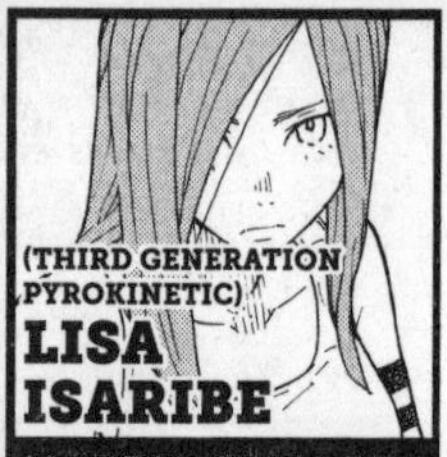

(THIRD GENERATION PYROKINETIC)
LISA ISARIBE

A former Knight of the Ashen Flame sent by Dr. Giovanni to spy on Vulcan, she has now joined Company 8 as she recovers from her trauma. She controls tentacles of flame.

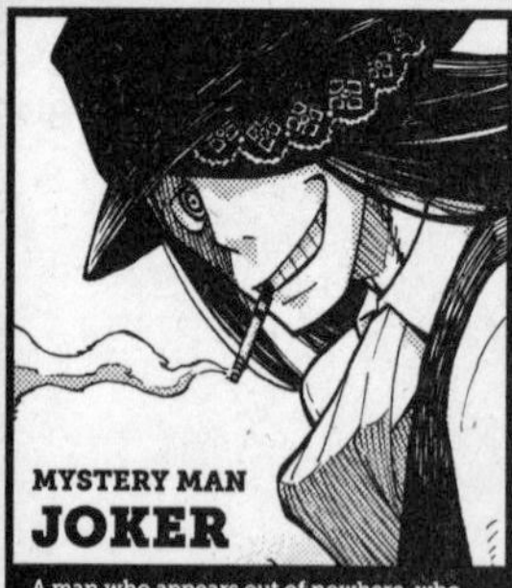

MYSTERY MAN
JOKER

A man who appears out of nowhere, who has turned against the Tokyo Empire in his search for the world's truth. He was raised as a member of the Holy Sol Temple's secret death squad, the Holy Sol's Shadow, but he left the organization.

+ UNITED 8 FRONT

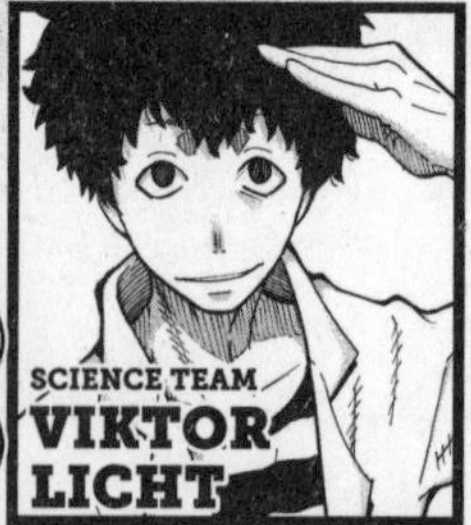

SCIENCE TEAM
VIKTOR LICHT

A suspicious genius deployed from Haijima Industries to fill the vacancy in Company 8's science department. Has confessed to being a Haijima spy.

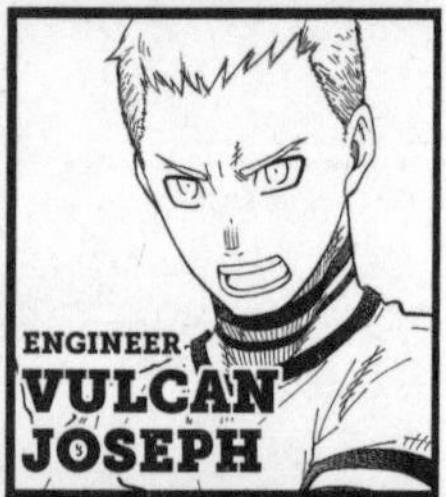

ENGINEER
VULCAN JOSEPH

The greatest engineer of the day, renowned as the God of Fire and the Forge. The weapons he created have increased Company 8's powers immensely.

SUMMARY...

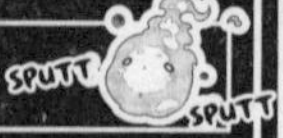
SPUTT
SPUTT

To fight the evermore powerful white-clad foe, the three rookies of Company 8 undergo training in Asakusa, where they grow beyond their former limits. Meanwhile, Emperor Raffles III has summoned Captain Burns and his Company 1 lieutenants to the Curia, where he declares that, for the sake of the Empire and the Great Sun God, they must join Haumea—an Adolla-Burst wielding apostle of the Great Sun God—and her White-Clad companions. The devout priest Burns devotes himself wholly to his faith and converts to their cause. Now that the Imperial Army serves the White-Clad organization, they take Ōbi into custody, and when Company 8 finds out, they immediately set out to rescue him....

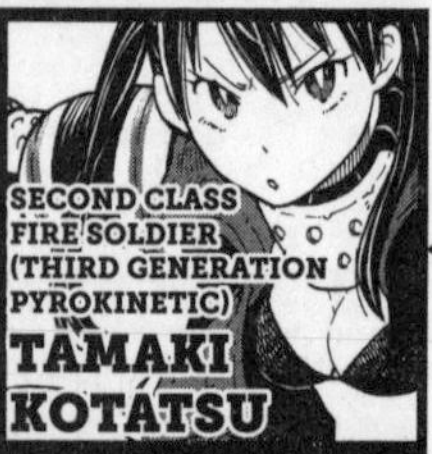

SECOND CLASS FIRE SOLDIER (THIRD GENERATION PYROKINETIC)
TAMAKI KOTATSU

A rookie from Company 1 currently in Company 8's care. Although she has a "lucky lecher lure" condition, she nevertheless has a pure heart. She controls nekomata-like flames. While training in Asakusa, she shed her bad habits.

← HAS HIM ON HER MIND

FIRE FORCE 21

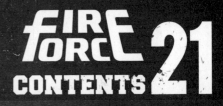

CONTENTS

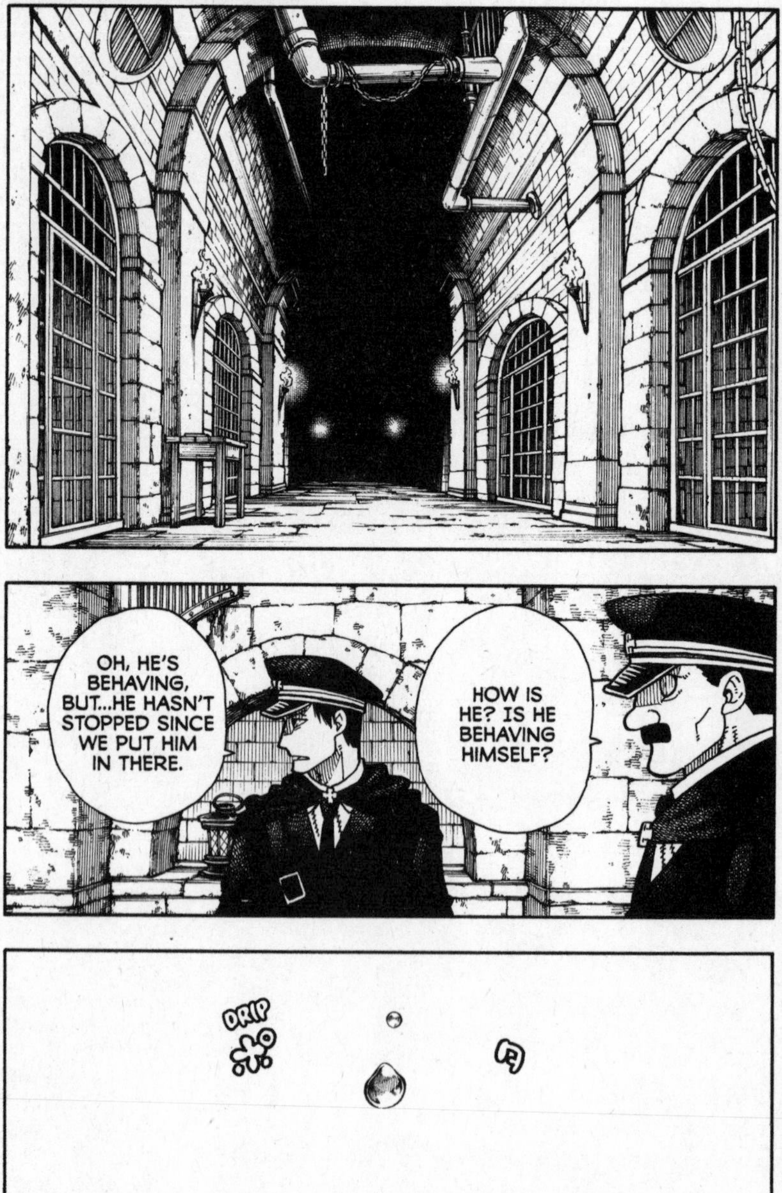
HOW IS HE? IS HE BEHAVING HIMSELF?
OH, HE'S BEHAVING, BUT...HE HASN'T STOPPED SINCE WE PUT HIM IN THERE.
DRIP

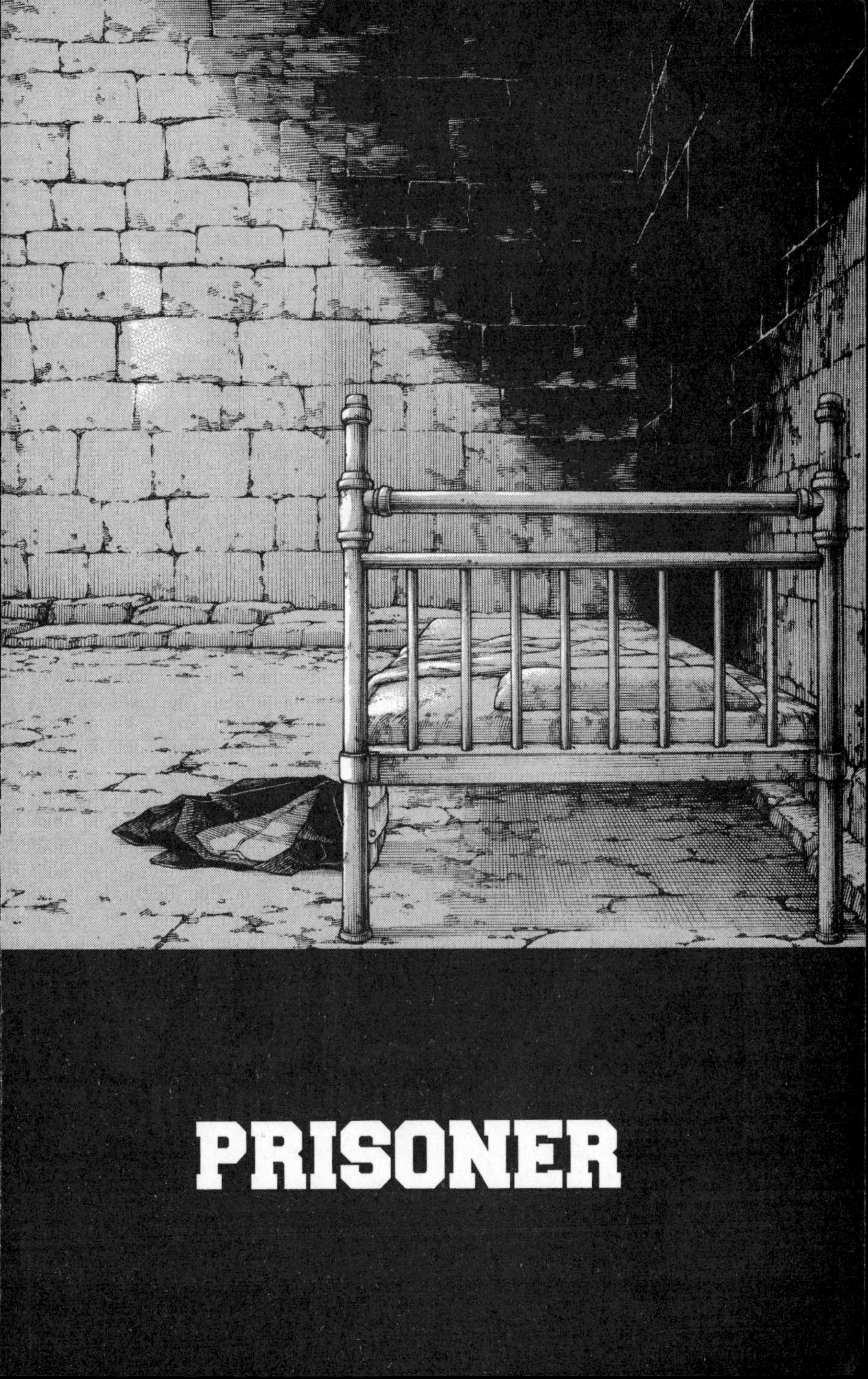

PRISONER

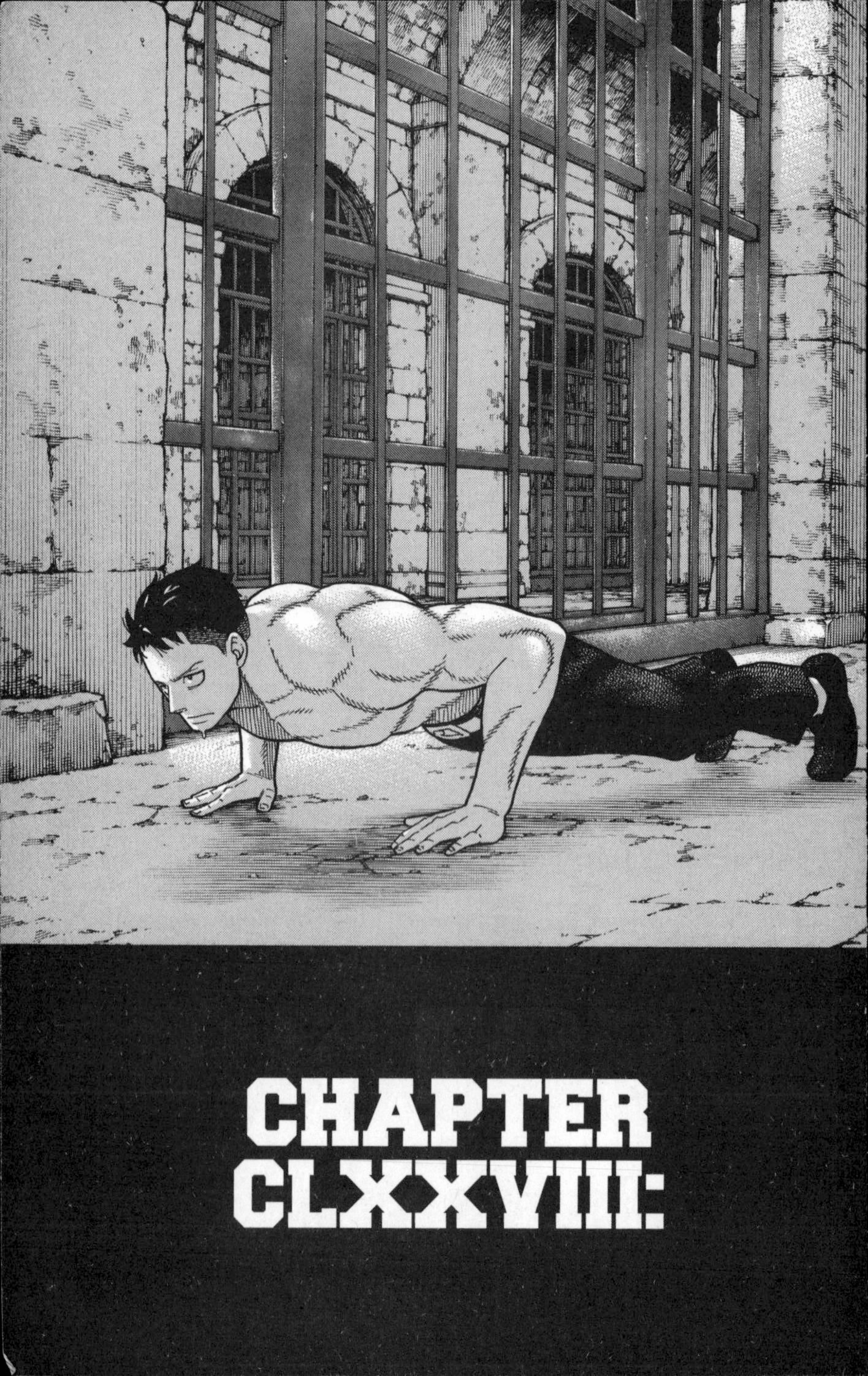

CHAPTER CLXXVIII:

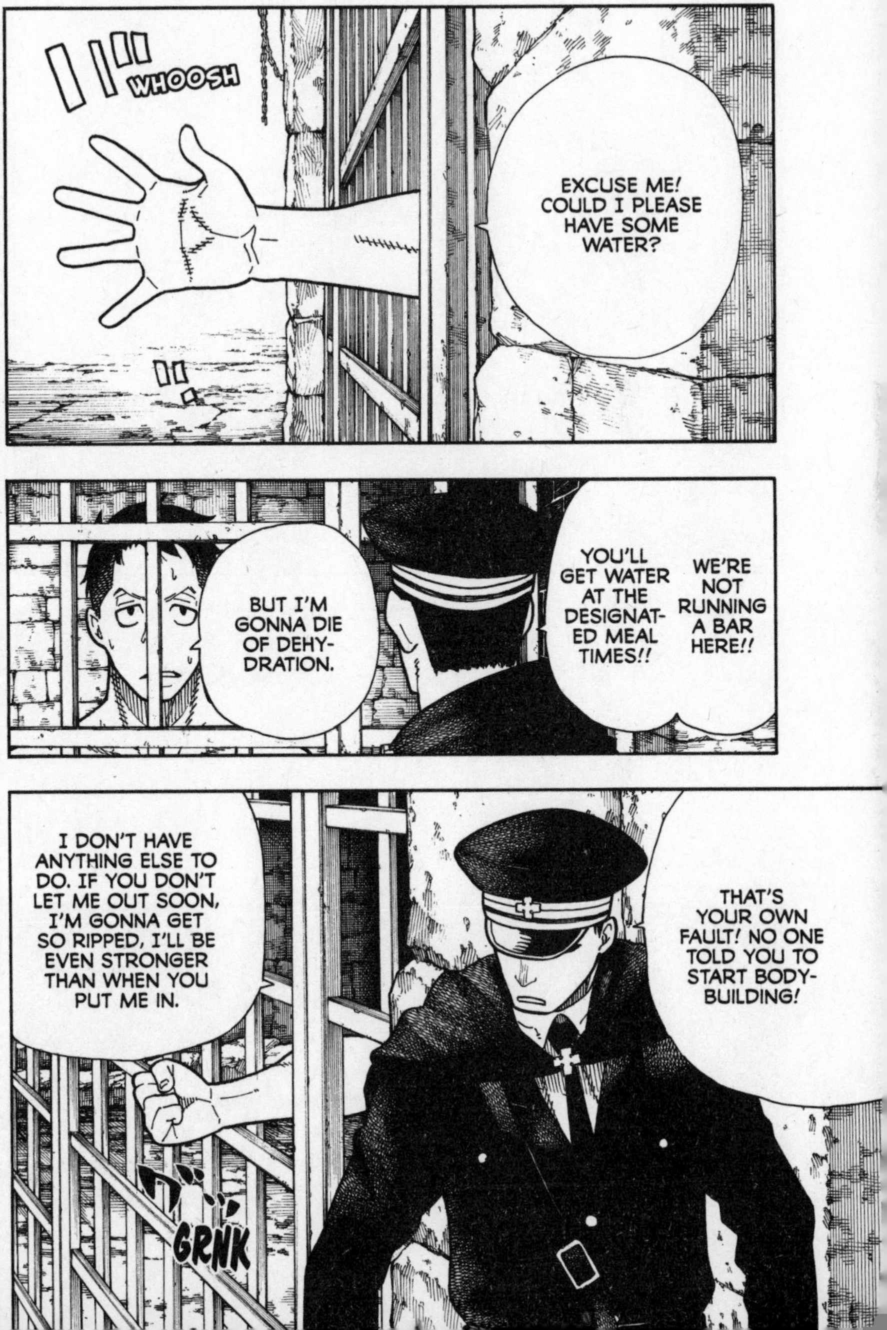
WHOOSH
EXCUSE ME! COULD I PLEASE HAVE SOME WATER?
WE'RE NOT RUNNING A BAR HERE!!
YOU'LL GET WATER AT THE DESIGNAT-ED MEAL TIMES!!
BUT I'M GONNA DIE OF DEHY-DRATION.
THAT'S YOUR OWN FAULT! NO ONE TOLD YOU TO START BODY-BUILDING!
I DON'T HAVE ANYTHING ELSE TO DO. IF YOU DON'T LET ME OUT SOON, I'M GONNA GET SO RIPPED, I'LL BE EVEN STRONGER THAN WHEN YOU PUT ME IN.
GRNK

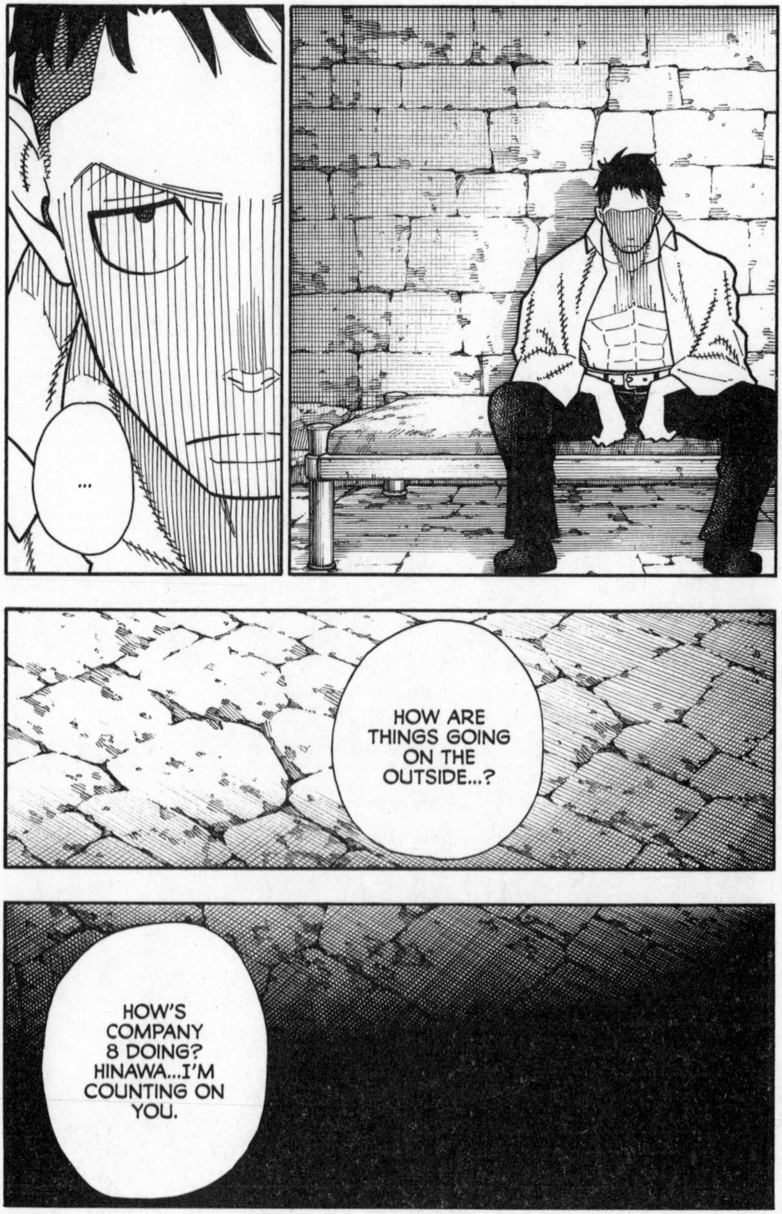
...
HOW ARE THINGS GOING ON THE OUTSIDE...?
HOW'S COMPANY 8 DOING? HINAWA...I'M COUNTING ON YOU.

SPECIAL FIRE FORCE CAPTAIN ARRESTED
AKITARU ŌBI (31) UNDER ARREST
AND IN TODAY'S NEWS, SPECIAL FIRE FORCE COMPANY 8 CAPTAIN AKITARU ŌBI HAS BEEN ARRESTED ON SUSPICION OF...
...KIDNAPPING AND IMPRISONING ONE SHINRA KUSAKABE, A WIELDER OF THE SACRED FLAME COMMONLY KNOWN AS THE ADOLLA BURST.
IT IS ALSO BELIEVED THAT THE OTHER MEMBERS OF SPECIAL FIRE FORCE COMPANY 8 HAVE TAKEN SHINRA KUSAKABE AND FLED.
KIDNAPPING A GUY WITH THE SACRED FLAME AND LOCKING HIM UP...
IT WAS AN OFFICIAL FIRE FORCE COMPANY, TOO. THIS IS A SCARY WORLD WE LIVE IN.

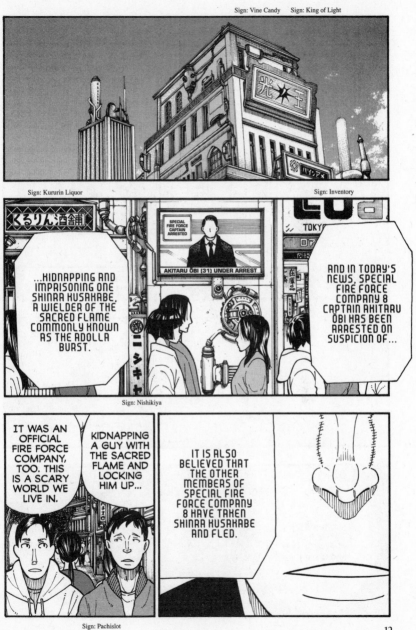

Sign: Vine Candy Sign: King of Light

Sign: Kururin Liquor Sign: Inventory

Sign: Nishikiya

Sign: Pachislot

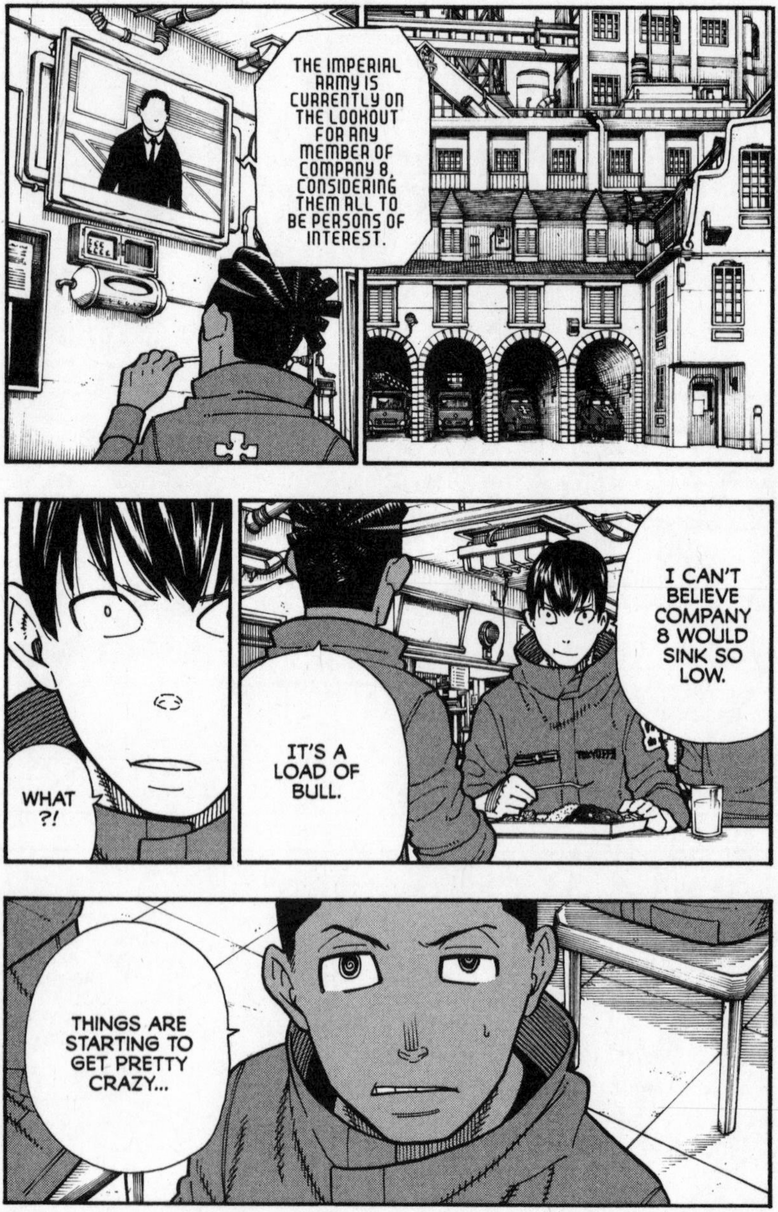
THE IMPERIAL ARMY IS CURRENTLY ON THE LOOKOUT FOR ANY MEMBER OF COMPANY 8, CONSIDERING THEM ALL TO BE PERSONS OF INTEREST.
I CAN'T BELIEVE COMPANY 8 WOULD SINK SO LOW.
IT'S A LOAD OF BULL.
WHAT ?!
THINGS ARE STARTING TO GET PRETTY CRAZY...

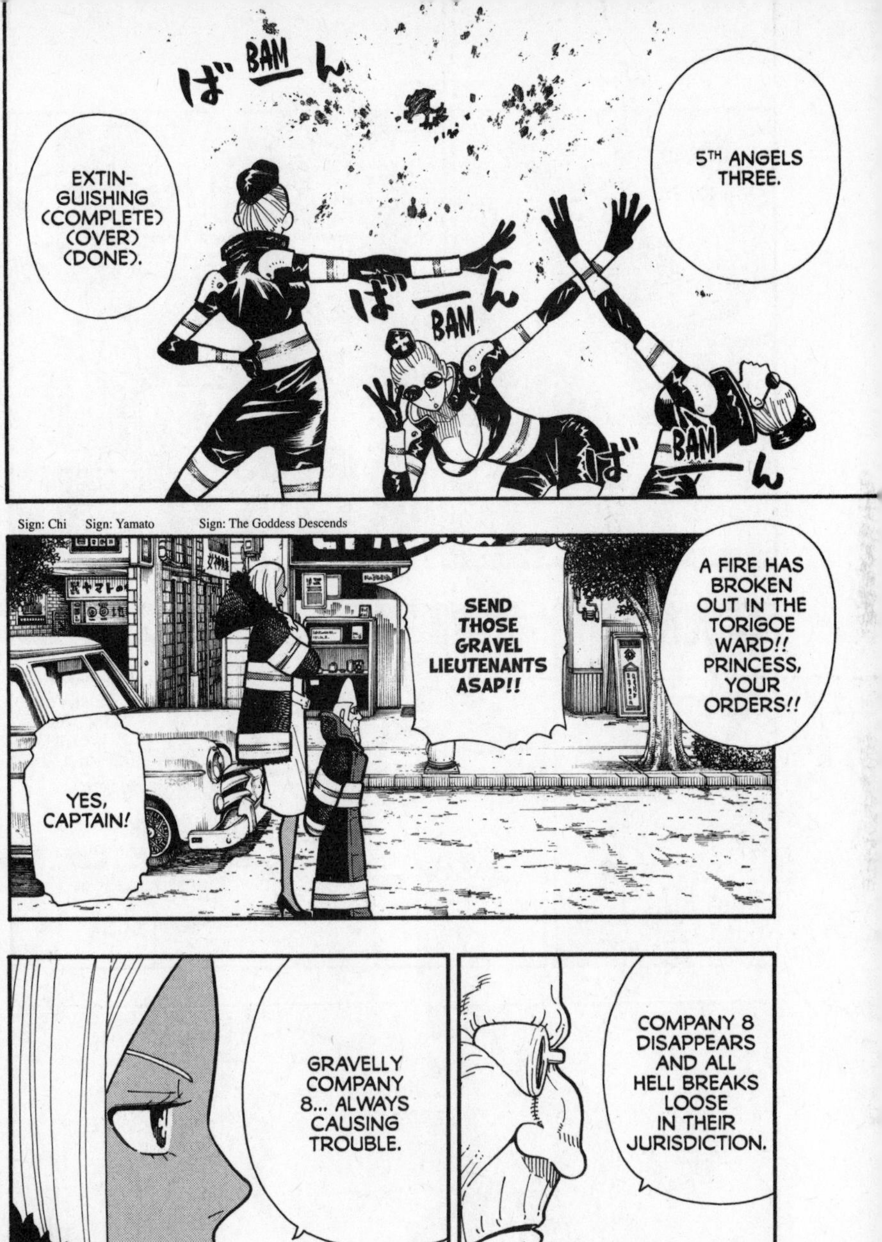
ばBAMん
5TH ANGELS THREE.
ばBAMん
EXTIN-GUISHING (COMPLETE) (OVER) (DONE).
ばBAMん
Sign: Chi Sign: Yamato Sign: The Goddess Descends
A FIRE HAS BROKEN OUT IN THE TORIGOE WARD!! PRINCESS, YOUR ORDERS!!
SEND THOSE GRAVEL LIEUTENANTS ASAP!!
YES, CAPTAIN!
COMPANY 8 DISAPPEARS AND ALL HELL BREAKS LOOSE IN THEIR JURISDICTION.
GRAVELLY COMPANY 8... ALWAYS CAUSING TROUBLE.

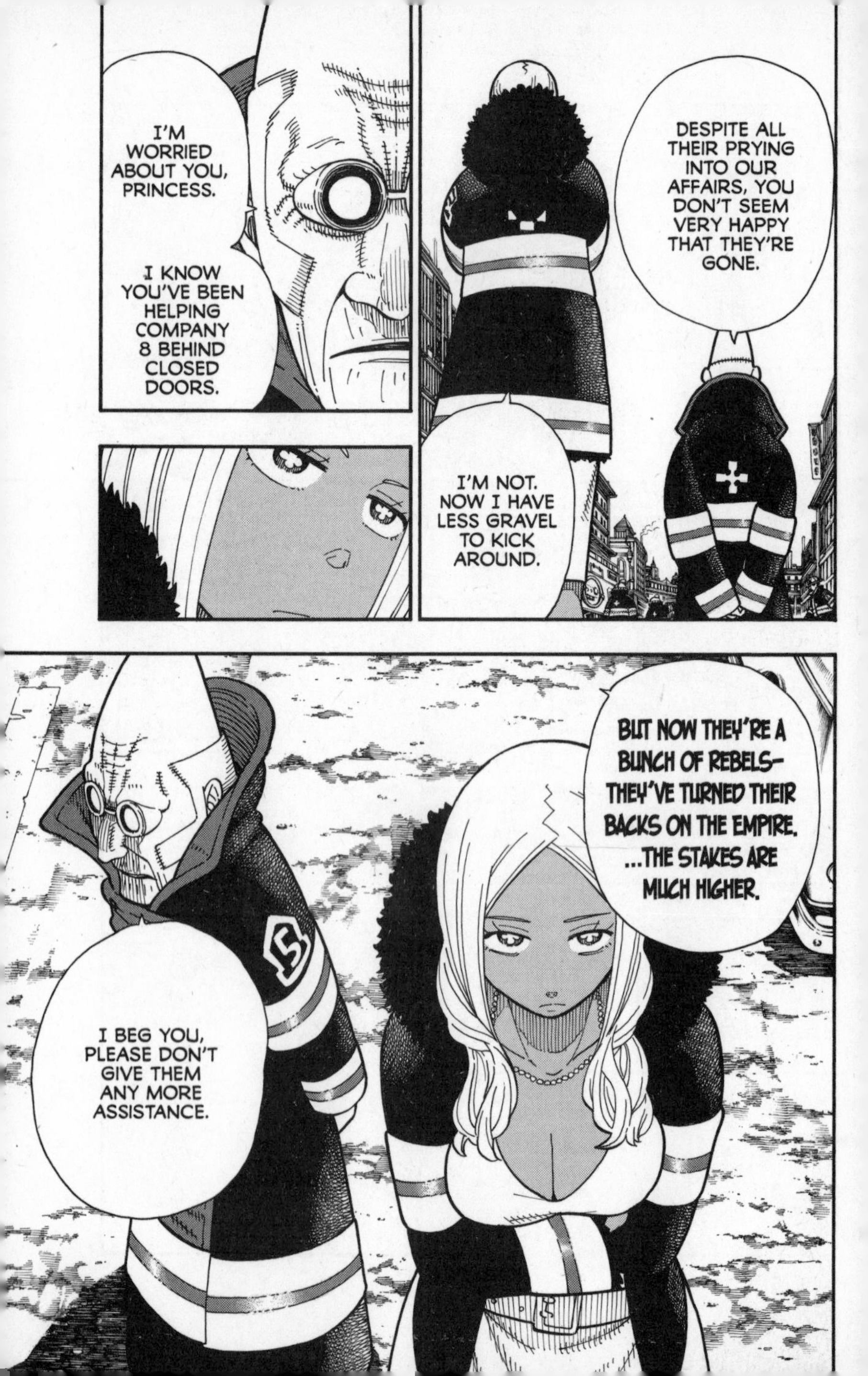
DESPITE ALL THEIR PRYING INTO OUR AFFAIRS, YOU DON'T SEEM VERY HAPPY THAT THEY'RE GONE.
I'M NOT. NOW I HAVE LESS GRAVEL TO KICK AROUND.
I'M WORRIED ABOUT YOU, PRINCESS.
I KNOW YOU'VE BEEN HELPING COMPANY 8 BEHIND CLOSED DOORS.
BUT NOW THEY'RE A BUNCH OF REBELS— THEY'VE TURNED THEIR BACKS ON THE EMPIRE. ...THE STAKES ARE MUCH HIGHER.
I BEG YOU, PLEASE DON'T GIVE THEM ANY MORE ASSISTANCE.

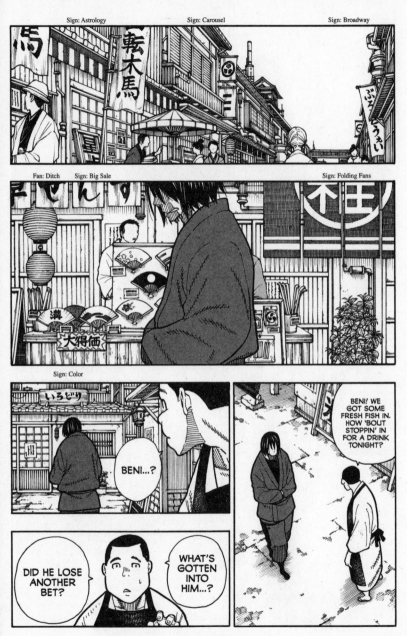

Sign: Broadway
Sign: Carousel
Sign: Astrology
Sign: Folding Fans
Sign: Big Sale
Fan: Ditch
BENI! WE GOT SOME FRESH FISH IN. HOW 'BOUT STOPPIN' IN FOR A DRINK TONIGHT?
Sign: Color
BENI...?
WHAT'S GOTTEN INTO HIM...?
DID HE LOSE ANOTHER BET?

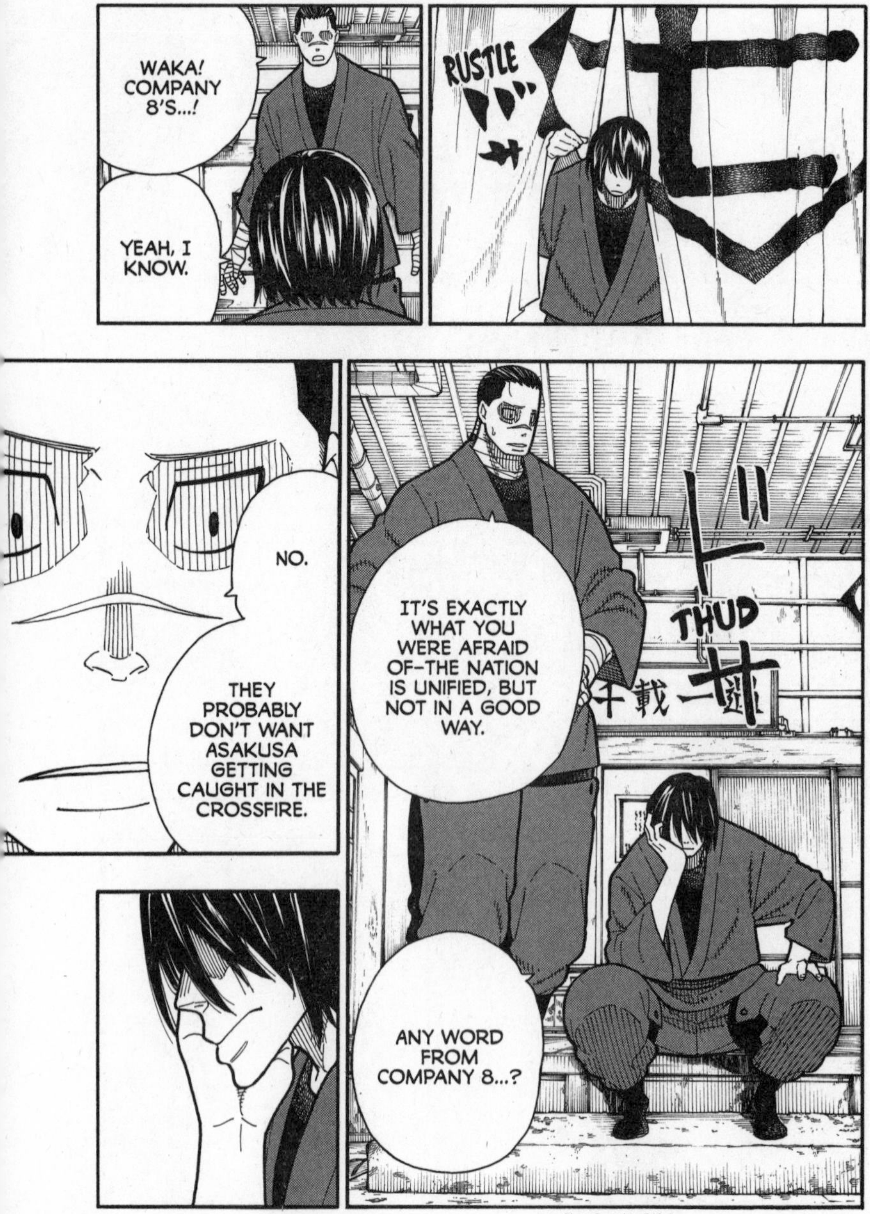
RUSTLE
WAKA! COMPANY 8'S...!
YEAH, I KNOW.
THUD
IT'S EXACTLY WHAT YOU WERE AFRAID OF–THE NATION IS UNIFIED, BUT NOT IN A GOOD WAY.
ANY WORD FROM COMPANY 8...?
NO.
THEY PROBABLY DON'T WANT ASAKUSA GETTING CAUGHT IN THE CROSSFIRE.
Sign: Once in a Lifetime

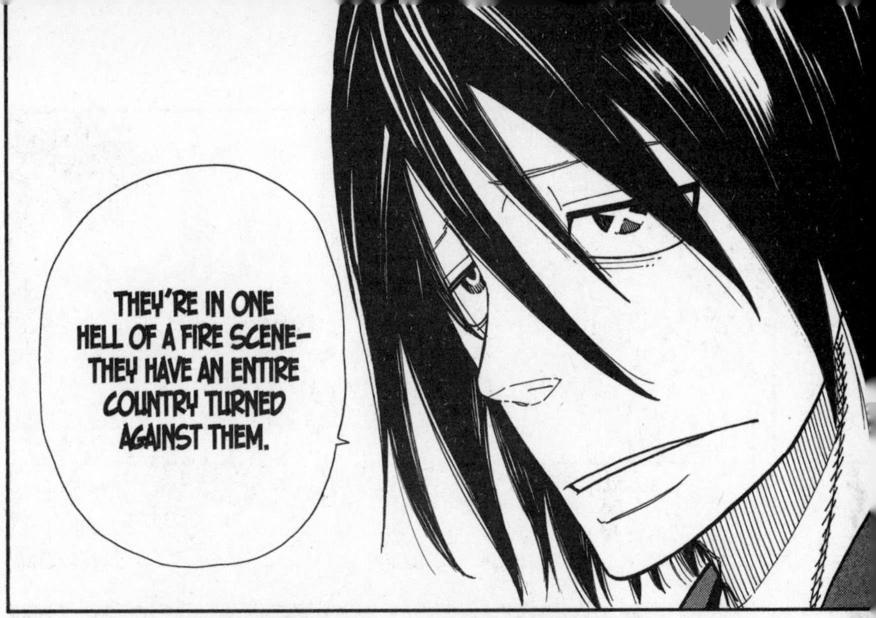
THEY'RE IN ONE HELL OF A FIRE SCENE– THEY HAVE AN ENTIRE COUNTRY TURNED AGAINST THEM.

Sign: Liquor

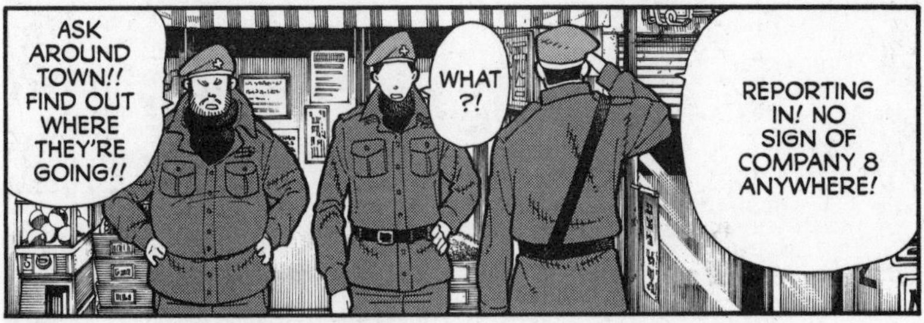
REPORTING IN! NO SIGN OF COMPANY 8 ANYWHERE!
WHAT?!
ASK AROUND TOWN!! FIND OUT WHERE THEY'RE GOING!!

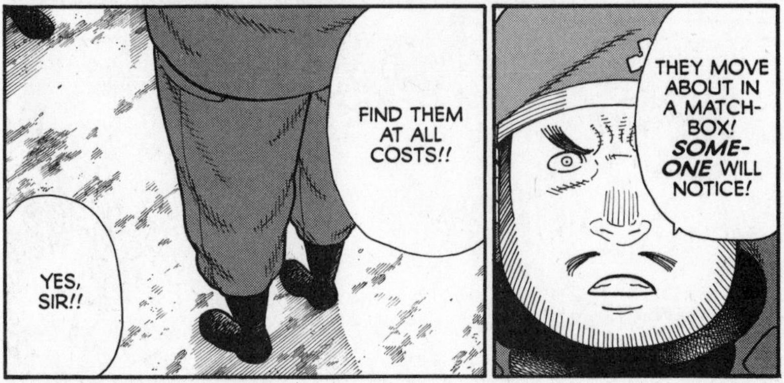
THEY MOVE ABOUT IN A MATCH-BOX! *SOME-ONE* WILL NOTICE!
FIND THEM AT ALL COSTS!!
YES, SIR!!

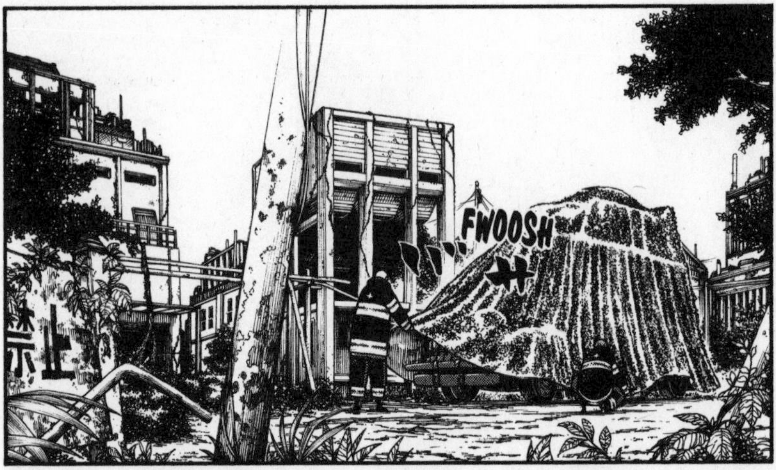
FWOOSH

Sign: No Trespassing

Sign: Danger

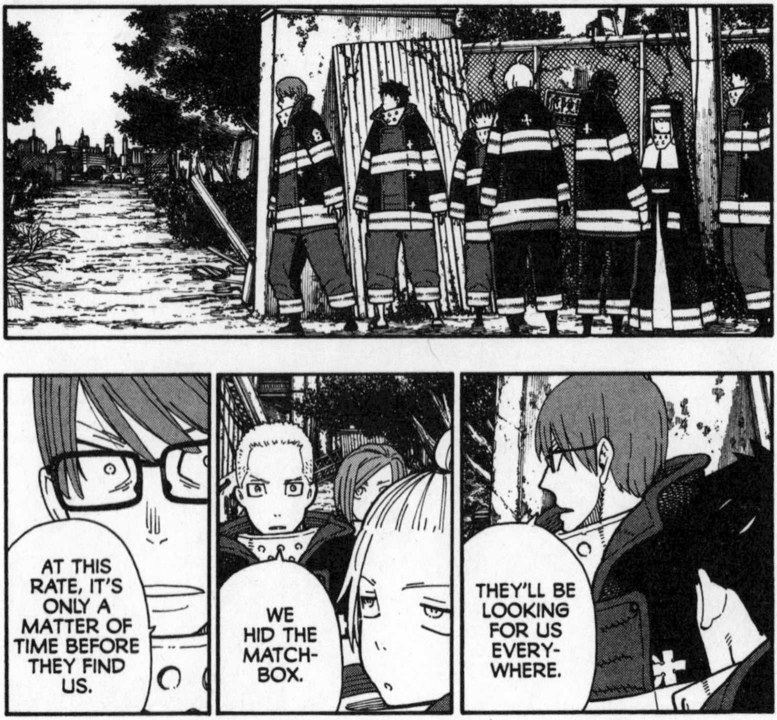
THEY'LL BE LOOKING FOR US EVERY-WHERE.
WE HID THE MATCH-BOX.
AT THIS RATE, IT'S ONLY A MATTER OF TIME BEFORE THEY FIND US.

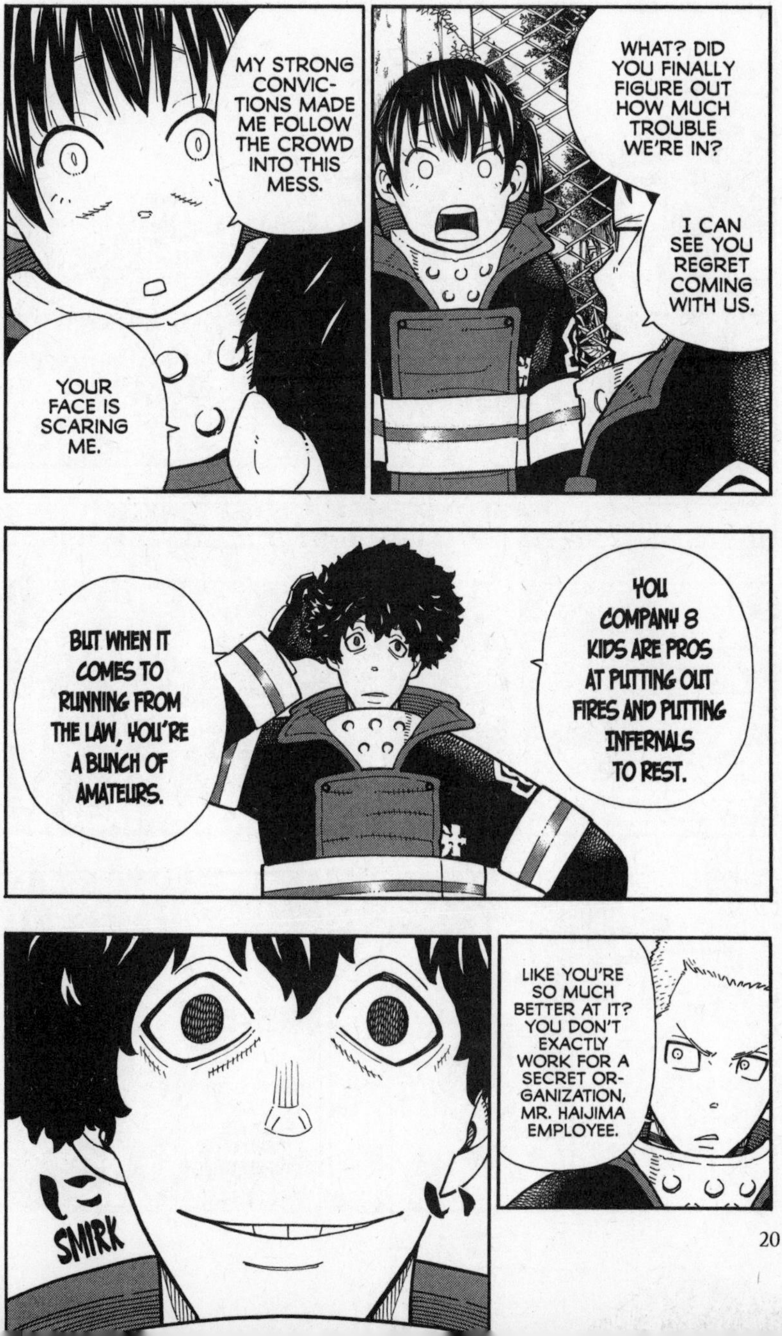
WHAT? DID YOU FINALLY FIGURE OUT HOW MUCH TROUBLE WE'RE IN?
I CAN SEE YOU REGRET COMING WITH US.
MY STRONG CONVICTIONS MADE ME FOLLOW THE CROWD INTO THIS MESS.
YOUR FACE IS SCARING ME.
YOU COMPANY 8 KIDS ARE PROS AT PUTTING OUT FIRES AND PUTTING INFERNALS TO REST.
BUT WHEN IT COMES TO RUNNING FROM THE LAW, YOU'RE A BUNCH OF AMATEURS.
LIKE YOU'RE SO MUCH BETTER AT IT? YOU DON'T EXACTLY WORK FOR A SECRET ORGANIZATION, MR. HAIJIMA EMPLOYEE.
SMIRK

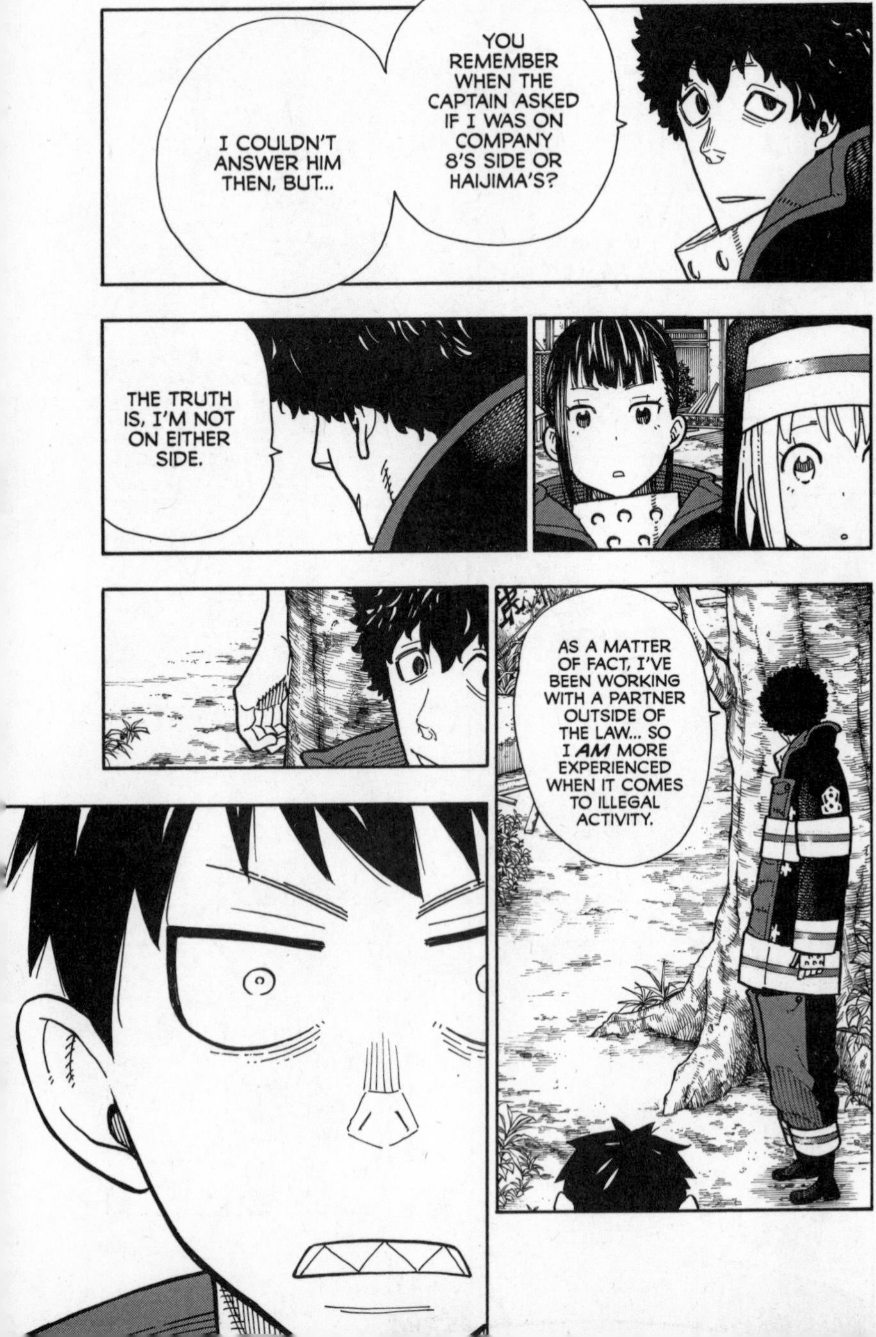
YOU REMEMBER WHEN THE CAPTAIN ASKED IF I WAS ON COMPANY 8'S SIDE OR HAIJIMA'S?
I COULDN'T ANSWER HIM THEN, BUT...
THE TRUTH IS, I'M NOT ON EITHER SIDE.
AS A MATTER OF FACT, I'VE BEEN WORKING WITH A PARTNER OUTSIDE OF THE LAW... SO I *AM* MORE EXPERIENCED WHEN IT COMES TO ILLEGAL ACTIVITY.

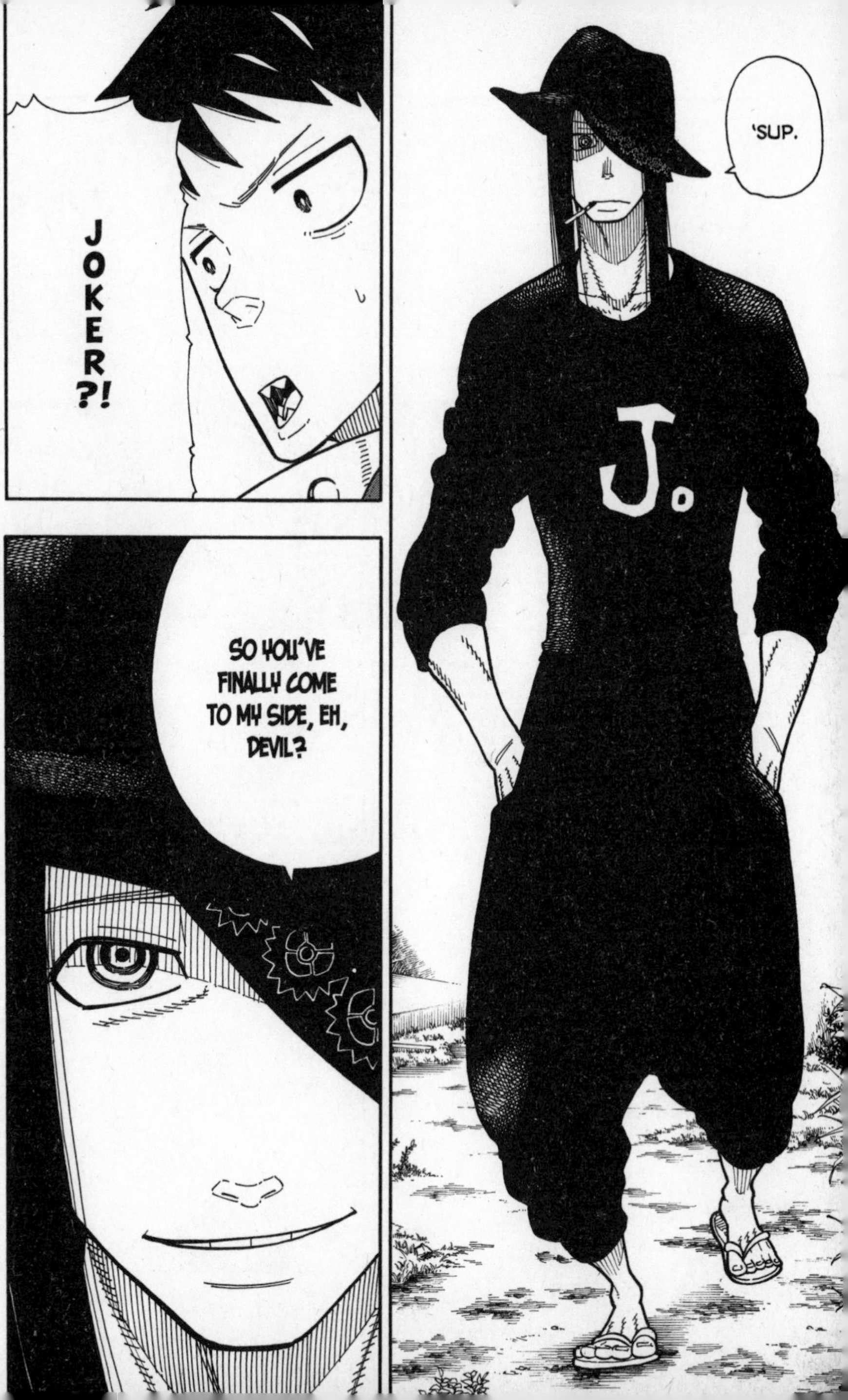
'SUP.
JOKER?!
SO YOU'VE FINALLY COME TO MY SIDE, EH, DEVIL?

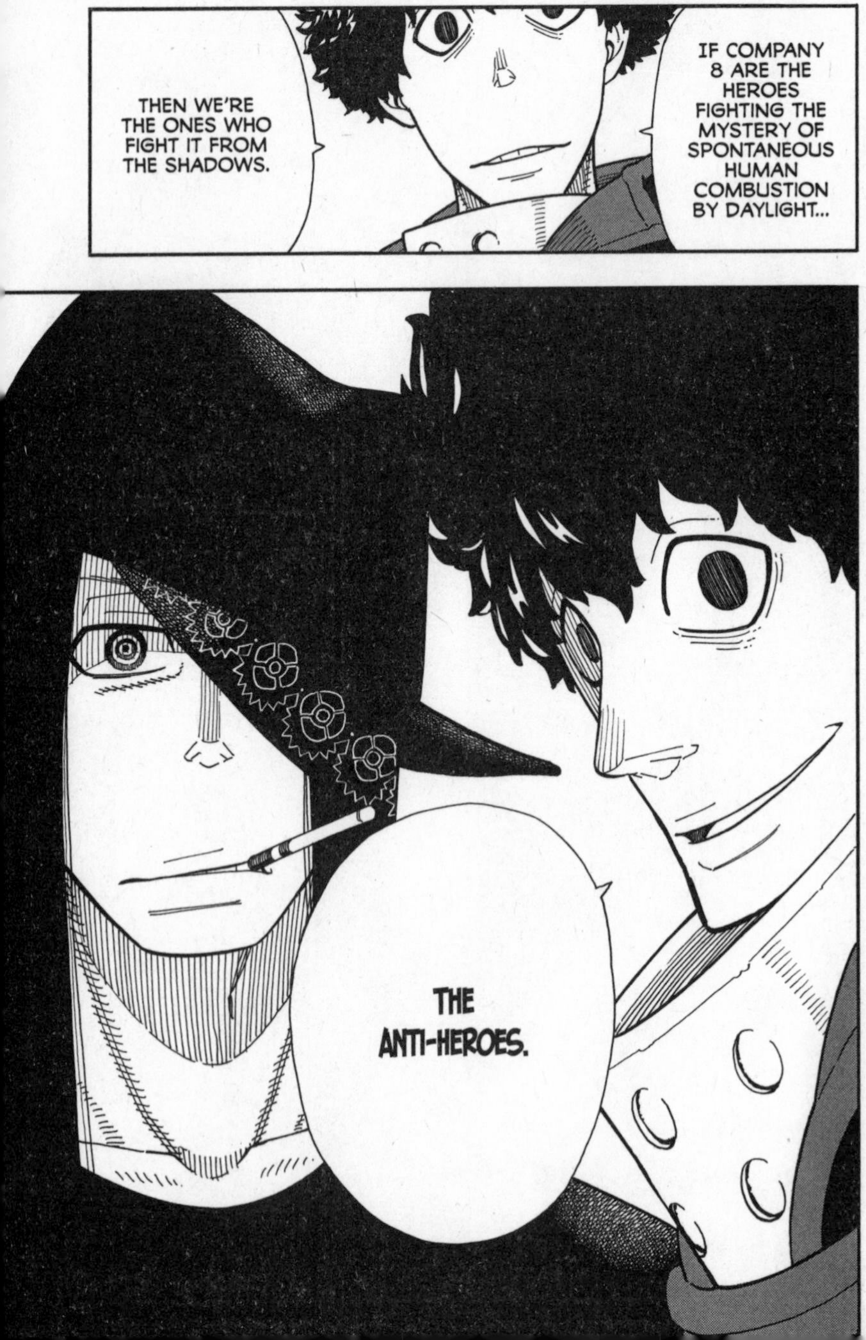
IF COMPANY 8 ARE THE HEROES FIGHTING THE MYSTERY OF SPONTANEOUS HUMAN COMBUSTION BY DAYLIGHT...
THEN WE'RE THE ONES WHO FIGHT IT FROM THE SHADOWS.
THE ANTI-HEROES.

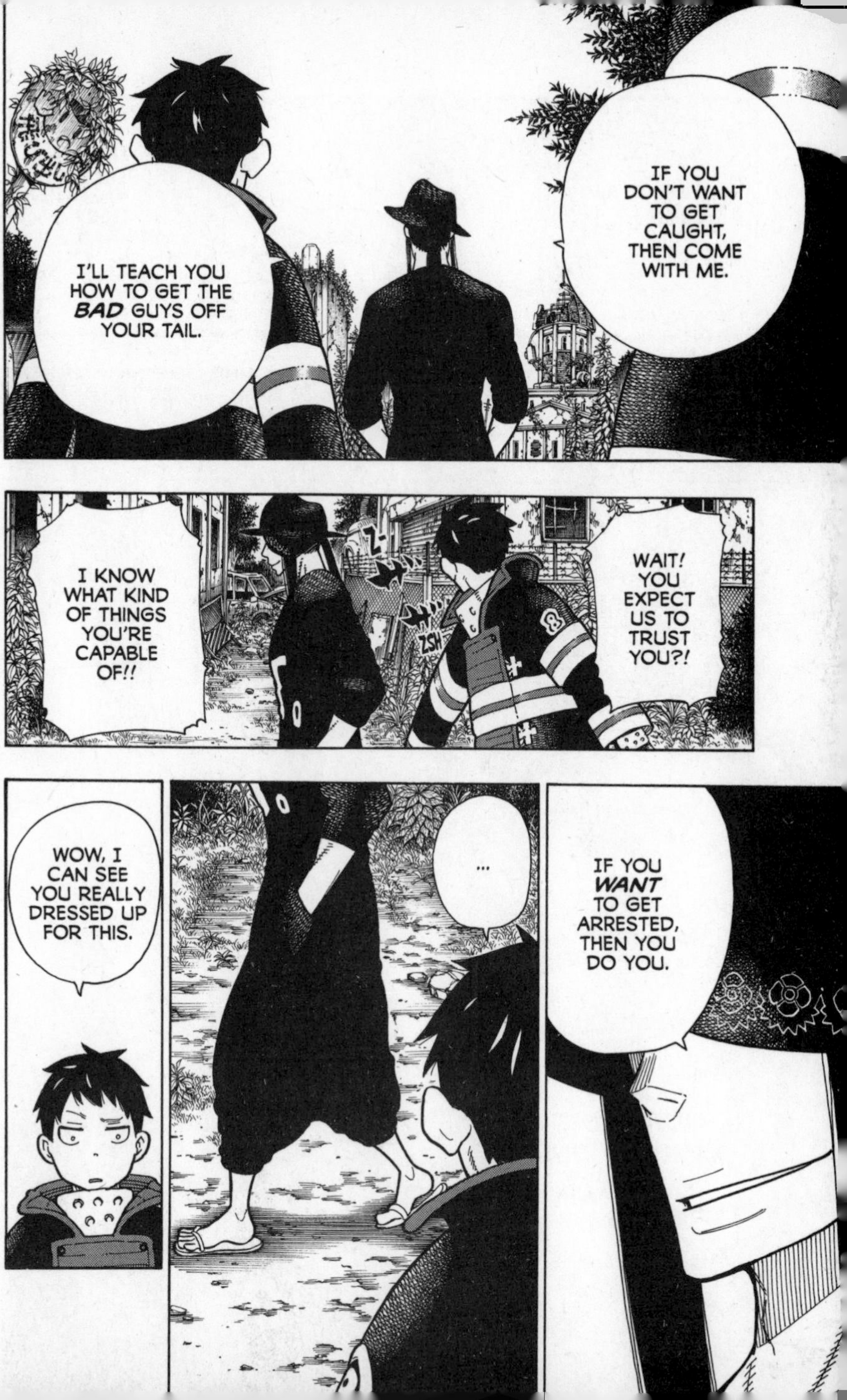
IF YOU DON'T WANT TO GET CAUGHT, THEN COME WITH ME.
I'LL TEACH YOU HOW TO GET THE *BAD* GUYS OFF YOUR TAIL.
WAIT! YOU EXPECT US TO TRUST YOU?!
ZSH
I KNOW WHAT KIND OF THINGS YOU'RE CAPABLE OF!!
IF YOU *WANT* TO GET ARRESTED, THEN YOU DO YOU.
...
WOW, I CAN SEE YOU REALLY DRESSED UP FOR THIS.

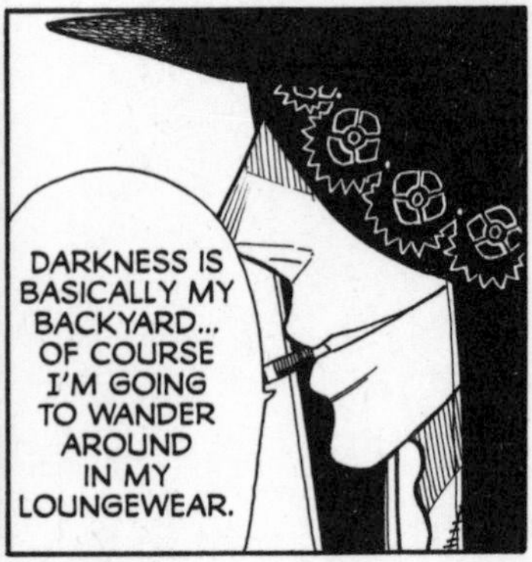
DARKNESS IS BASICALLY MY BACKYARD... OF COURSE I'M GOING TO WANDER AROUND IN MY LOUNGEWEAR.

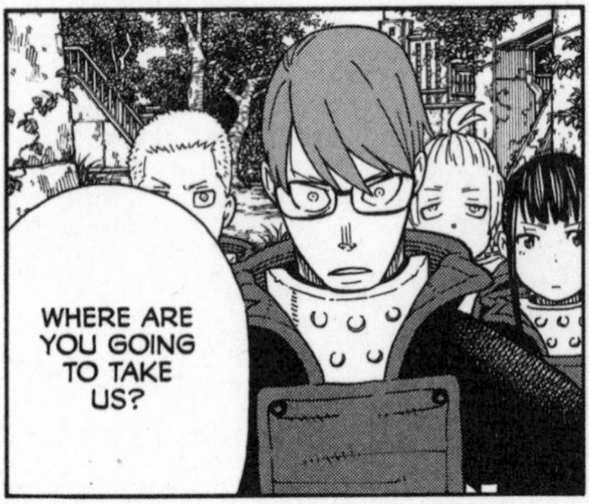
WHERE ARE YOU GOING TO TAKE US?

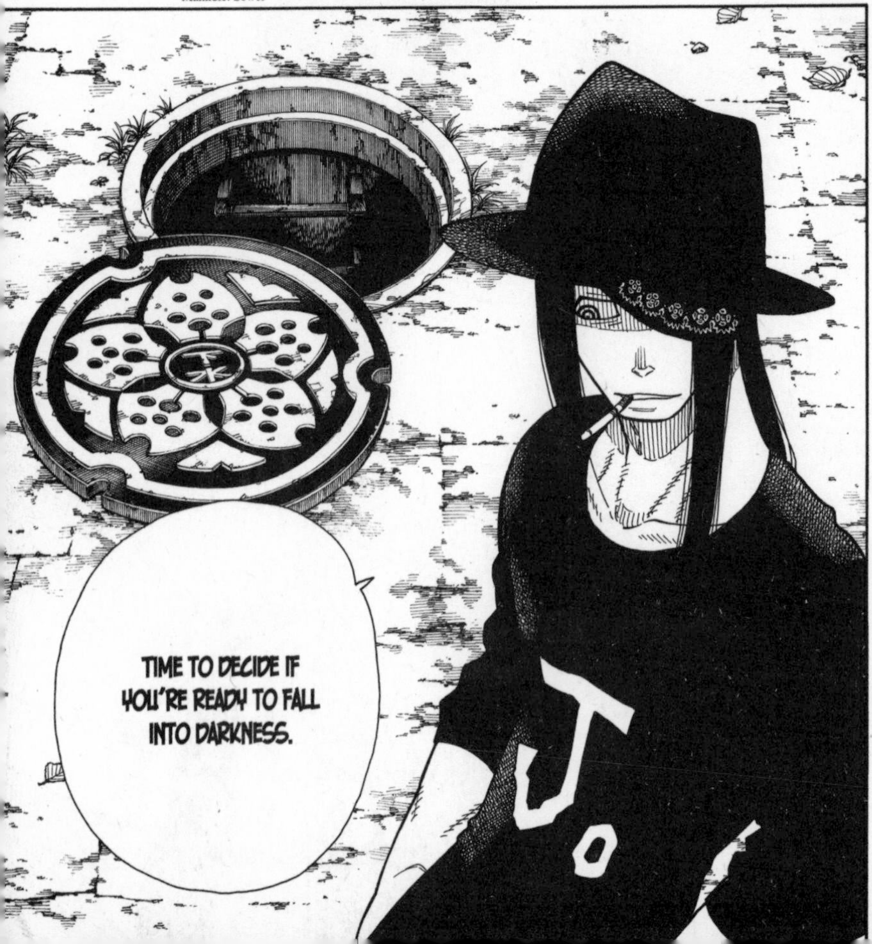
TIME TO DECIDE IF YOU'RE READY TO FALL INTO DARKNESS.

Manhole: Sewer

FIRE FORCE

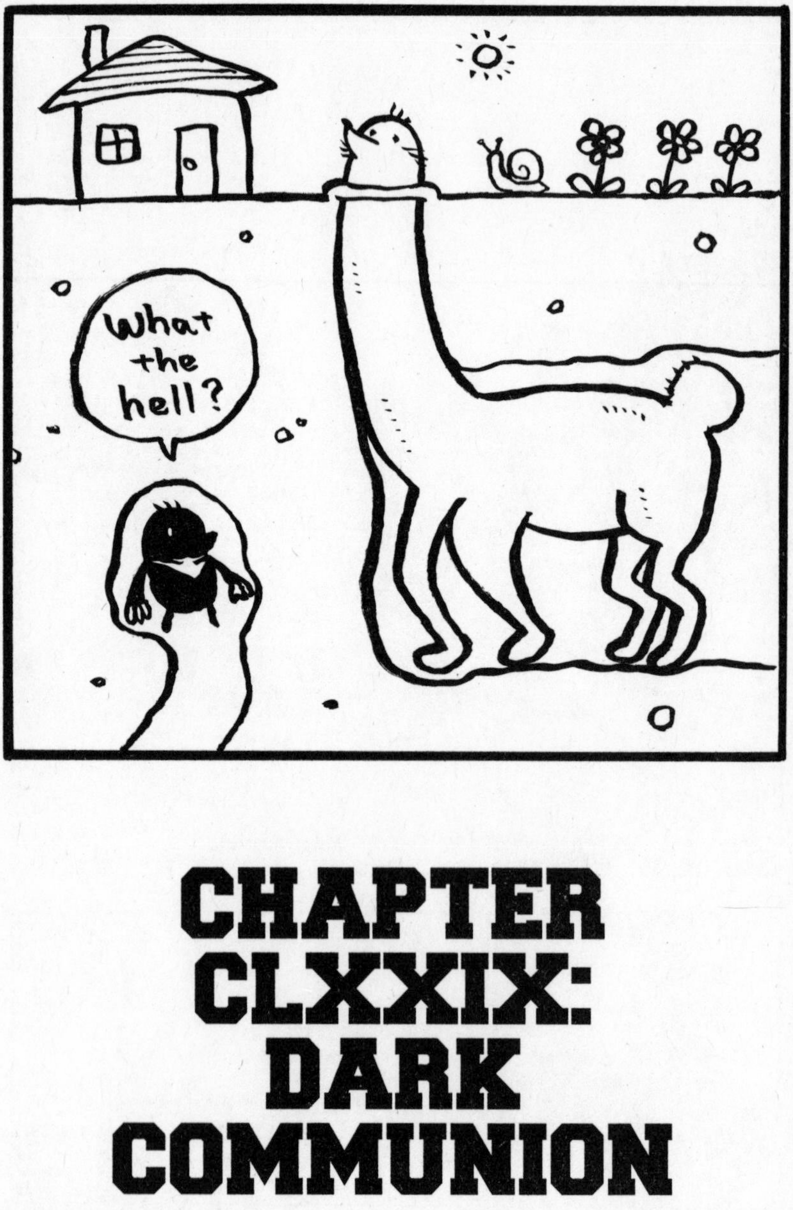
What the hell?

CHAPTER CLXXIX: DARK COMMUNION

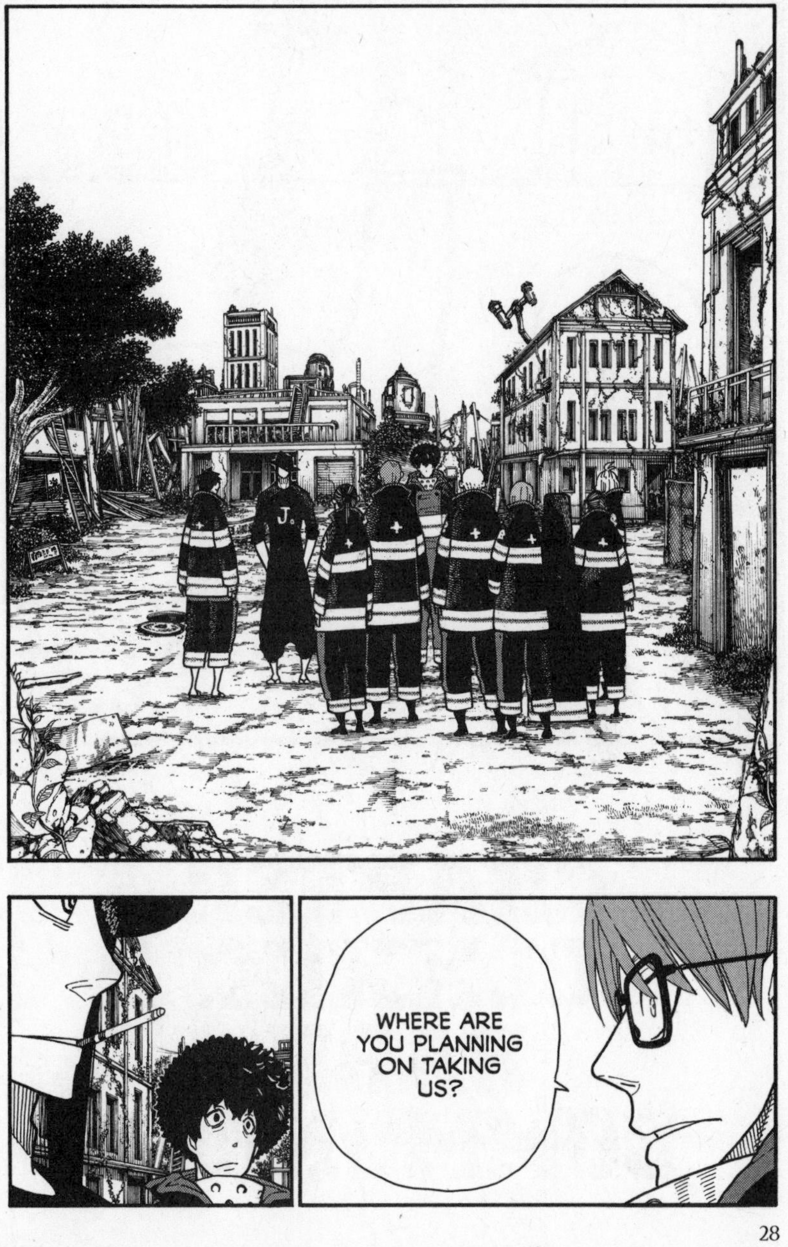
WHERE ARE YOU PLANNING ON TAKING US?

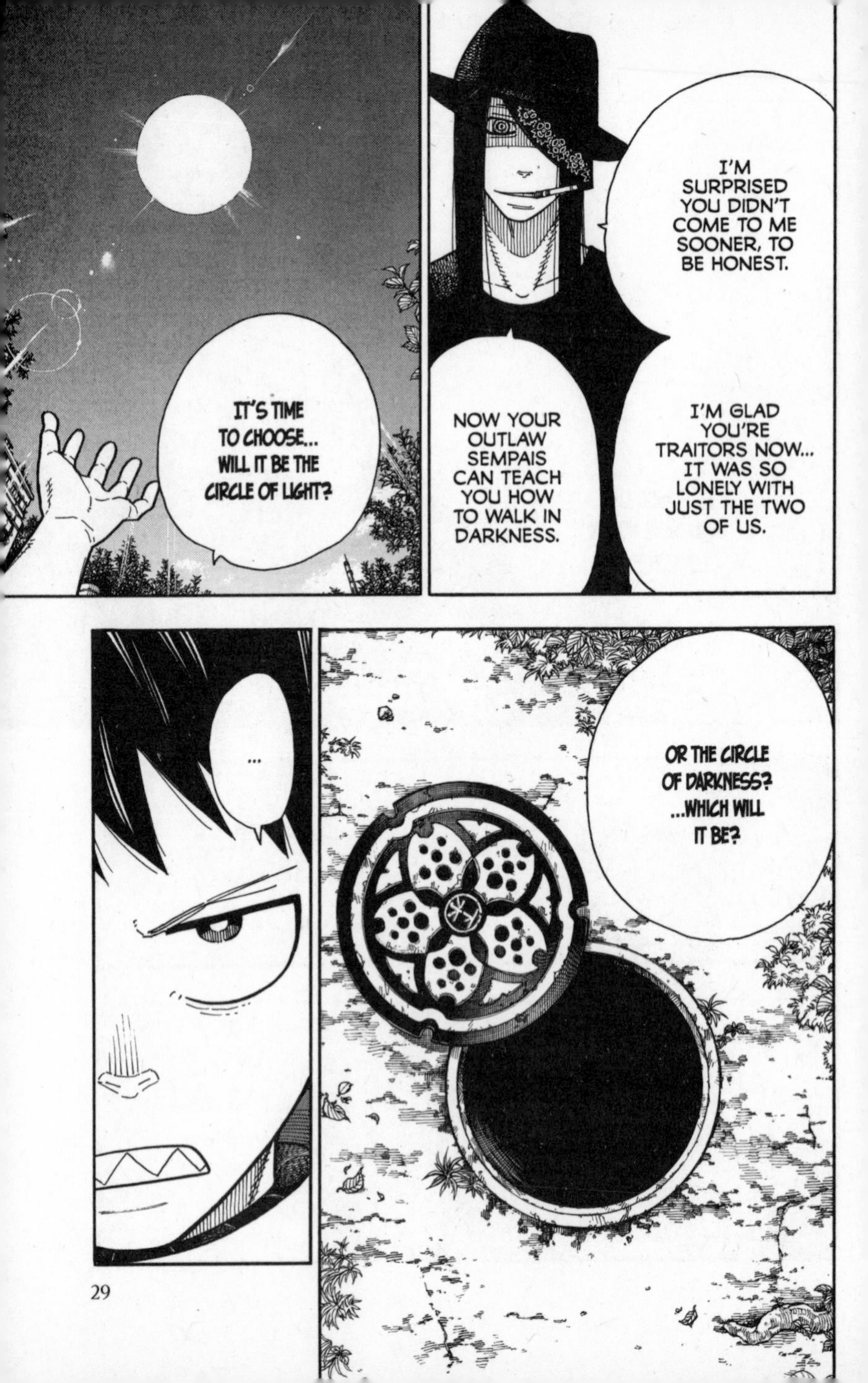
I'M SURPRISED YOU DIDN'T COME TO ME SOONER, TO BE HONEST.
I'M GLAD YOU'RE TRAITORS NOW... IT WAS SO LONELY WITH JUST THE TWO OF US.
NOW YOUR OUTLAW SEMPAIS CAN TEACH YOU HOW TO WALK IN DARKNESS.
IT'S TIME TO CHOOSE... WILL IT BE THE CIRCLE OF LIGHT?
OR THE CIRCLE OF DARKNESS? ...WHICH WILL IT BE?
...

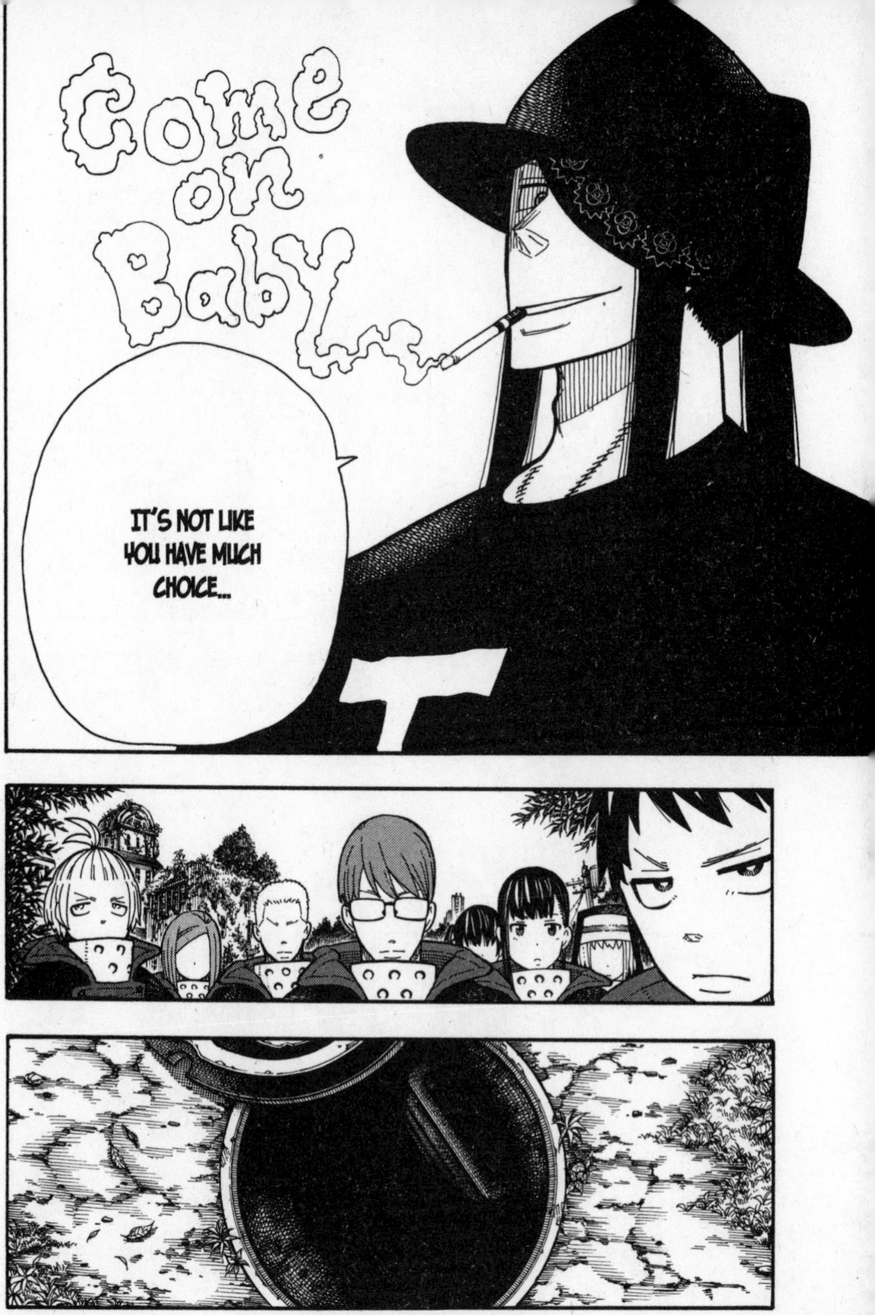
Come on Baby
IT'S NOT LIKE YOU HAVE MUCH CHOICE...

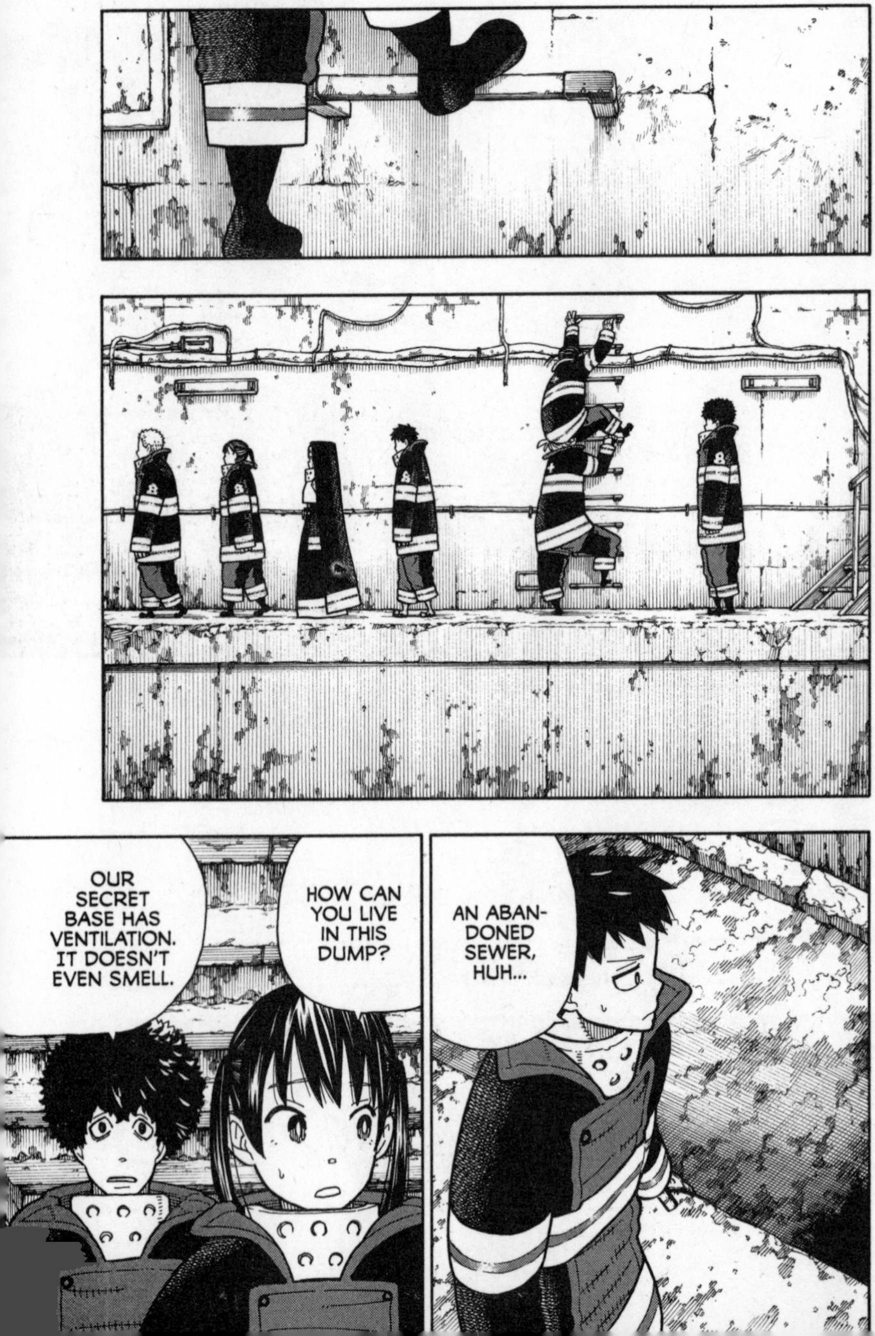
AN ABAN-DONED SEWER, HUH...
HOW CAN YOU LIVE IN THIS DUMP?
OUR SECRET BASE HAS VENTILATION. IT DOESN'T EVEN SMELL.

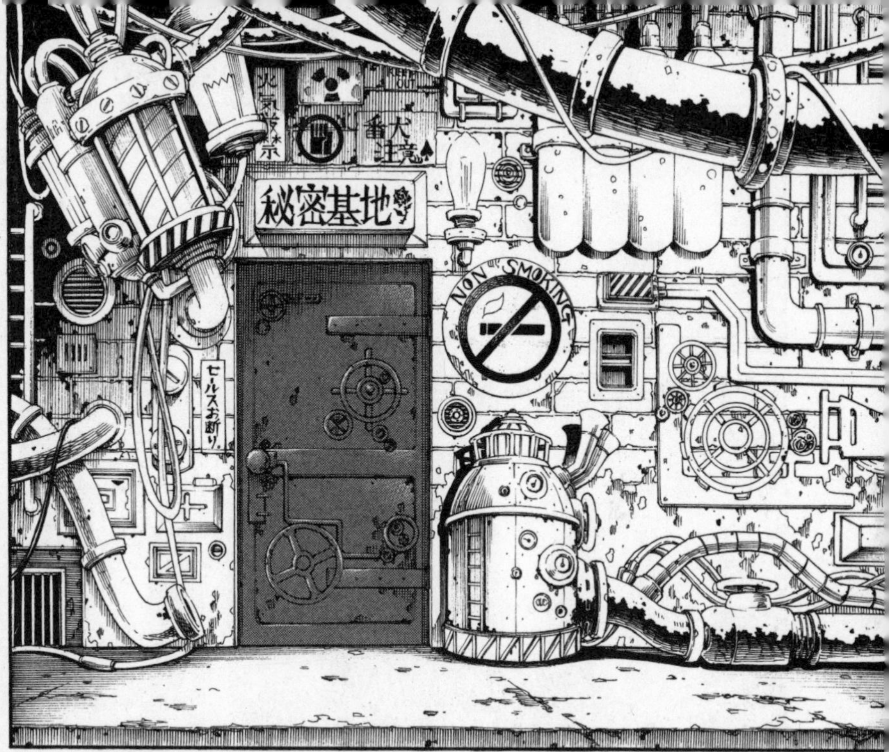
火気厳禁
番犬注意
秘密基地
セールスお断り
NON SMOKING

Sign: No Solicitors Sign: Secret Base Sign: No Fire Sign: Beware of Dog

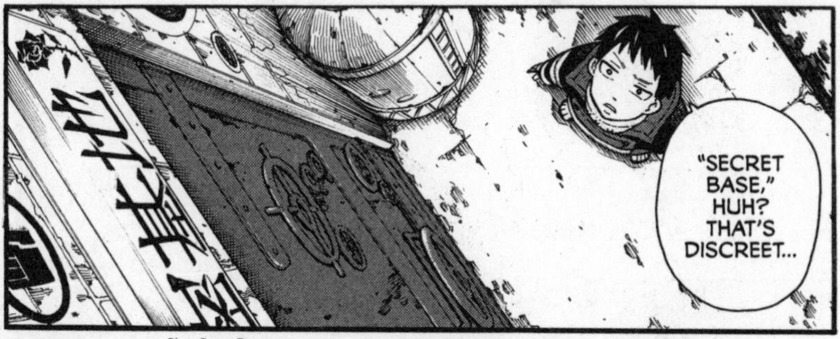
"SECRET BASE," HUH? THAT'S DISCREET...

Sign: Secret Base

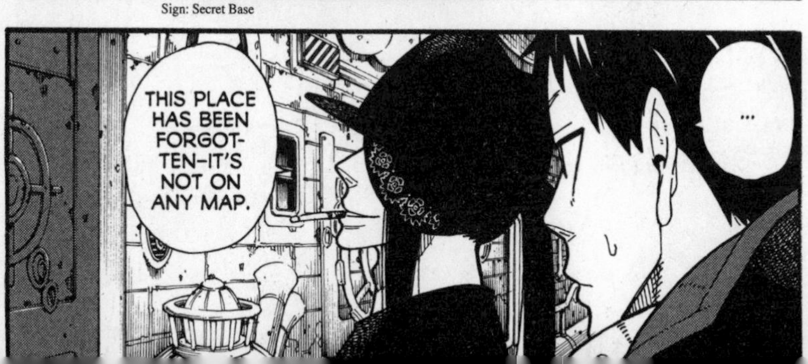
...
THIS PLACE HAS BEEN FORGOT-TEN—IT'S NOT ON ANY MAP.

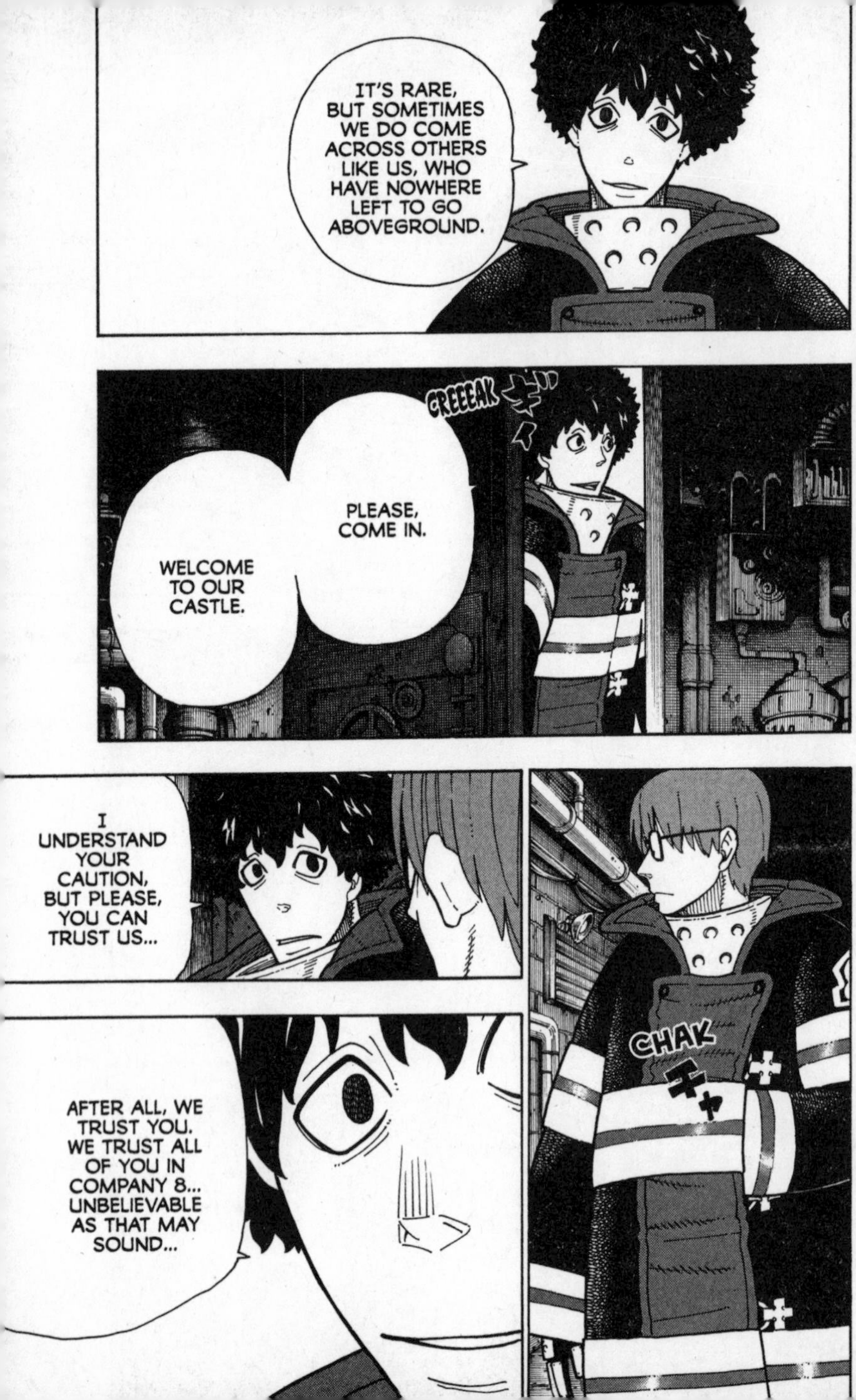

IT'S RARE, BUT SOMETIMES WE DO COME ACROSS OTHERS LIKE US, WHO HAVE NOWHERE LEFT TO GO ABOVEGROUND.
CREEEAK
PLEASE, COME IN.
WELCOME TO OUR CASTLE.
CHAK
I UNDERSTAND YOUR CAUTION, BUT PLEASE, YOU CAN TRUST US...
AFTER ALL, WE TRUST YOU. WE TRUST ALL OF YOU IN COMPANY 8... UNBELIEVABLE AS THAT MAY SOUND...

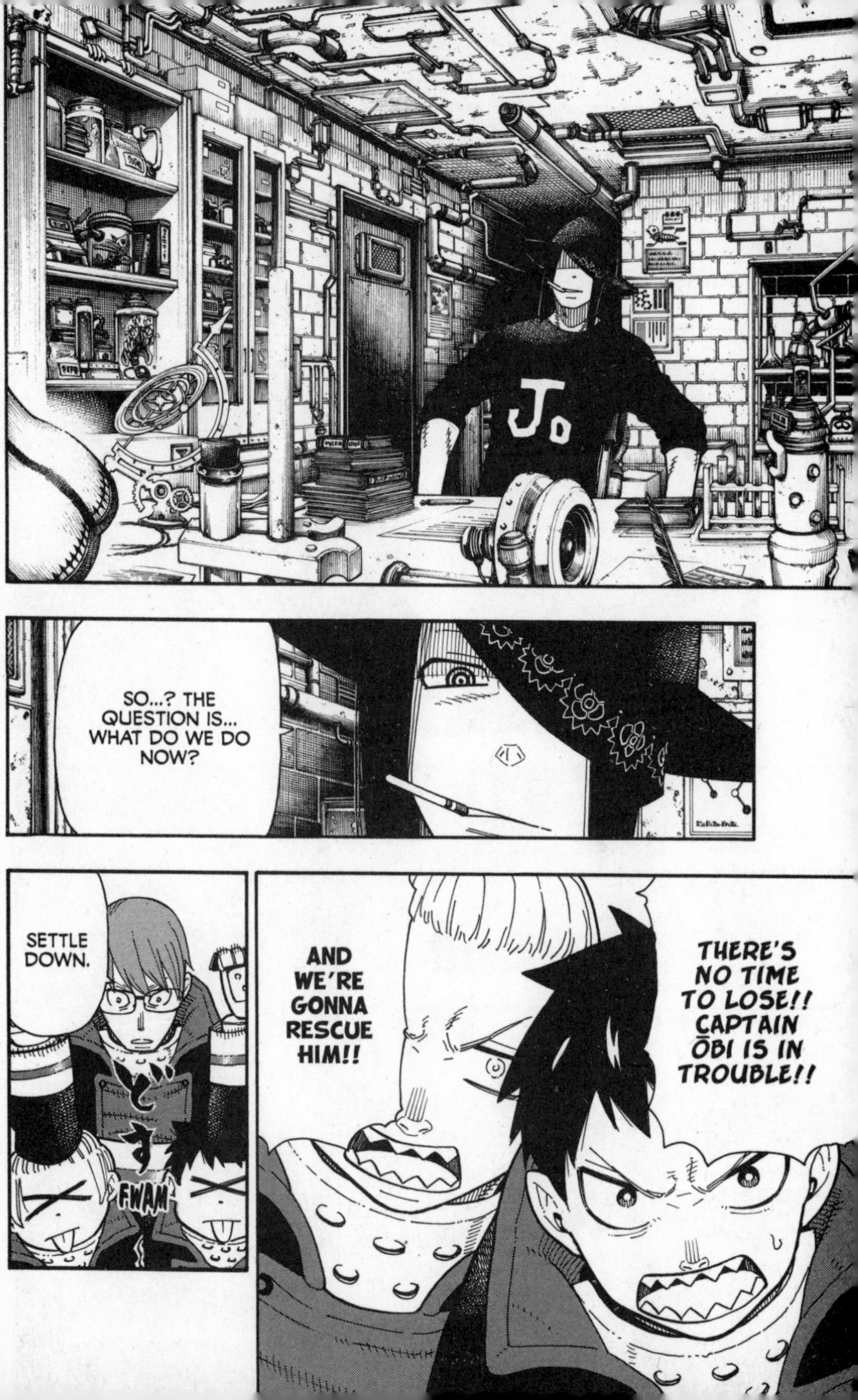
SO...? THE QUESTION IS... WHAT DO WE DO NOW?
THERE'S NO TIME TO LOSE!! CAPTAIN ŌBI IS IN TROUBLE!!
AND WE'RE GONNA RESCUE HIM!!
SETTLE DOWN.
どす
FWAM

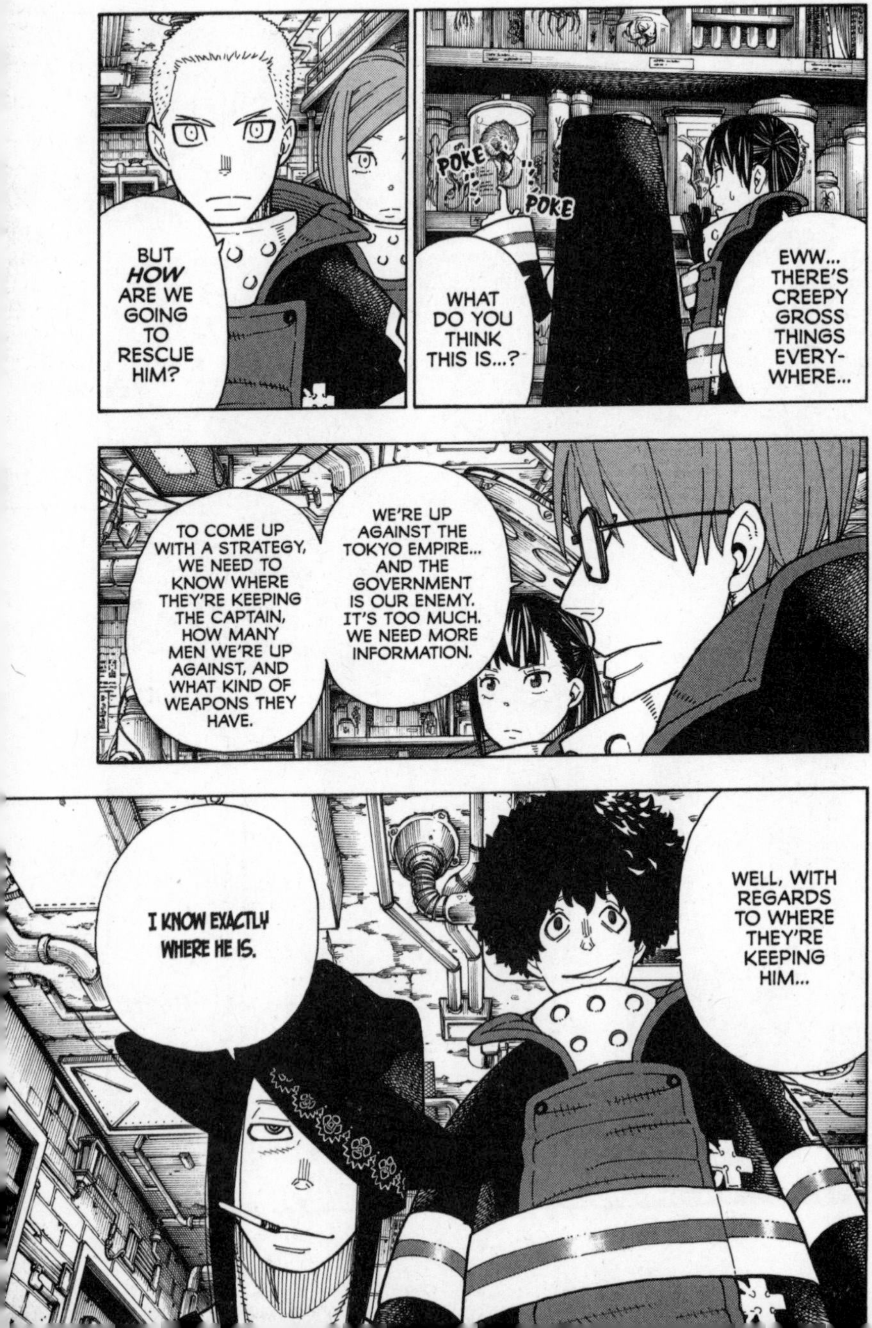
EWW... THERE'S CREEPY GROSS THINGS EVERY-WHERE...
POKE
POKE
WHAT DO YOU THINK THIS IS...?
BUT *HOW* ARE WE GOING TO RESCUE HIM?
WE'RE UP AGAINST THE TOKYO EMPIRE... AND THE GOVERNMENT IS OUR ENEMY. IT'S TOO MUCH. WE NEED MORE INFORMATION.
TO COME UP WITH A STRATEGY, WE NEED TO KNOW WHERE THEY'RE KEEPING THE CAPTAIN, HOW MANY MEN WE'RE UP AGAINST, AND WHAT KIND OF WEAPONS THEY HAVE.
WELL, WITH REGARDS TO WHERE THEY'RE KEEPING HIM...
I KNOW EXACTLY WHERE HE IS.

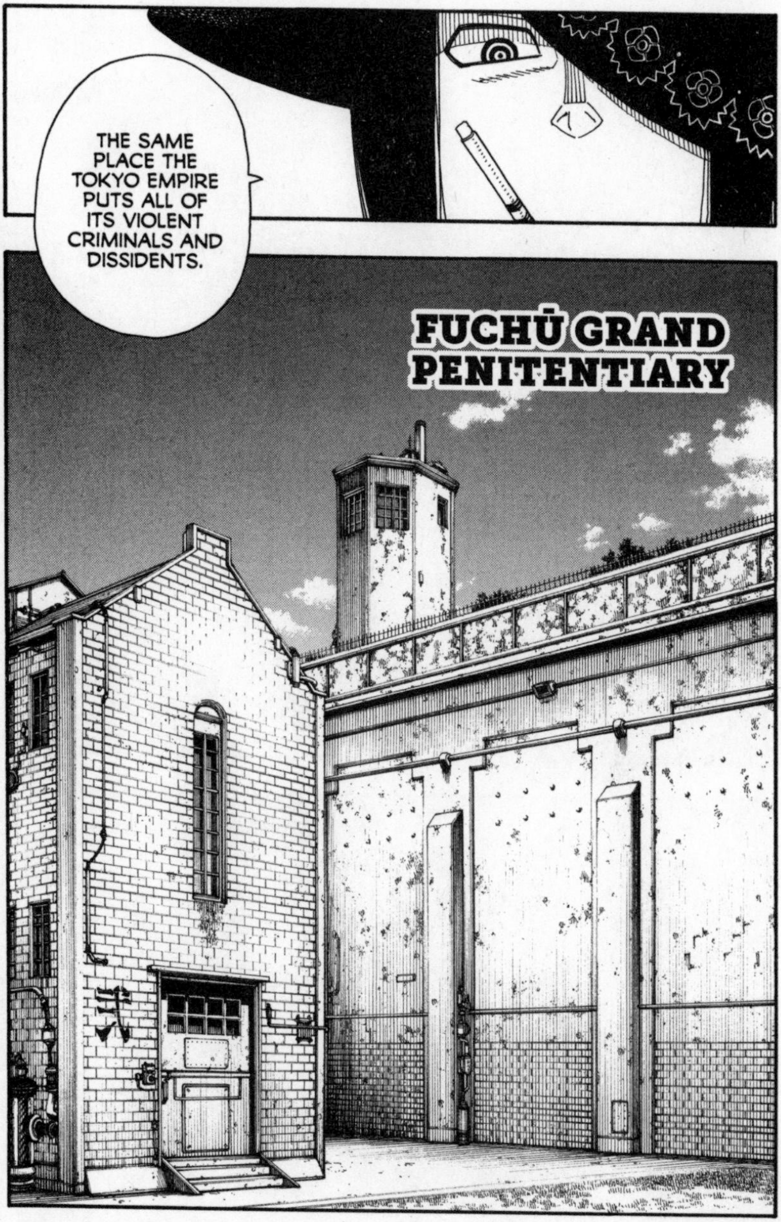
THE SAME PLACE THE TOKYO EMPIRE PUTS ALL OF ITS VIOLENT CRIMINALS AND DISSIDENTS.
FUCHŪ GRAND PENITENTIARY

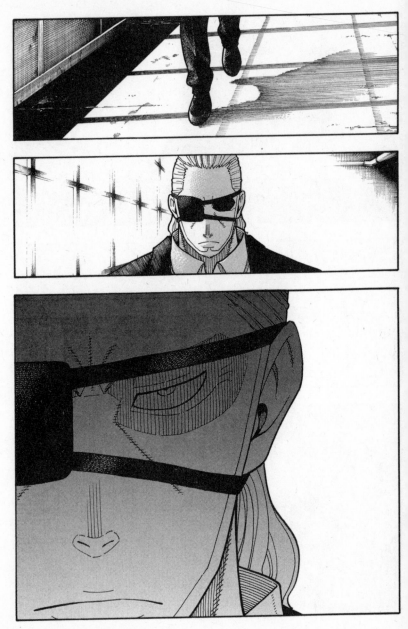

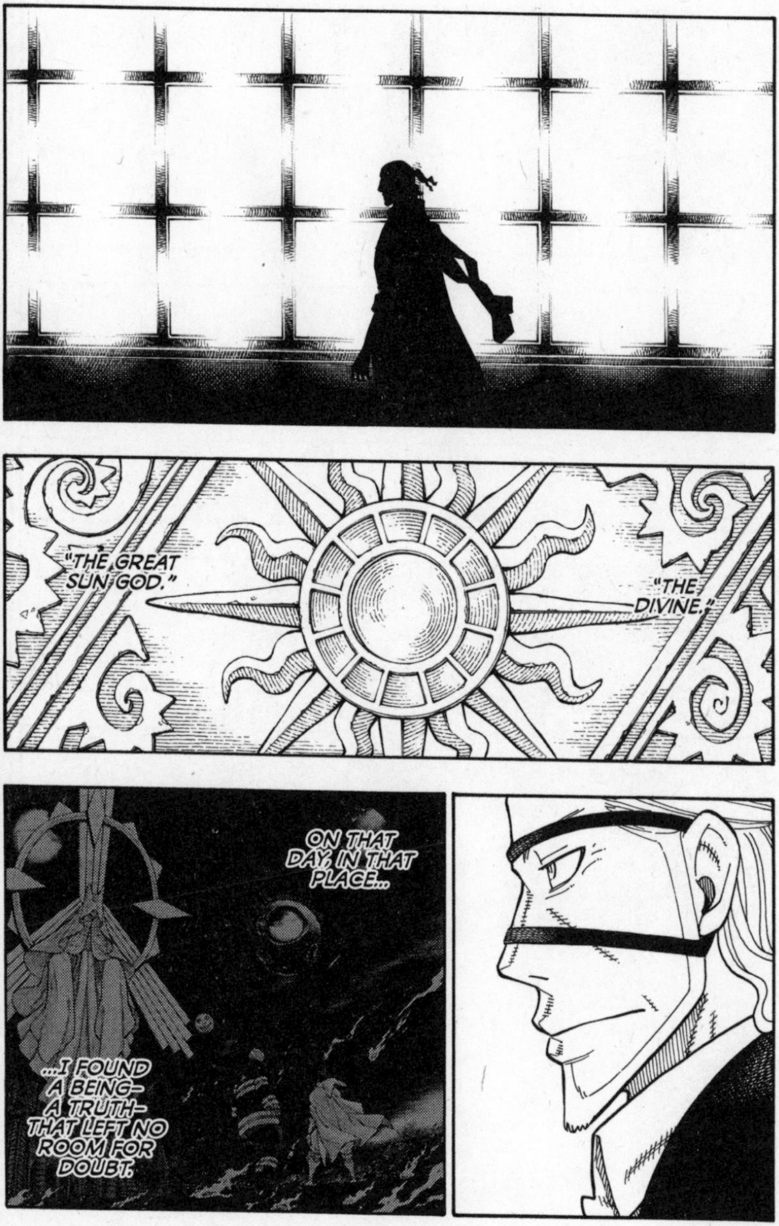
"THE DIVINE."
"THE GREAT SUN GOD."
ON THAT DAY, IN THAT PLACE...
...I FOUND A BEING—A TRUTH—THAT LEFT NO ROOM FOR DOUBT.

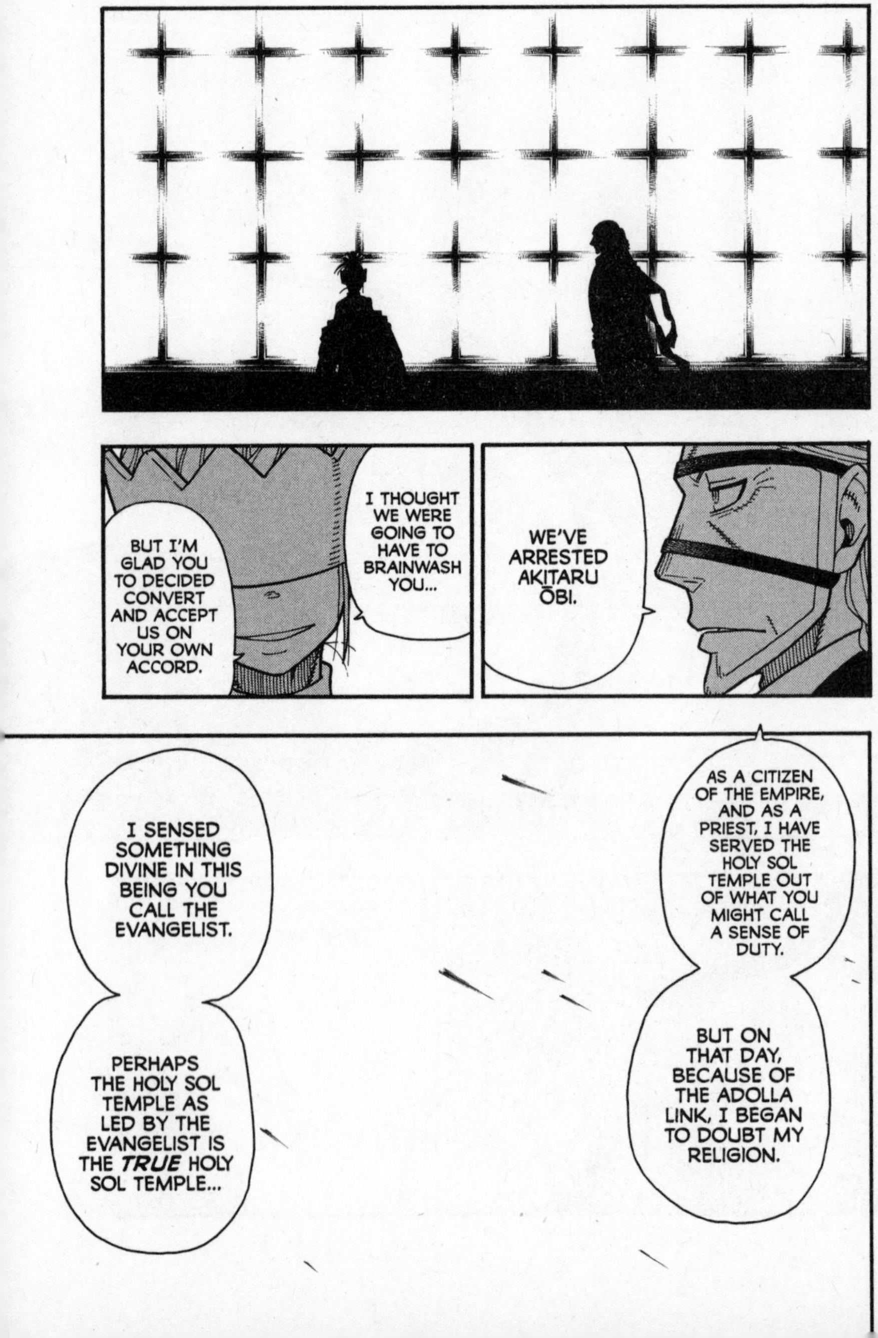
WE'VE ARRESTED AKITARU ŌBI.
I THOUGHT WE WERE GOING TO HAVE TO BRAINWASH YOU...
BUT I'M GLAD YOU TO DECIDED CONVERT AND ACCEPT US ON YOUR OWN ACCORD.
AS A CITIZEN OF THE EMPIRE, AND AS A PRIEST, I HAVE SERVED THE HOLY SOL TEMPLE OUT OF WHAT YOU MIGHT CALL A SENSE OF DUTY.
BUT ON THAT DAY, BECAUSE OF THE ADOLLA LINK, I BEGAN TO DOUBT MY RELIGION.
I SENSED SOMETHING DIVINE IN THIS BEING YOU CALL THE EVANGELIST.
PERHAPS THE HOLY SOL TEMPLE AS LED BY THE EVANGELIST IS THE *TRUE* HOLY SOL TEMPLE...

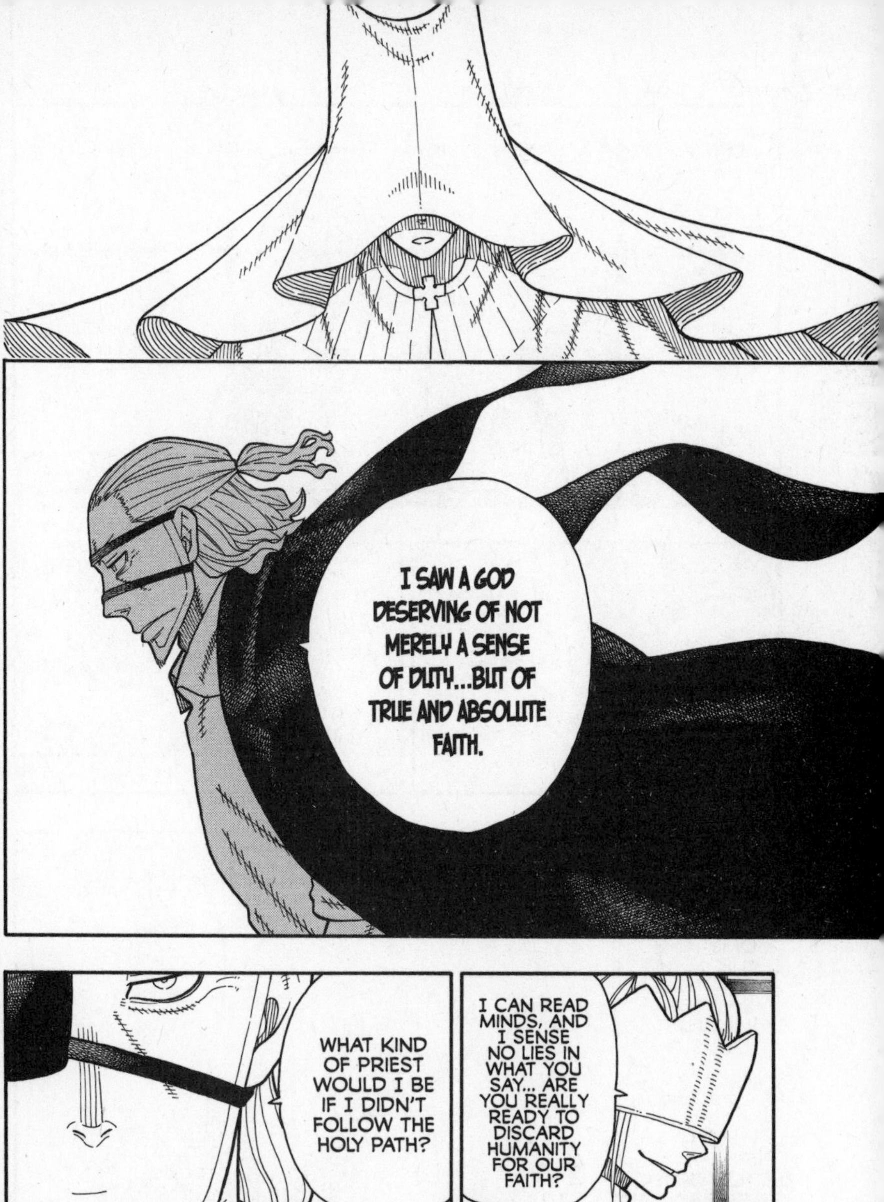
I SAW A GOD DESERVING OF NOT MERELY A SENSE OF DUTY...BUT OF TRUE AND ABSOLUTE FAITH.
I CAN READ MINDS, AND I SENSE NO LIES IN WHAT YOU SAY... ARE YOU REALLY READY TO DISCARD HUMANITY FOR OUR FAITH?
WHAT KIND OF PRIEST WOULD I BE IF I DIDN'T FOLLOW THE HOLY PATH?

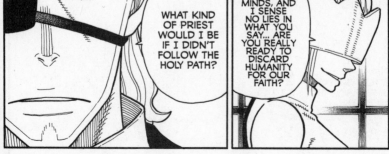

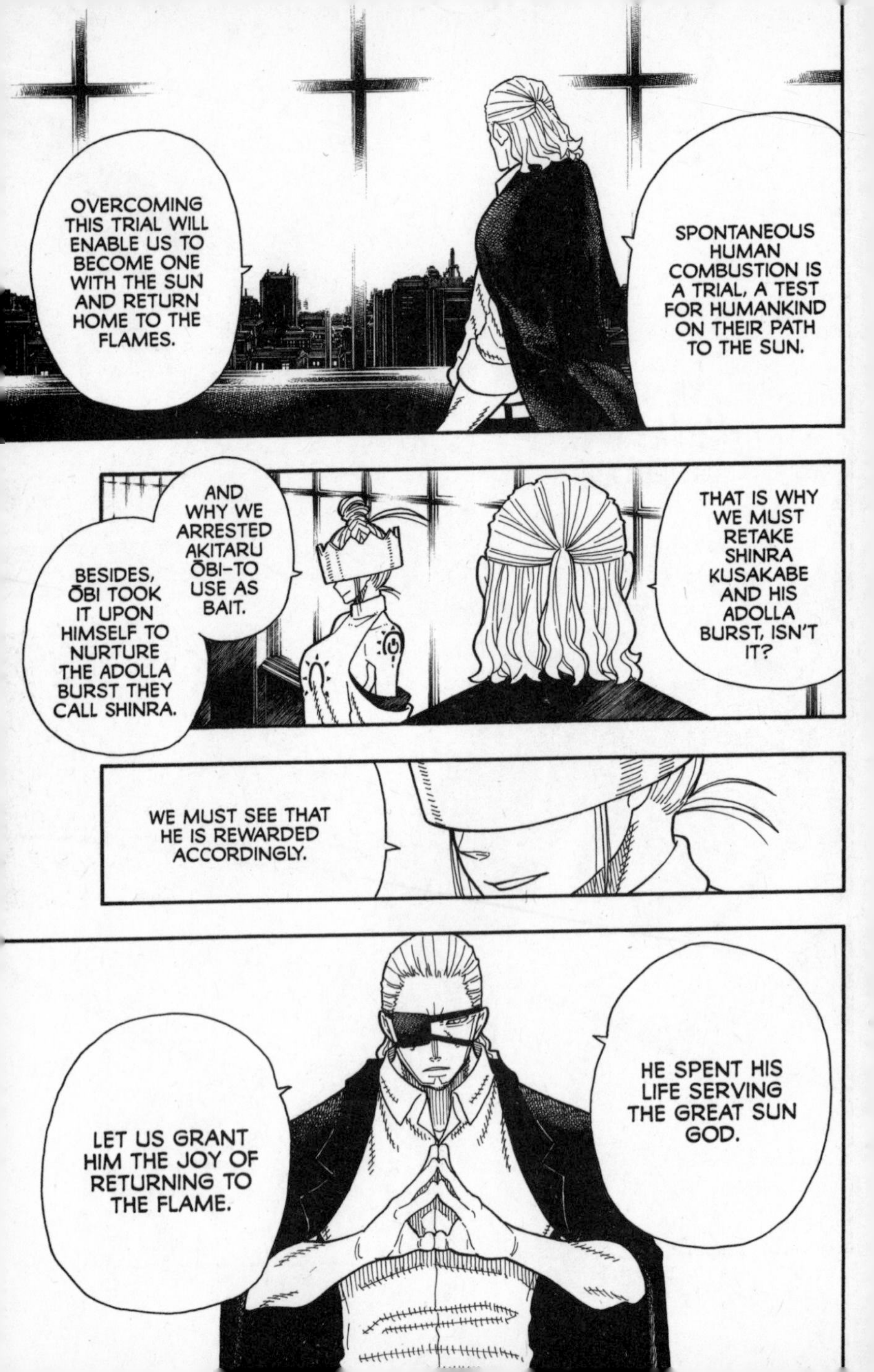
SPONTANEOUS HUMAN COMBUSTION IS A TRIAL, A TEST FOR HUMANKIND ON THEIR PATH TO THE SUN.
OVERCOMING THIS TRIAL WILL ENABLE US TO BECOME ONE WITH THE SUN AND RETURN HOME TO THE FLAMES.
THAT IS WHY WE MUST RETAKE SHINRA KUSAKABE AND HIS ADOLLA BURST, ISN'T IT?
AND WHY WE ARRESTED AKITARU ŌBI–TO USE AS BAIT.
BESIDES, ŌBI TOOK IT UPON HIMSELF TO NURTURE THE ADOLLA BURST THEY CALL SHINRA.
WE MUST SEE THAT HE IS REWARDED ACCORDINGLY.
HE SPENT HIS LIFE SERVING THE GREAT SUN GOD.
LET US GRANT HIM THE JOY OF RETURNING TO THE FLAME.

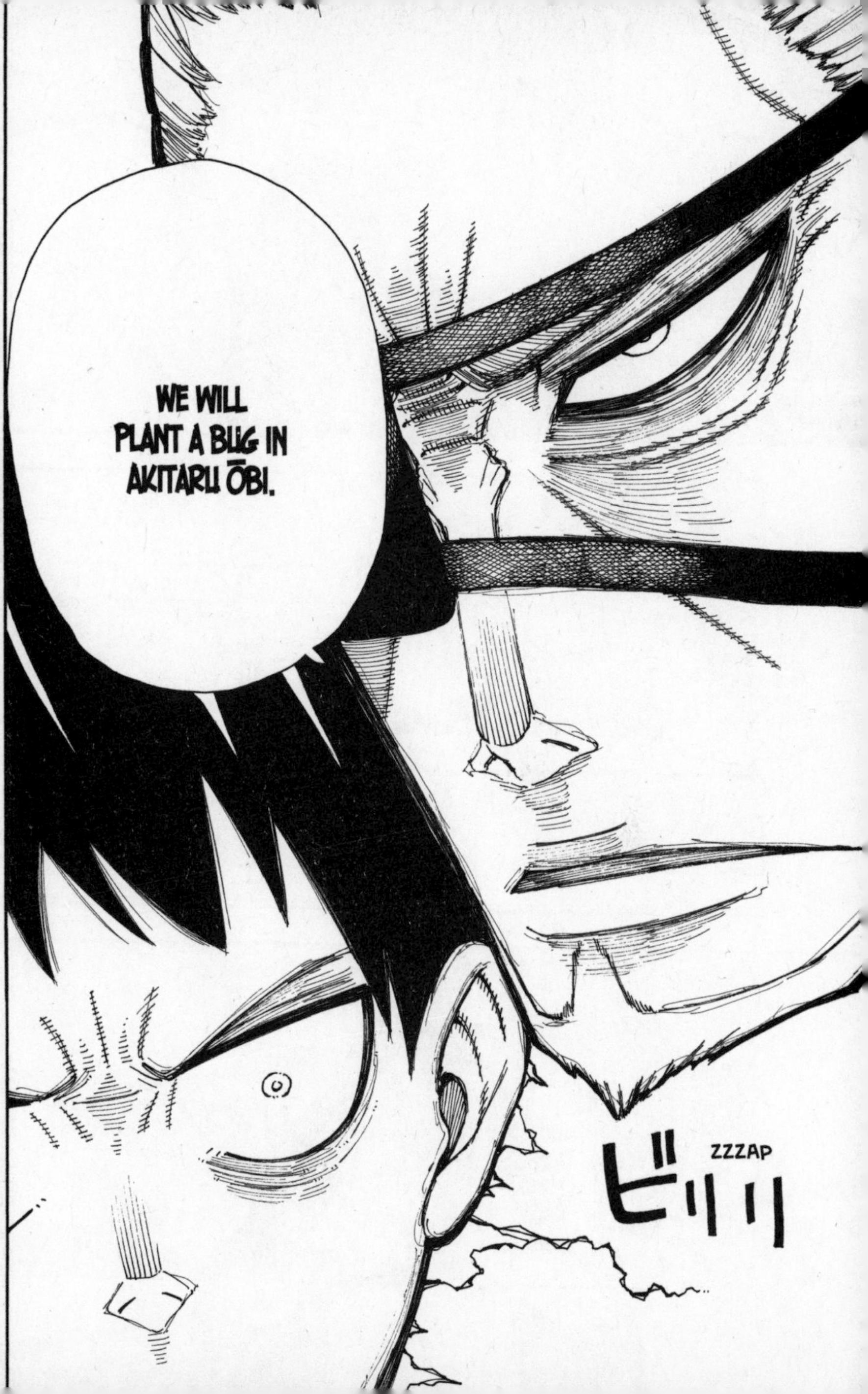
WE WILL PLANT A BUG IN AKITARU ŌBI.
ビリリ
ZZZAP

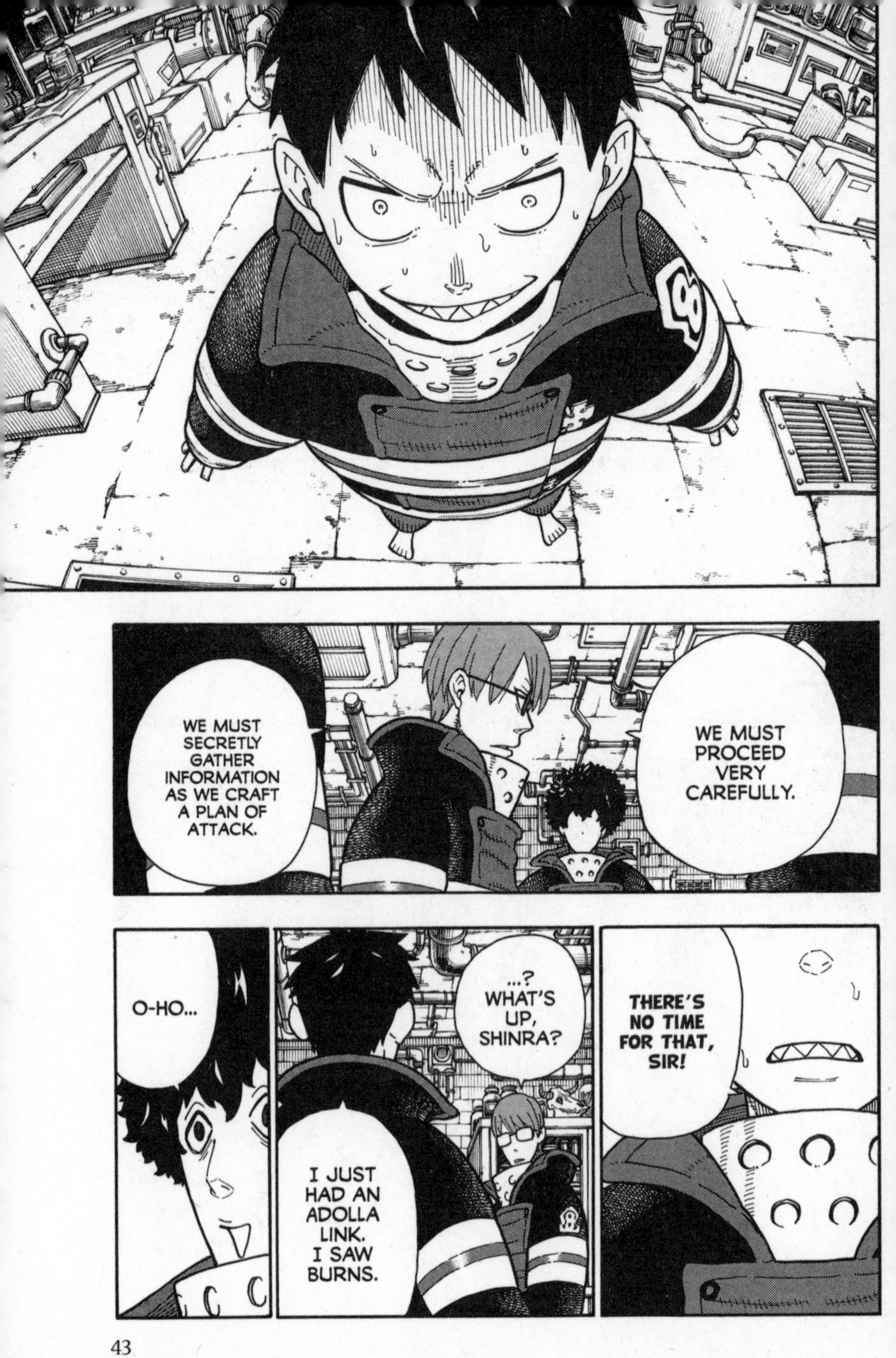
WE MUST PROCEED VERY CAREFULLY.
WE MUST SECRETLY GATHER INFORMATION AS WE CRAFT A PLAN OF ATTACK.
THERE'S NO TIME FOR THAT, SIR!
...? WHAT'S UP, SHINRA?
I JUST HAD AN ADOLLA LINK. I SAW BURNS.
O-HO...

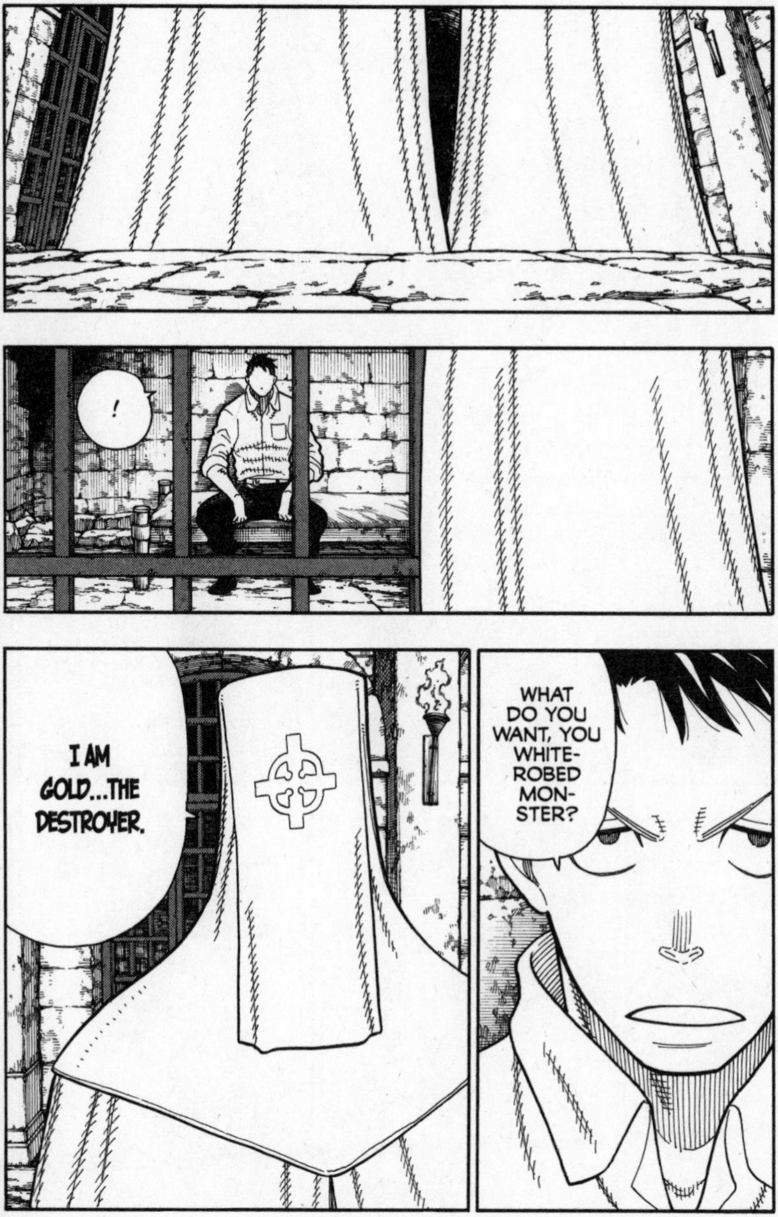
!
WHAT DO YOU WANT, YOU WHITE-ROBED MONSTER?
I AM GOLD...THE DESTROYER.

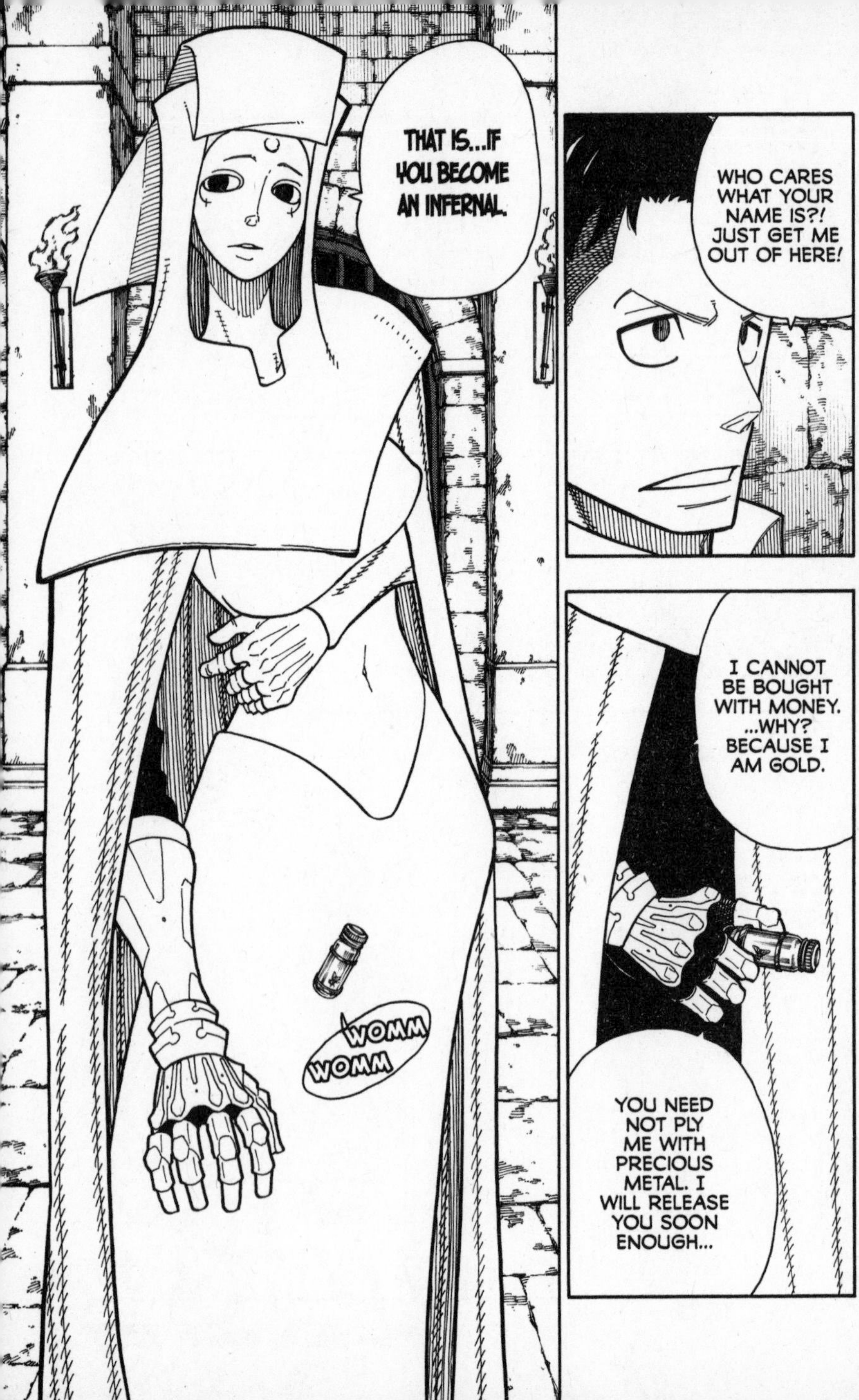
WHO CARES WHAT YOUR NAME IS?! JUST GET ME OUT OF HERE!
I CANNOT BE BOUGHT WITH MONEY. ...WHY? BECAUSE I AM GOLD.
YOU NEED NOT PLY ME WITH PRECIOUS METAL. I WILL RELEASE YOU SOON ENOUGH...
THAT IS...IF YOU BECOME AN INFERNAL.
WOMM
WOMM

FIRE FORCE

CHAPTER CLXXX: THE DESTROYERS

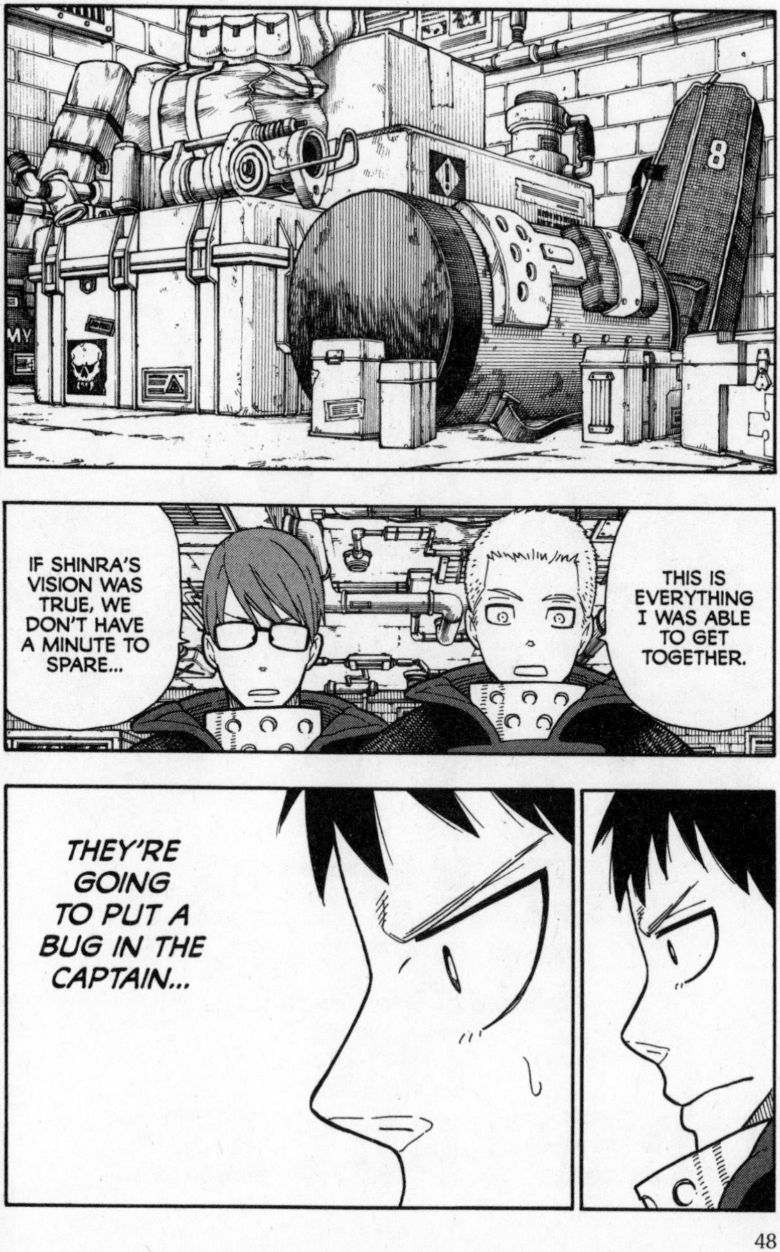
THIS IS EVERYTHING I WAS ABLE TO GET TOGETHER.
IF SHINRA'S VISION WAS TRUE, WE DON'T HAVE A MINUTE TO SPARE...
THEY'RE GOING TO PUT A BUG IN THE CAPTAIN...

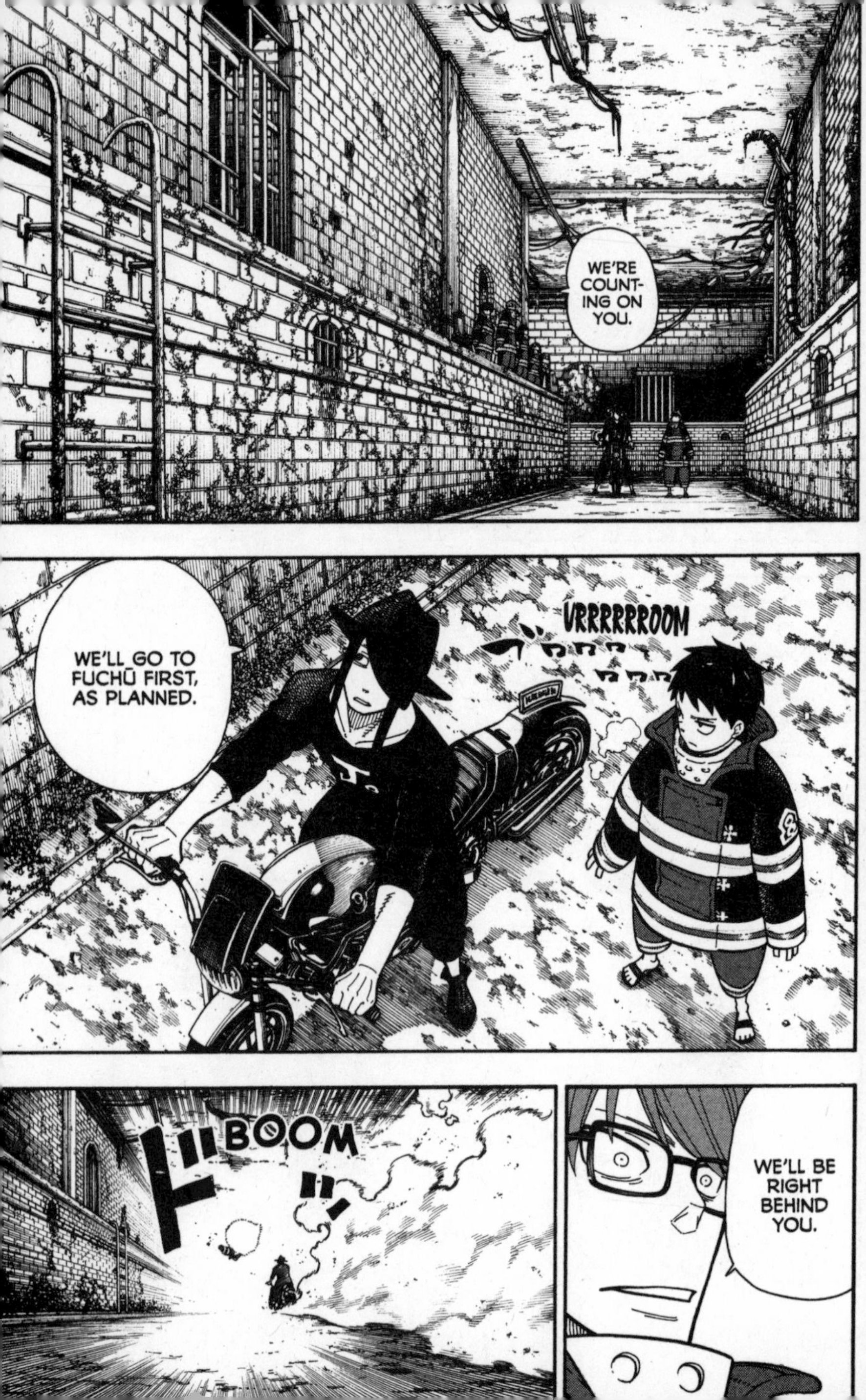
WE'RE COUNTING ON YOU.
VRRRRRROOM
WE'LL GO TO FUCHŪ FIRST, AS PLANNED.
WE'LL BE RIGHT BEHIND YOU.
BOOM

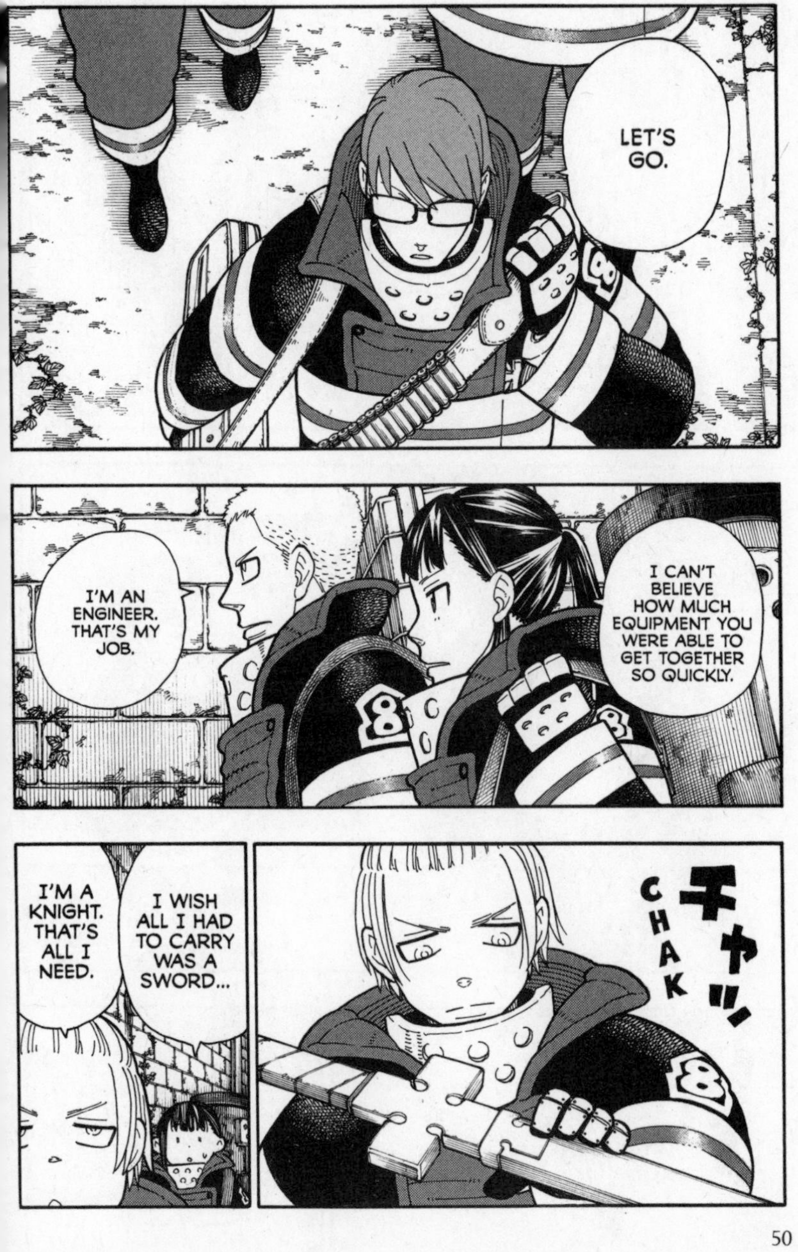
LET'S GO.
I CAN'T BELIEVE HOW MUCH EQUIPMENT YOU WERE ABLE TO GET TOGETHER SO QUICKLY.
I'M AN ENGINEER. THAT'S MY JOB.
CHAK
I WISH ALL I HAD TO CARRY WAS A SWORD...
I'M A KNIGHT. THAT'S ALL I NEED.

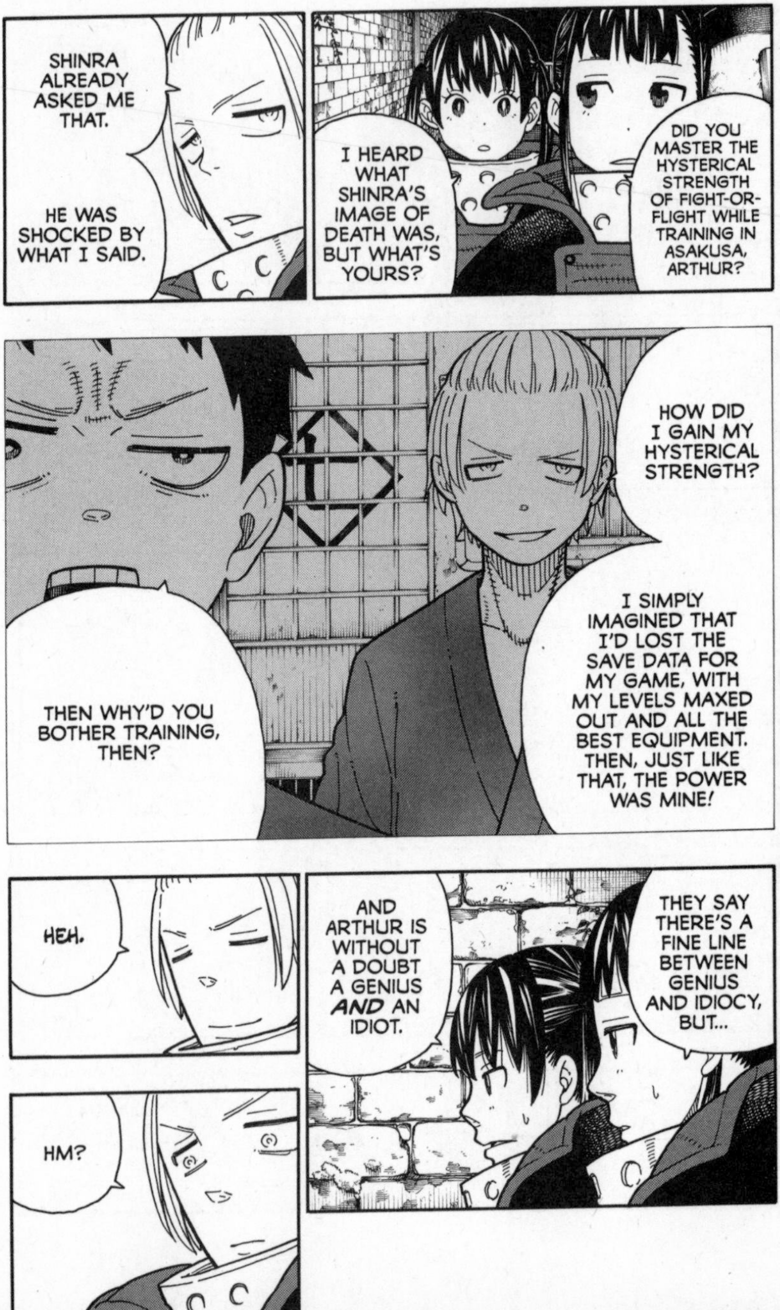
DID YOU MASTER THE HYSTERICAL STRENGTH OF FIGHT-OR-FLIGHT WHILE TRAINING IN ASAKUSA, ARTHUR?
I HEARD WHAT SHINRA'S IMAGE OF DEATH WAS, BUT WHAT'S YOURS?
SHINRA ALREADY ASKED ME THAT.
HE WAS SHOCKED BY WHAT I SAID.
HOW DID I GAIN MY HYSTERICAL STRENGTH?
I SIMPLY IMAGINED THAT I'D LOST THE SAVE DATA FOR MY GAME, WITH MY LEVELS MAXED OUT AND ALL THE BEST EQUIPMENT. THEN, JUST LIKE THAT, THE POWER WAS MINE!
THEN WHY'D YOU BOTHER TRAINING, THEN?
THEY SAY THERE'S A FINE LINE BETWEEN GENIUS AND IDIOCY, BUT...
AND ARTHUR IS WITHOUT A DOUBT A GENIUS ***AND*** AN IDIOT.
HEH.
HM?

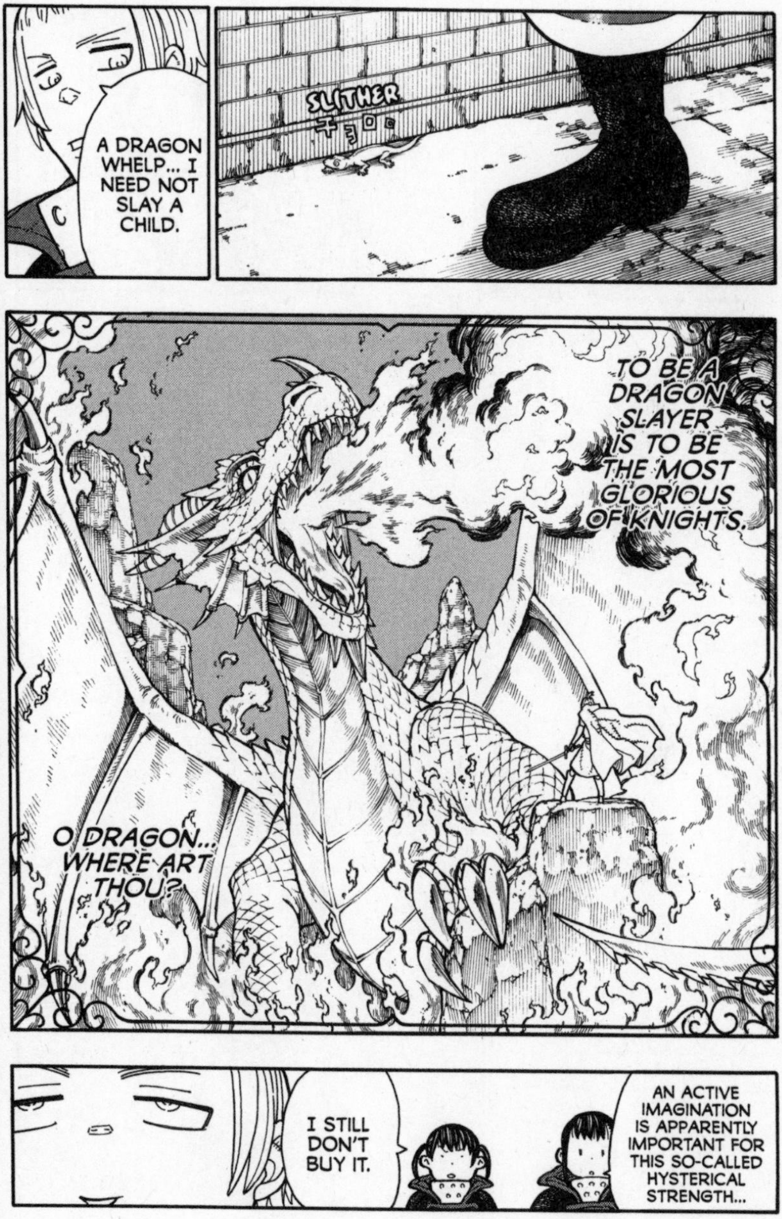
SLITHER
A DRAGON WHELP... I NEED NOT SLAY A CHILD.
TO BE A DRAGON SLAYER IS TO BE THE MOST GLORIOUS OF KNIGHTS.
O DRAGON... WHERE ART THOU?
AN ACTIVE IMAGINATION IS APPARENTLY IMPORTANT FOR THIS SO-CALLED HYSTERICAL STRENGTH...
I STILL DON'T BUY IT.

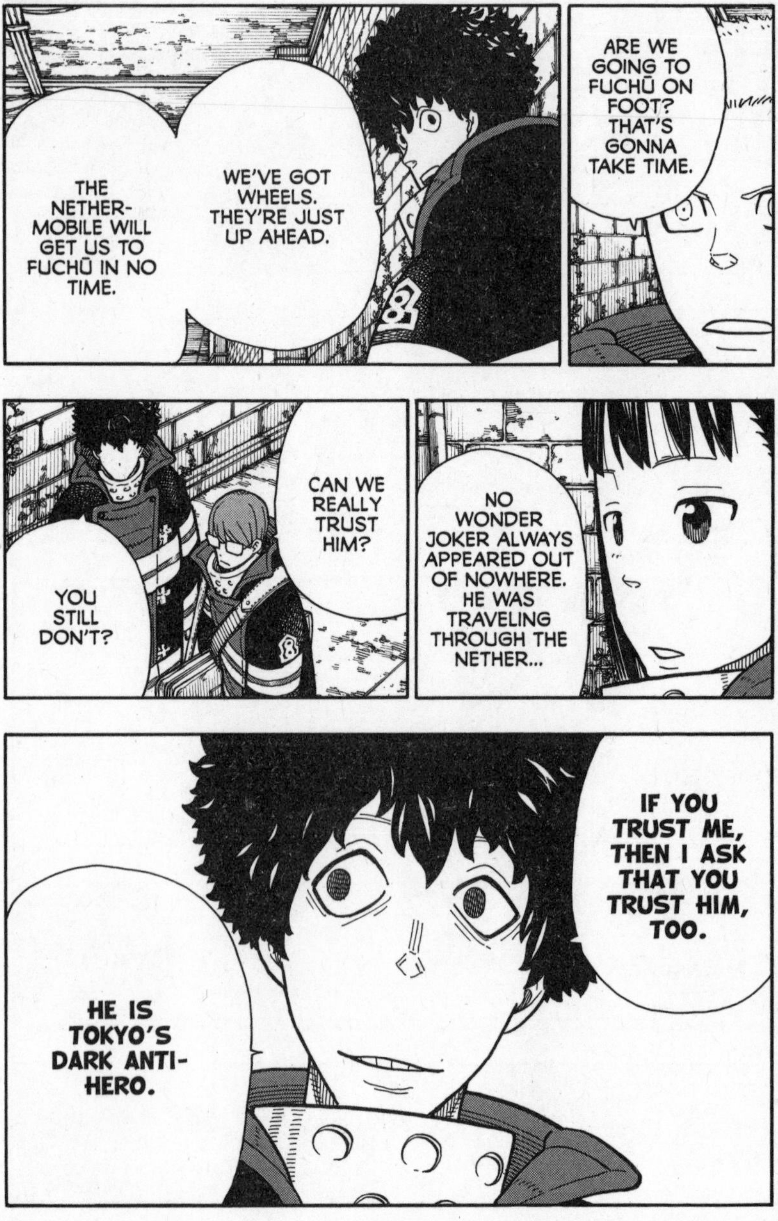
ARE WE GOING TO FUCHŪ ON FOOT? THAT'S GONNA TAKE TIME.
WE'VE GOT WHEELS. THEY'RE JUST UP AHEAD.
THE NETHER-MOBILE WILL GET US TO FUCHŪ IN NO TIME.
NO WONDER JOKER ALWAYS APPEARED OUT OF NOWHERE. HE WAS TRAVELING THROUGH THE NETHER...
CAN WE REALLY TRUST HIM?
YOU STILL DON'T?
IF YOU TRUST ME, THEN I ASK THAT YOU TRUST HIM, TOO.
HE IS TOKYO'S DARK ANTI-HERO.

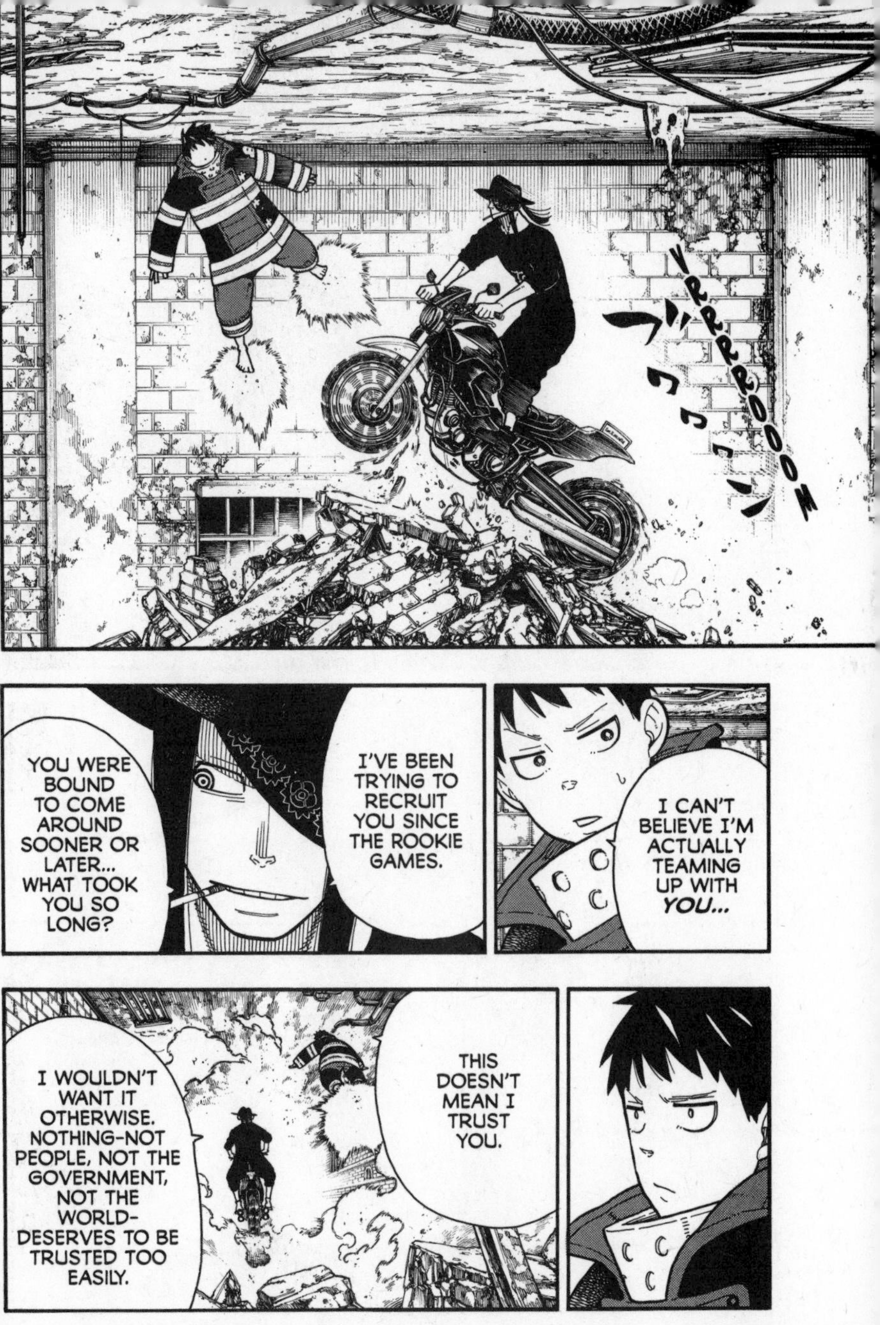
VRRRROOOOM
I CAN'T BELIEVE I'M ACTUALLY TEAMING UP WITH *YOU...*
I'VE BEEN TRYING TO RECRUIT YOU SINCE THE ROOKIE GAMES.
YOU WERE BOUND TO COME AROUND SOONER OR LATER... WHAT TOOK YOU SO LONG?
THIS DOESN'T MEAN I TRUST YOU.
I WOULDN'T WANT IT OTHERWISE. NOTHING-NOT PEOPLE, NOT THE GOVERNMENT, NOT THE WORLD-DESERVES TO BE TRUSTED TOO EASILY.

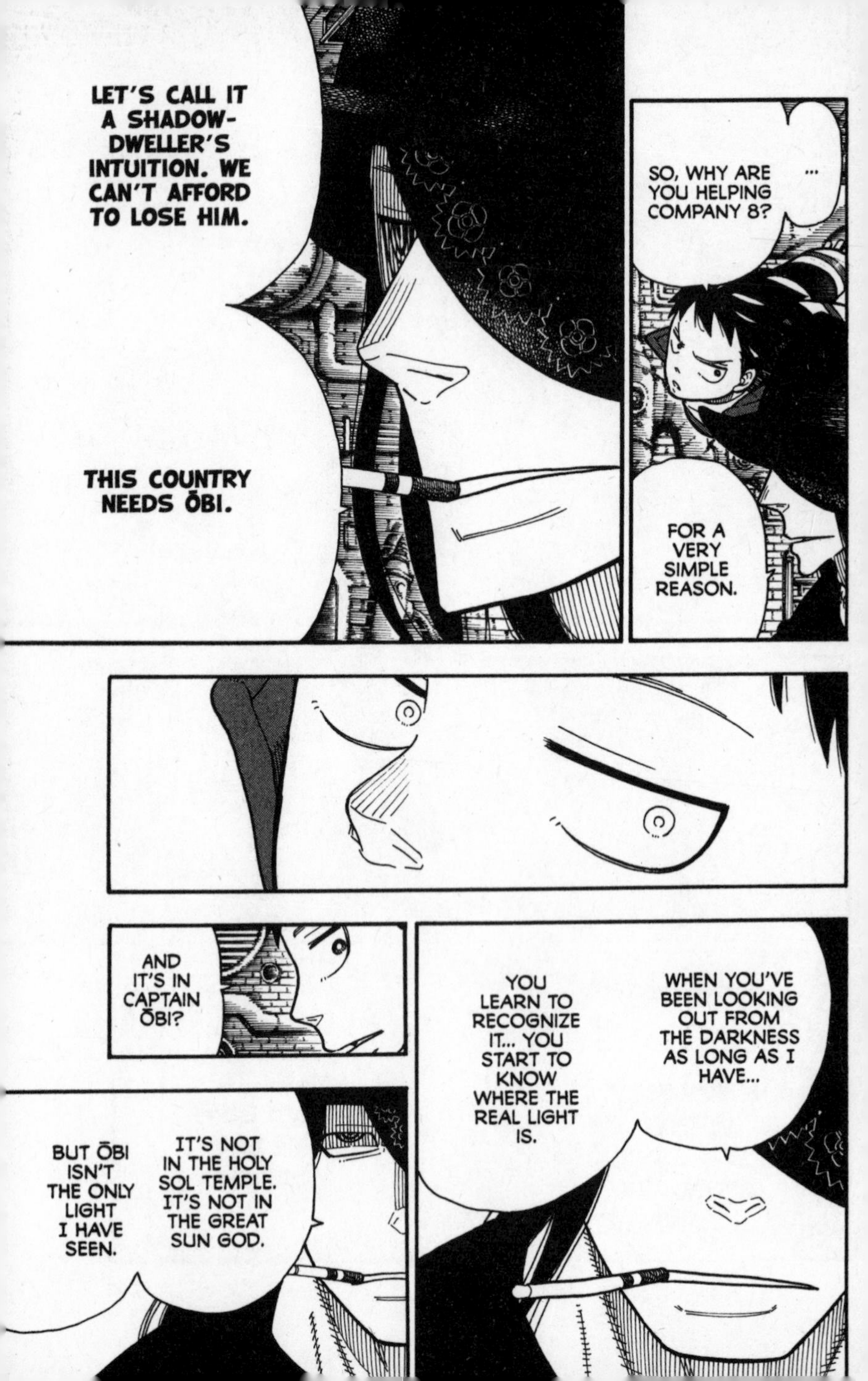
...
SO, WHY ARE YOU HELPING COMPANY 8?
FOR A VERY SIMPLE REASON.
LET'S CALL IT A SHADOW-DWELLER'S INTUITION. WE CAN'T AFFORD TO LOSE HIM.
THIS COUNTRY NEEDS ŌBI.
WHEN YOU'VE BEEN LOOKING OUT FROM THE DARKNESS AS LONG AS I HAVE...
YOU LEARN TO RECOGNIZE IT... YOU START TO KNOW WHERE THE REAL LIGHT IS.
AND IT'S IN CAPTAIN ŌBI?
IT'S NOT IN THE HOLY SOL TEMPLE. IT'S NOT IN THE GREAT SUN GOD.
BUT ŌBI ISN'T THE ONLY LIGHT I HAVE SEEN.

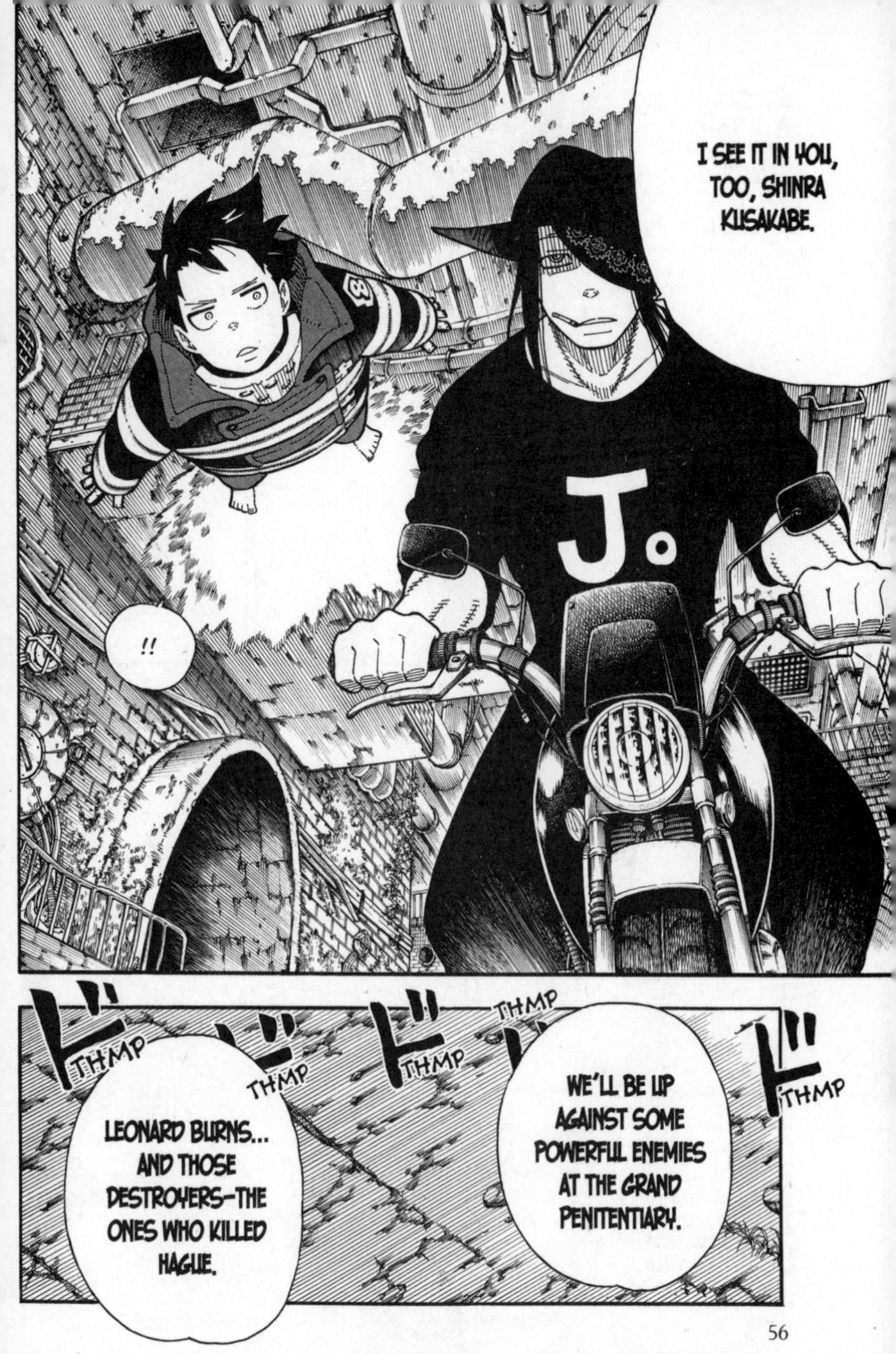

I SEE IT IN YOU, TOO, SHINRA KUSAKABE.
!!
THMP
THMP
WE'LL BE UP AGAINST SOME POWERFUL ENEMIES AT THE GRAND PENITENTIARY.
THMP
THMP
THMP
LEONARD BURNS... AND THOSE DESTROYERS—THE ONES WHO KILLED HAGUE.

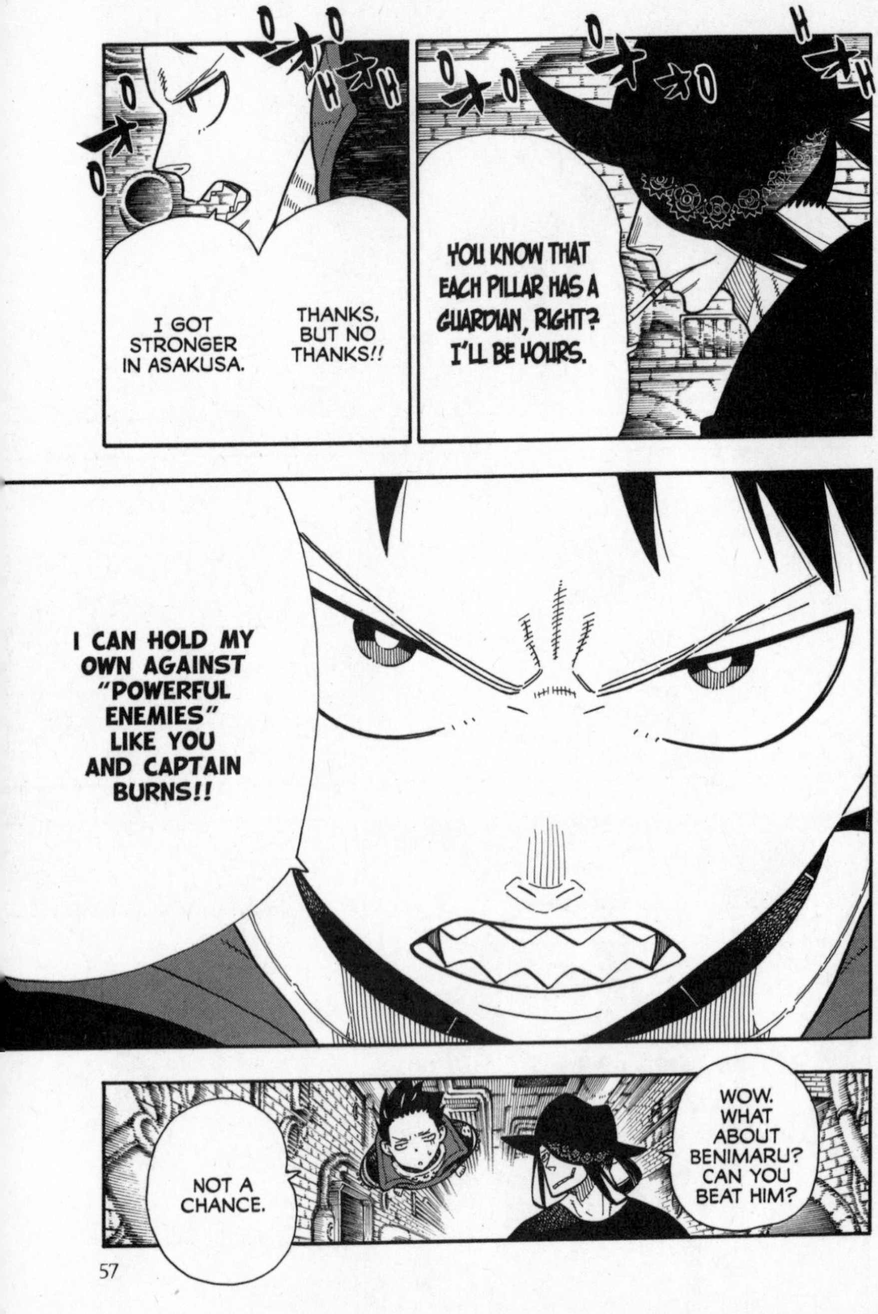
YOU KNOW THAT EACH PILLAR HAS A GUARDIAN, RIGHT? I'LL BE YOURS.
THANKS, BUT NO THANKS!!
I GOT STRONGER IN ASAKUSA.
I CAN HOLD MY OWN AGAINST "POWERFUL ENEMIES" LIKE YOU AND CAPTAIN BURNS!!
WOW. WHAT ABOUT BENIMARU? CAN YOU BEAT HIM?
NOT A CHANCE.

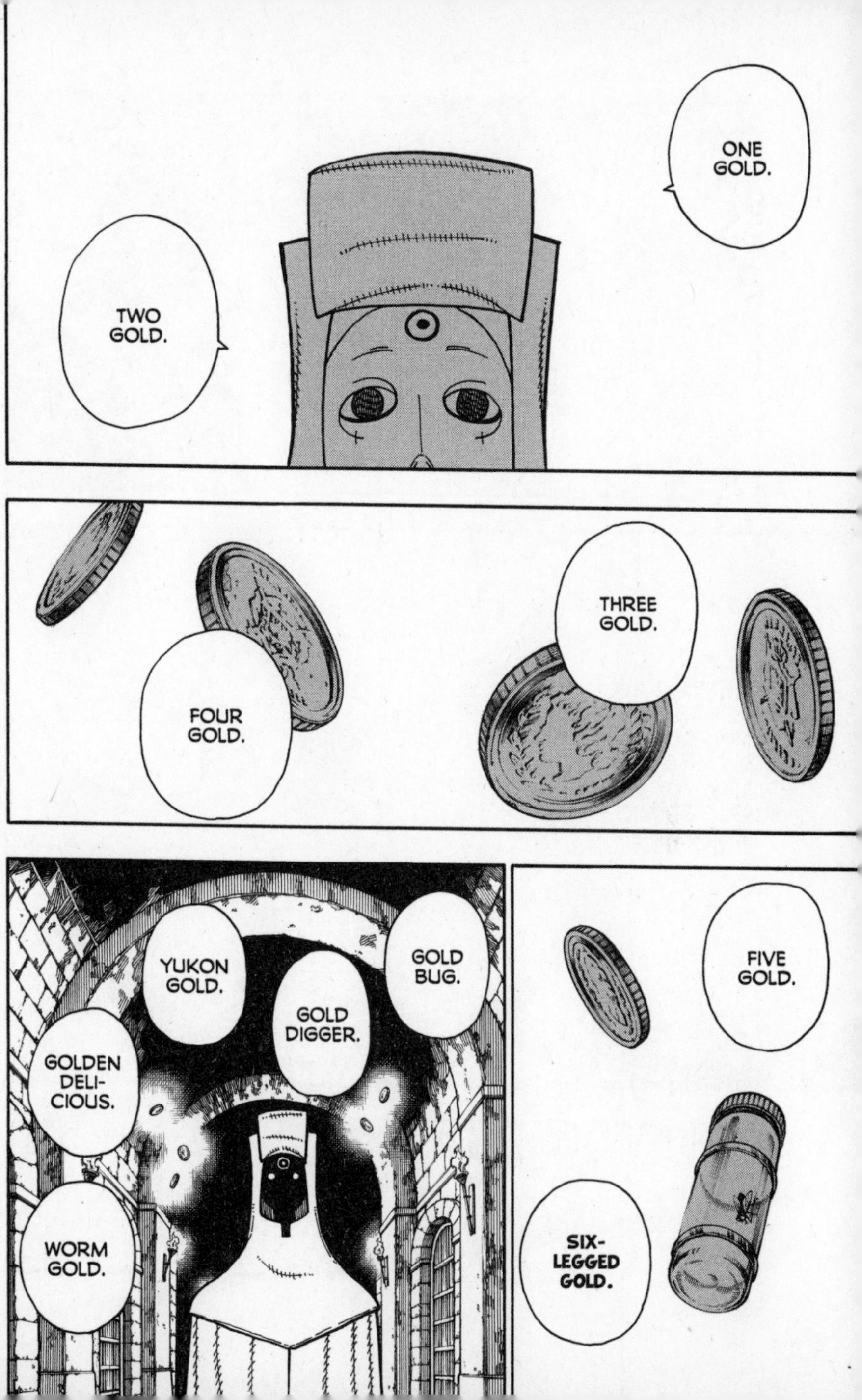
ONE GOLD.
TWO GOLD.
THREE GOLD.
FOUR GOLD.
FIVE GOLD.
SIX-LEGGED GOLD.
GOLD BUG.
GOLD DIGGER.
YUKON GOLD.
GOLDEN DELI-CIOUS.
WORM GOLD.

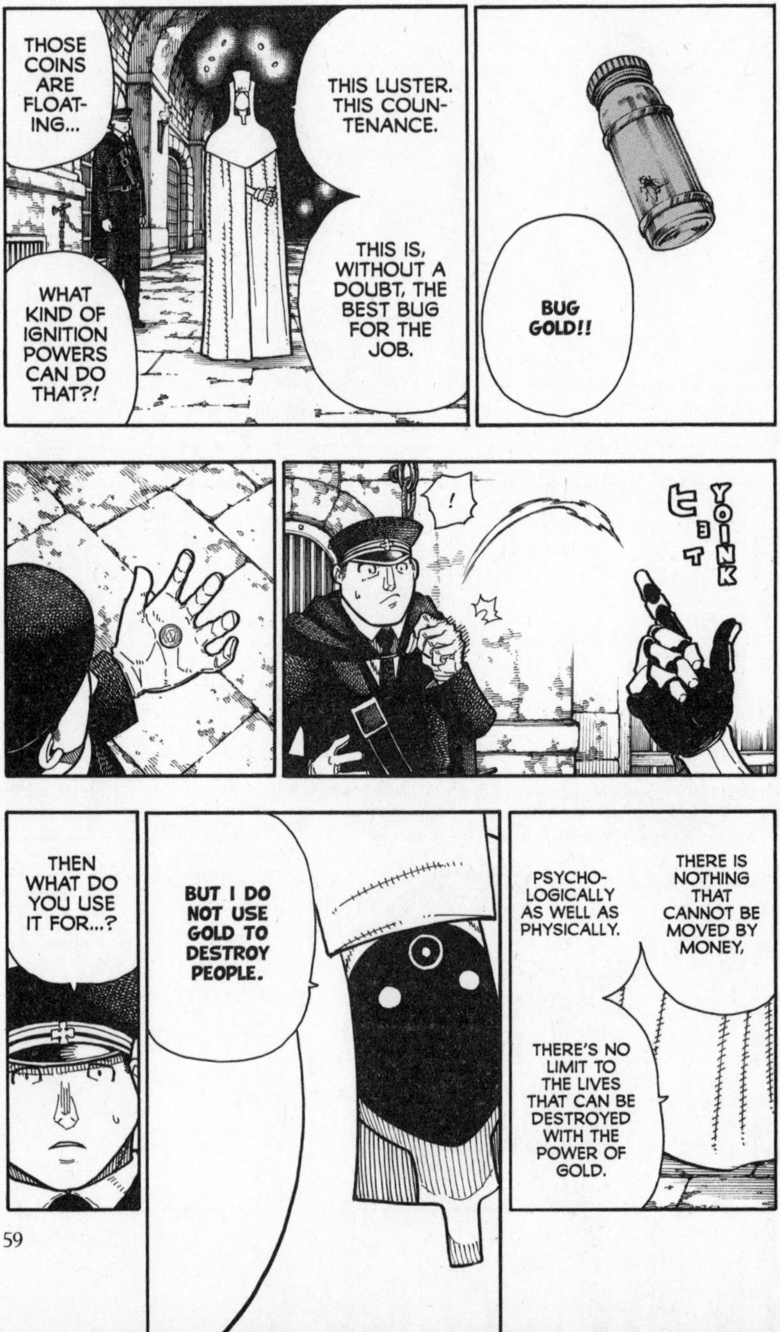
BUG GOLD!!
THIS LUSTER. THIS COUNTENANCE.
THIS IS, WITHOUT A DOUBT, THE BEST BUG FOR THE JOB.
THOSE COINS ARE FLOATING...
WHAT KIND OF IGNITION POWERS CAN DO THAT?!
YOINK
!
THERE IS NOTHING THAT CANNOT BE MOVED BY MONEY,
PSYCHOLOGICALLY AS WELL AS PHYSICALLY.
THERE'S NO LIMIT TO THE LIVES THAT CAN BE DESTROYED WITH THE POWER OF GOLD.
BUT I DO NOT USE GOLD TO DESTROY PEOPLE.
THEN WHAT DO YOU USE IT FOR...?

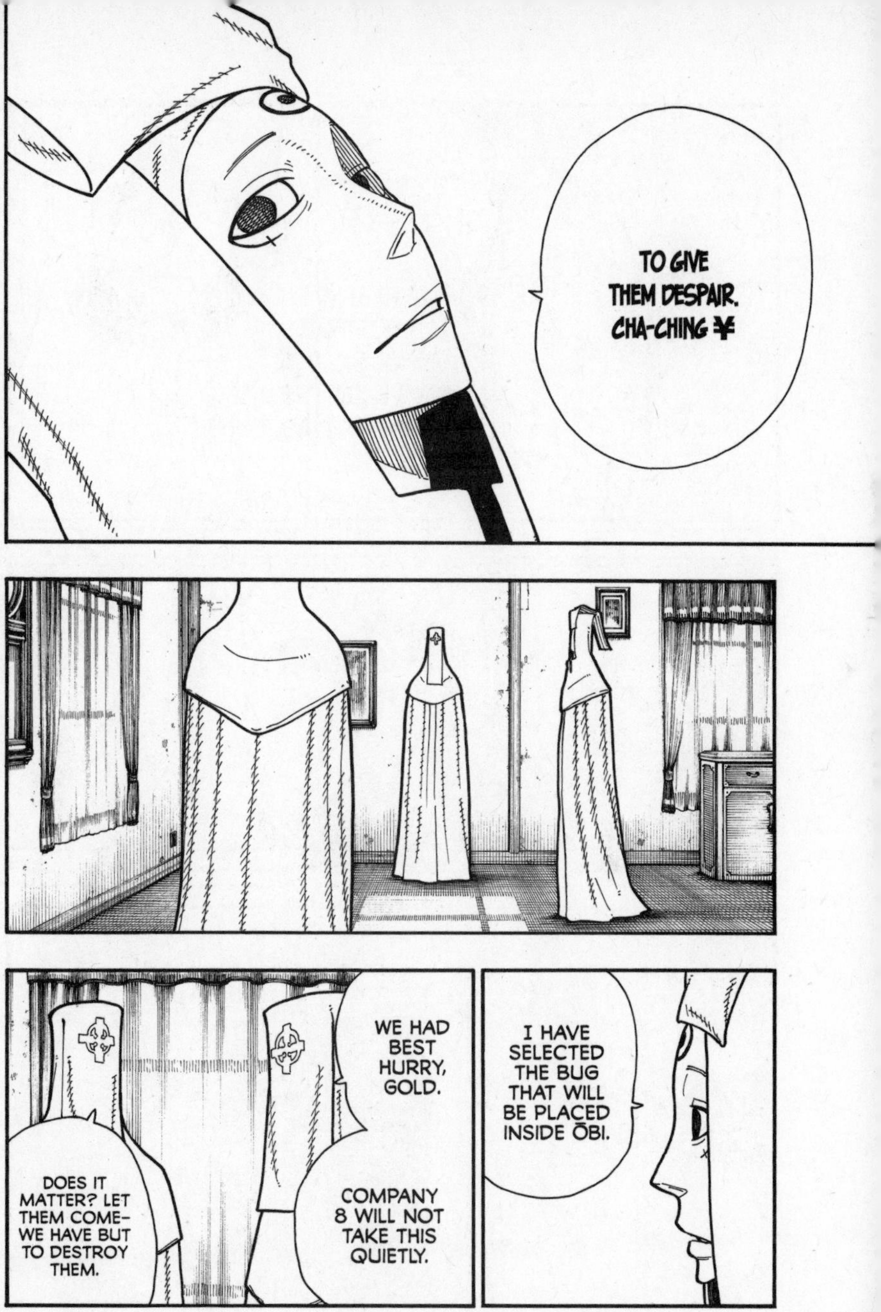
TO GIVE THEM DESPAIR. CHA-CHING ¥
I HAVE SELECTED THE BUG THAT WILL BE PLACED INSIDE ŌBI.
WE HAD BEST HURRY, GOLD.
COMPANY 8 WILL NOT TAKE THIS QUIETLY.
DOES IT MATTER? LET THEM COME— WE HAVE BUT TO DESTROY THEM.

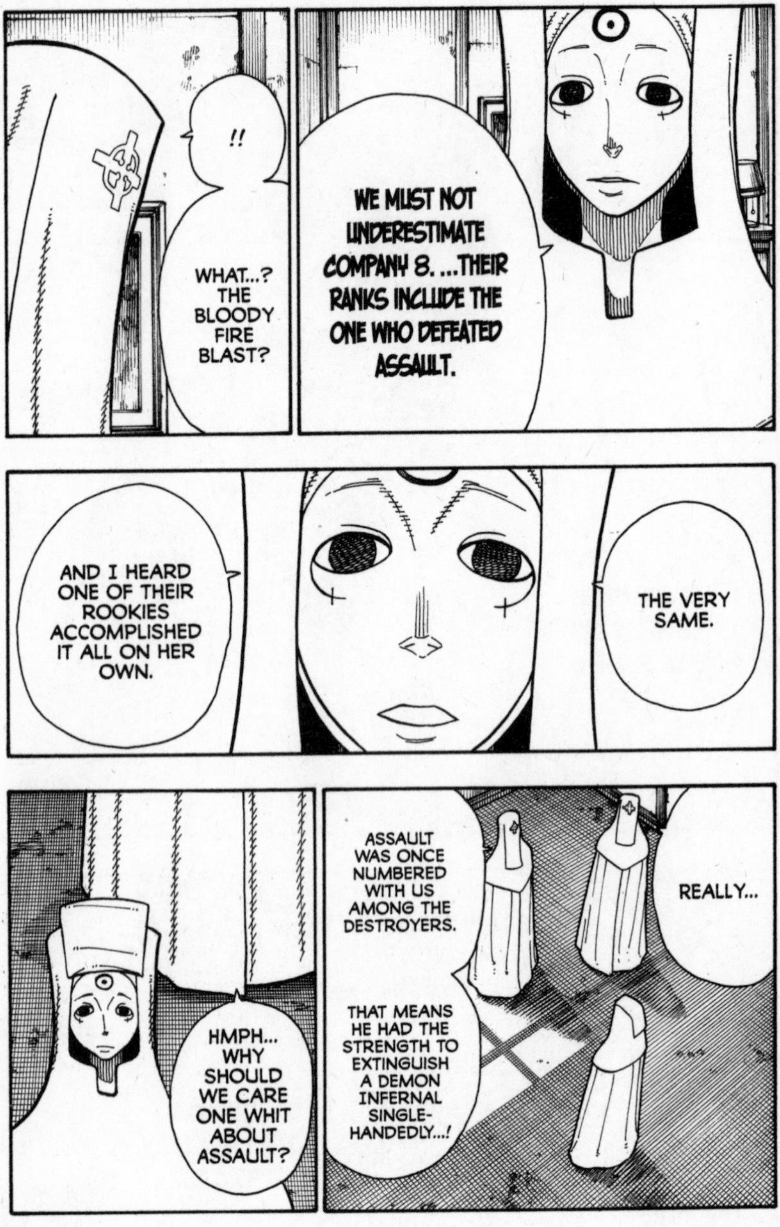
WE MUST NOT UNDERESTIMATE COMPANY 8. ...THEIR RANKS INCLUDE THE ONE WHO DEFEATED ASSAULT.
!!
WHAT...? THE BLOODY FIRE BLAST?
THE VERY SAME.
AND I HEARD ONE OF THEIR ROOKIES ACCOMPLISHED IT ALL ON HER OWN.
REALLY...
ASSAULT WAS ONCE NUMBERED WITH US AMONG THE DESTROYERS.
THAT MEANS HE HAD THE STRENGTH TO EXTINGUISH A DEMON INFERNAL SINGLE-HANDEDLY...!
HMPH... WHY SHOULD WE CARE ONE WHIT ABOUT ASSAULT?

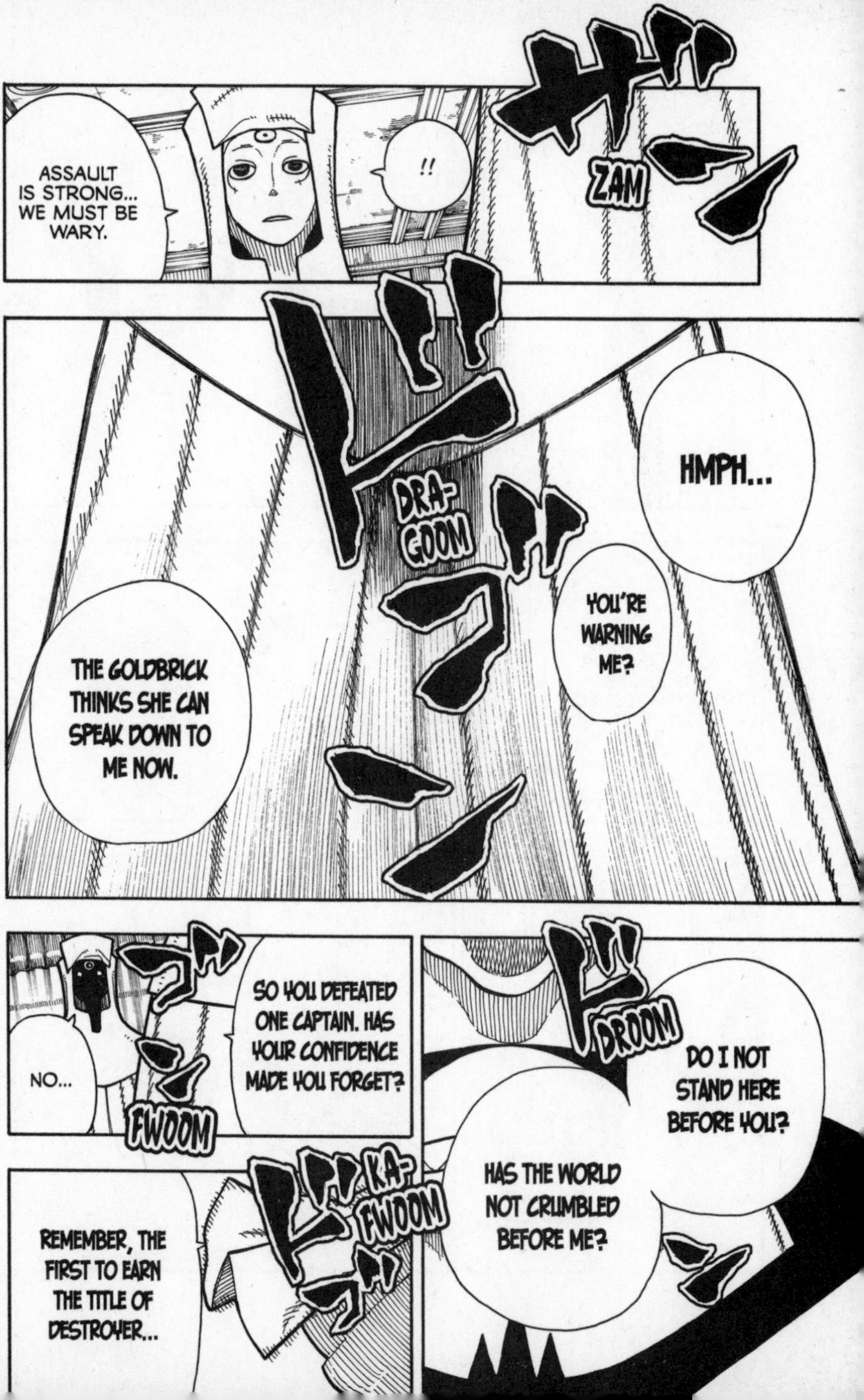
ZAM
!!
ASSAULT IS STRONG... WE MUST BE WARY.
HMPH...
DRA-GOOM
YOU'RE WARNING ME?
THE GOLDBRICK THINKS SHE CAN SPEAK DOWN TO ME NOW.
DROOM
DO I NOT STAND HERE BEFORE YOU?
HAS THE WORLD NOT CRUMBLED BEFORE ME?
SO YOU DEFEATED ONE CAPTAIN. HAS YOUR CONFIDENCE MADE YOU FORGET?
NO...
FWOOM
KA-FWOOM
REMEMBER, THE FIRST TO EARN THE TITLE OF DESTROYER...

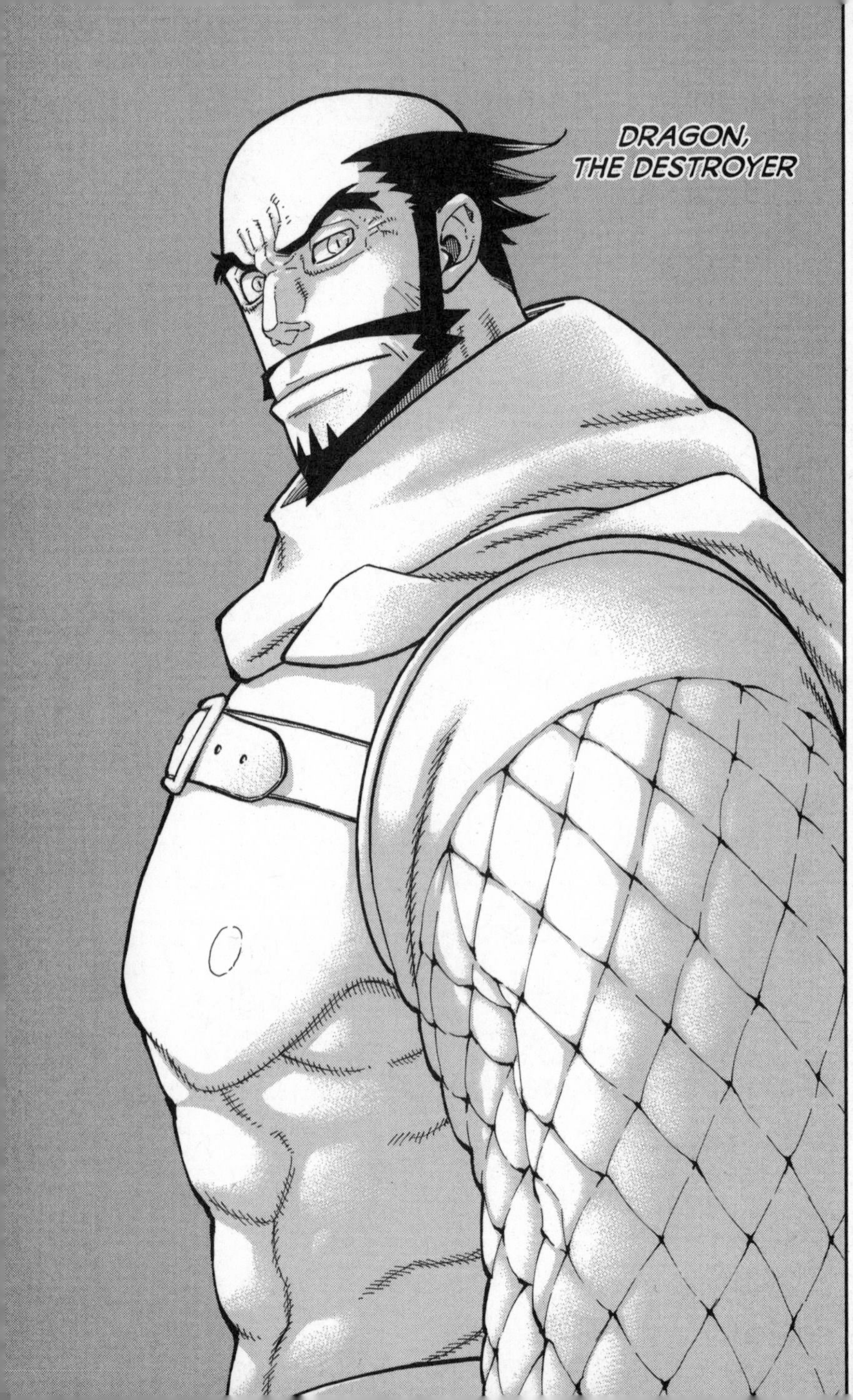
DRAGON,
THE DESTROYER

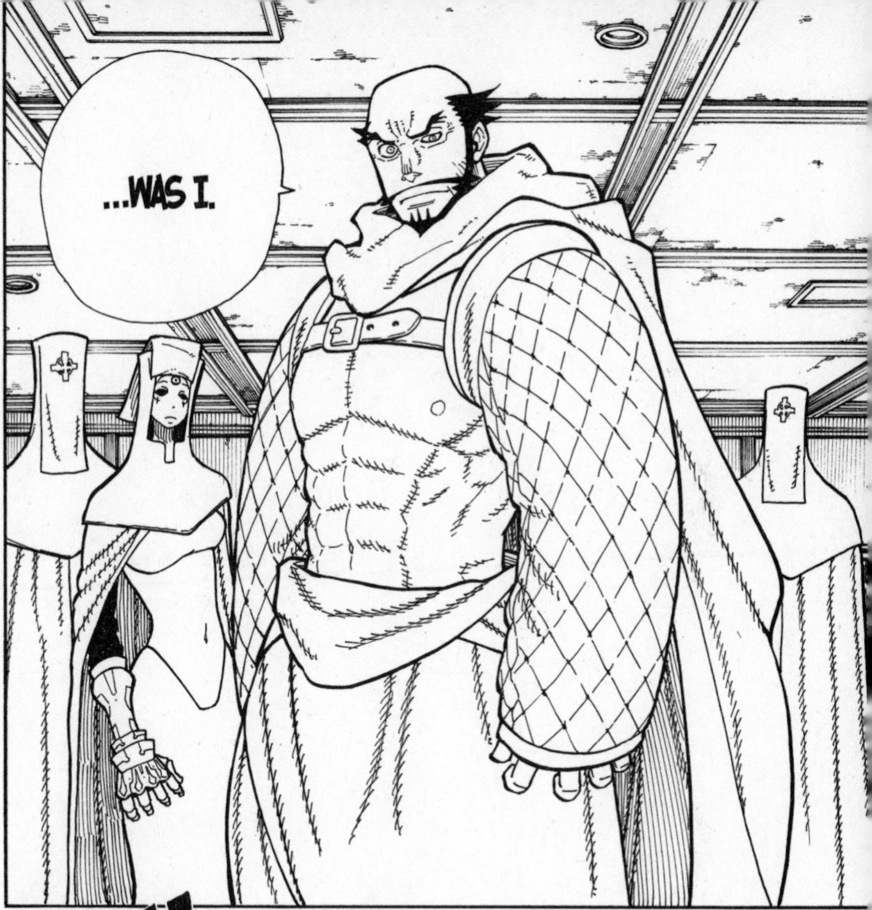
...WAS I.
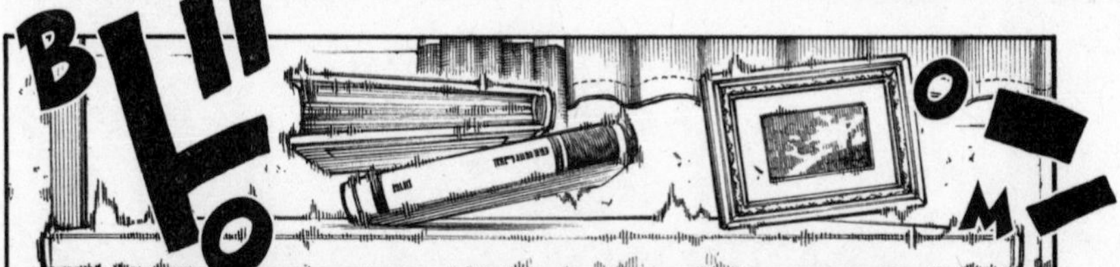
BLOOOM
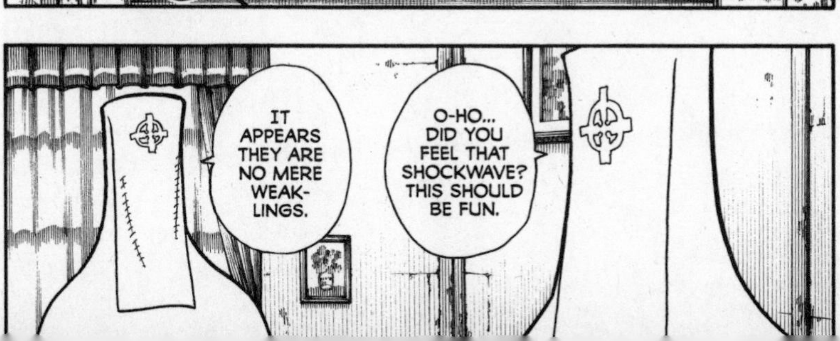
O-HO... DID YOU FEEL THAT SHOCKWAVE? THIS SHOULD BE FUN.
IT APPEARS THEY ARE NO MERE WEAK-LINGS.

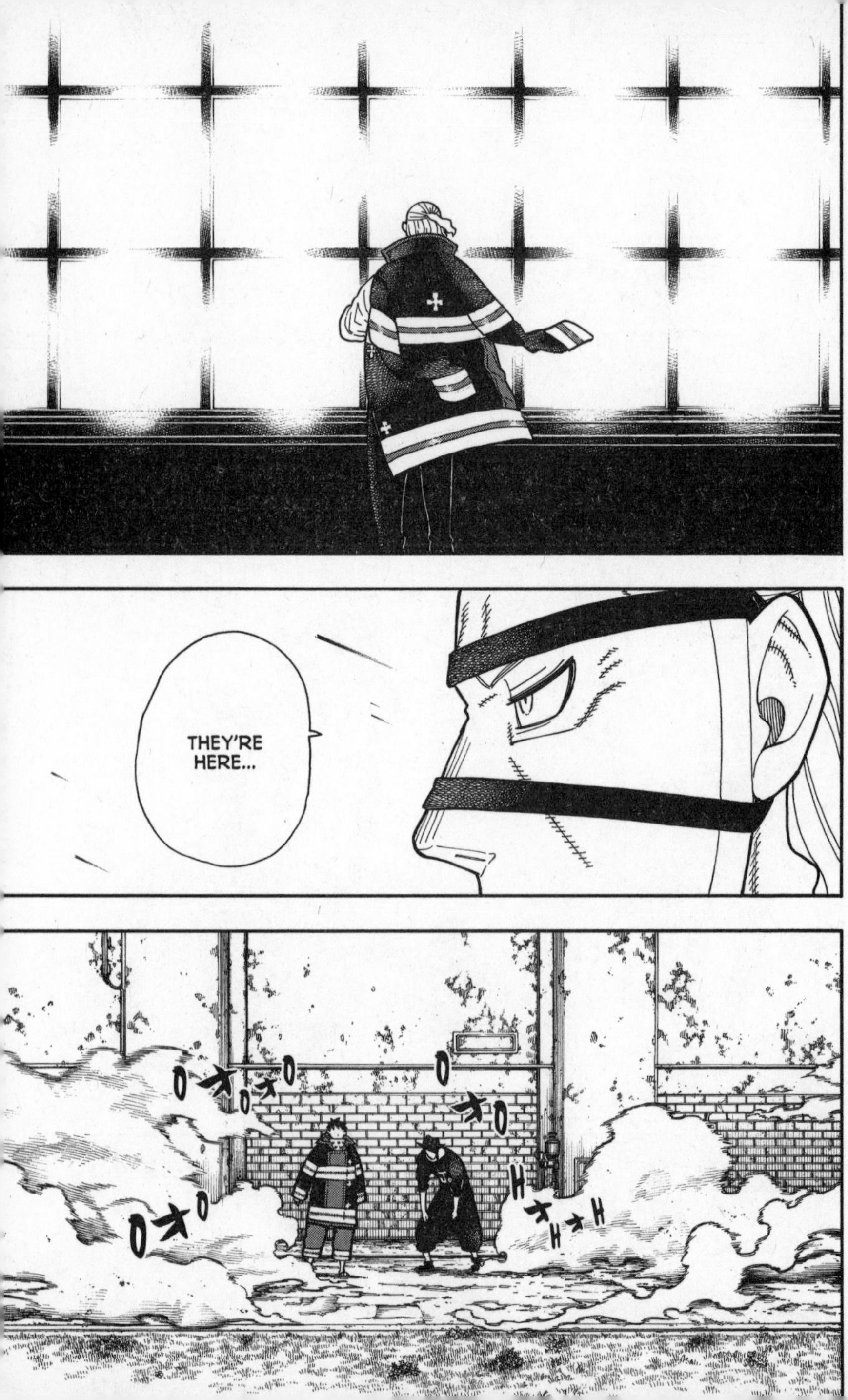
THEY'RE HERE...

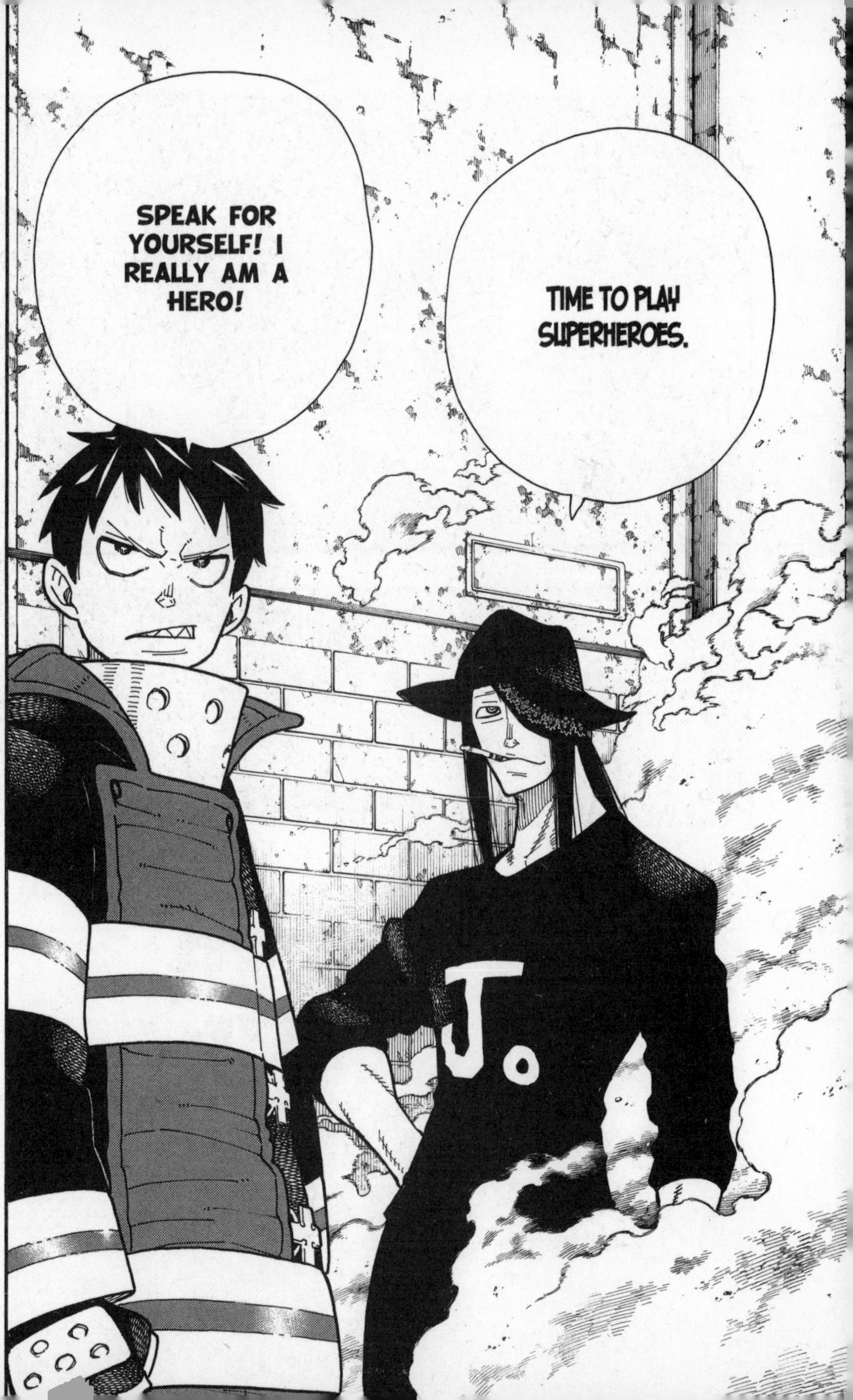
TIME TO PLAY SUPERHEROES.
SPEAK FOR YOURSELF! I REALLY AM A HERO!

CHAPTER CLXXXI: FLAME INCARNATE

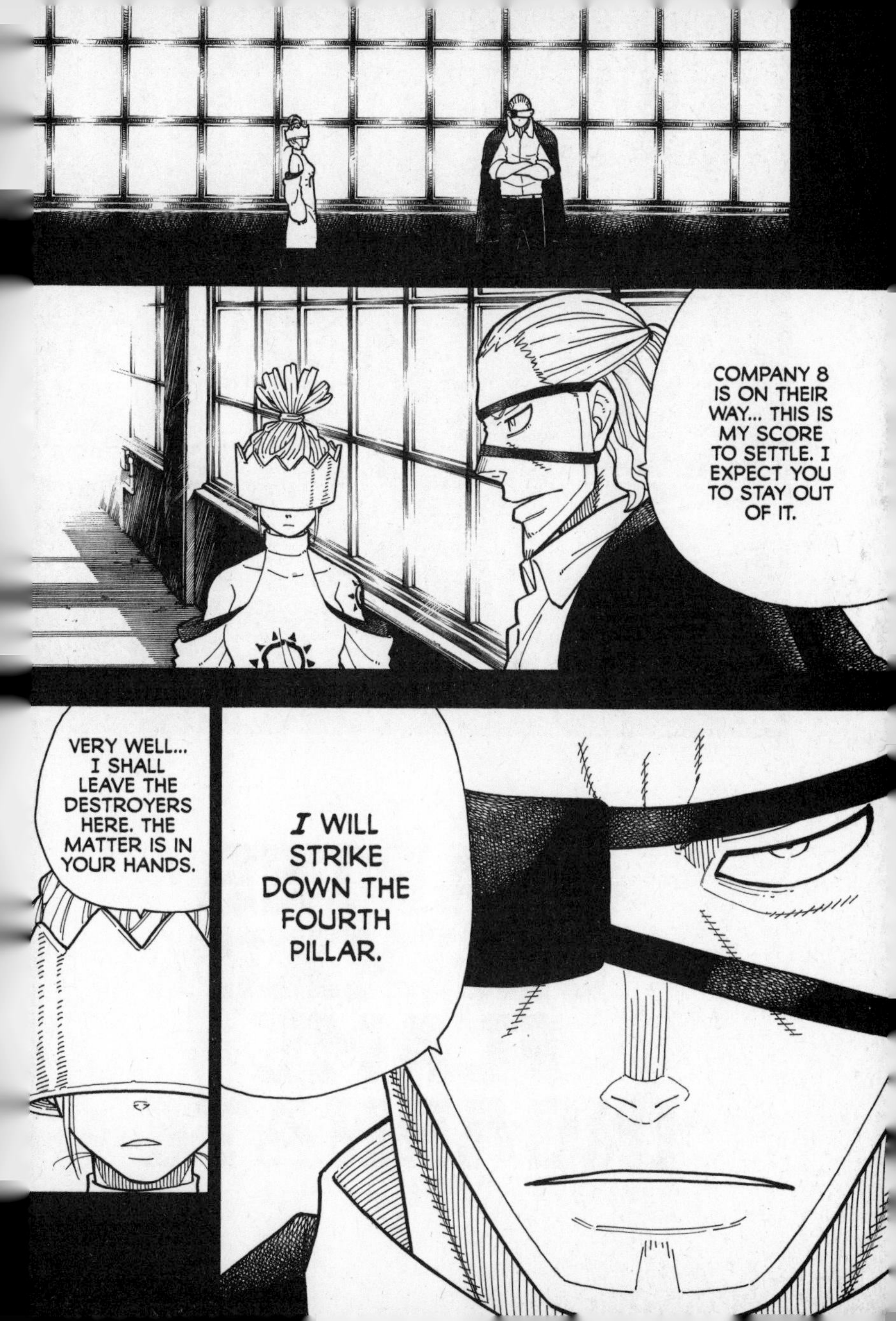
COMPANY 8 IS ON THEIR WAY... THIS IS MY SCORE TO SETTLE. I EXPECT YOU TO STAY OUT OF IT.
I WILL STRIKE DOWN THE FOURTH PILLAR.
VERY WELL... I SHALL LEAVE THE DESTROYERS HERE. THE MATTER IS IN YOUR HANDS.

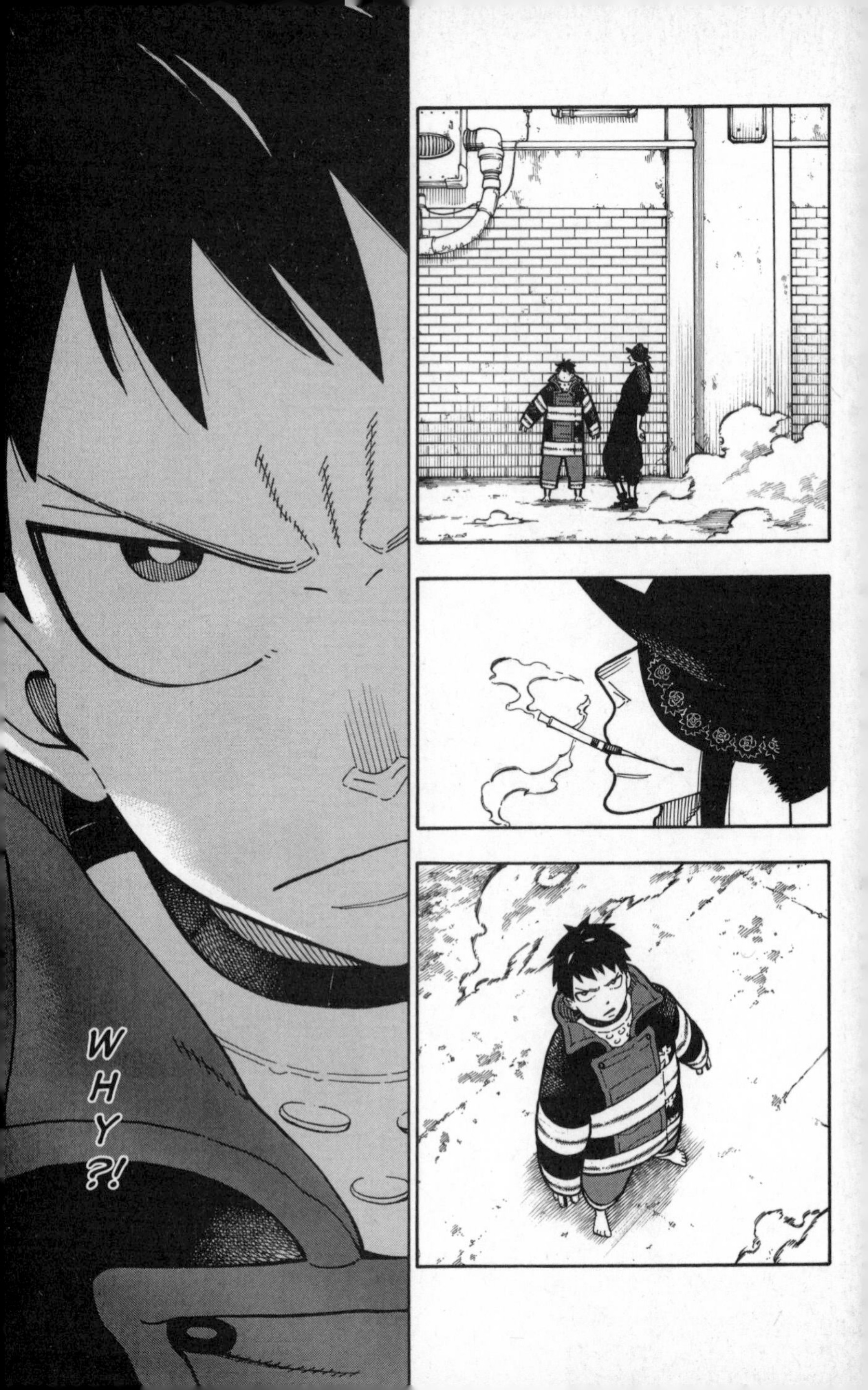
WHY?!

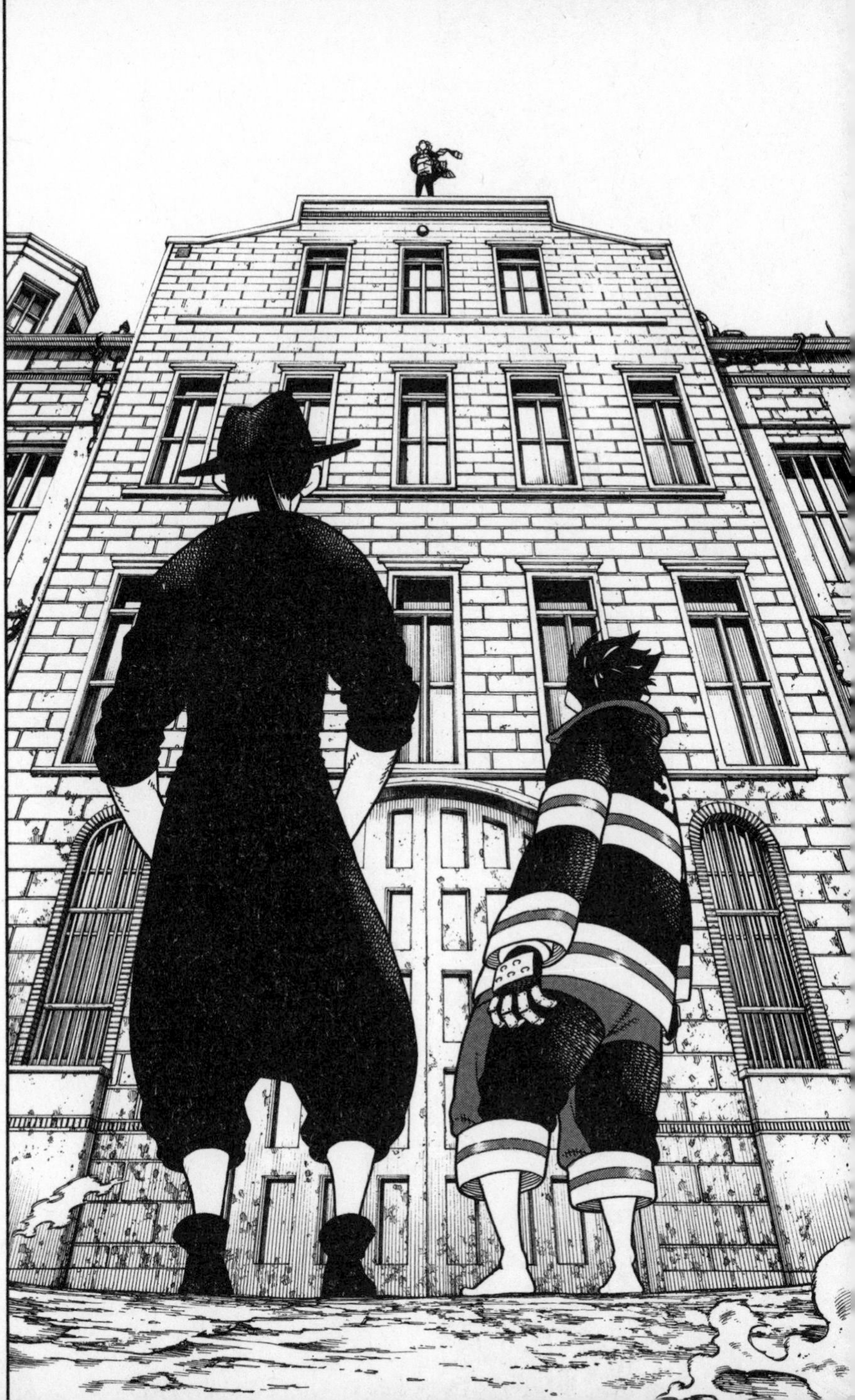

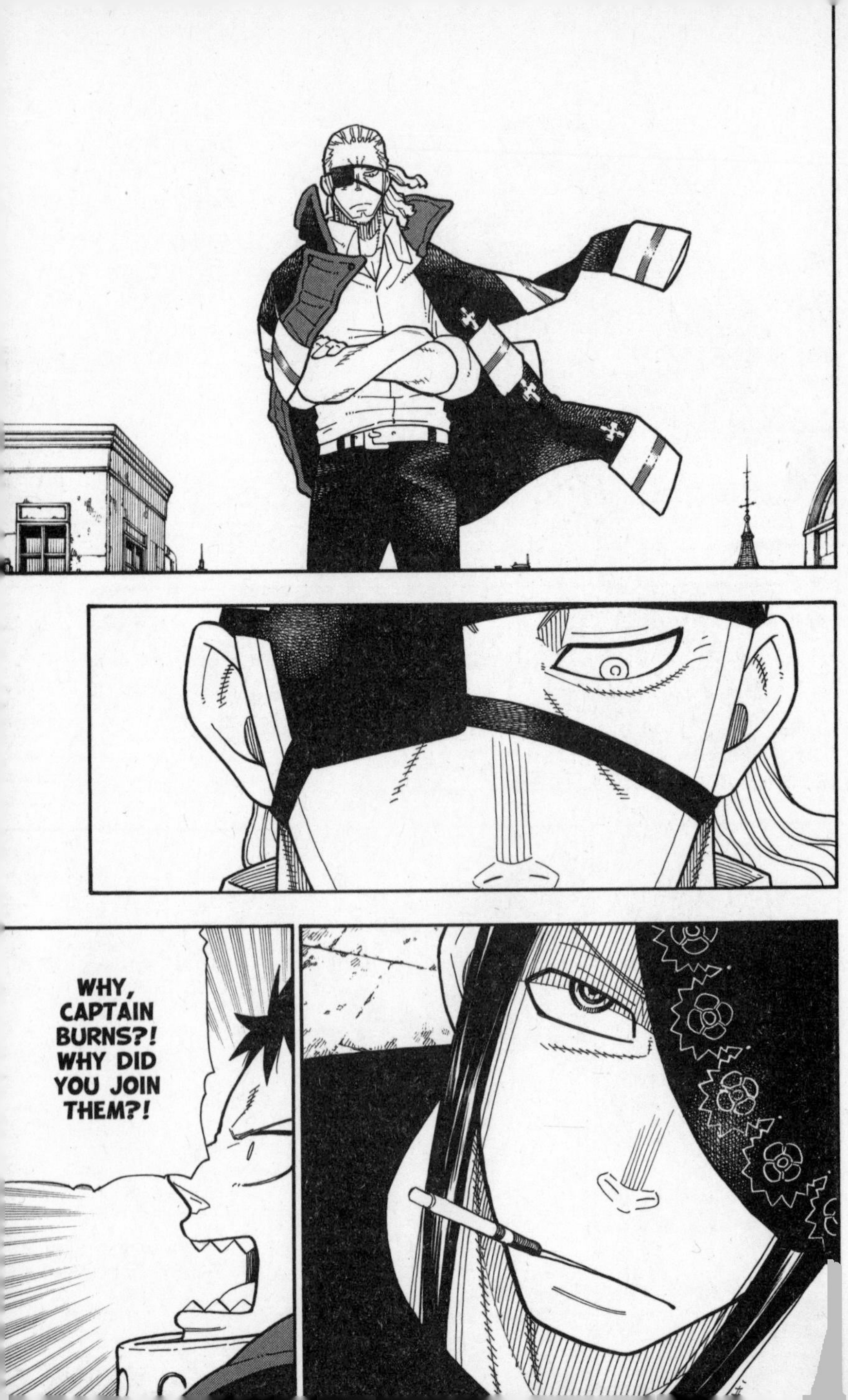
WHY, CAPTAIN BURNS?! WHY DID YOU JOIN THEM?!

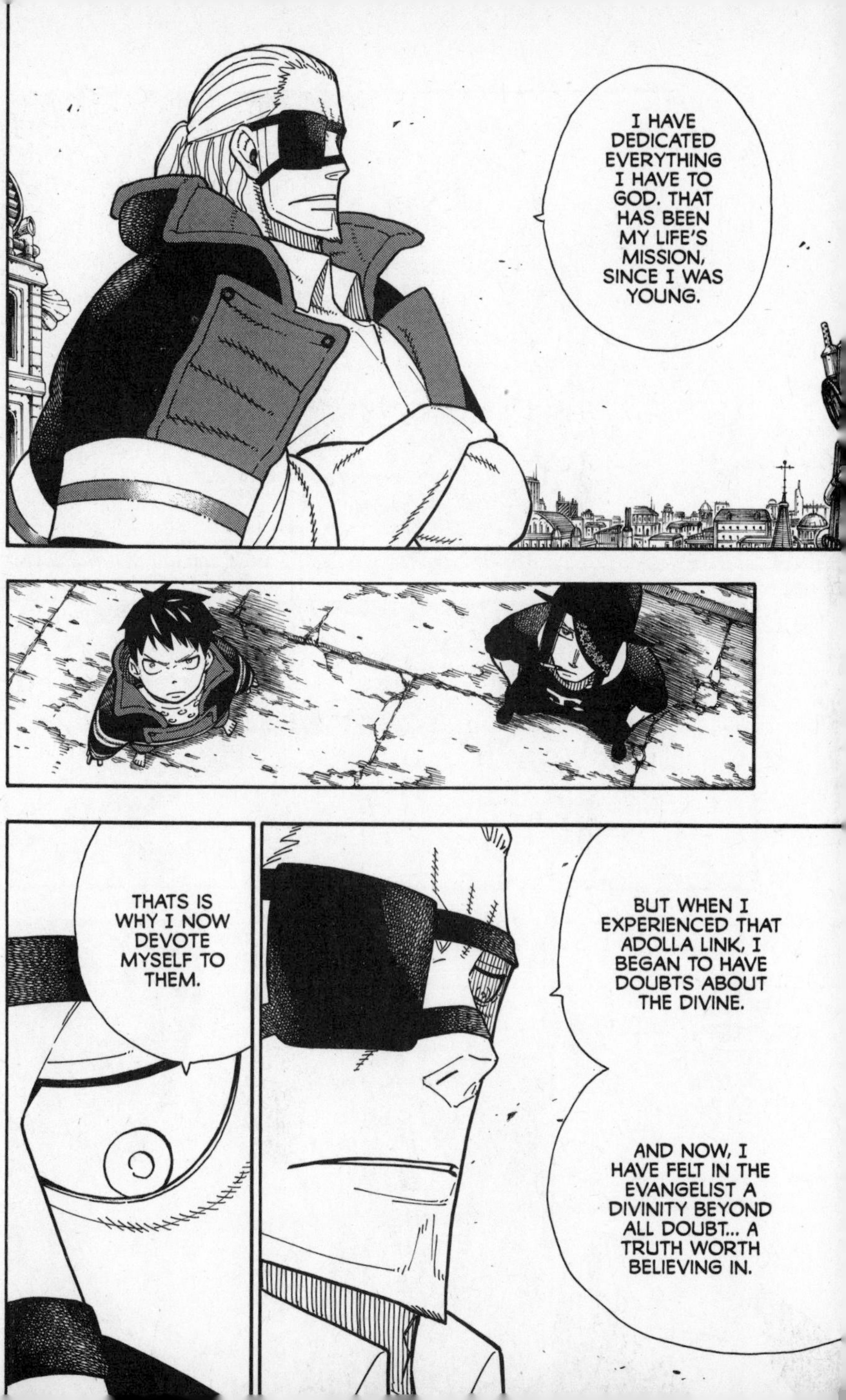
I HAVE DEDICATED EVERYTHING I HAVE TO GOD. THAT HAS BEEN MY LIFE'S MISSION, SINCE I WAS YOUNG.
BUT WHEN I EXPERIENCED THAT ADOLLA LINK, I BEGAN TO HAVE DOUBTS ABOUT THE DIVINE.
AND NOW, I HAVE FELT IN THE EVANGELIST A DIVINITY BEYOND ALL DOUBT... A TRUTH WORTH BELIEVING IN.
THATS IS WHY I NOW DEVOTE MYSELF TO THEM.

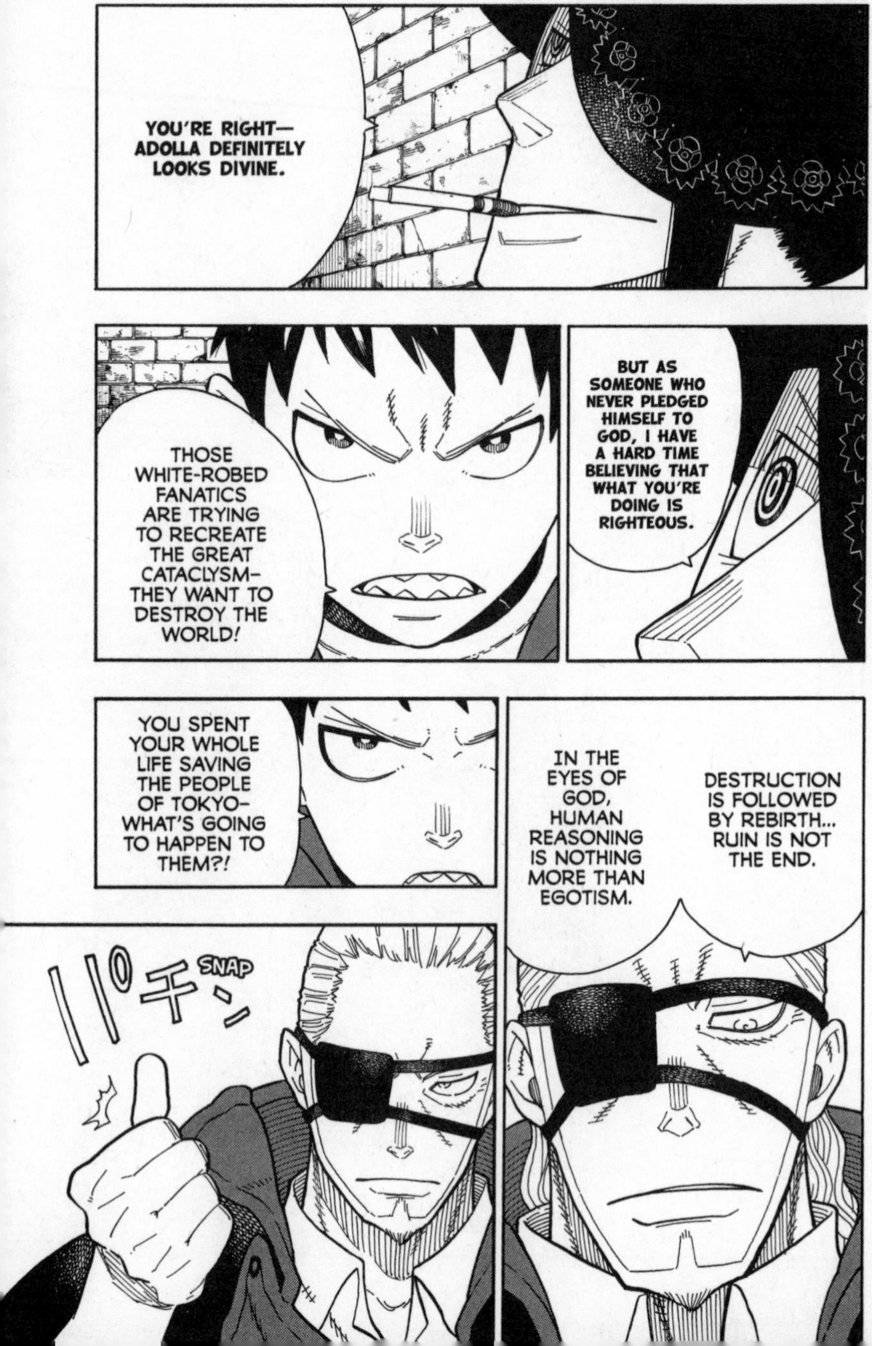
YOU'RE RIGHT— ADOLLA DEFINITELY LOOKS DIVINE.
BUT AS SOMEONE WHO NEVER PLEDGED HIMSELF TO GOD, I HAVE A HARD TIME BELIEVING THAT WHAT YOU'RE DOING IS RIGHTEOUS.
THOSE WHITE-ROBED FANATICS ARE TRYING TO RECREATE THE GREAT CATACLYSM— THEY WANT TO DESTROY THE WORLD!
DESTRUCTION IS FOLLOWED BY REBIRTH... RUIN IS NOT THE END.
IN THE EYES OF GOD, HUMAN REASONING IS NOTHING MORE THAN EGOTISM.
YOU SPENT YOUR WHOLE LIFE SAVING THE PEOPLE OF TOKYO— WHAT'S GOING TO HAPPEN TO THEM?!
パチン
SNAP

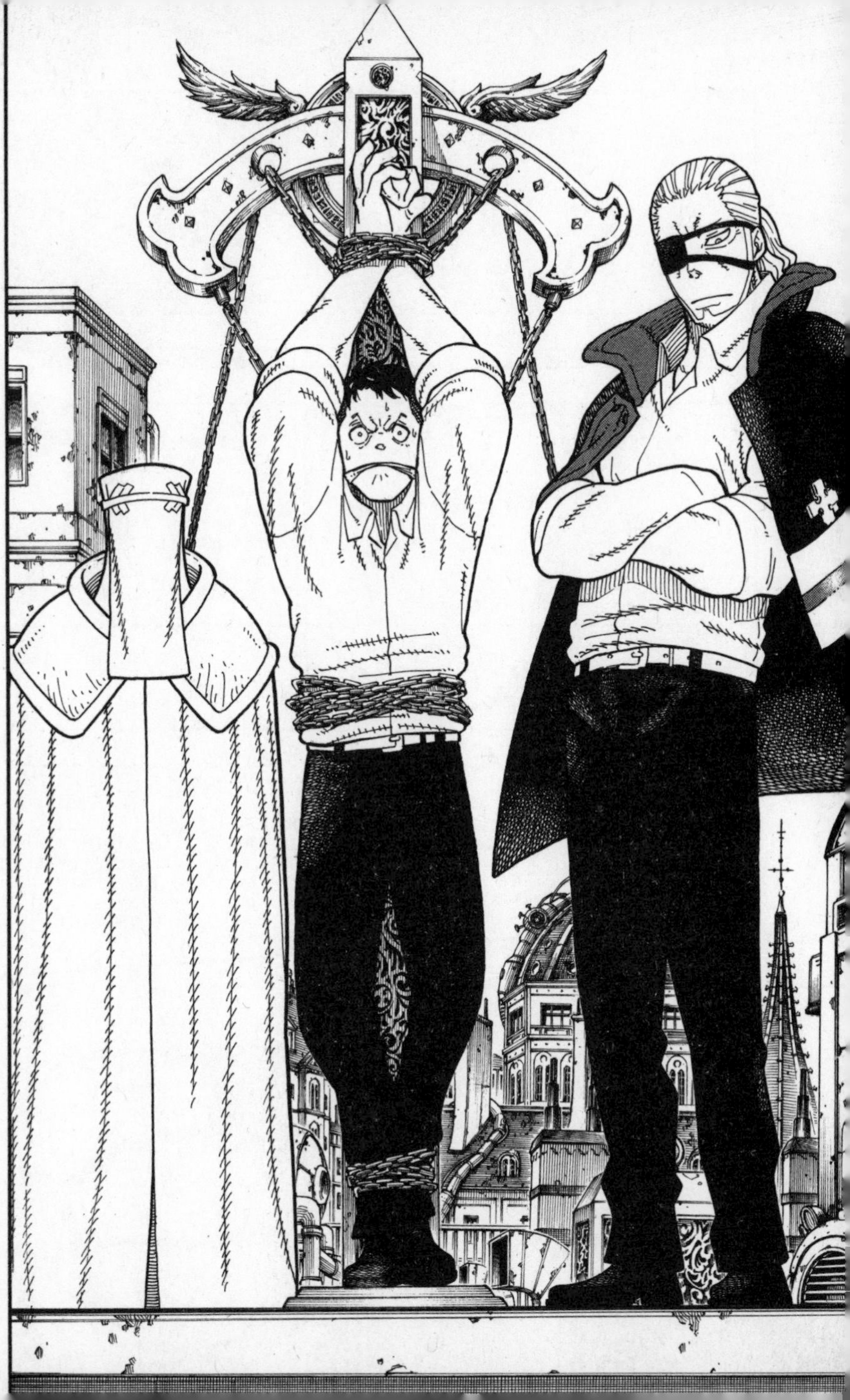

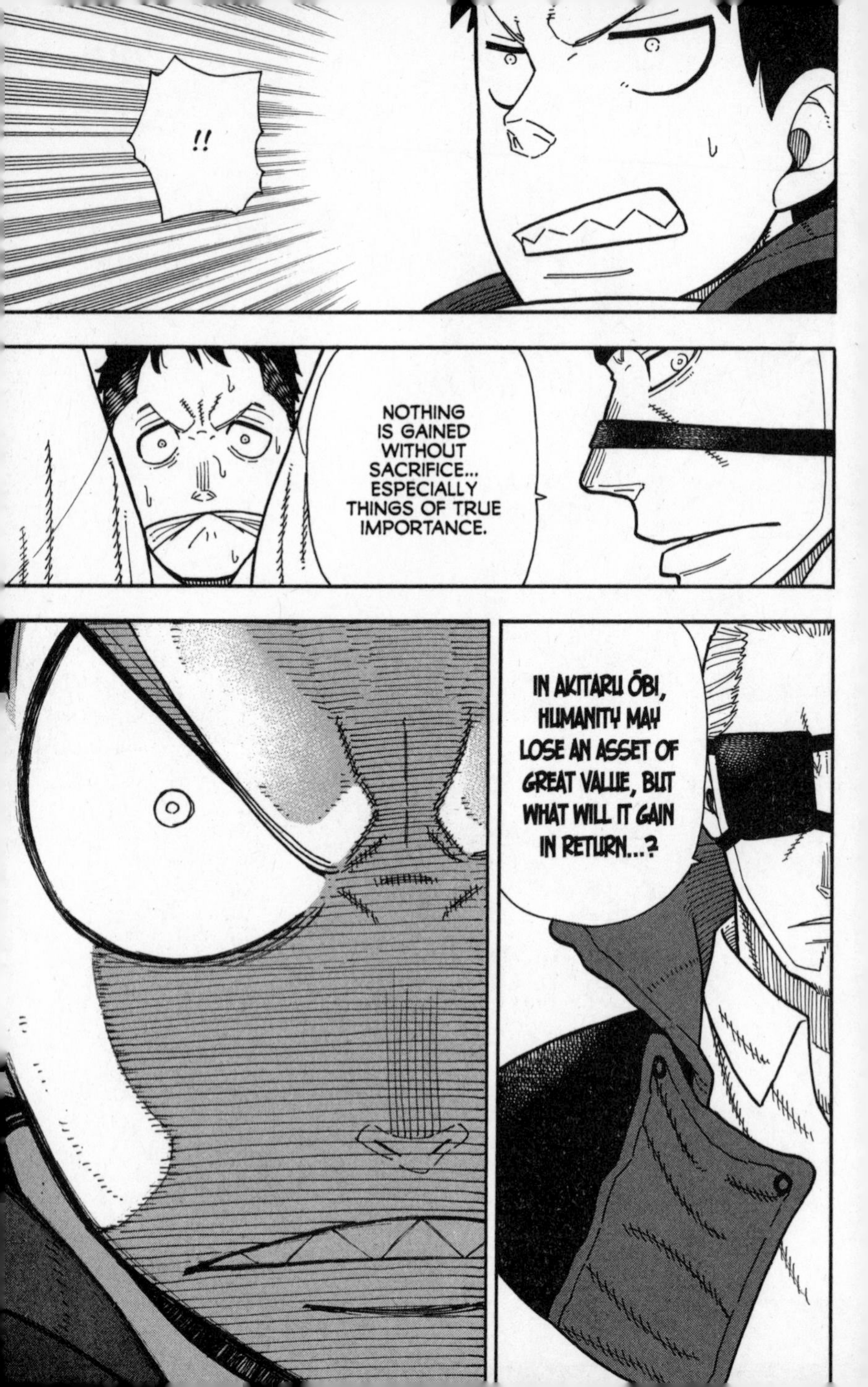
!!
NOTHING IS GAINED WITHOUT SACRIFICE... ESPECIALLY THINGS OF TRUE IMPORTANCE.
IN AKITARU ŌBI, HUMANITY MAY LOSE AN ASSET OF GREAT VALUE, BUT WHAT WILL IT GAIN IN RETURN...?

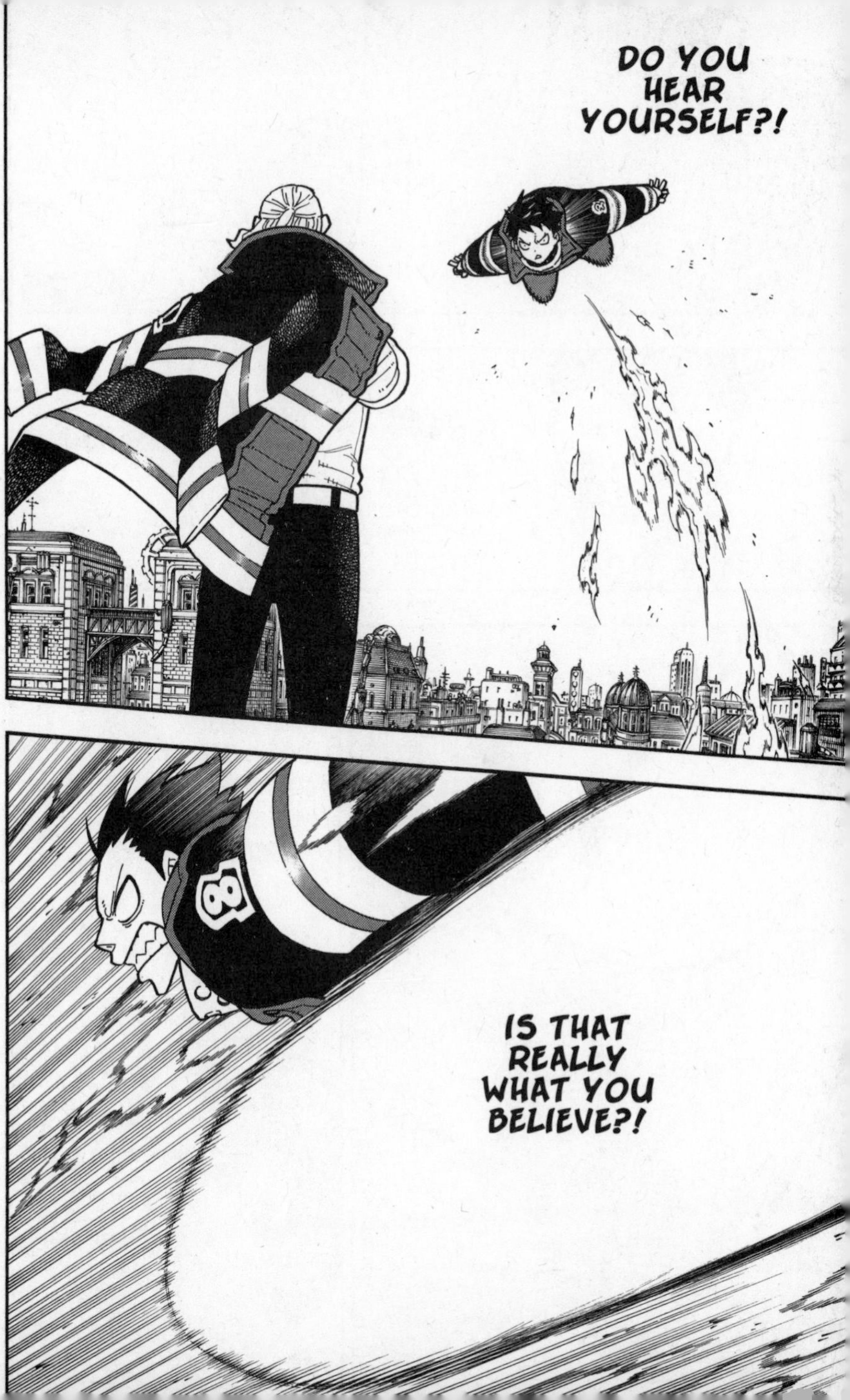
DO YOU HEAR YOURSELF?!
IS THAT REALLY WHAT YOU BELIEVE?!

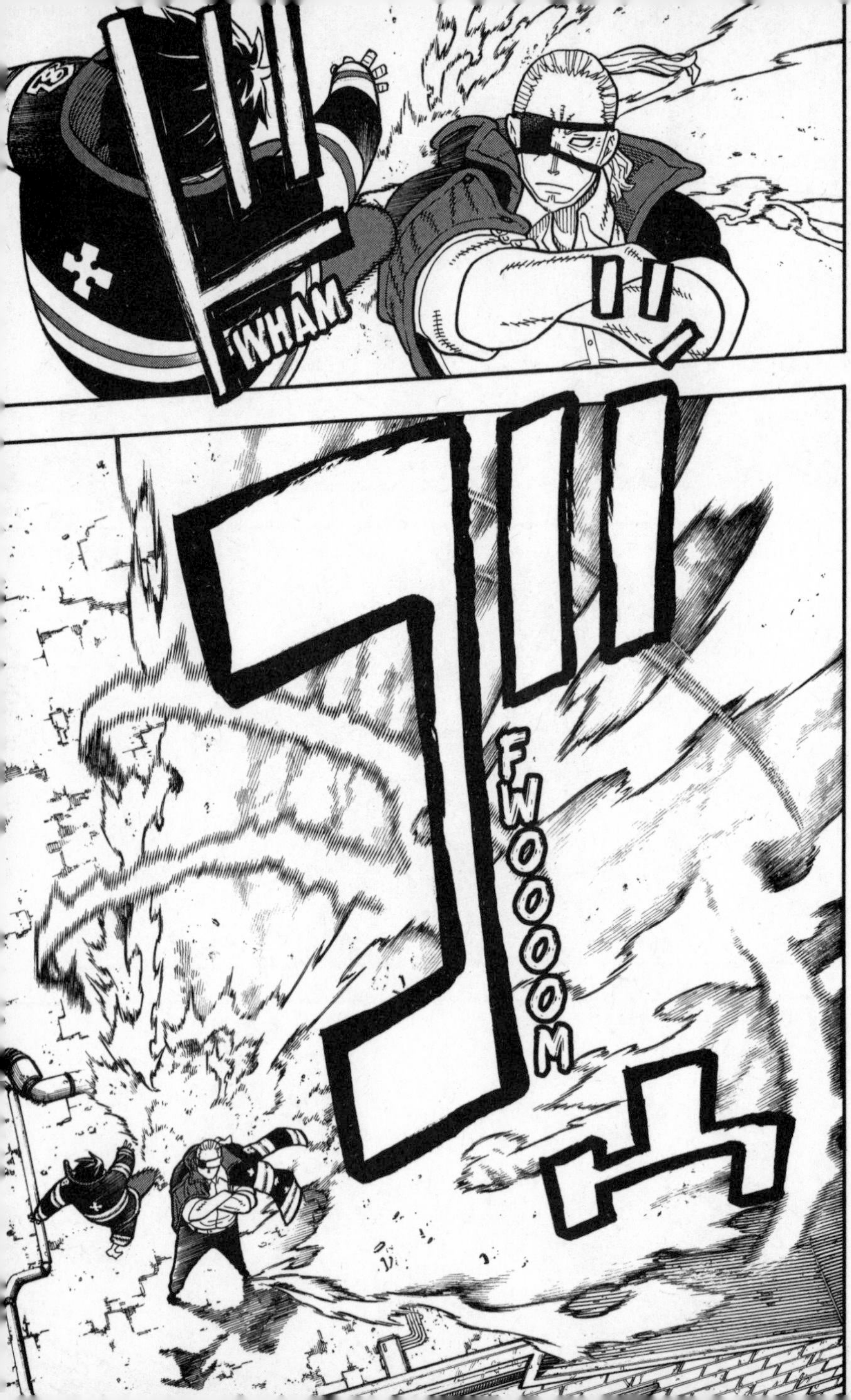
WHAM
FWOOOOM

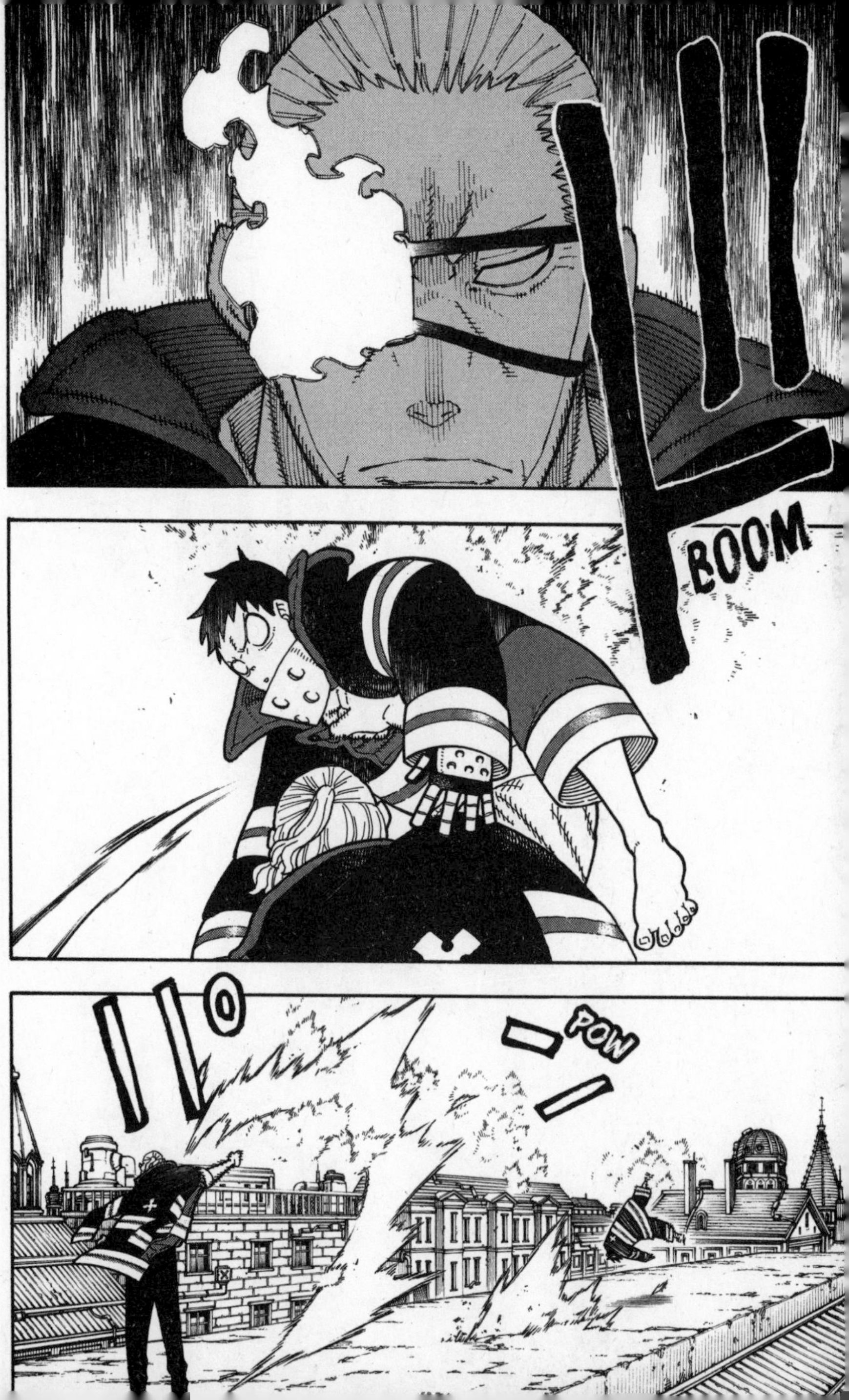
BOOM
POW

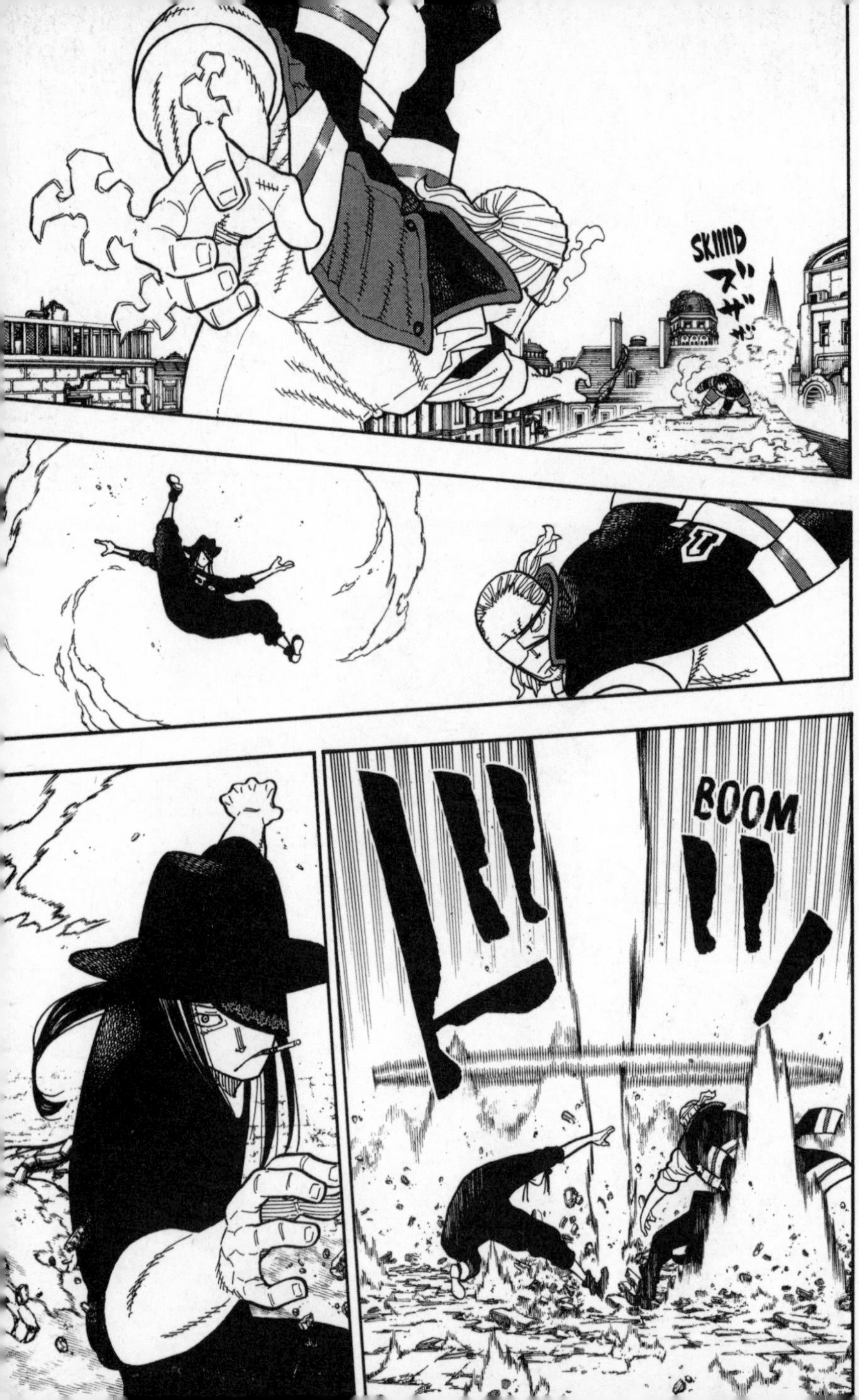
SKIIIID
ズザザ
BOOM

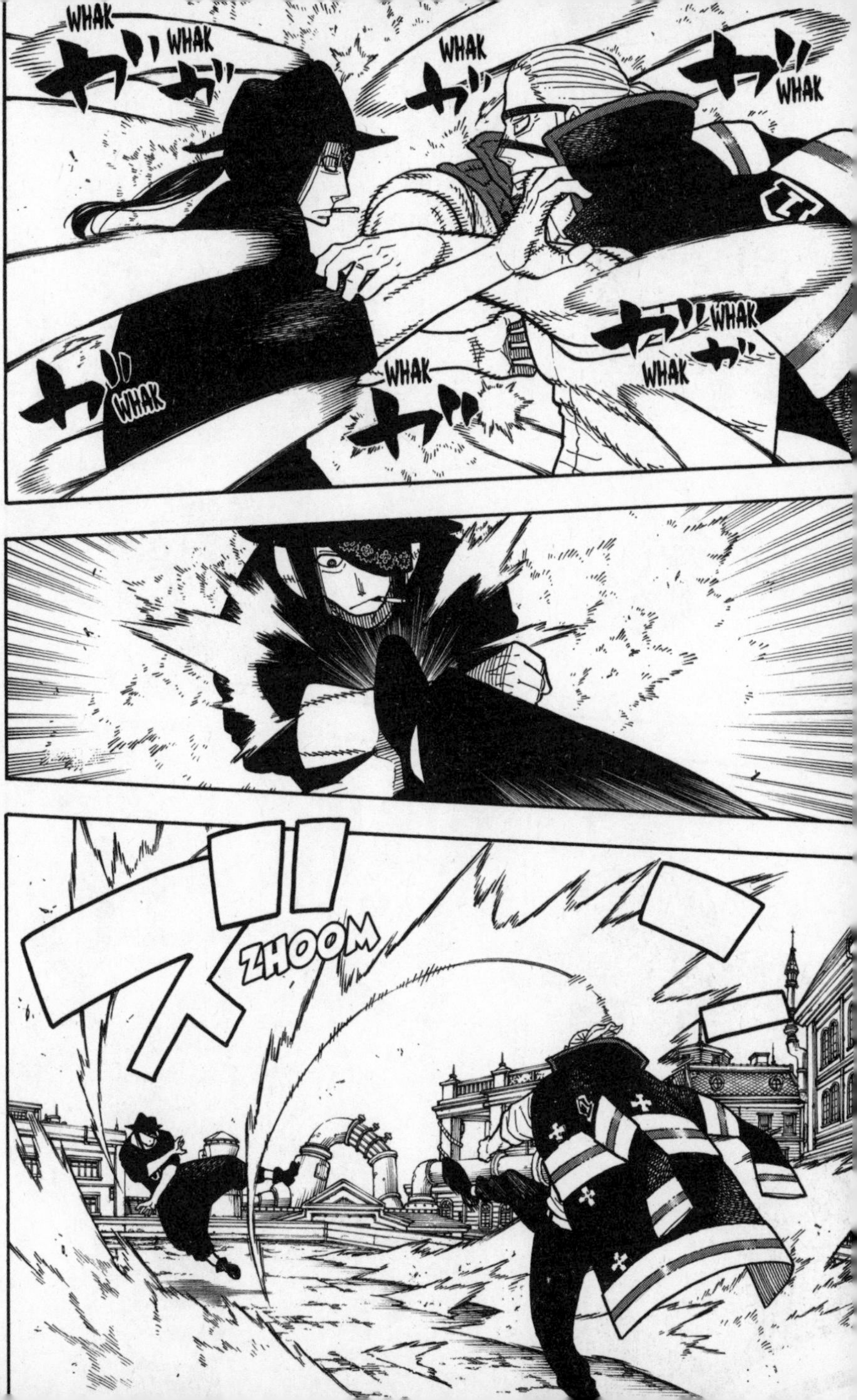
WHAK
WHAK
WHAK
WHAK
WHAK
WHAK
WHAK
WHAK
WHAK
ZHOOM

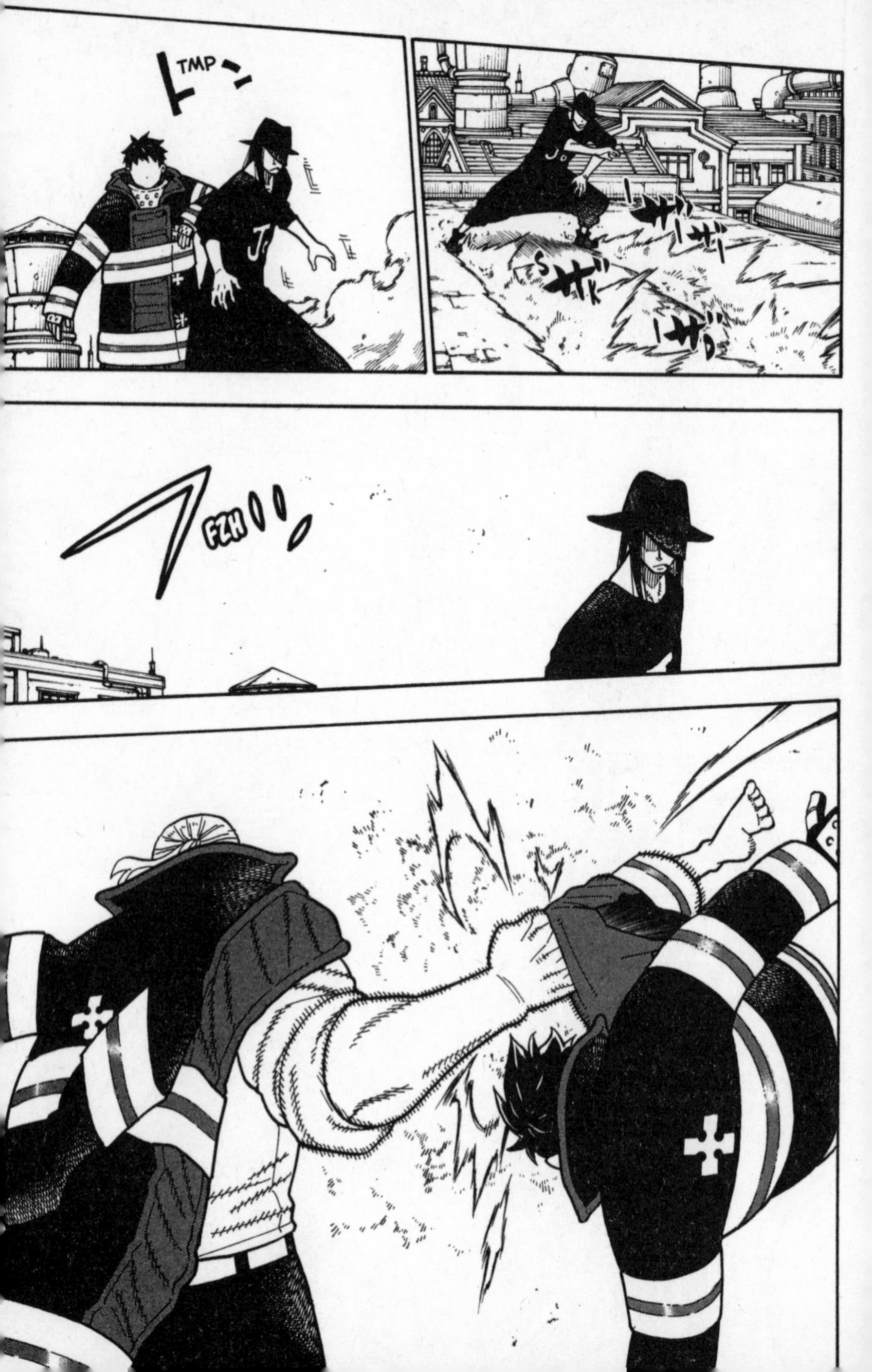
SK
D
TMP
FZH

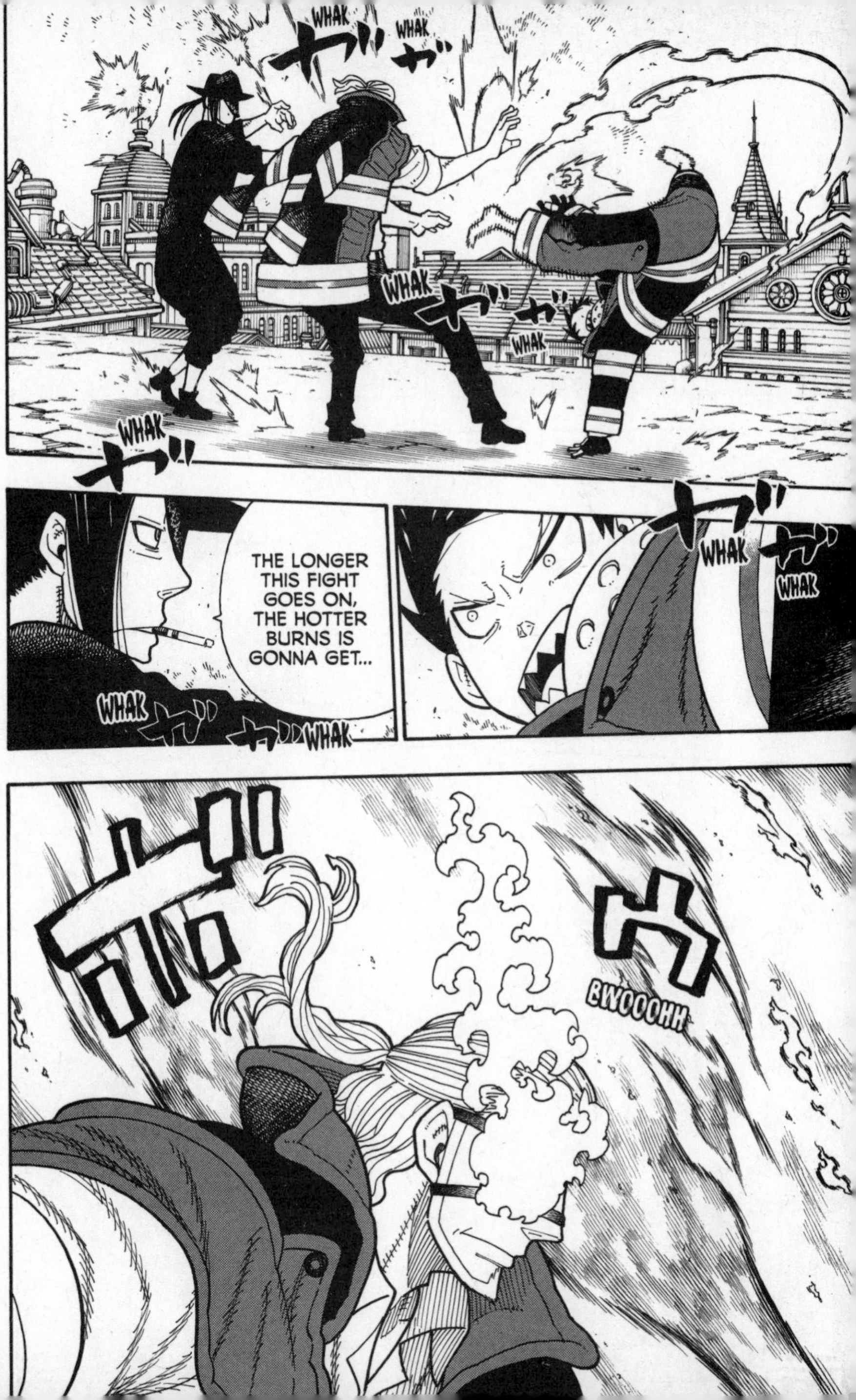
WHAK
WHAK
WHAK
WHAK
WHAK
WHAK
WHAK
THE LONGER THIS FIGHT GOES ON, THE HOTTER BURNS IS GONNA GET...
WHAK
WHAK
BWOOOHH

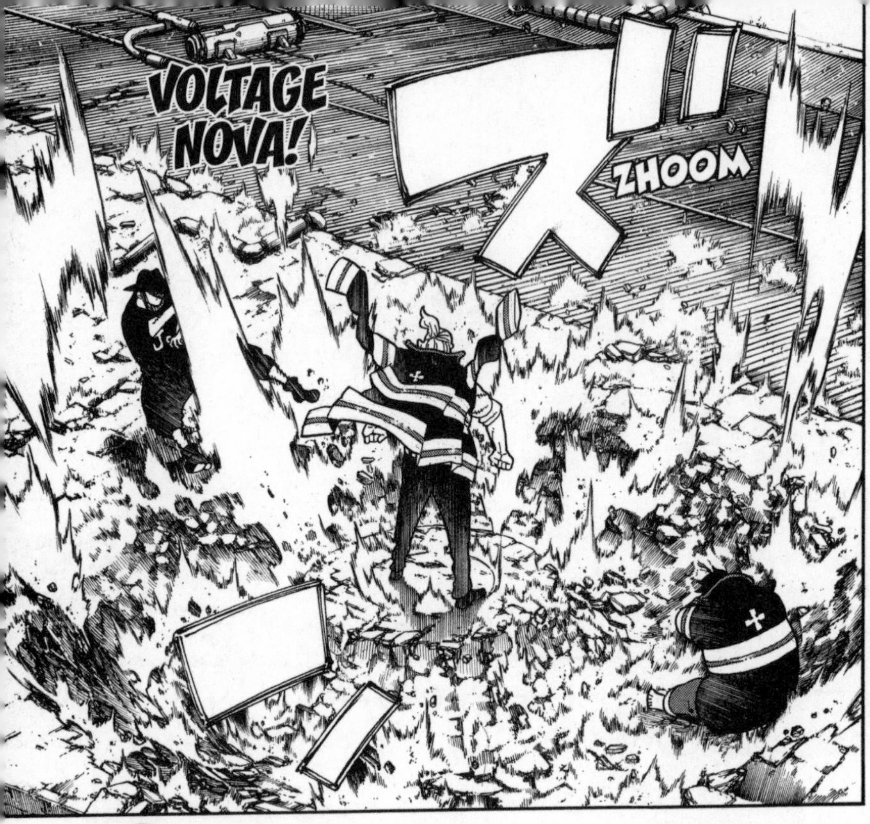
VOLTAGE NOVA!
ZHOOM

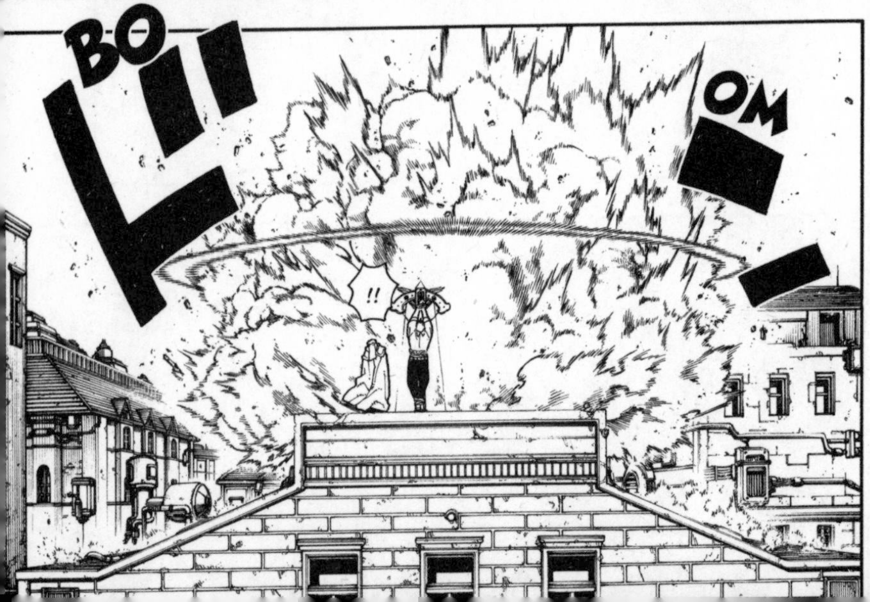
BO-
OM
!!

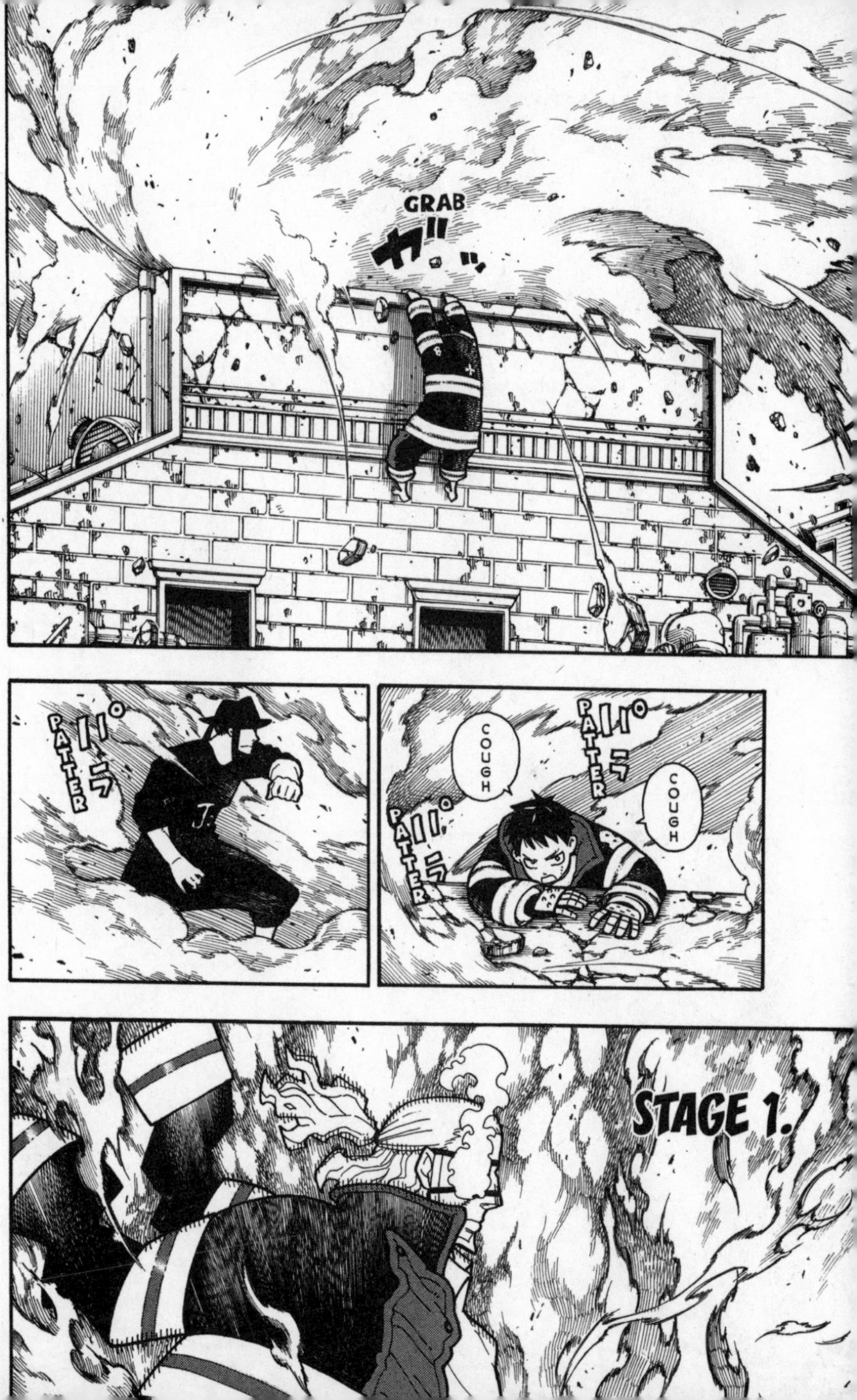
GRAB
PATTER
COUGH
COUGH
PATTER
PATTER
STAGE 1.

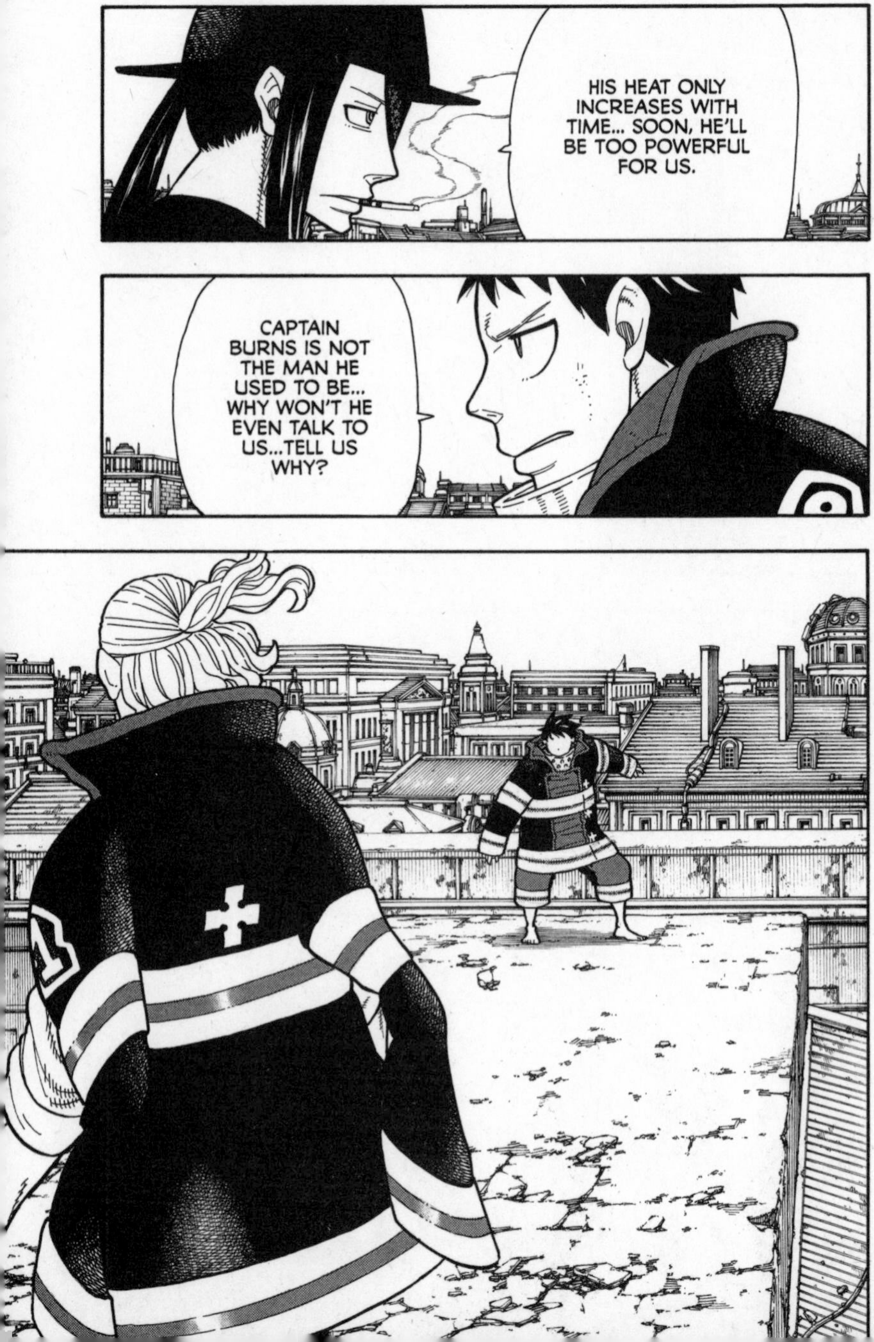
HIS HEAT ONLY INCREASES WITH TIME... SOON, HE'LL BE TOO POWERFUL FOR US.
CAPTAIN BURNS IS NOT THE MAN HE USED TO BE... WHY WON'T HE EVEN TALK TO US...TELL US WHY?

FIRE FORCE

CHAPTER CLXXXII: DEATH AND FLAME

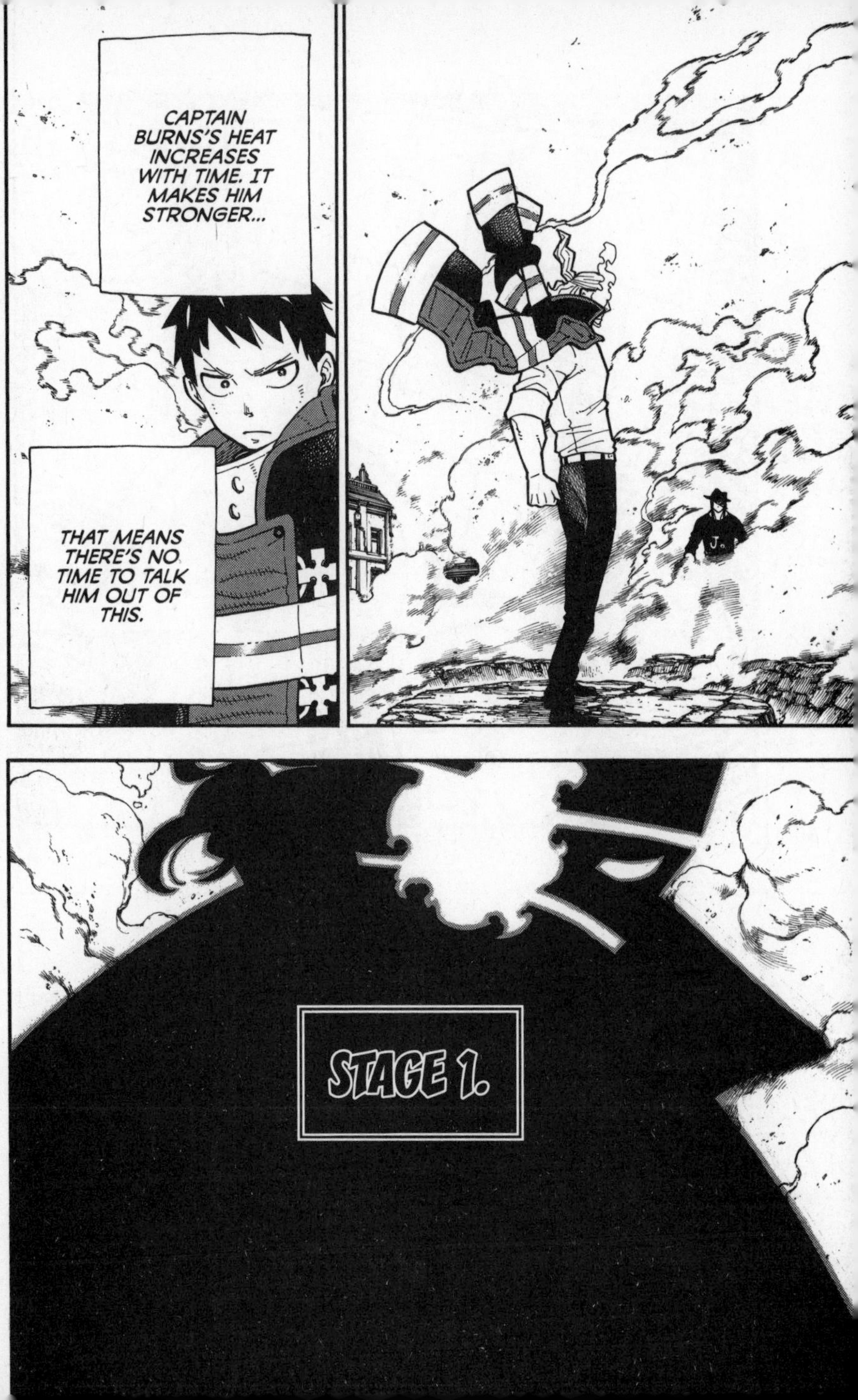
CAPTAIN BURNS'S HEAT INCREASES WITH TIME. IT MAKES HIM STRONGER...
THAT MEANS THERE'S NO TIME TO TALK HIM OUT OF THIS.
STAGE 1.

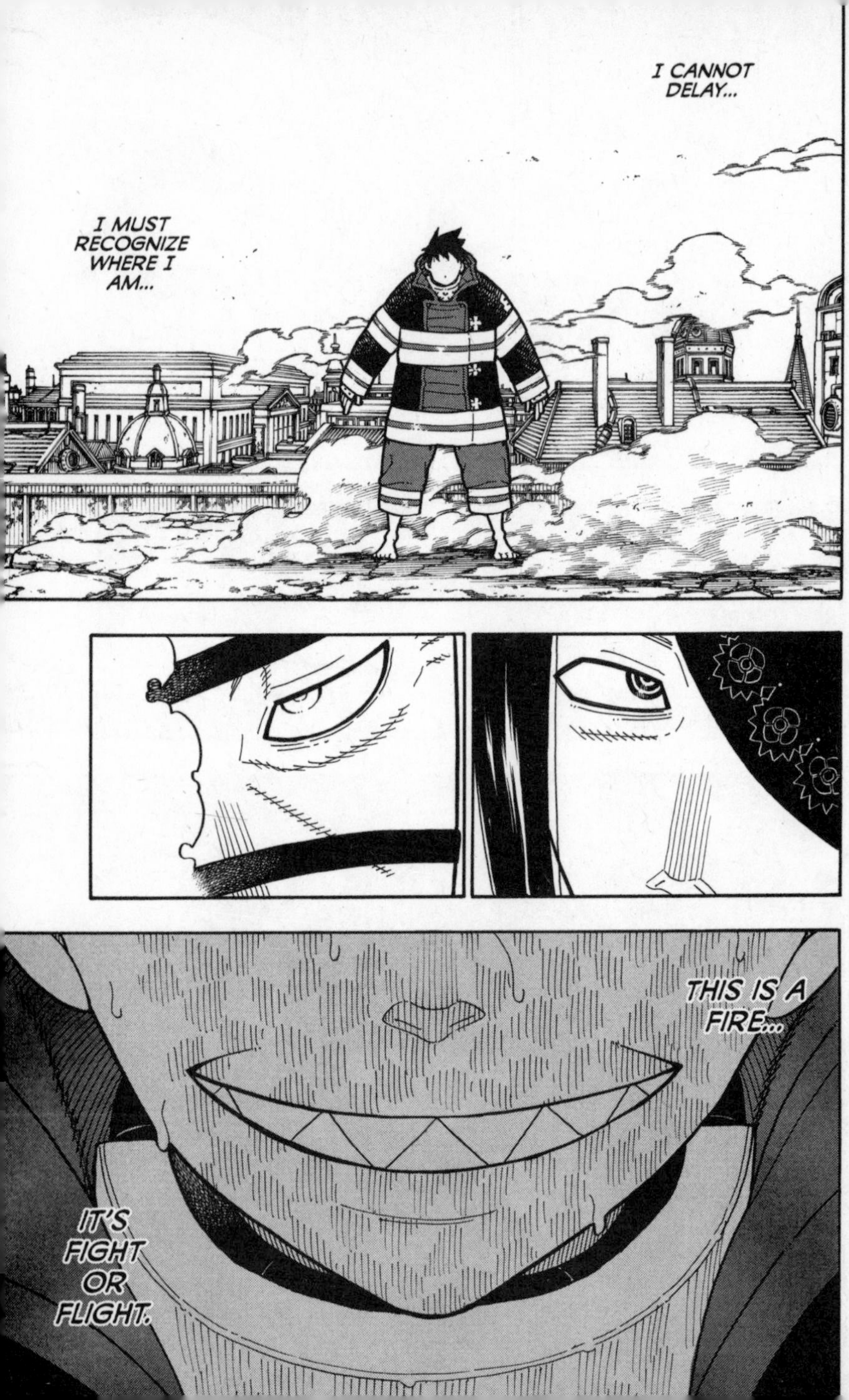
I CANNOT DELAY...
I MUST RECOGNIZE WHERE I AM...
THIS IS A FIRE...
IT'S FIGHT OR FLIGHT.

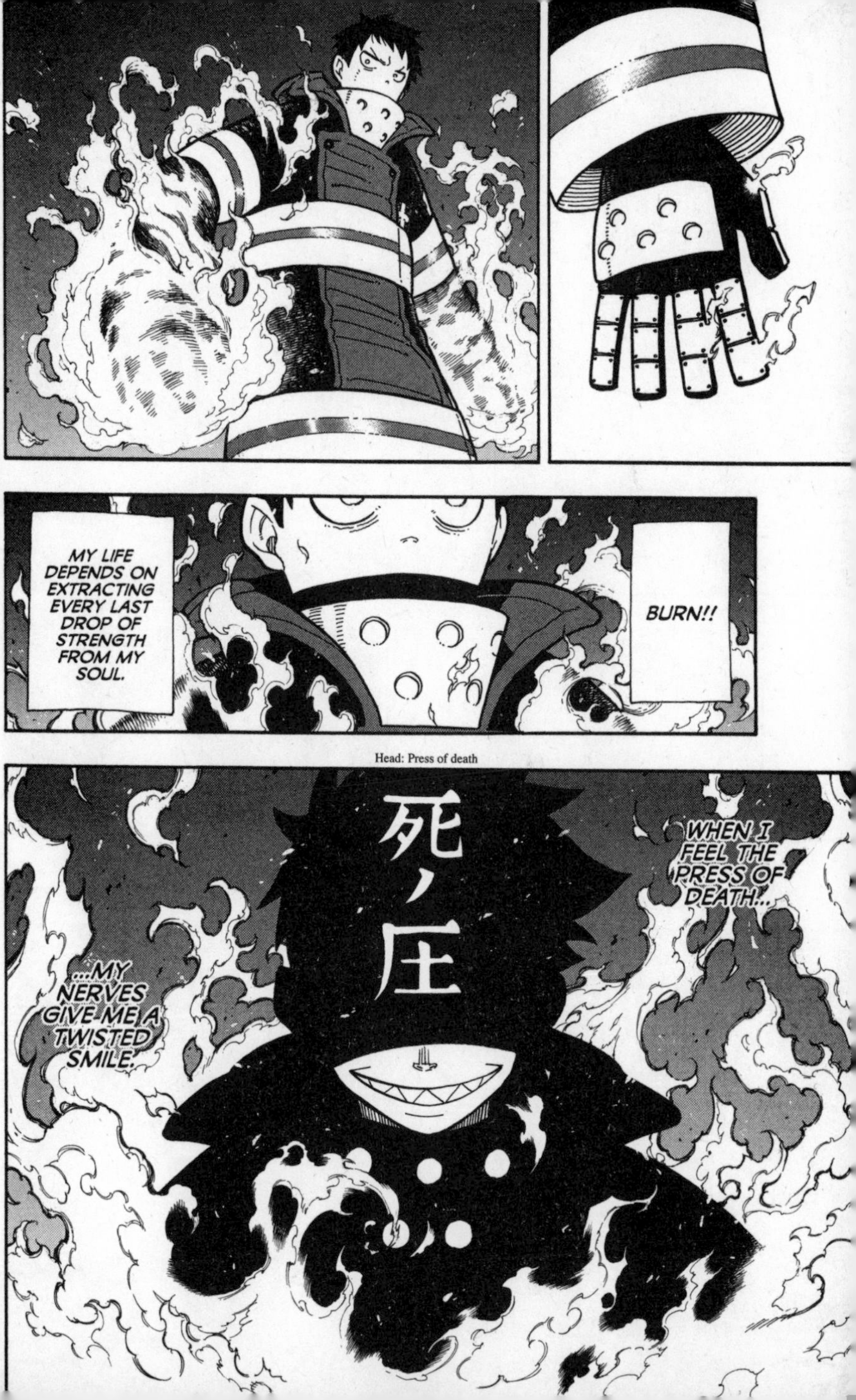
MY LIFE DEPENDS ON EXTRACTING EVERY LAST DROP OF STRENGTH FROM MY SOUL.
BURN!!
Head: Press of death
死ノ圧
WHEN I FEEL THE PRESS OF DEATH...
...MY NERVES GIVE ME A TWISTED SMILE.

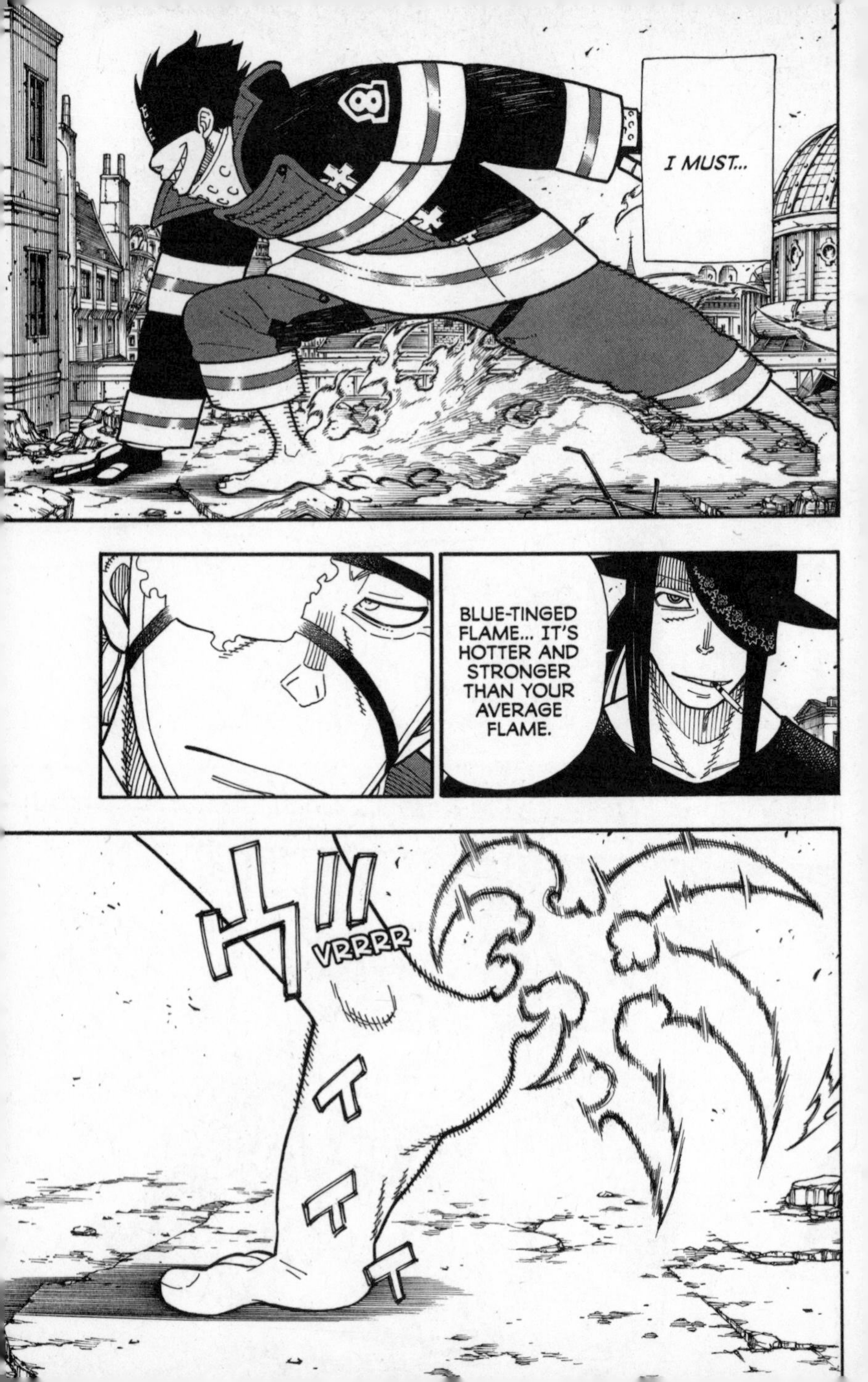
I MUST...
BLUE-TINGED FLAME... IT'S HOTTER AND STRONGER THAN YOUR AVERAGE FLAME.
VRRRR

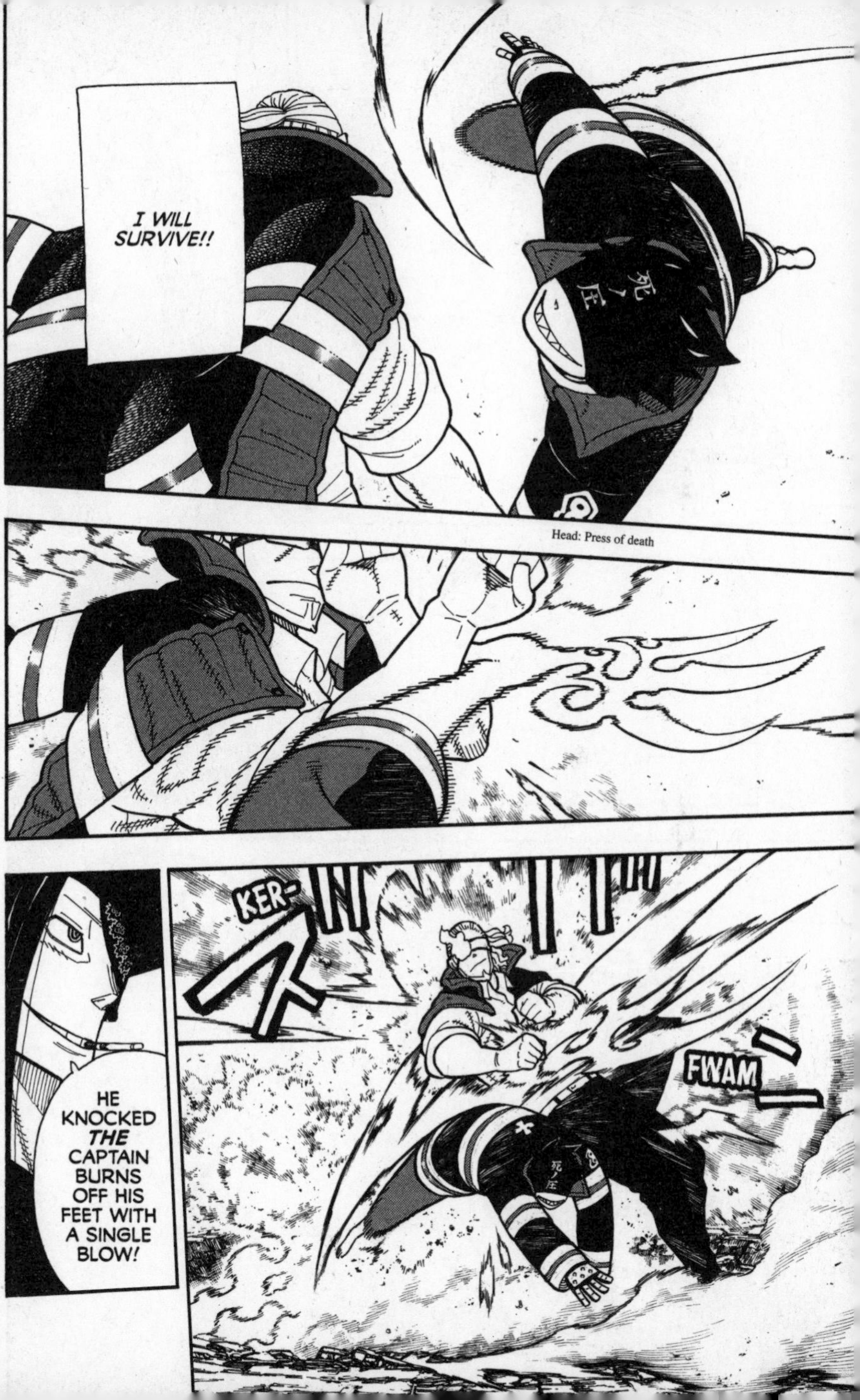
I WILL SURVIVE!!
死ノ圧
Head: Press of death
KER-
FWAM
HE KNOCKED *THE* CAPTAIN BURNS OFF HIS FEET WITH A SINGLE BLOW!

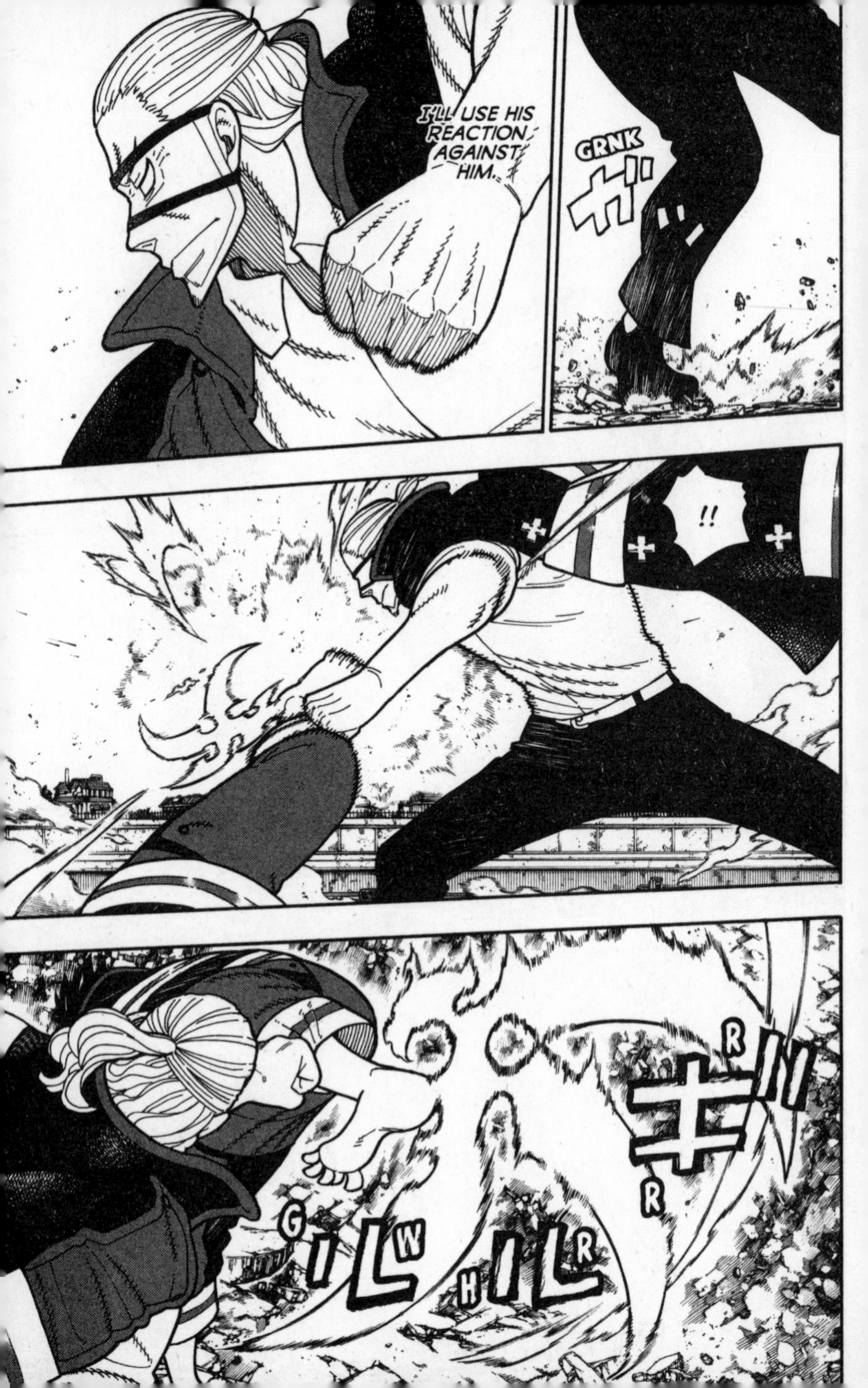
GRNK
I'LL USE HIS REACTION AGAINST HIM.
!!
GILWHILR

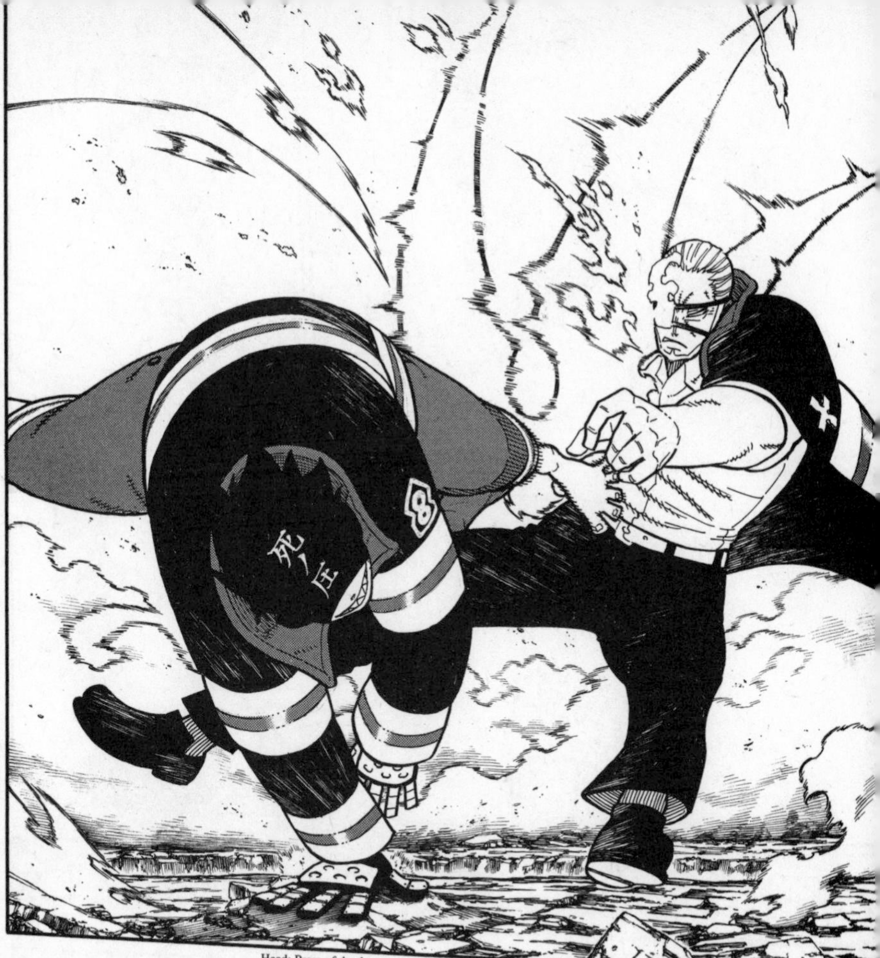
死ノ圧

Head: Press of death

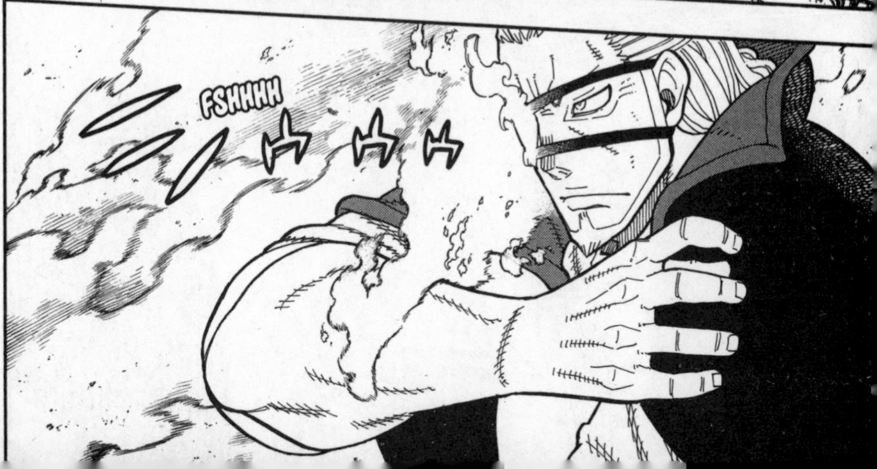
FSHHHH

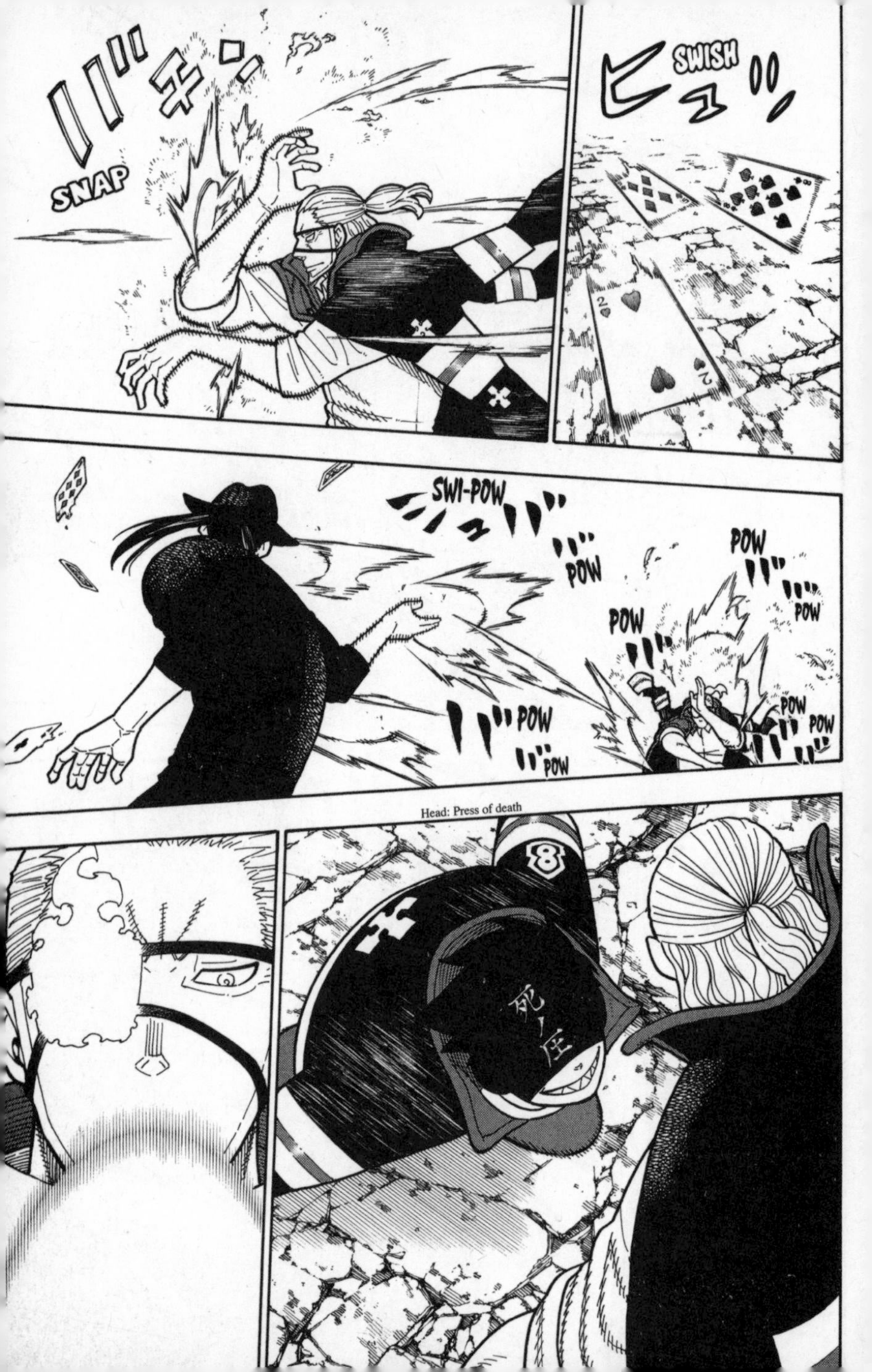
SWISH
SNAP
POW
POW
POW
POW
POW
SWI-POW
POW
POW
POW
Head: Press of death

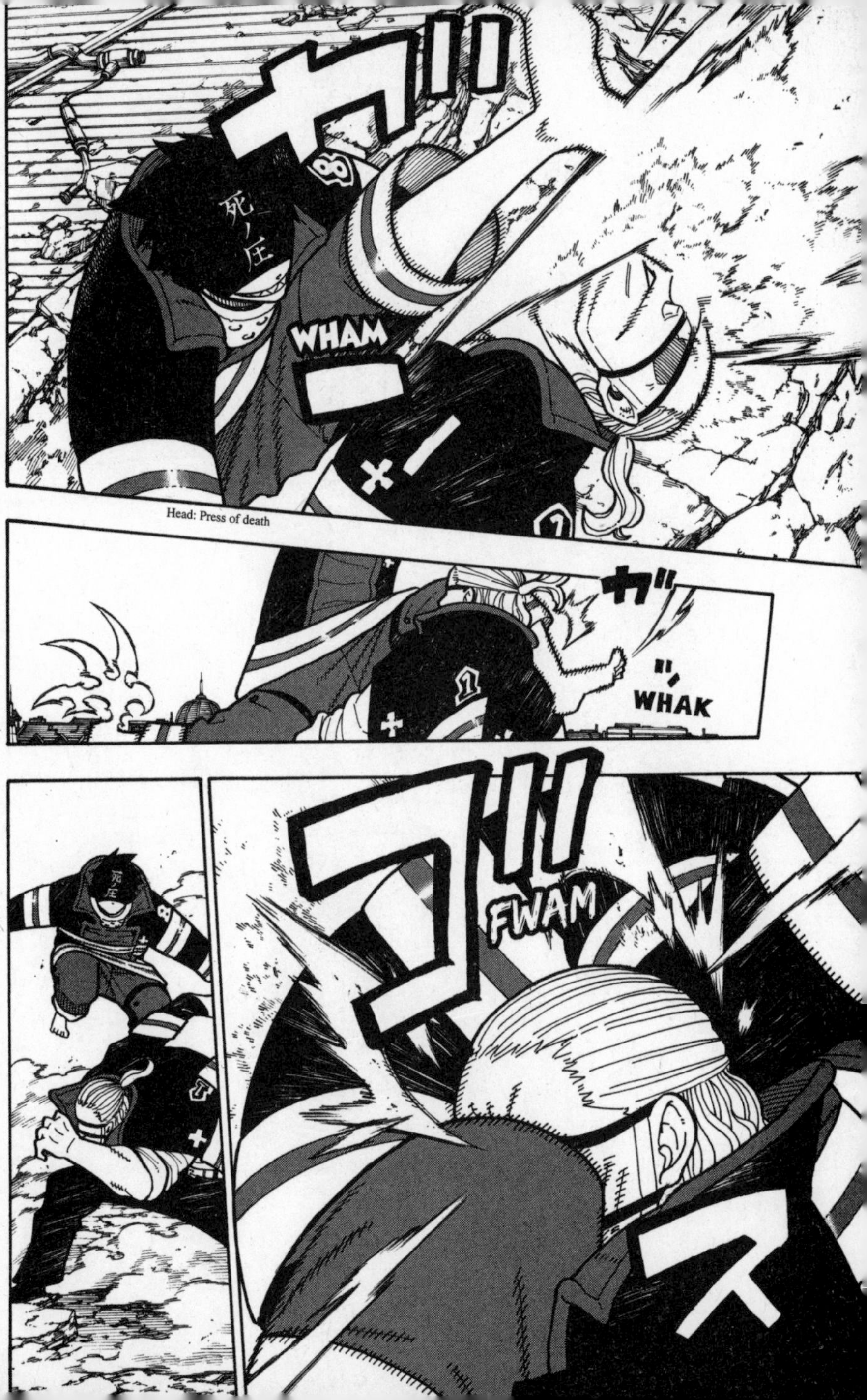
WHAM
Head: Press of death
WHAK
FWAM

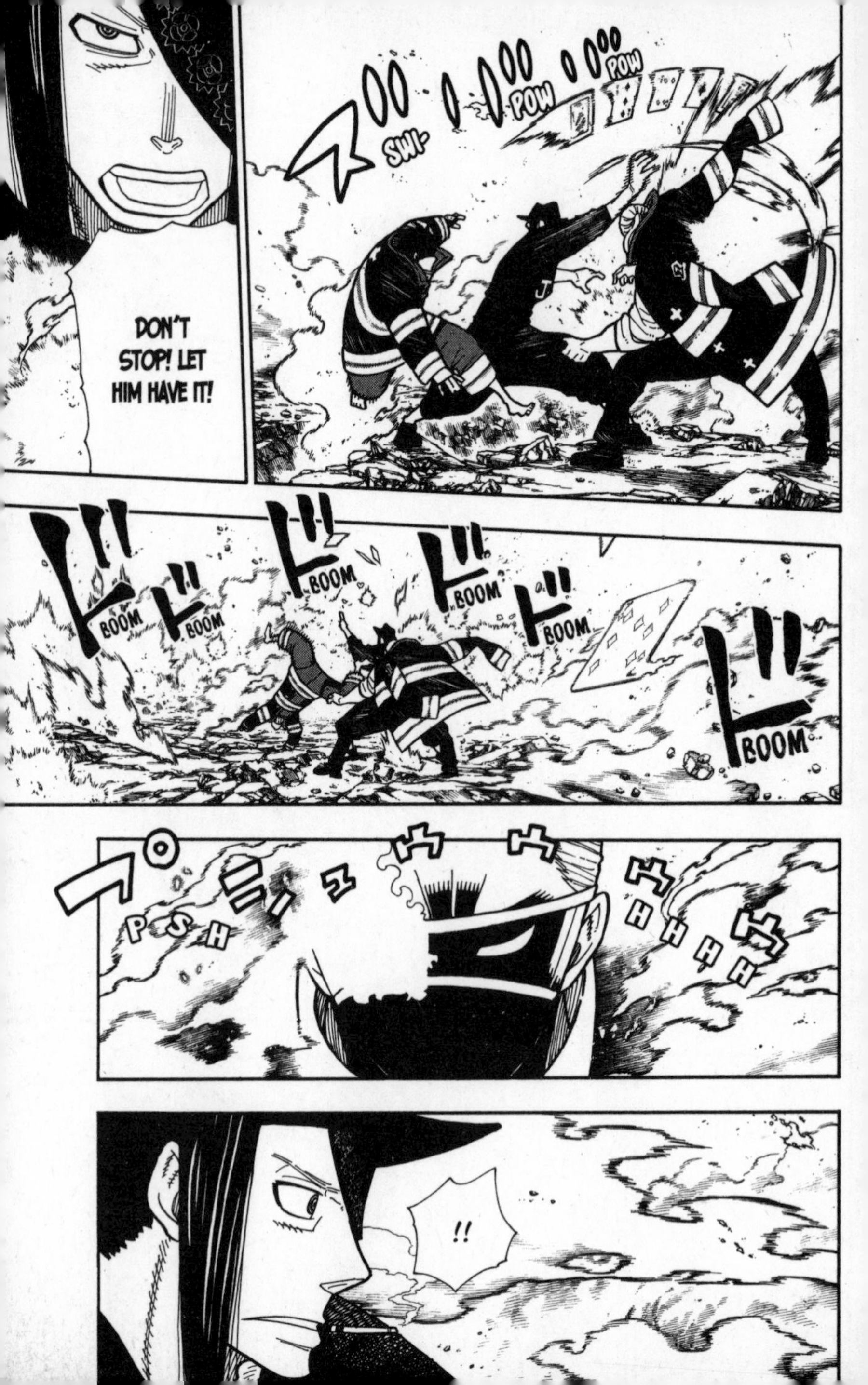
SWI-
POW
POW
DON'T STOP! LET HIM HAVE IT!
BOOM
BOOM
BOOM
BOOM
BOOM
BOOM
PSH
HHHH
!!

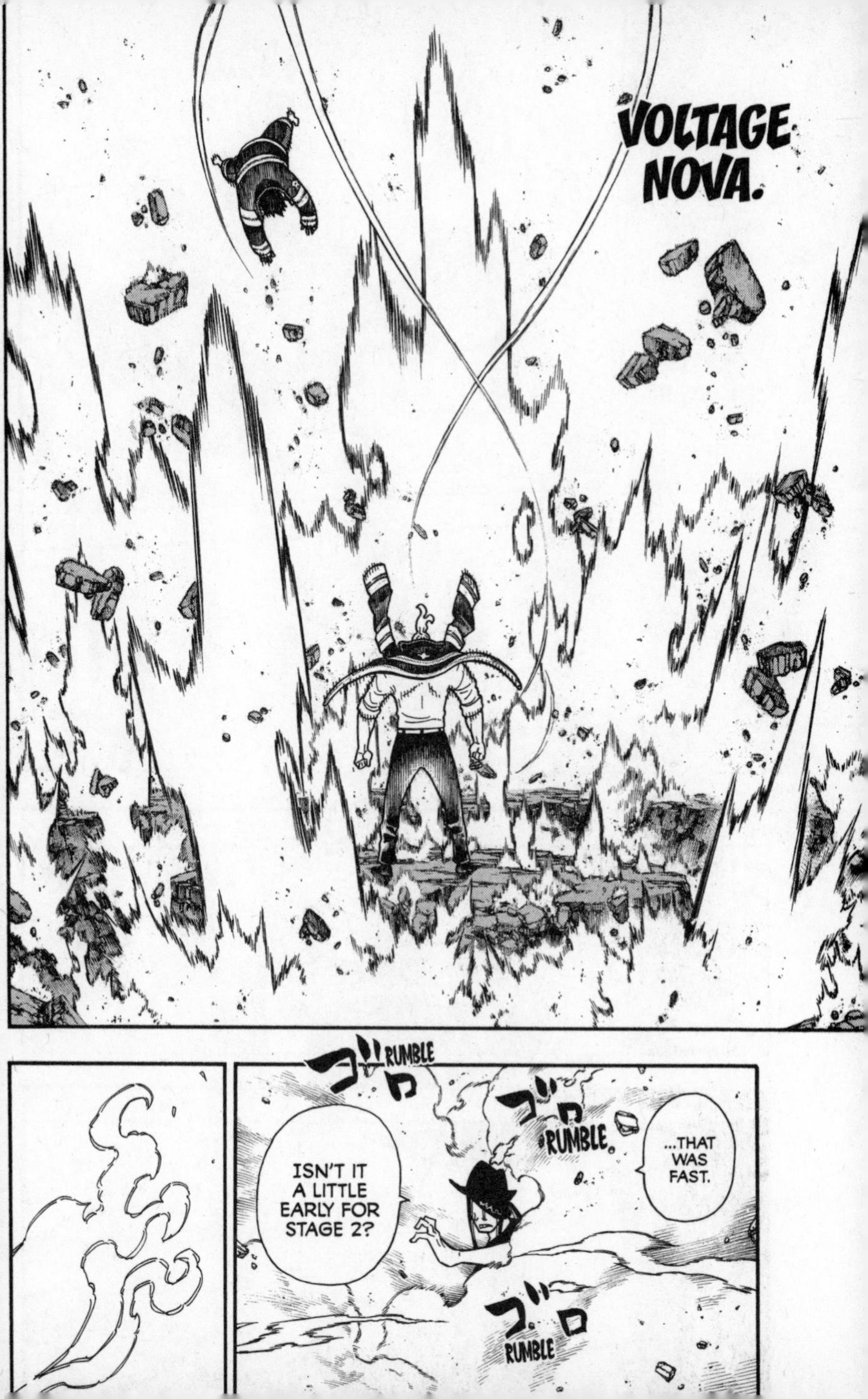
VOLTAGE NOVA.
RUMBLE
RUMBLE
...THAT WAS FAST.
ISN'T IT A LITTLE EARLY FOR STAGE 2?
RUMBLE

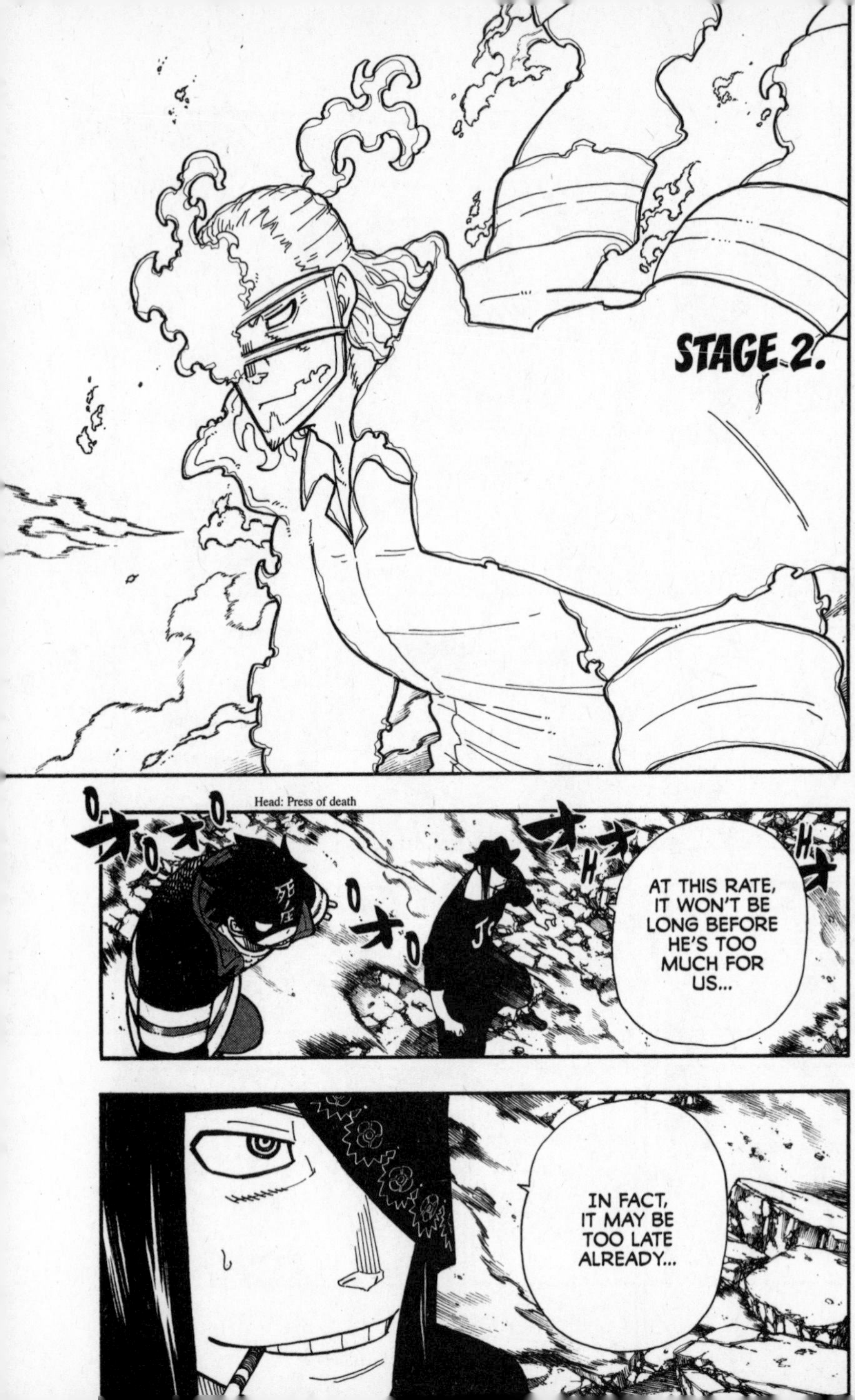
STAGE 2.
Head: Press of death
AT THIS RATE, IT WON'T BE LONG BEFORE HE'S TOO MUCH FOR US...
IN FACT, IT MAY BE TOO LATE ALREADY...

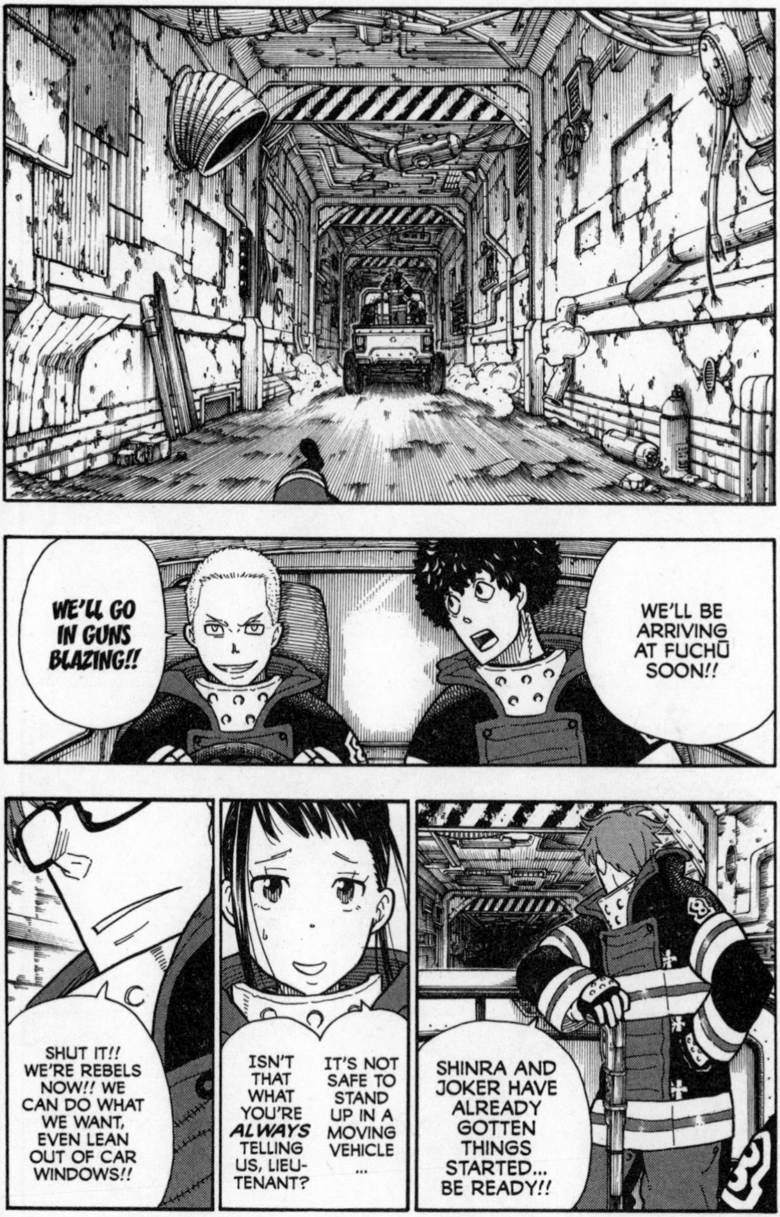
WE'LL BE ARRIVING AT FUCHŪ SOON!!
WE'LL GO IN GUNS BLAZING!!
SHINRA AND JOKER HAVE ALREADY GOTTEN THINGS STARTED... BE READY!!
IT'S NOT SAFE TO STAND UP IN A MOVING VEHICLE ...
ISN'T THAT WHAT YOU'RE *ALWAYS* TELLING US, LIEU-TENANT?
SHUT IT!! WE'RE REBELS NOW!! WE CAN DO WHAT WE WANT, EVEN LEAN OUT OF CAR WINDOWS!!

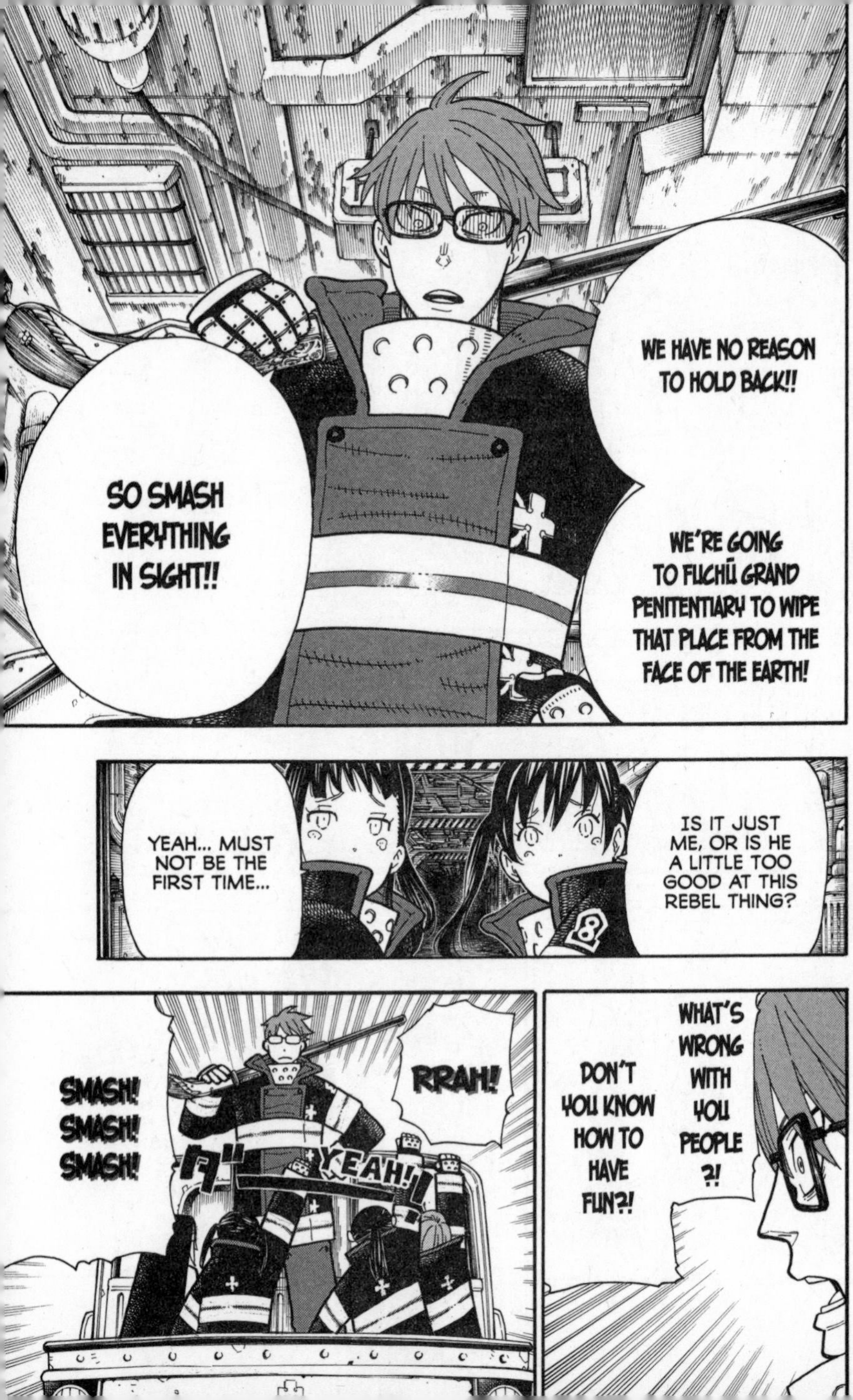
WE HAVE NO REASON TO HOLD BACK!!
WE'RE GOING TO FUCHŪ GRAND PENITENTIARY TO WIPE THAT PLACE FROM THE FACE OF THE EARTH!
SO SMASH EVERYTHING IN SIGHT!!
IS IT JUST ME, OR IS HE A LITTLE TOO GOOD AT THIS REBEL THING?
YEAH... MUST NOT BE THE FIRST TIME...
WHAT'S WRONG WITH YOU PEOPLE?!
DON'T YOU KNOW HOW TO HAVE FUN?!
RRAH!
YEAH!!
SMASH! SMASH! SMASH!

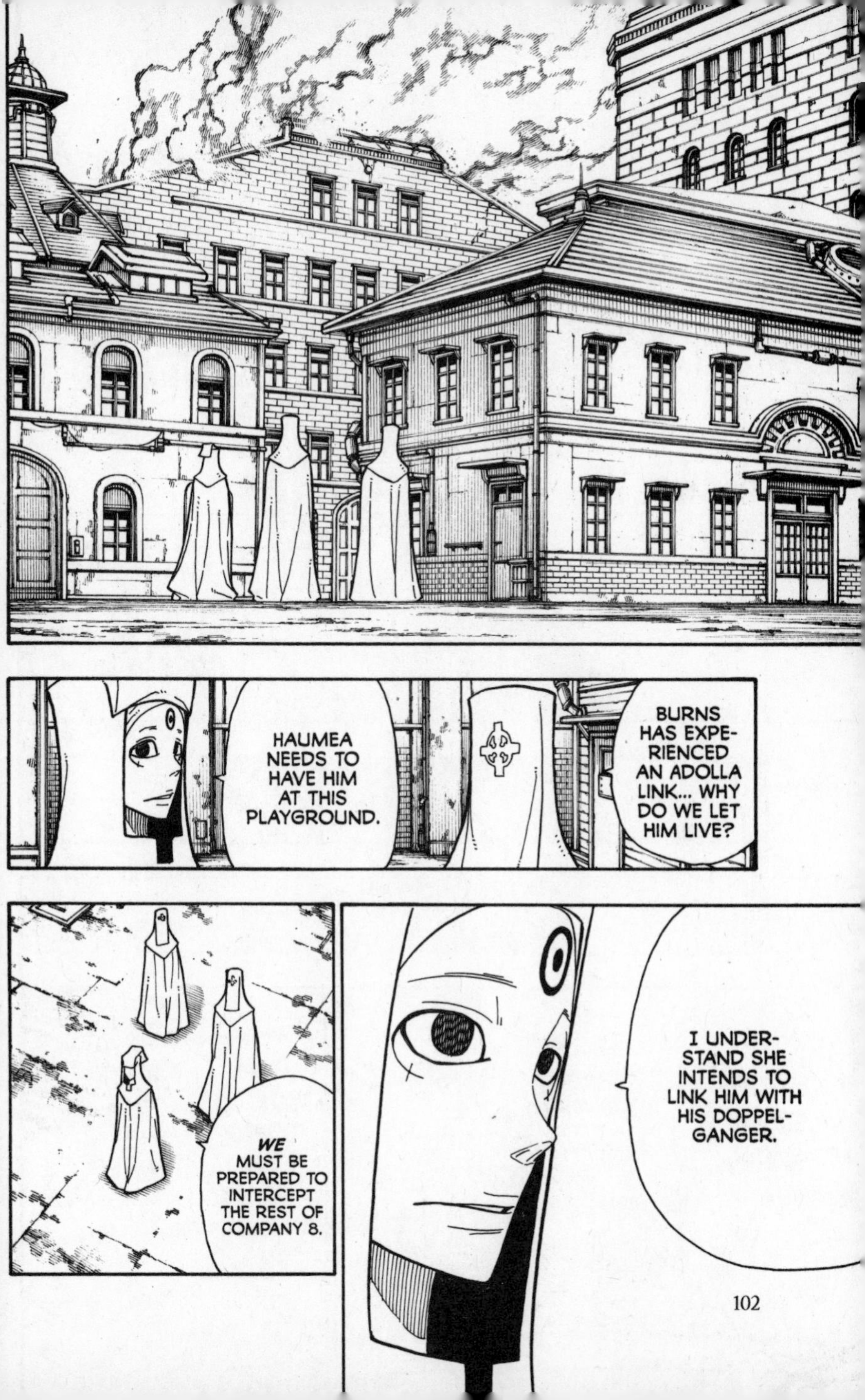
BURNS HAS EXPERIENCED AN ADOLLA LINK... WHY DO WE LET HIM LIVE?
HAUMEA NEEDS TO HAVE HIM AT THIS PLAYGROUND.
I UNDERSTAND SHE INTENDS TO LINK HIM WITH HIS DOPPELGANGER.
WE MUST BE PREPARED TO INTERCEPT THE REST OF COMPANY 8.

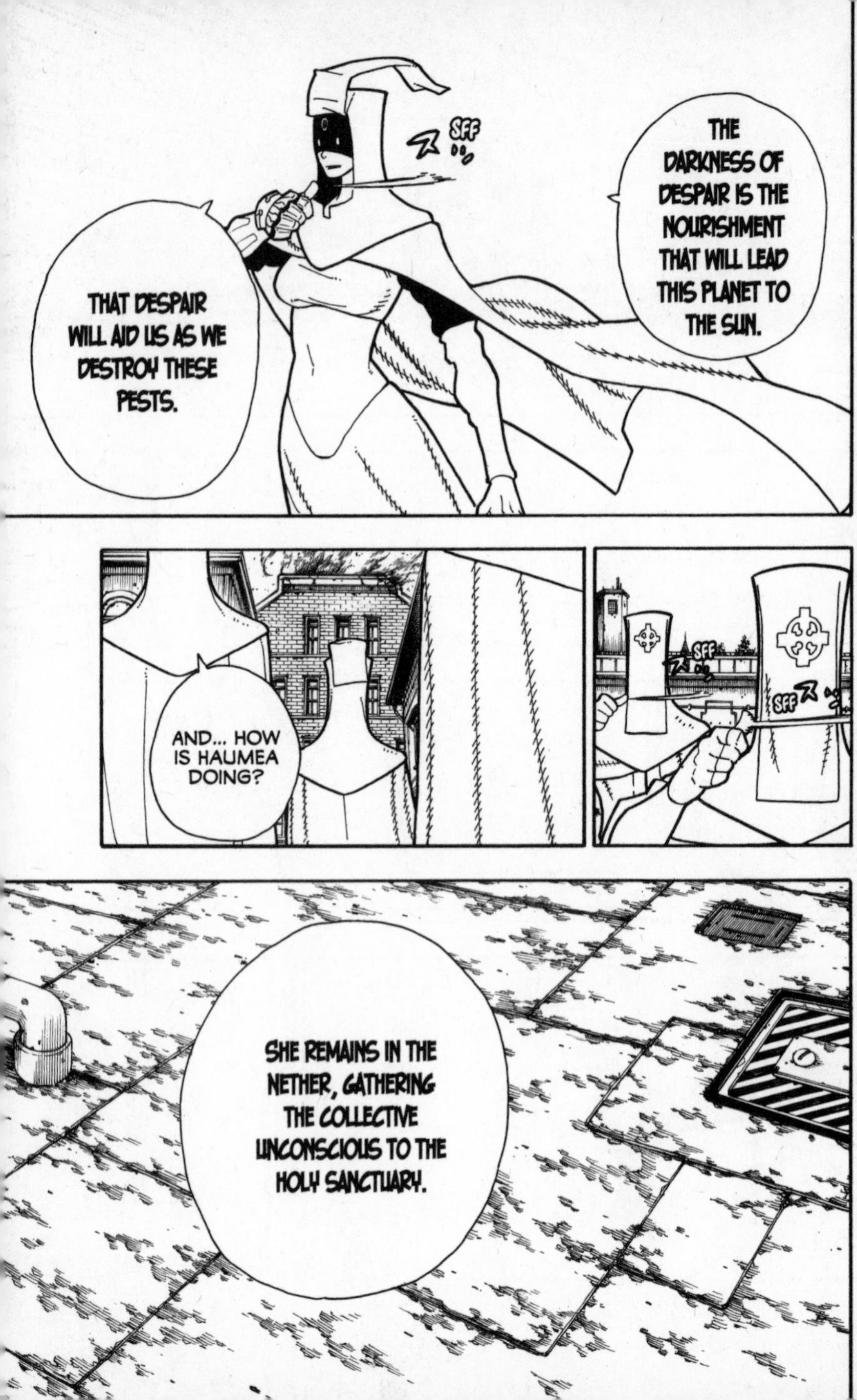
SFF
THE DARKNESS OF DESPAIR IS THE NOURISHMENT THAT WILL LEAD THIS PLANET TO THE SUN.
THAT DESPAIR WILL AID US AS WE DESTROY THESE PESTS.
SFF
SFF
AND... HOW IS HAUMEA DOING?
SHE REMAINS IN THE NETHER, GATHERING THE COLLECTIVE UNCONSCIOUS TO THE HOLY SANCTUARY.

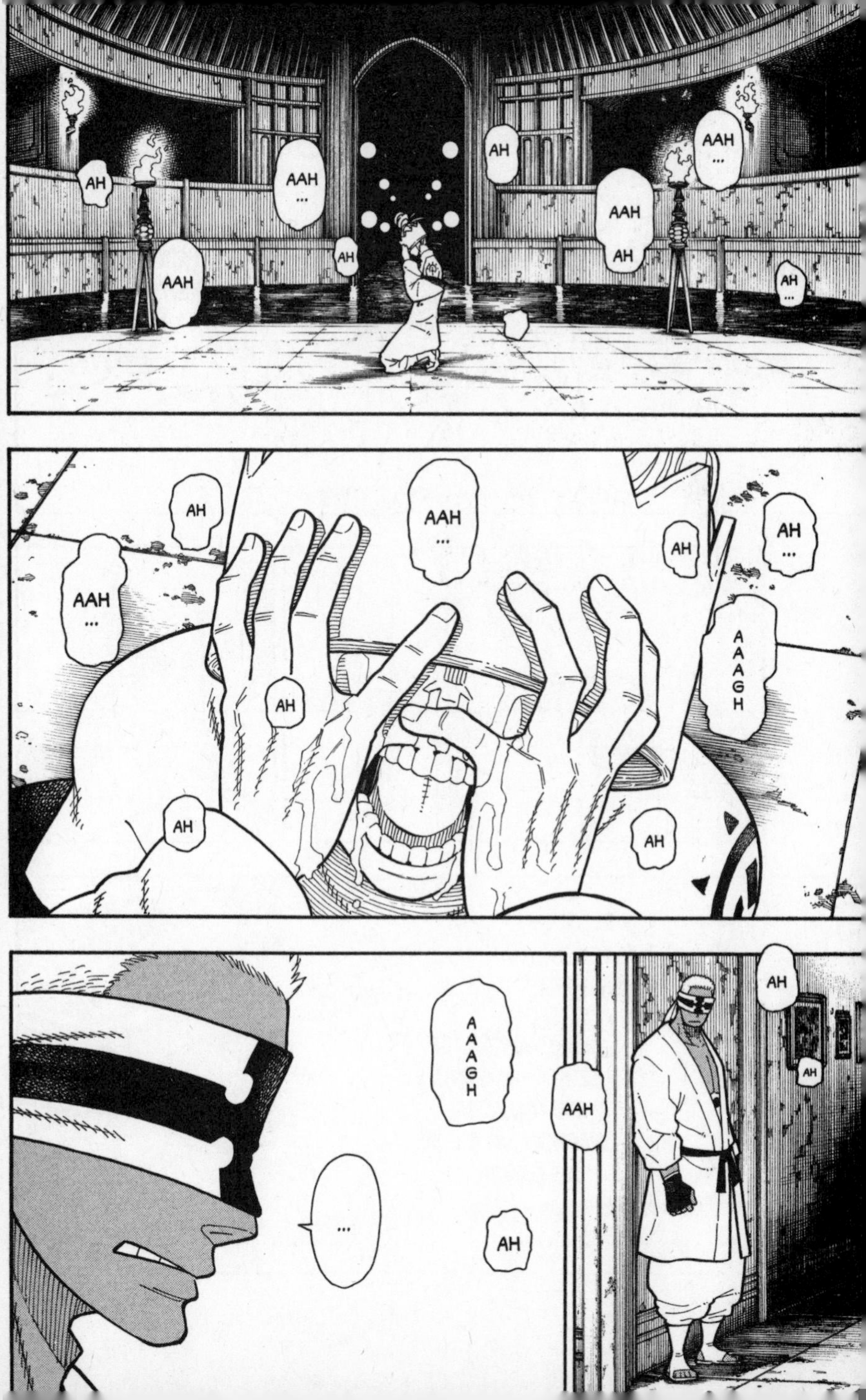
AAH ...
AH
AAH AH
AH ...
AAH ...
AH
AH
AAH
AH ...
AH
AAAGH
AAH ...
AH
AAH ...
AH
AH
AH
AH
AH
AAH
AAAGH
AH
...

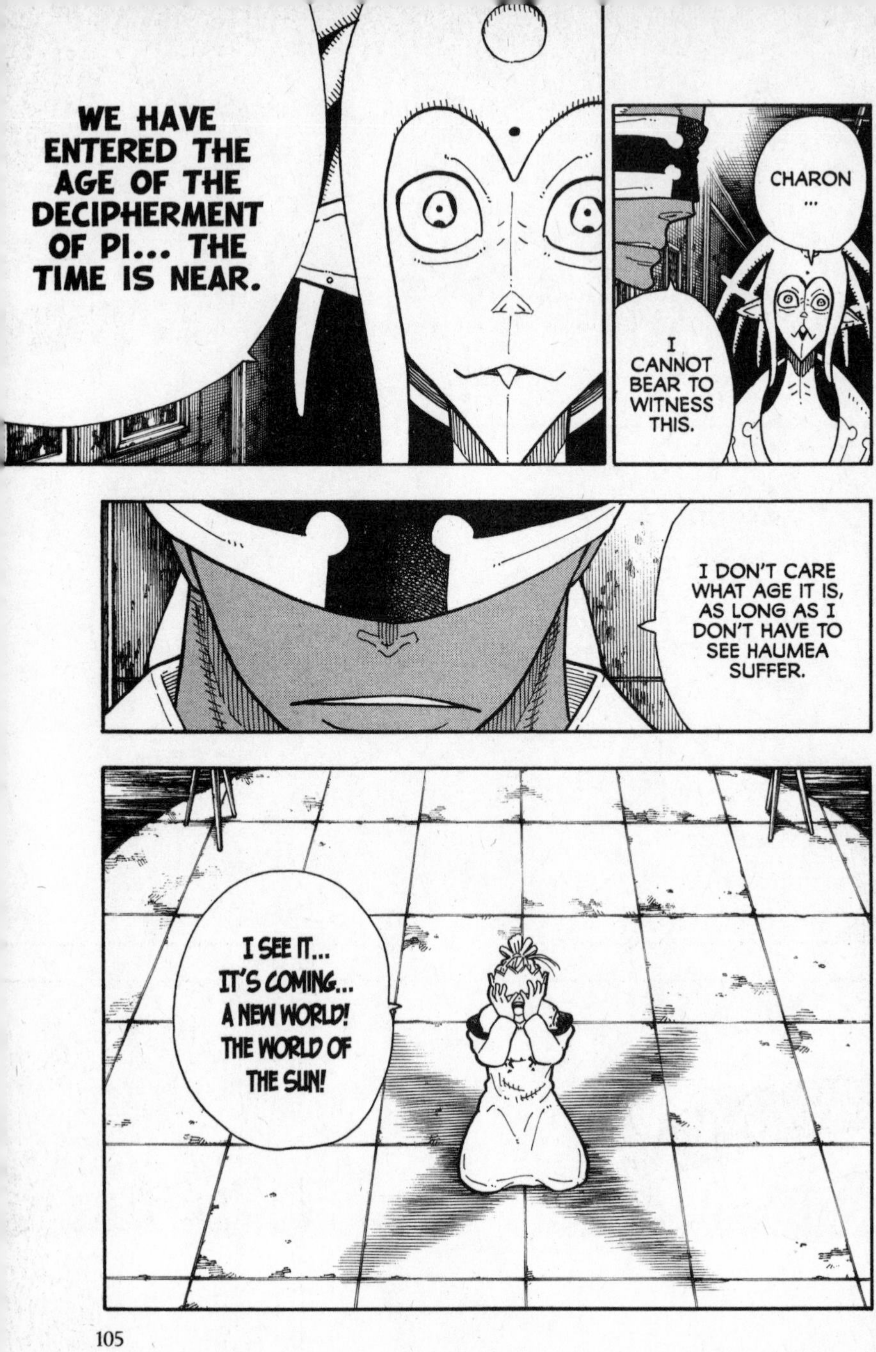
CHARON ...
I CANNOT BEAR TO WITNESS THIS.
WE HAVE ENTERED THE AGE OF THE DECIPHERMENT OF PI... THE TIME IS NEAR.
I DON'T CARE WHAT AGE IT IS, AS LONG AS I DON'T HAVE TO SEE HAUMEA SUFFER.
I SEE IT... IT'S COMING... A NEW WORLD! THE WORLD OF THE SUN!

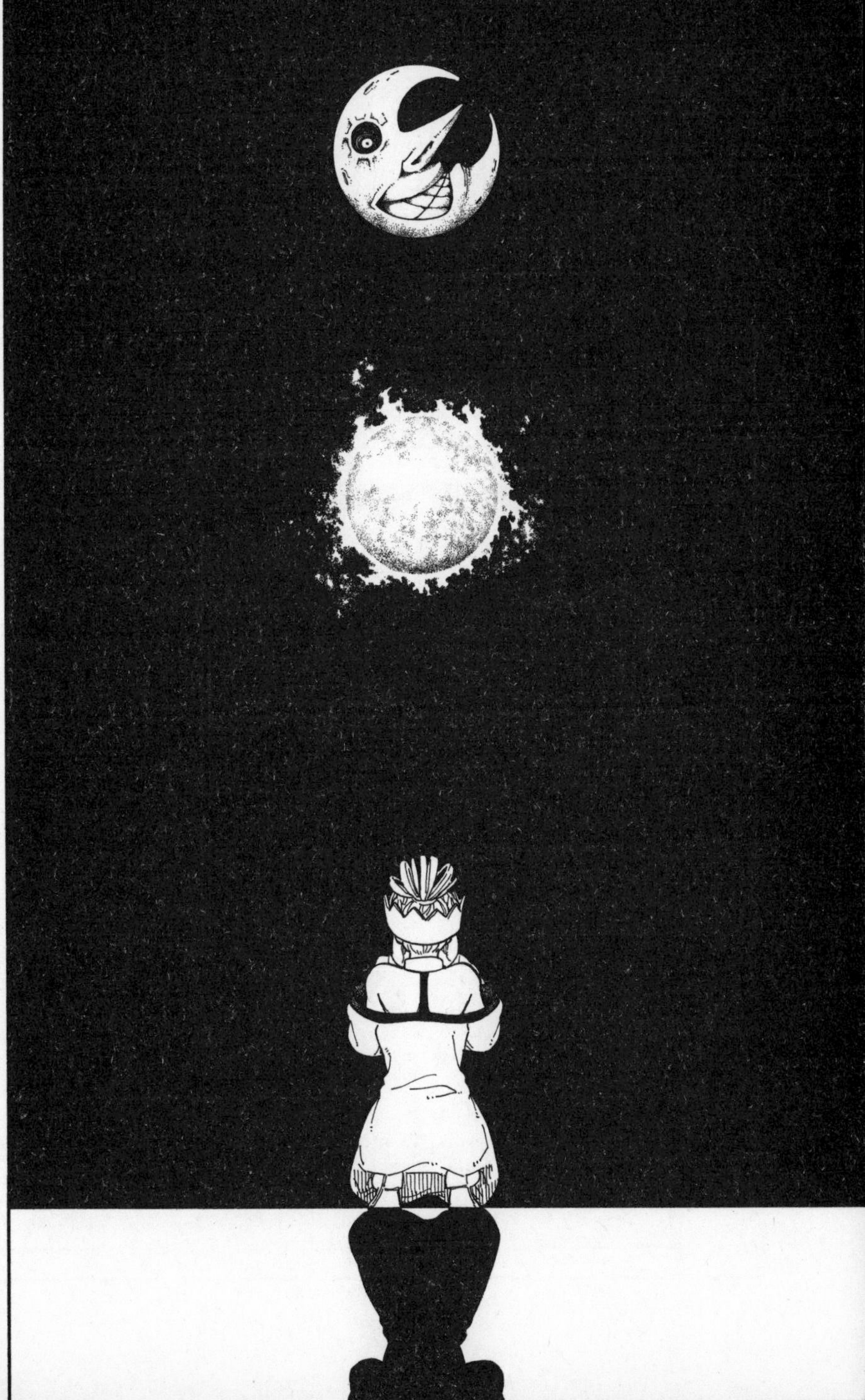

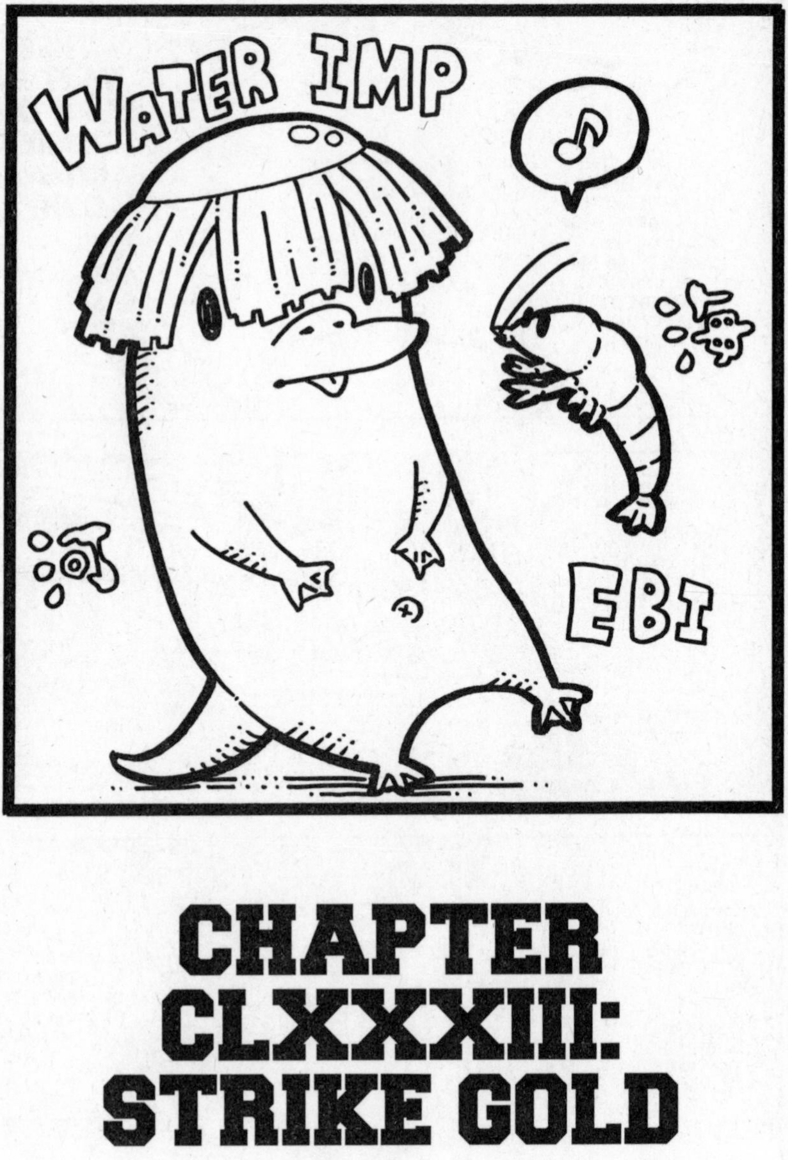
WATER IMP
EBI

CHAPTER CLXXXIII: STRIKE GOLD

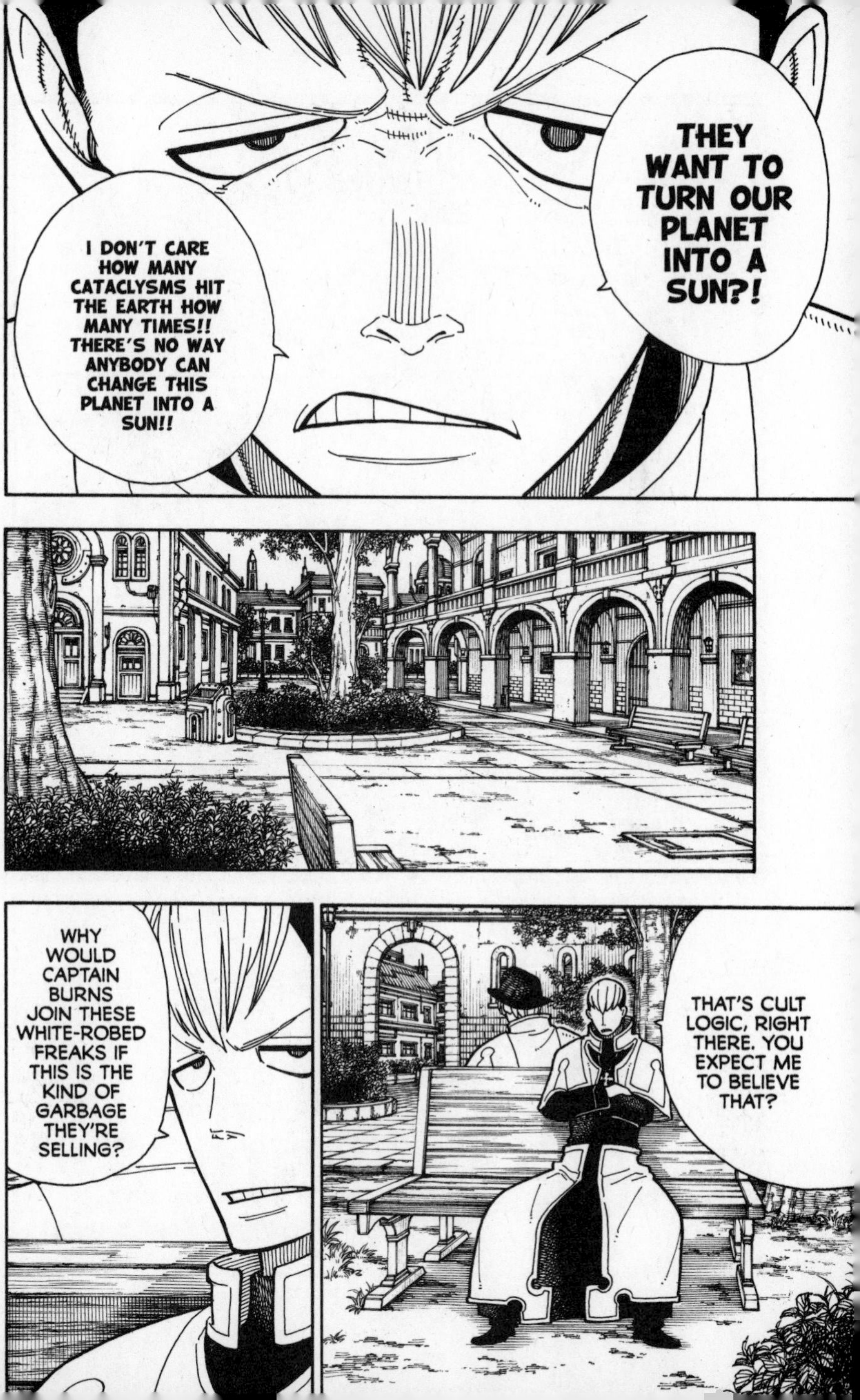
THEY WANT TO TURN OUR PLANET INTO A SUN?!
I DON'T CARE HOW MANY CATACLYSMS HIT THE EARTH HOW MANY TIMES!! THERE'S NO WAY ANYBODY CAN CHANGE THIS PLANET INTO A SUN!!
THAT'S CULT LOGIC, RIGHT THERE. YOU EXPECT ME TO BELIEVE THAT?
WHY WOULD CAPTAIN BURNS JOIN THESE WHITE-ROBED FREAKS IF THIS IS THE KIND OF GARBAGE THEY'RE SELLING?

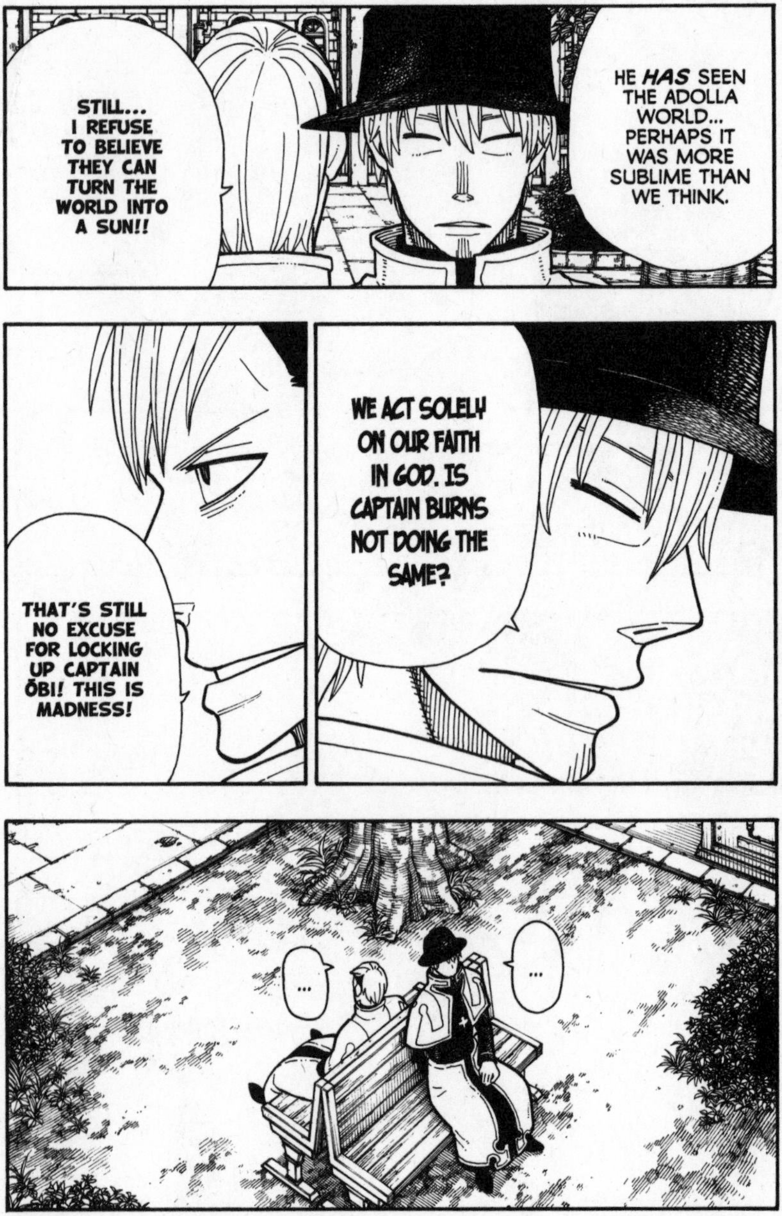
HE HAS SEEN THE ADOLLA WORLD... PERHAPS IT WAS MORE SUBLIME THAN WE THINK.
STILL... I REFUSE TO BELIEVE THEY CAN TURN THE WORLD INTO A SUN!!
WE ACT SOLELY ON OUR FAITH IN GOD. IS CAPTAIN BURNS NOT DOING THE SAME?
THAT'S STILL NO EXCUSE FOR LOCKING UP CAPTAIN ŌBI! THIS IS MADNESS!
...
...

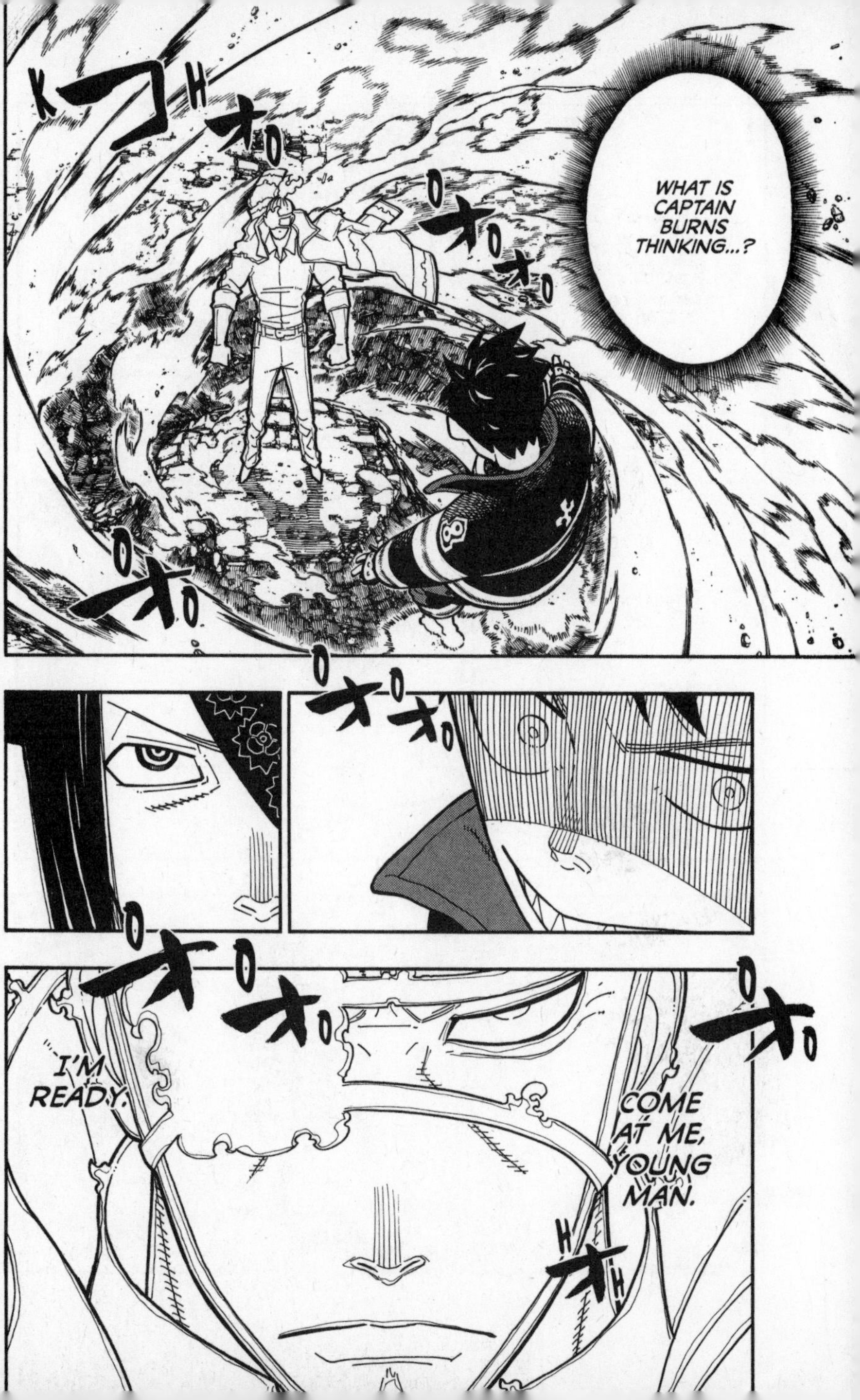
WHAT IS CAPTAIN BURNS THINKING...?
KOHOOO
OOO
OOO
COME AT ME, YOUNG MAN.
I'M READY.
HOH

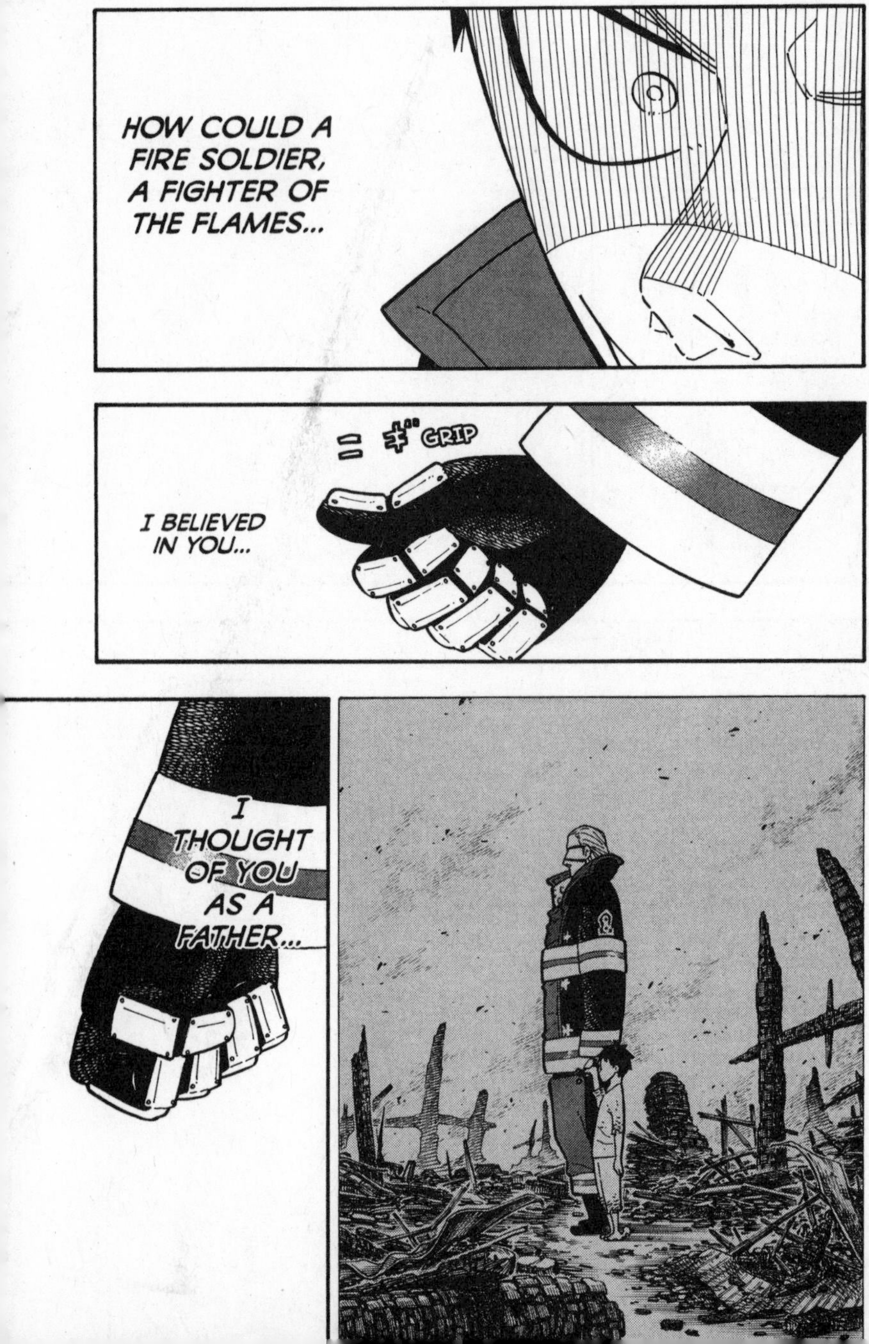
HOW COULD A FIRE SOLDIER, A FIGHTER OF THE FLAMES...
GRIP
I BELIEVED IN YOU...
I THOUGHT OF YOU AS A FATHER...

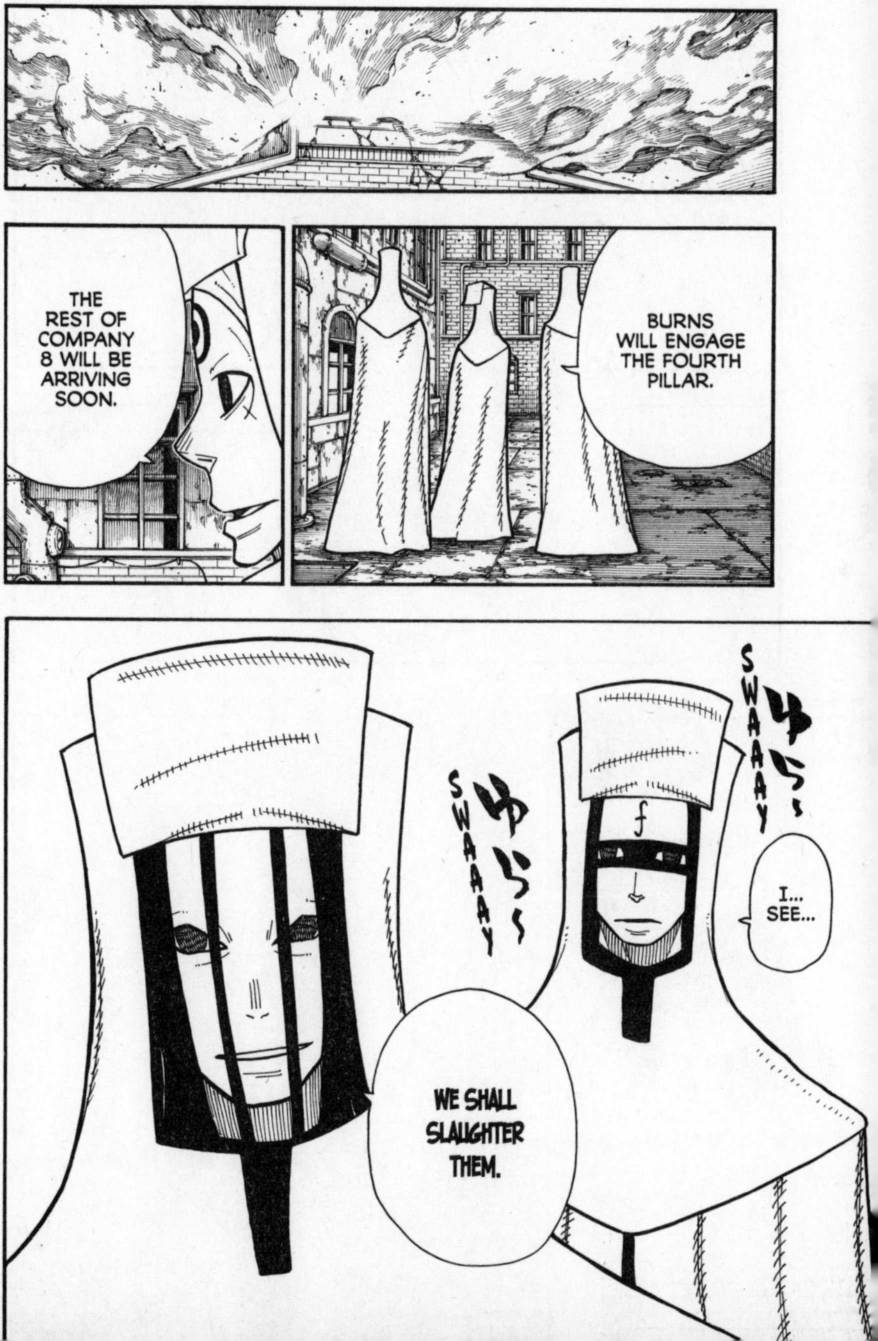
BURNS WILL ENGAGE THE FOURTH PILLAR.
THE REST OF COMPANY 8 WILL BE ARRIVING SOON.
SWAAAY
I... SEE...
SWAAAY
WE SHALL SLAUGHTER THEM.

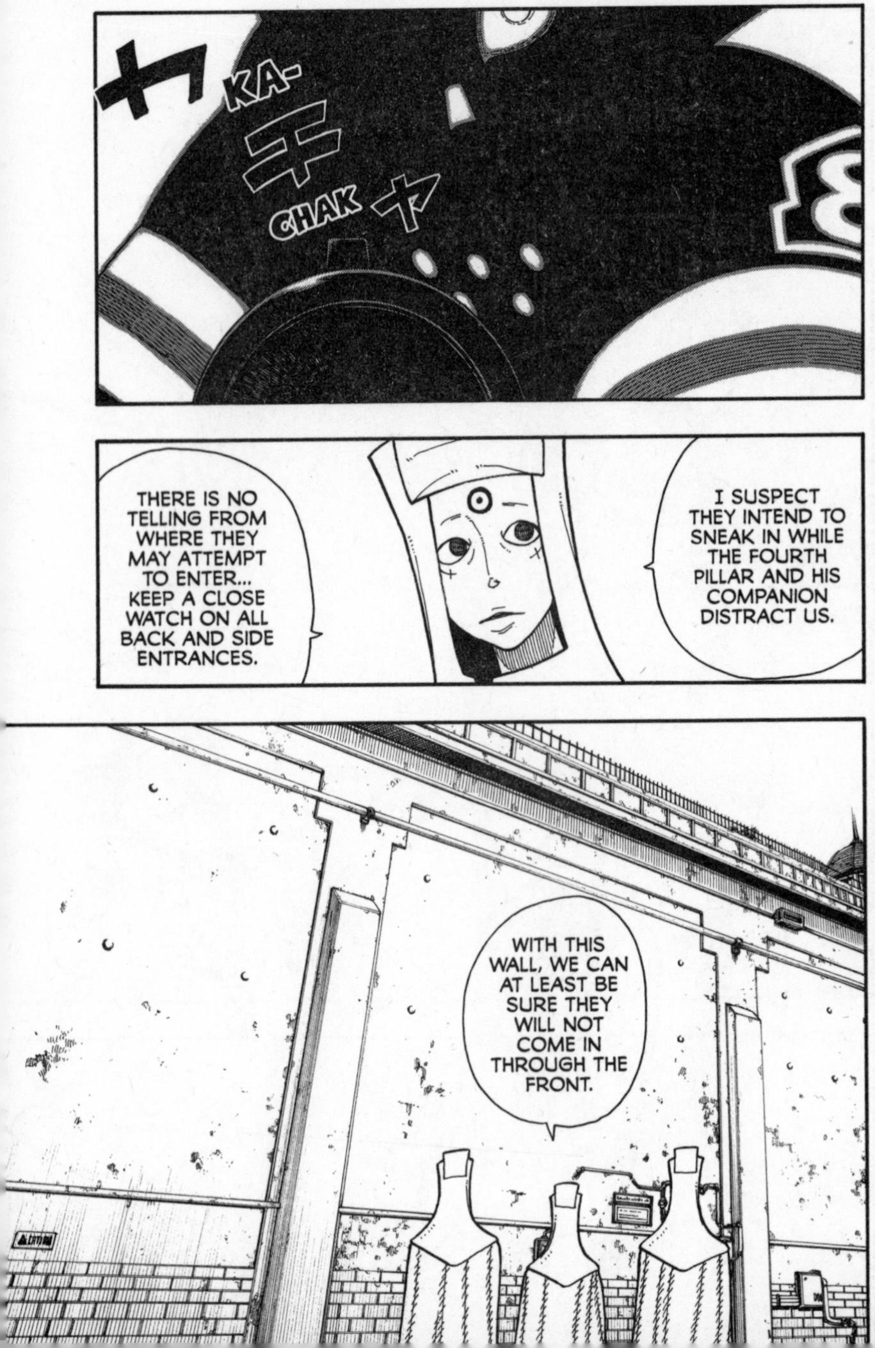
カチャ
KA-CHAK
I SUSPECT THEY INTEND TO SNEAK IN WHILE THE FOURTH PILLAR AND HIS COMPANION DISTRACT US.
THERE IS NO TELLING FROM WHERE THEY MAY ATTEMPT TO ENTER... KEEP A CLOSE WATCH ON ALL BACK AND SIDE ENTRANCES.
WITH THIS WALL, WE CAN AT LEAST BE SURE THEY WILL NOT COME IN THROUGH THE FRONT.

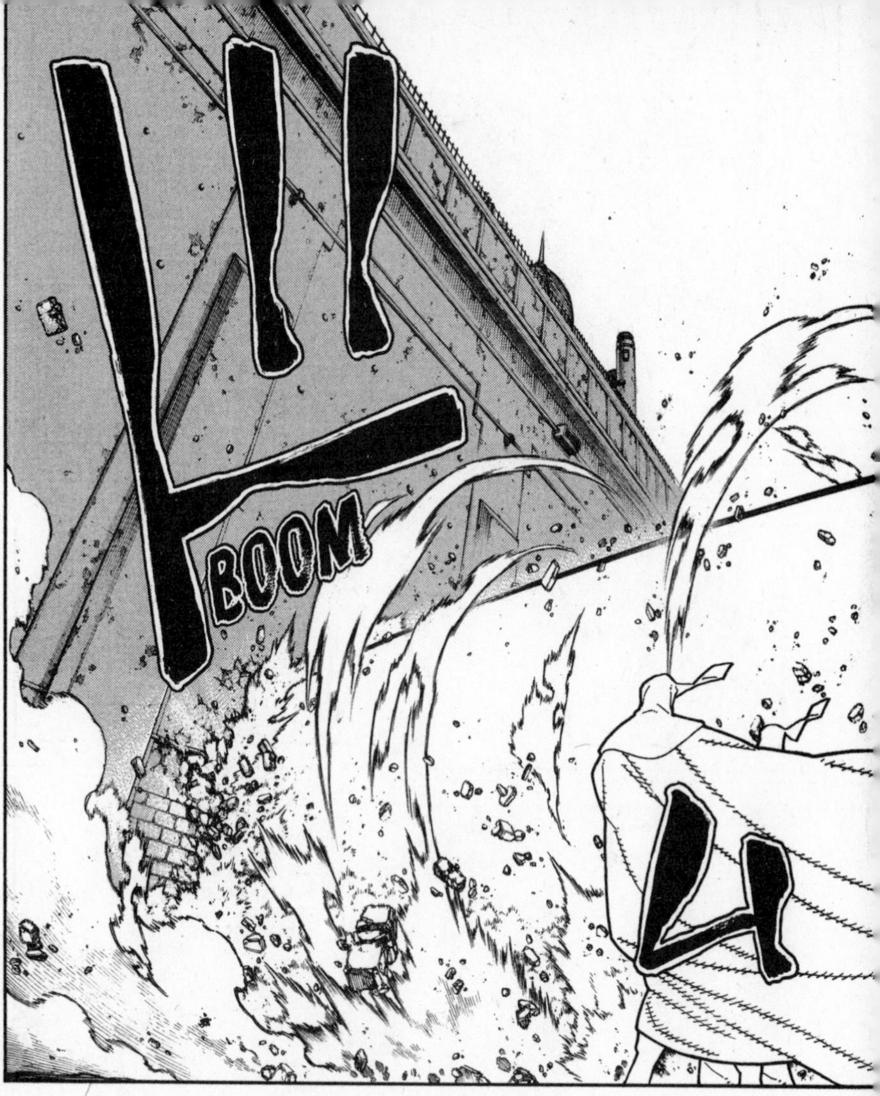
BOOM
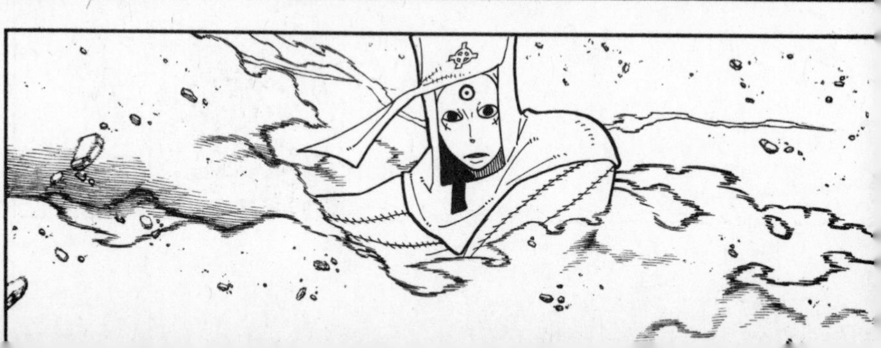

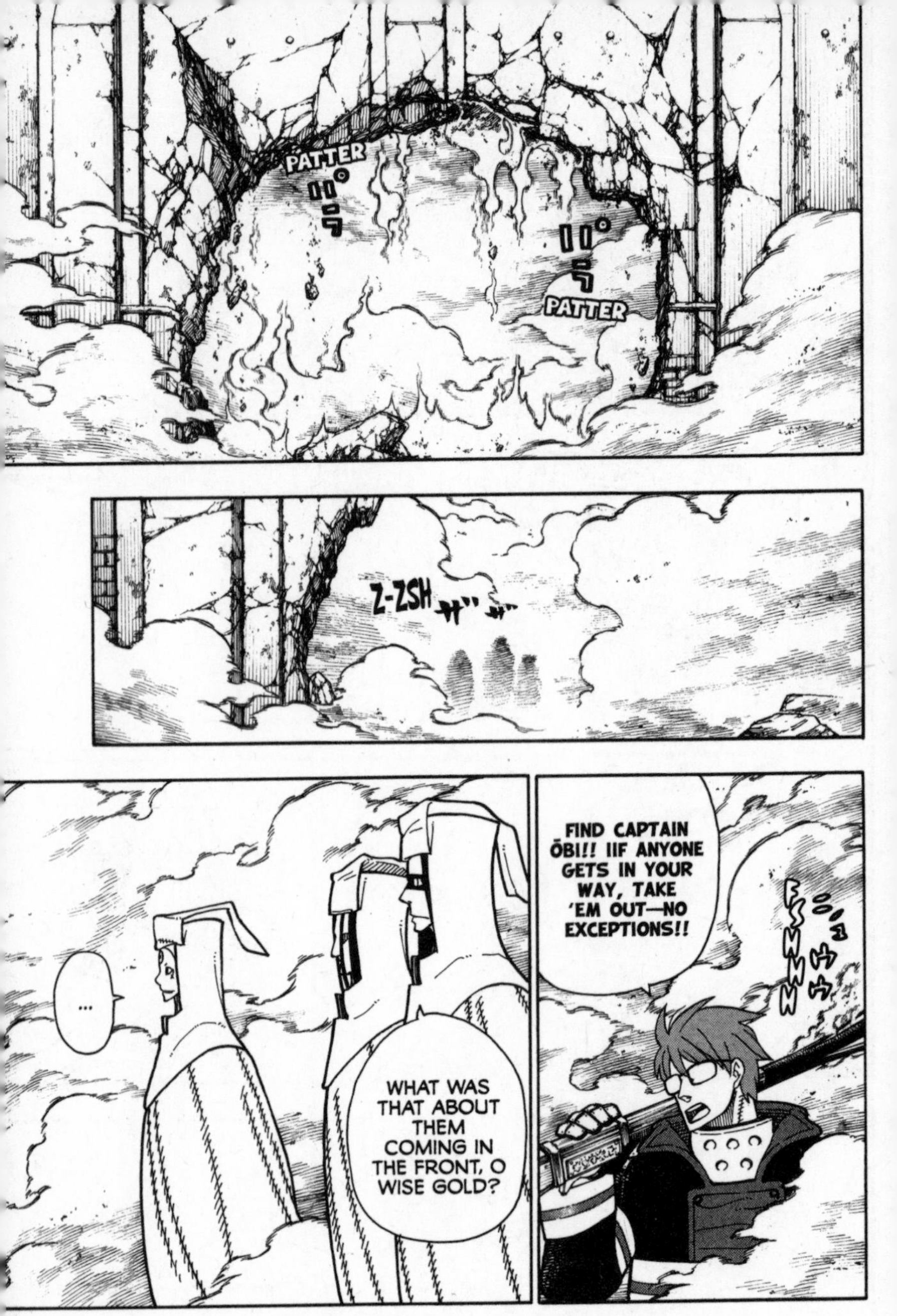
PATTER
PATTER
Z-ZSH
FIND CAPTAIN ŌBI!! IIF ANYONE GETS IN YOUR WAY, TAKE 'EM OUT—NO EXCEPTIONS!!
FSHHH
WHAT WAS THAT ABOUT THEM COMING IN THE FRONT, O WISE GOLD?
...

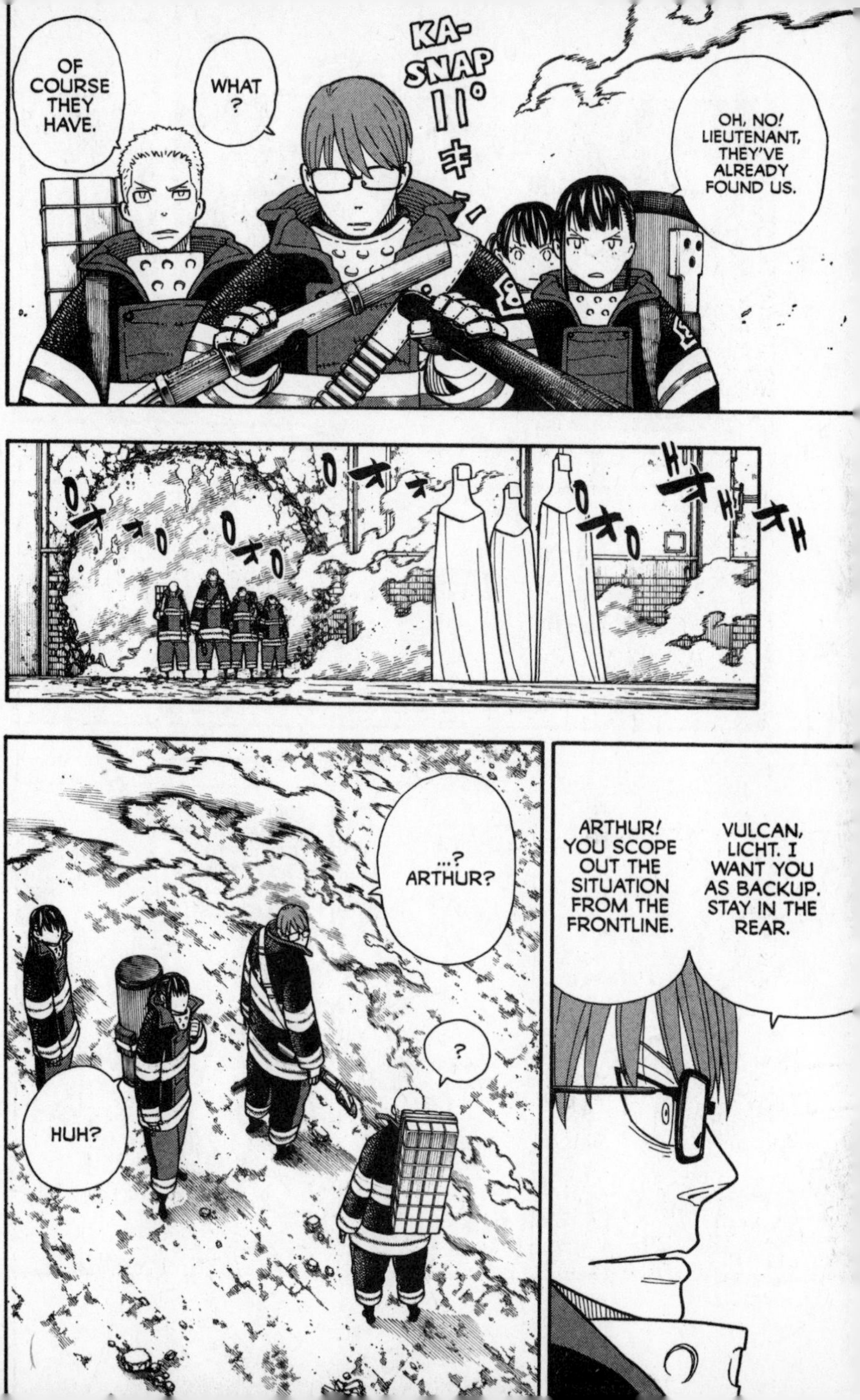
OH, NO! LIEUTENANT, THEY'VE ALREADY FOUND US.
KA-SNAP
WHAT?
OF COURSE THEY HAVE.
VULCAN, LICHT. I WANT YOU AS BACKUP. STAY IN THE REAR.
ARTHUR! YOU SCOPE OUT THE SITUATION FROM THE FRONTLINE.
...? ARTHUR?
?
HUH?

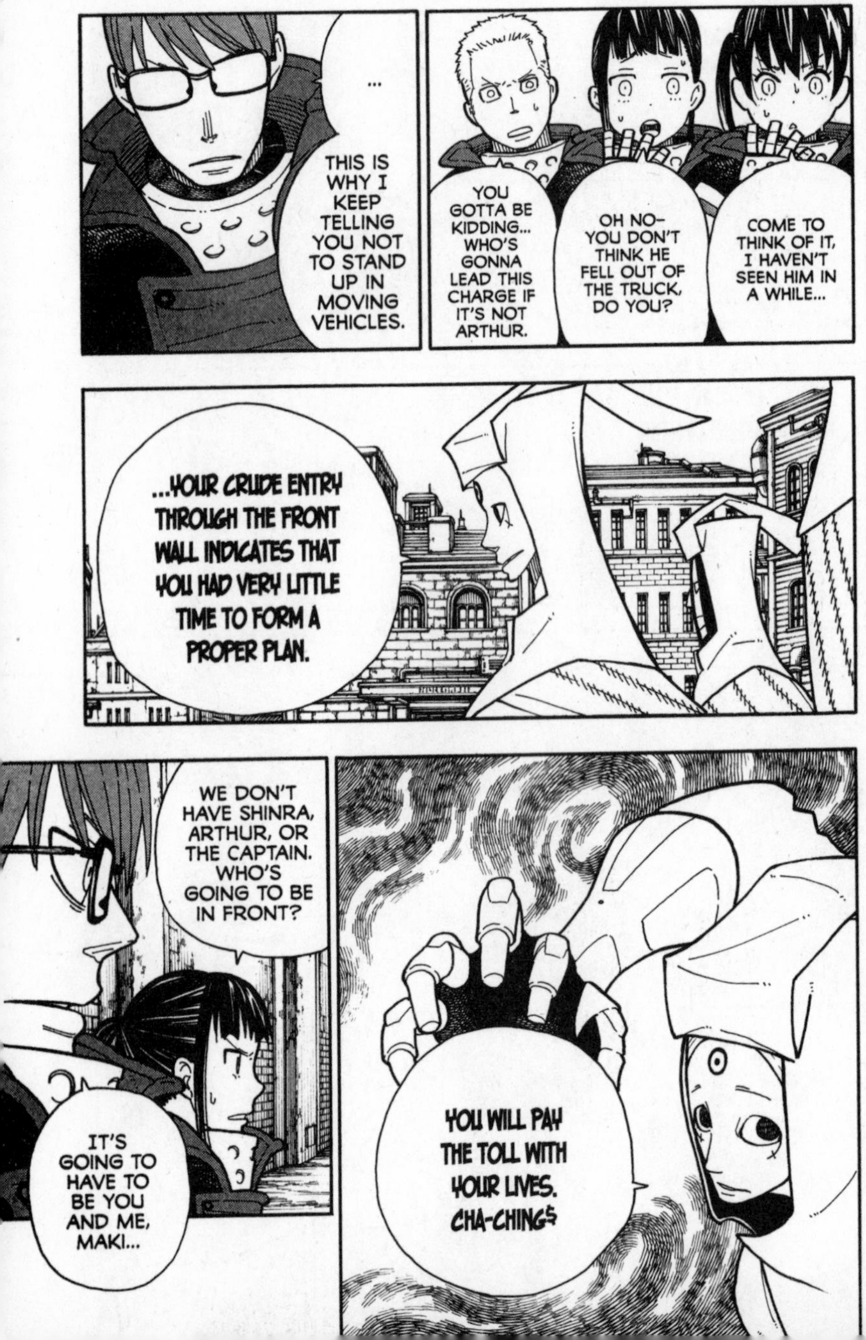
COME TO THINK OF IT, I HAVEN'T SEEN HIM IN A WHILE...
OH NO- YOU DON'T THINK HE FELL OUT OF THE TRUCK, DO YOU?
YOU GOTTA BE KIDDING... WHO'S GONNA LEAD THIS CHARGE IF IT'S NOT ARTHUR.
...
THIS IS WHY I KEEP TELLING YOU NOT TO STAND UP IN MOVING VEHICLES.
...YOUR CRUDE ENTRY THROUGH THE FRONT WALL INDICATES THAT YOU HAD VERY LITTLE TIME TO FORM A PROPER PLAN.
YOU WILL PAY THE TOLL WITH YOUR LIVES. CHA-CHING$
WE DON'T HAVE SHINRA, ARTHUR, OR THE CAPTAIN. WHO'S GOING TO BE IN FRONT?
IT'S GOING TO HAVE TO BE YOU AND ME, MAKI...

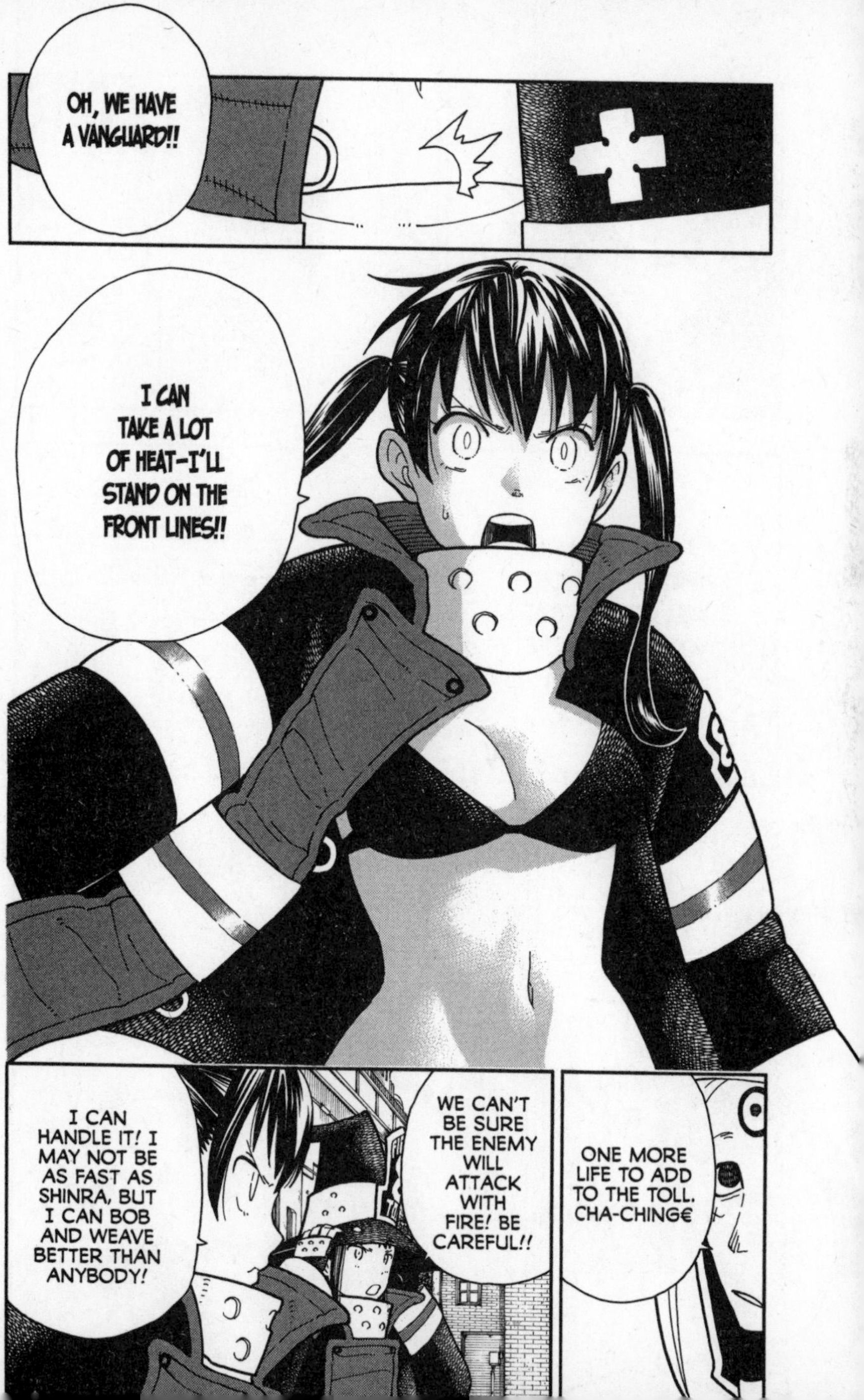
OH, WE HAVE A VANGUARD!!
I CAN TAKE A LOT OF HEAT—I'LL STAND ON THE FRONT LINES!!
ONE MORE LIFE TO ADD TO THE TOLL. CHA-CHING€
WE CAN'T BE SURE THE ENEMY WILL ATTACK WITH FIRE! BE CAREFUL!!
I CAN HANDLE IT! I MAY NOT BE AS FAST AS SHINRA, BUT I CAN BOB AND WEAVE BETTER THAN ANYBODY!

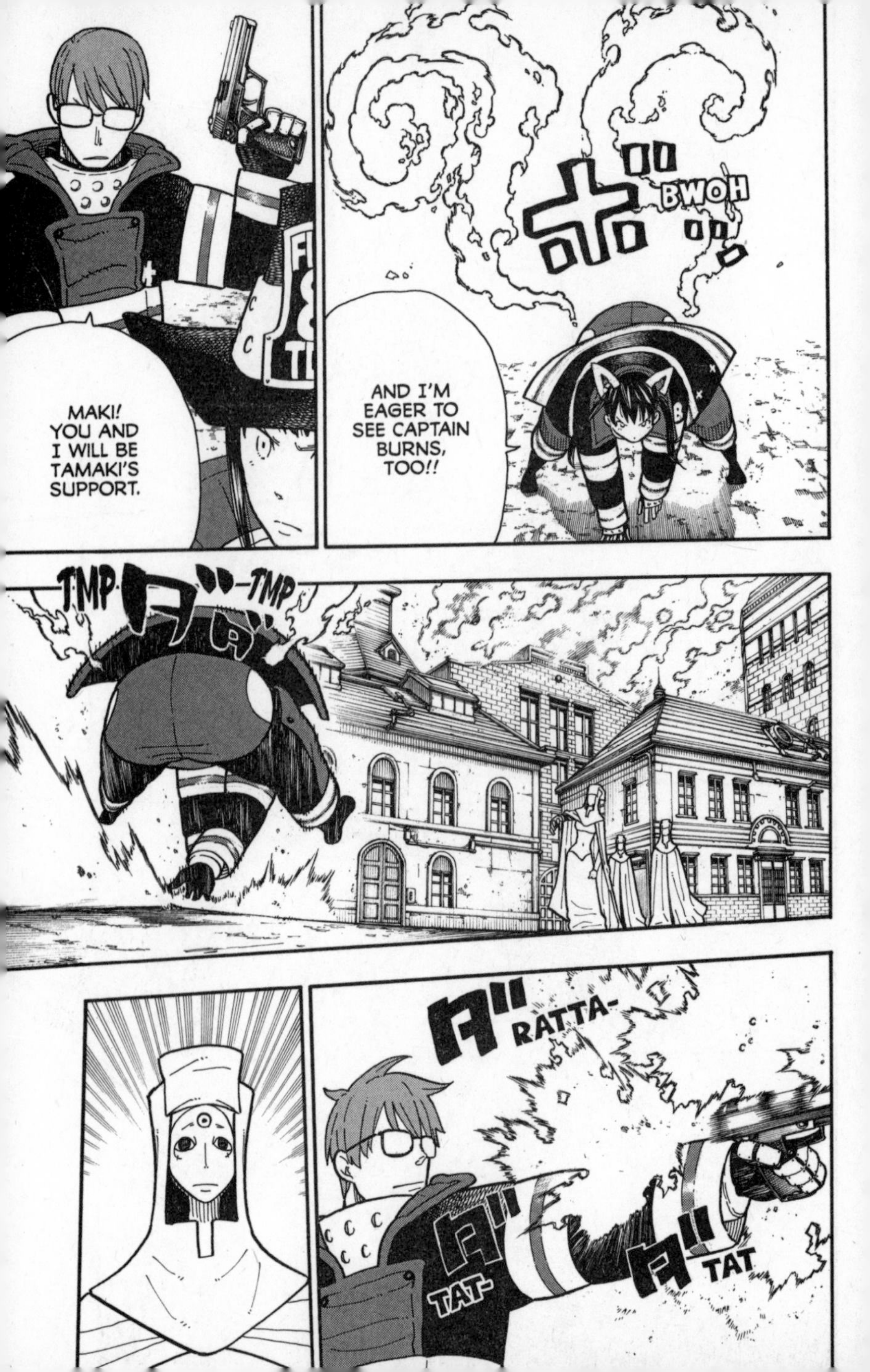
BWOH
AND I'M EAGER TO SEE CAPTAIN BURNS, TOO!!
MAKI! YOU AND I WILL BE TAMAKI'S SUPPORT.
TMP TMP
RATTA-
TAT-
TAT

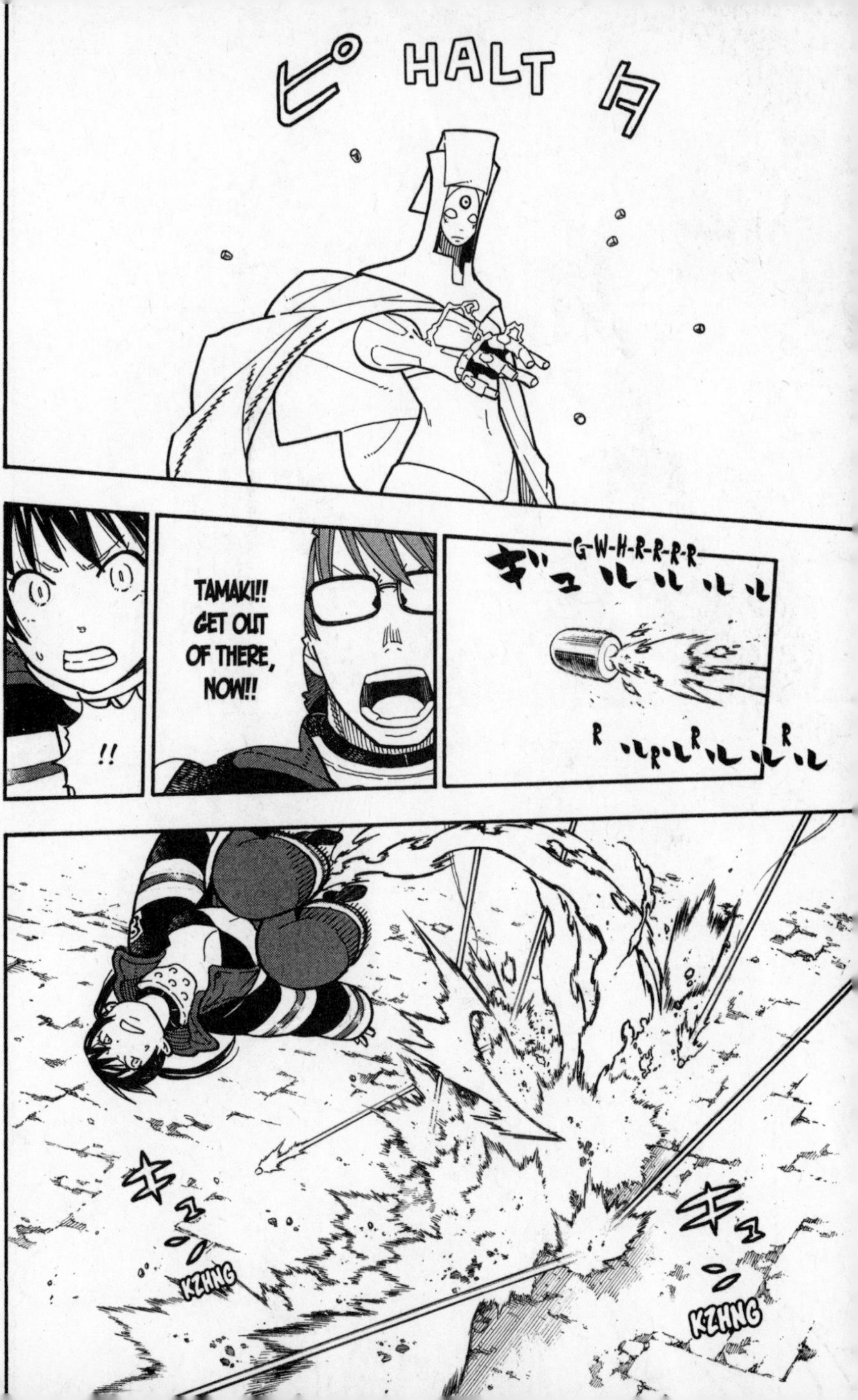
HALT
G-W-H-R-R-R-R
R R R R
TAMAKI!! GET OUT OF THERE, NOW!!
!!
KZHNG
KZHNG

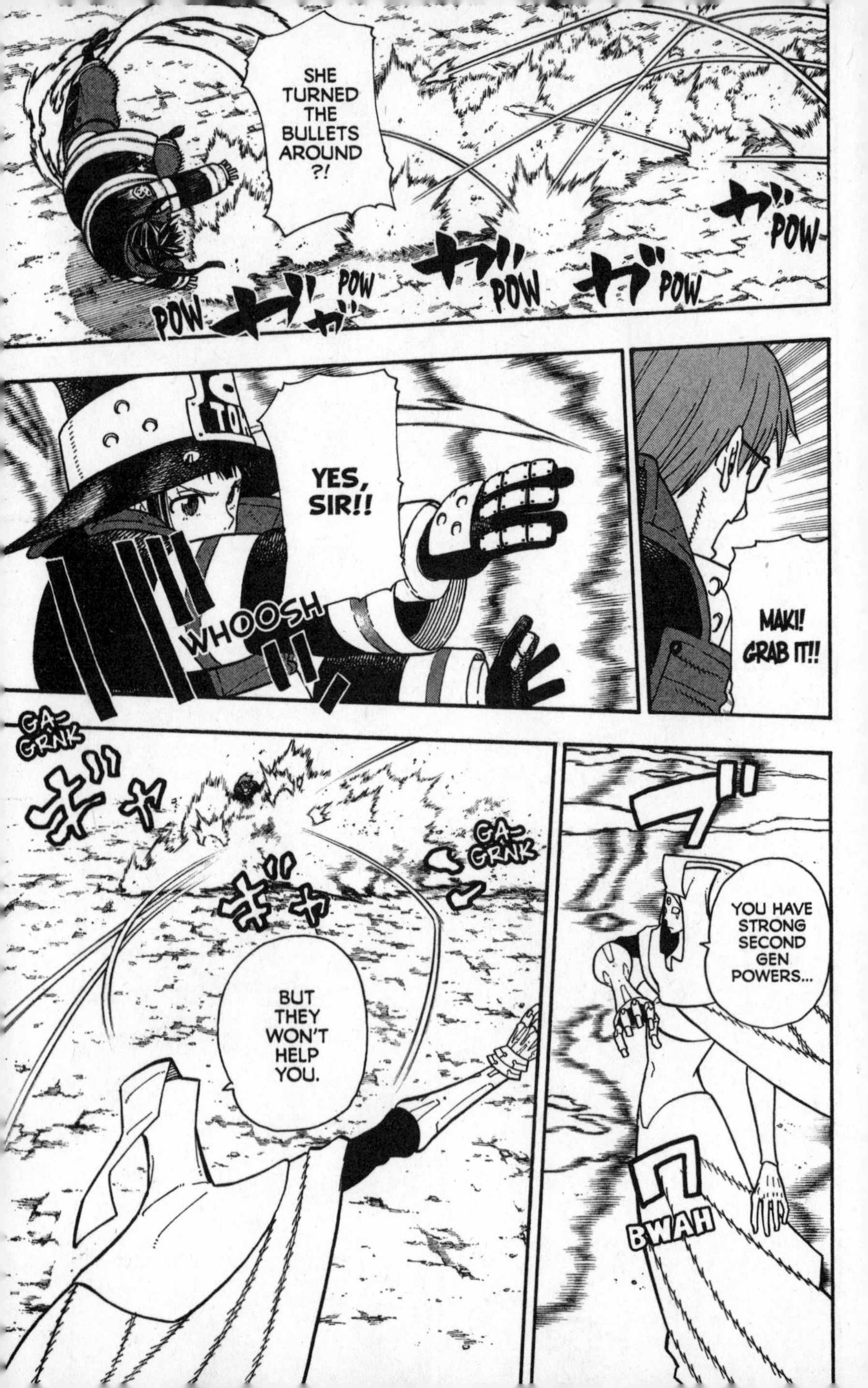
POW
POW
POW
SHE TURNED THE BULLETS AROUND ?!
POW
POW
MAKI! GRAB IT!!
YES, SIR!!
WHOOSH
YOU HAVE STRONG SECOND GEN POWERS...
BWAH
GA-GRNK
GA-GRNK
BUT THEY WON'T HELP YOU.

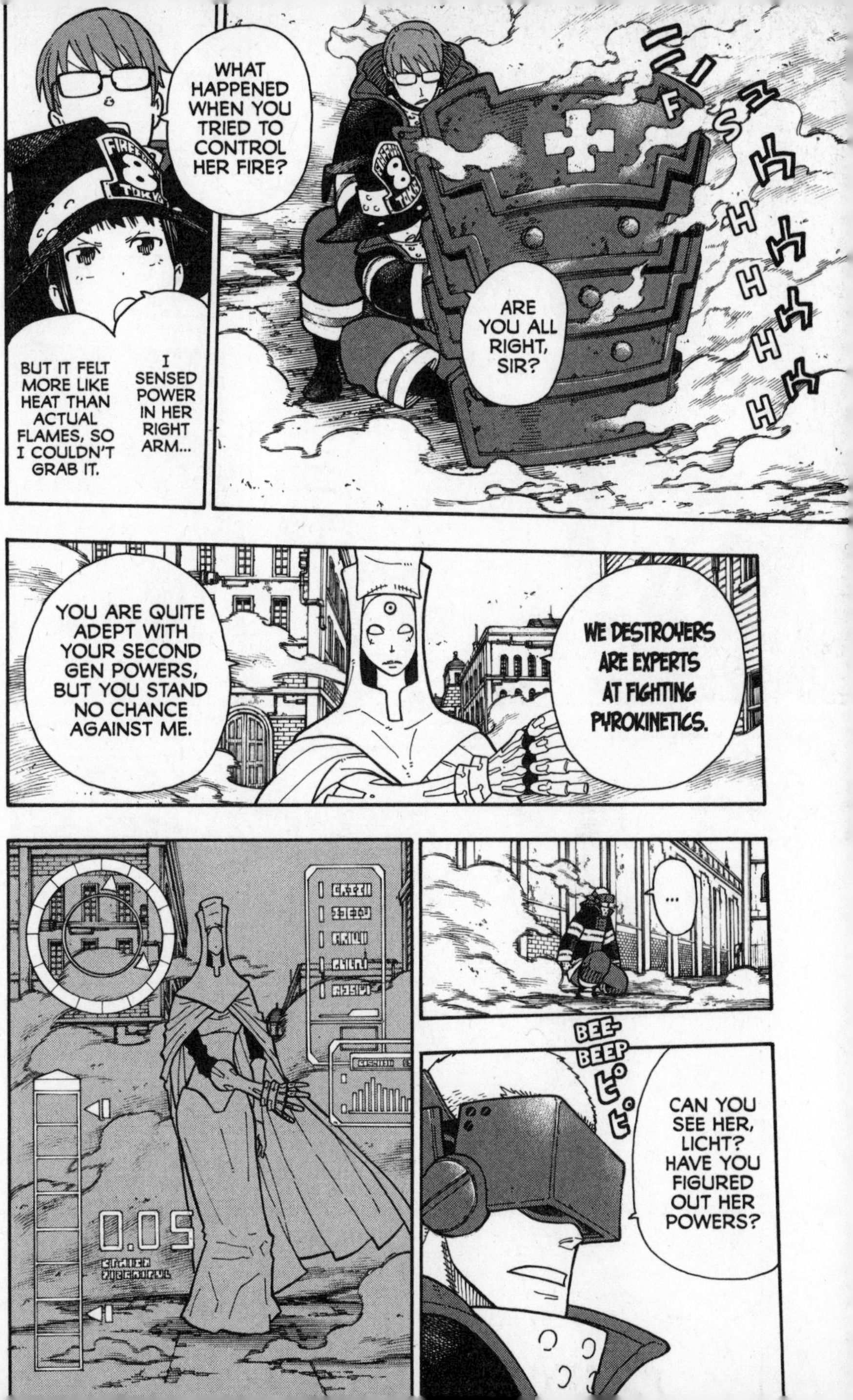
FSHHHHH
ARE YOU ALL RIGHT, SIR?
WHAT HAPPENED WHEN YOU TRIED TO CONTROL HER FIRE?
I SENSED POWER IN HER RIGHT ARM...
BUT IT FELT MORE LIKE HEAT THAN ACTUAL FLAMES, SO I COULDN'T GRAB IT.
WE DESTROYERS ARE EXPERTS AT FIGHTING PYROKINETICS.
YOU ARE QUITE ADEPT WITH YOUR SECOND GEN POWERS, BUT YOU STAND NO CHANCE AGAINST ME.
...
BEE-BEEP
CAN YOU SEE HER, LICHT? HAVE YOU FIGURED OUT HER POWERS?
0.05

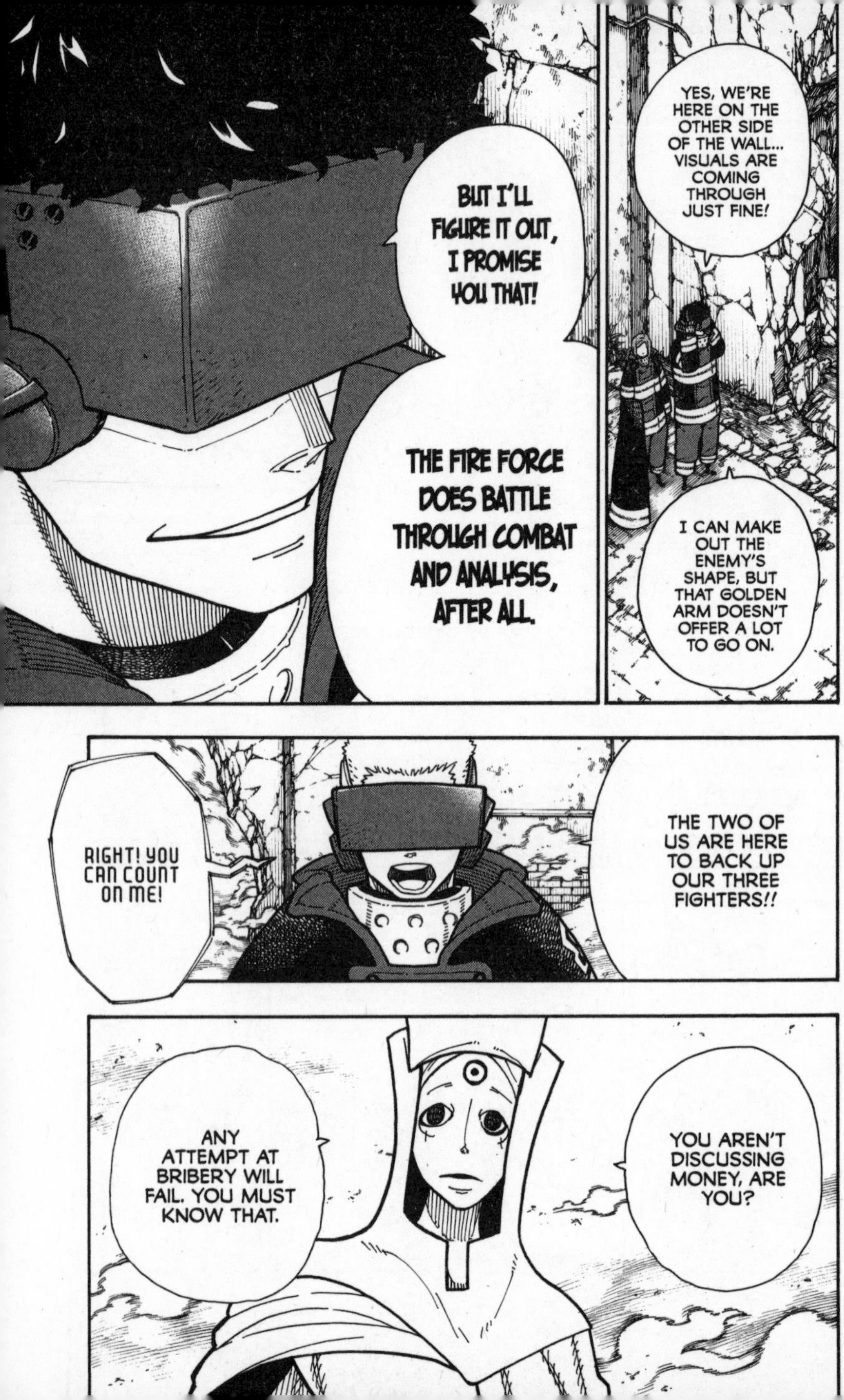
YES, WE'RE HERE ON THE OTHER SIDE OF THE WALL... VISUALS ARE COMING THROUGH JUST FINE!
I CAN MAKE OUT THE ENEMY'S SHAPE, BUT THAT GOLDEN ARM DOESN'T OFFER A LOT TO GO ON.
BUT I'LL FIGURE IT OUT, I PROMISE YOU THAT!
THE FIRE FORCE DOES BATTLE THROUGH COMBAT AND ANALYSIS, AFTER ALL.
THE TWO OF US ARE HERE TO BACK UP OUR THREE FIGHTERS!!
RIGHT! YOU CAN COUNT ON ME!
YOU AREN'T DISCUSSING MONEY, ARE YOU?
ANY ATTEMPT AT BRIBERY WILL FAIL. YOU MUST KNOW THAT.

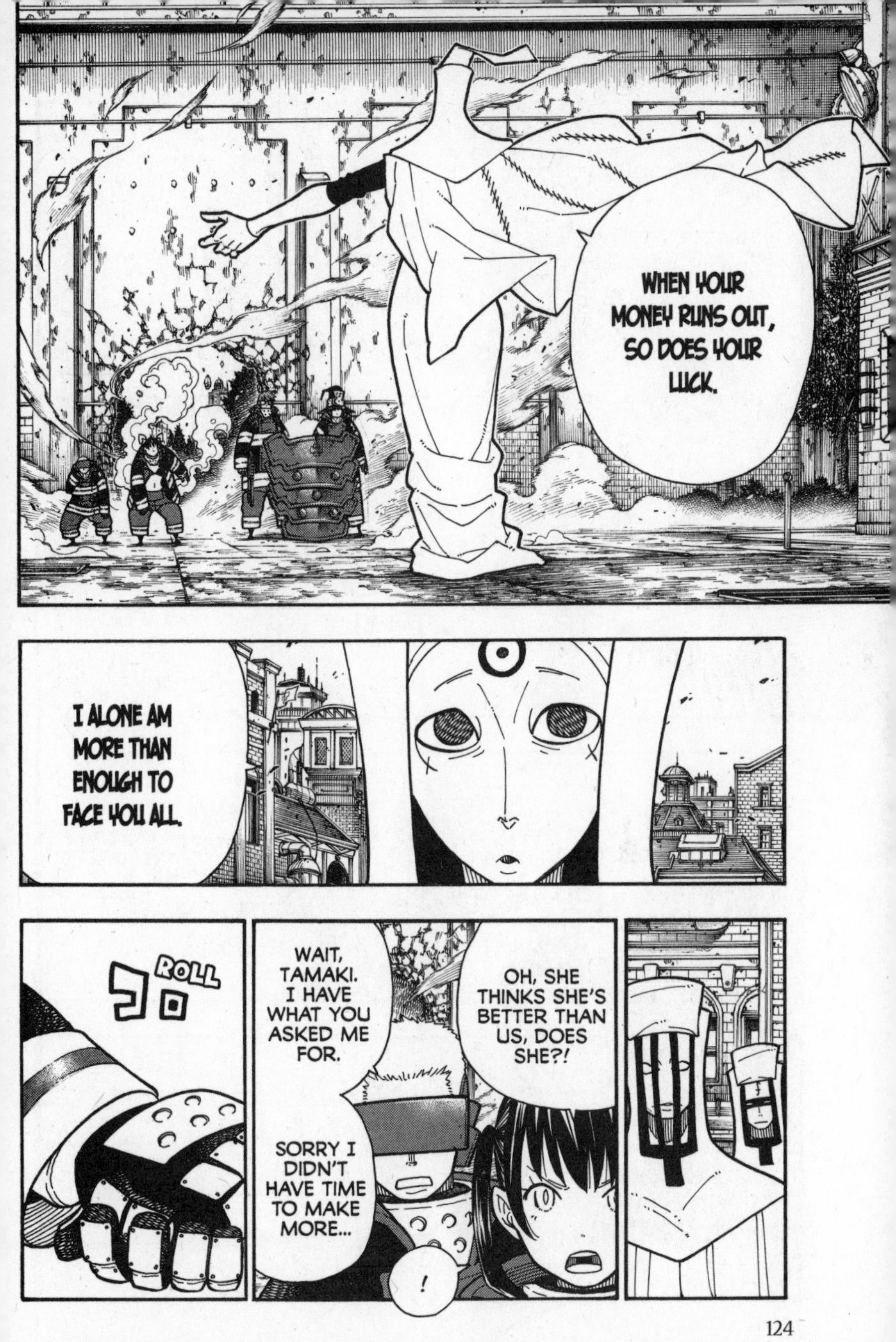
WHEN YOUR MONEY RUNS OUT, SO DOES YOUR LUCK.
I ALONE AM MORE THAN ENOUGH TO FACE YOU ALL.
OH, SHE THINKS SHE'S BETTER THAN US, DOES SHE?!
WAIT, TAMAKI. I HAVE WHAT YOU ASKED ME FOR.
SORRY I DIDN'T HAVE TIME TO MAKE MORE...
!
ROLL

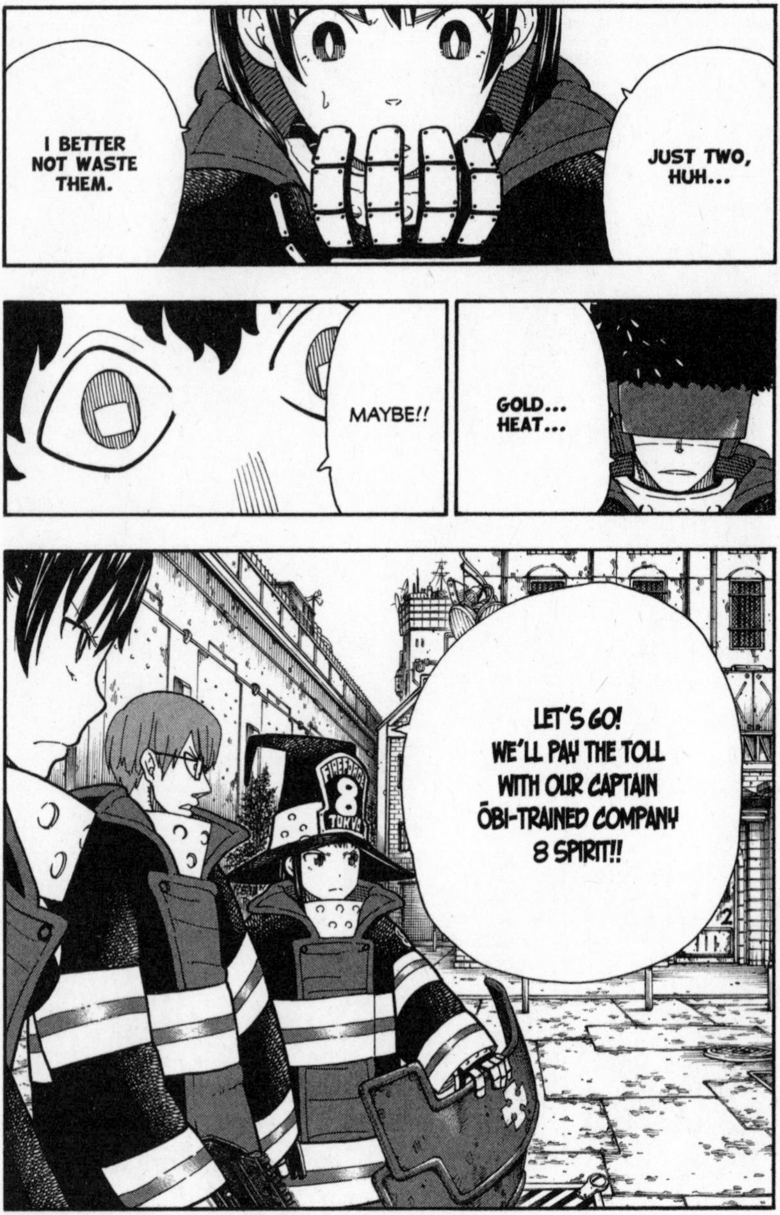
JUST TWO, HUH...
I BETTER NOT WASTE THEM.
GOLD... HEAT...
MAYBE!!
LET'S GO! WE'LL PAY THE TOLL WITH OUR CAPTAIN ŌBI-TRAINED COMPANY 8 SPIRIT!!

FIRE FORCE

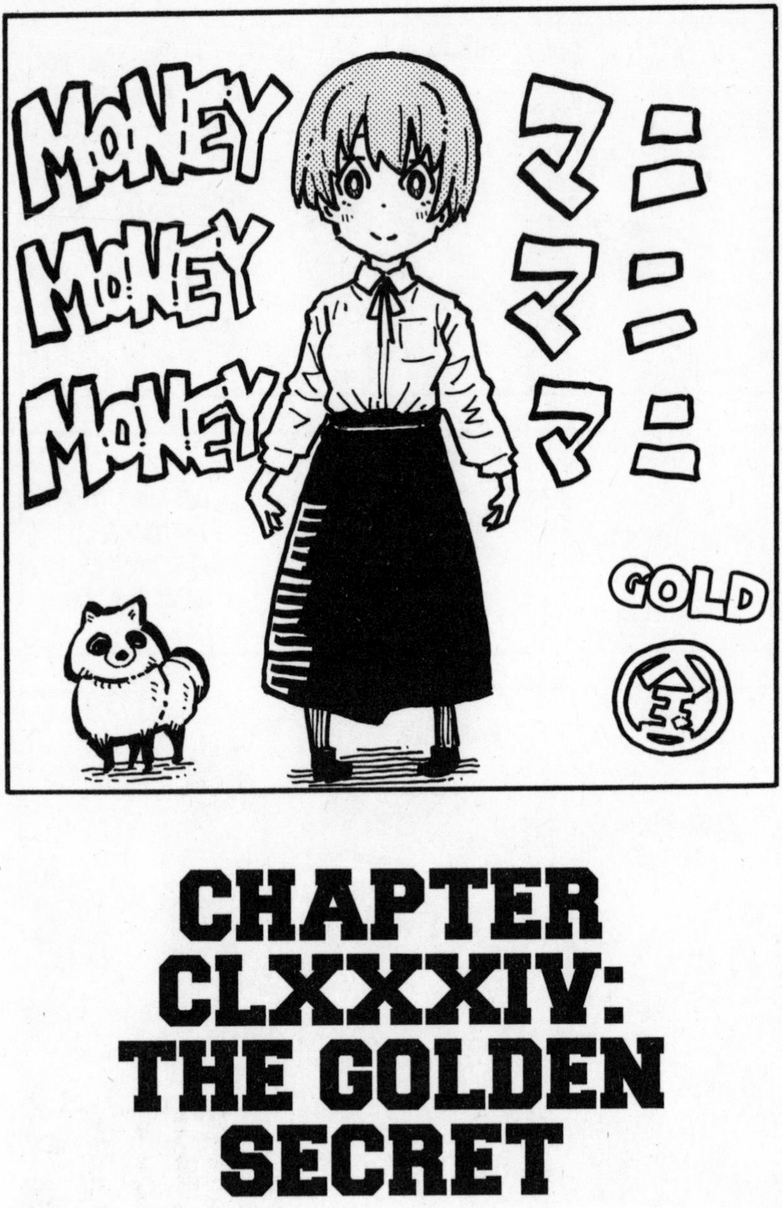
MONEY
MONEY
MONEY
マニ
マニ
マニ
GOLD

CHAPTER CLXXXIV: THE GOLDEN SECRET

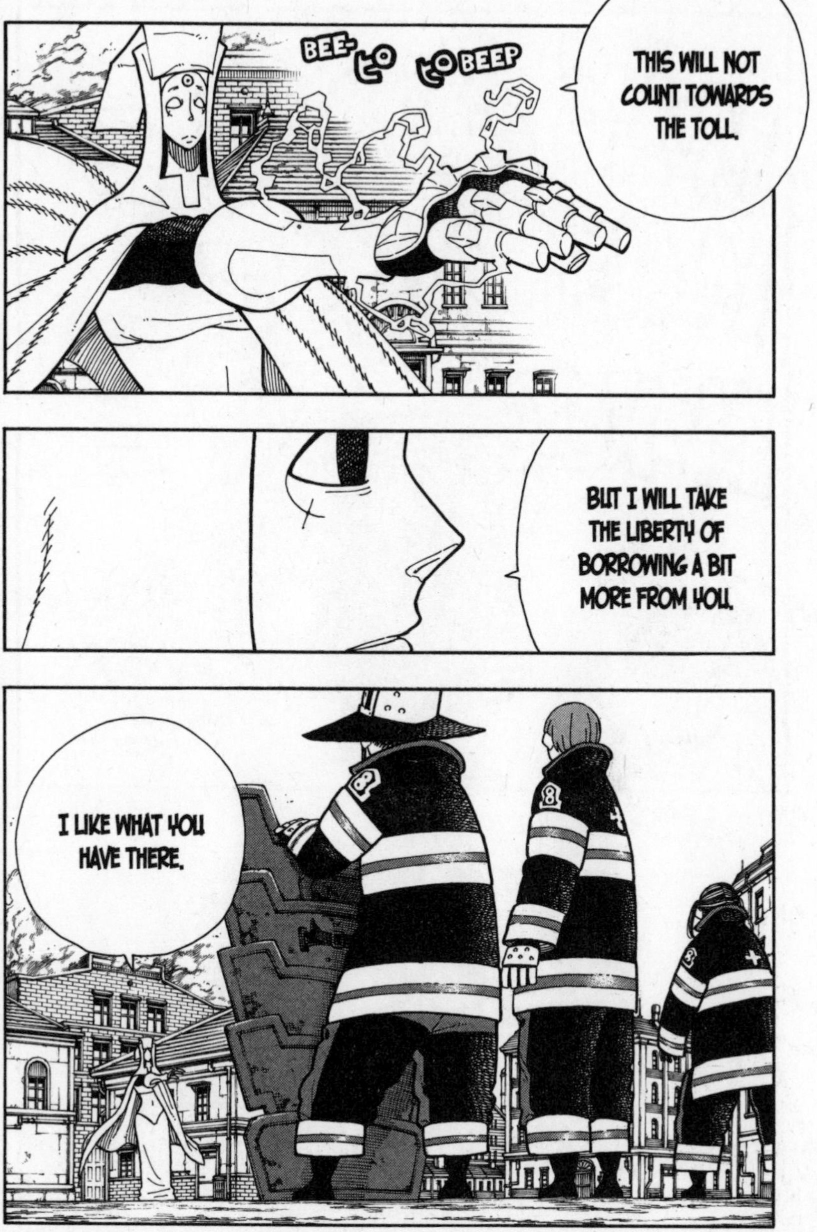
THIS WILL NOT COUNT TOWARDS THE TOLL.
BEE-
BEEP
BUT I WILL TAKE THE LIBERTY OF BORROWING A BIT MORE FROM YOU.
I LIKE WHAT YOU HAVE THERE.

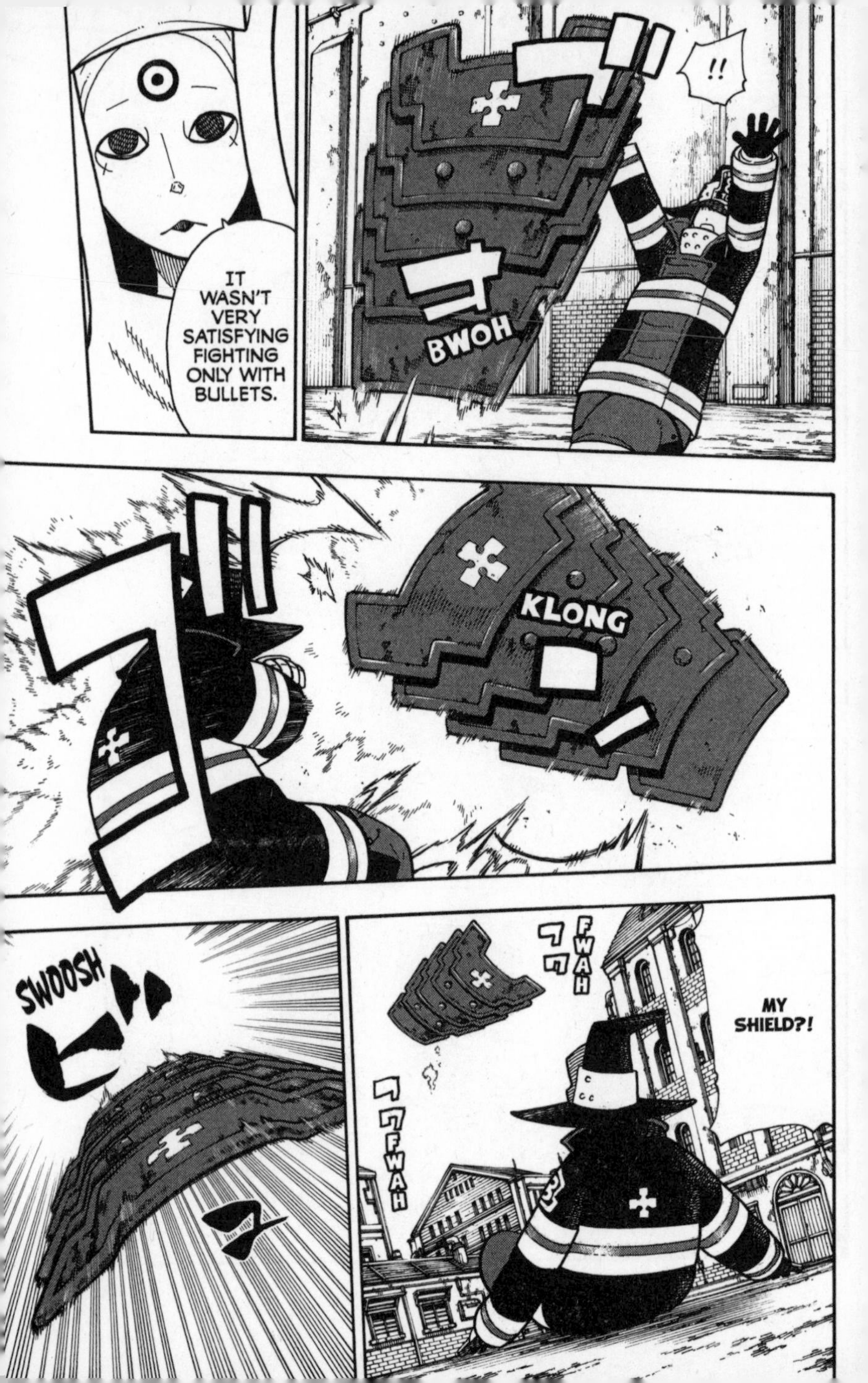
!!
BWOH
IT WASN'T VERY SATISFYING FIGHTING ONLY WITH BULLETS.
KLONG
FWAH
FWAH
MY SHIELD?!
SWOOSH

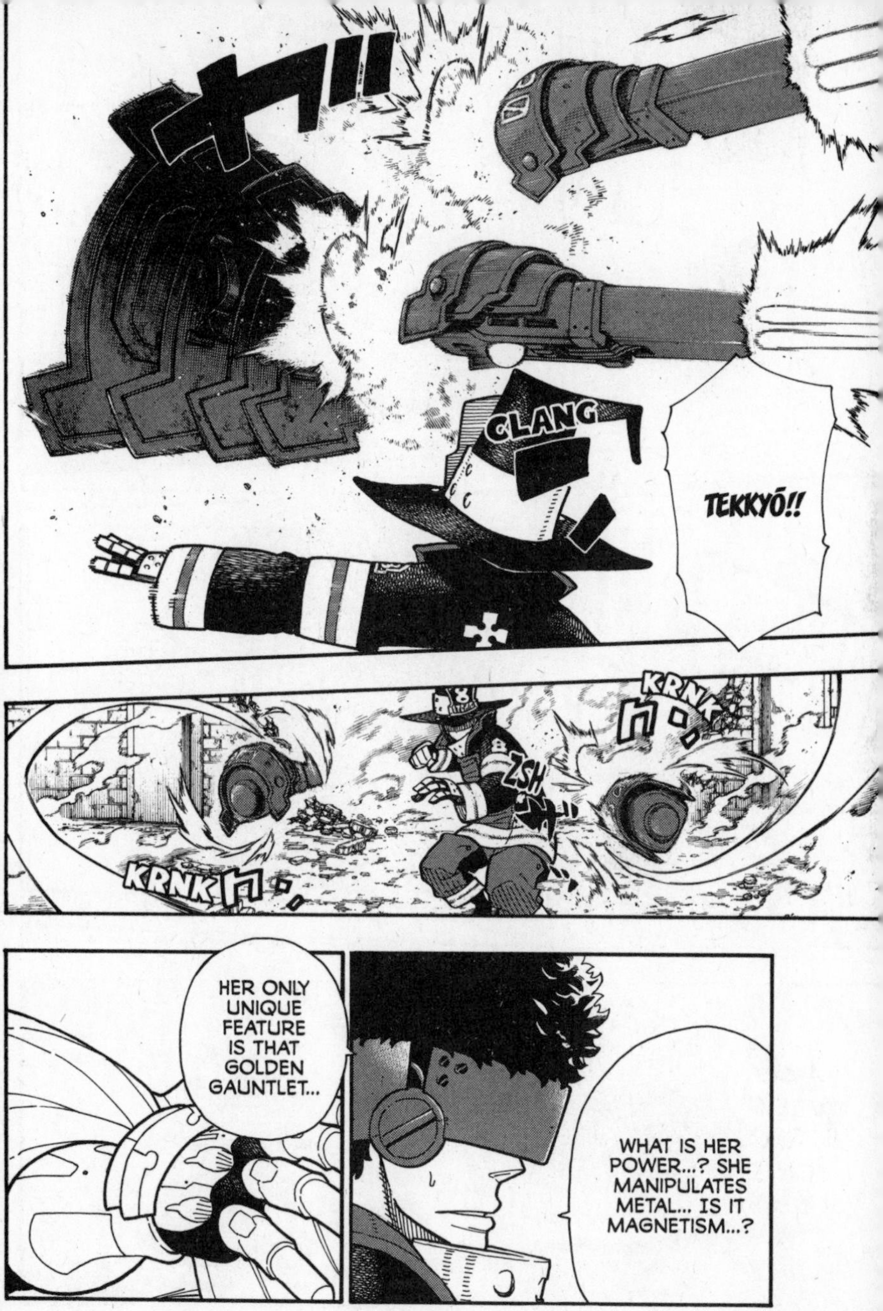
TEKKYŌ!!
CLANG
KRNK
ZSH
KRNK
WHAT IS HER POWER...? SHE MANIPULATES METAL... IS IT MAGNETISM...?
HER ONLY UNIQUE FEATURE IS THAT GOLDEN GAUNTLET...

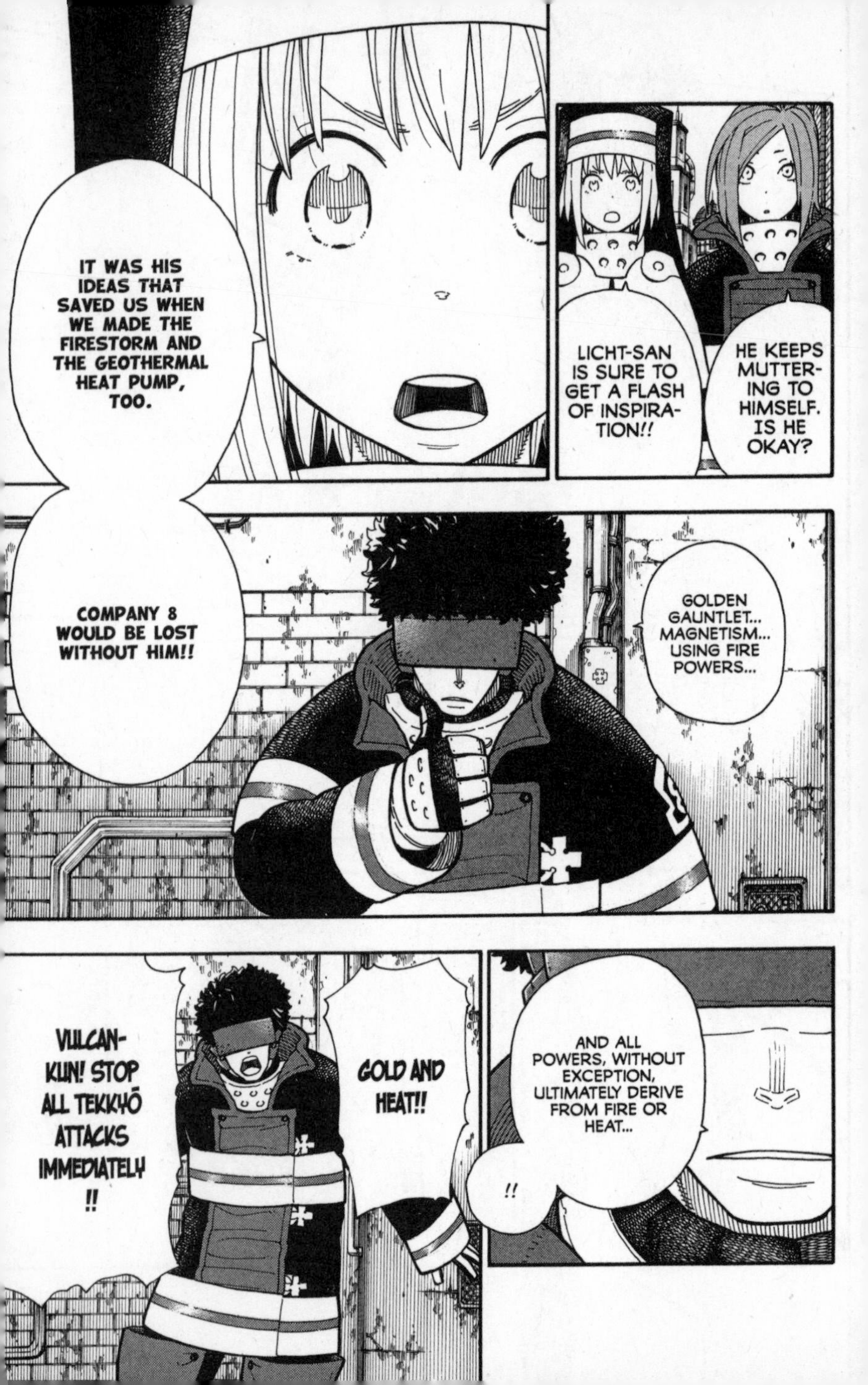
HE KEEPS MUTTERING TO HIMSELF. IS HE OKAY?
LICHT-SAN IS SURE TO GET A FLASH OF INSPIRATION!!
IT WAS HIS IDEAS THAT SAVED US WHEN WE MADE THE FIRESTORM AND THE GEOTHERMAL HEAT PUMP, TOO.
COMPANY 8 WOULD BE LOST WITHOUT HIM!!
GOLDEN GAUNTLET... MAGNETISM... USING FIRE POWERS...
AND ALL POWERS, WITHOUT EXCEPTION, ULTIMATELY DERIVE FROM FIRE OR HEAT...
!!
GOLD AND HEAT!!
VULCAN-KUN! STOP ALL TEKKYŌ ATTACKS IMMEDIATELY!!

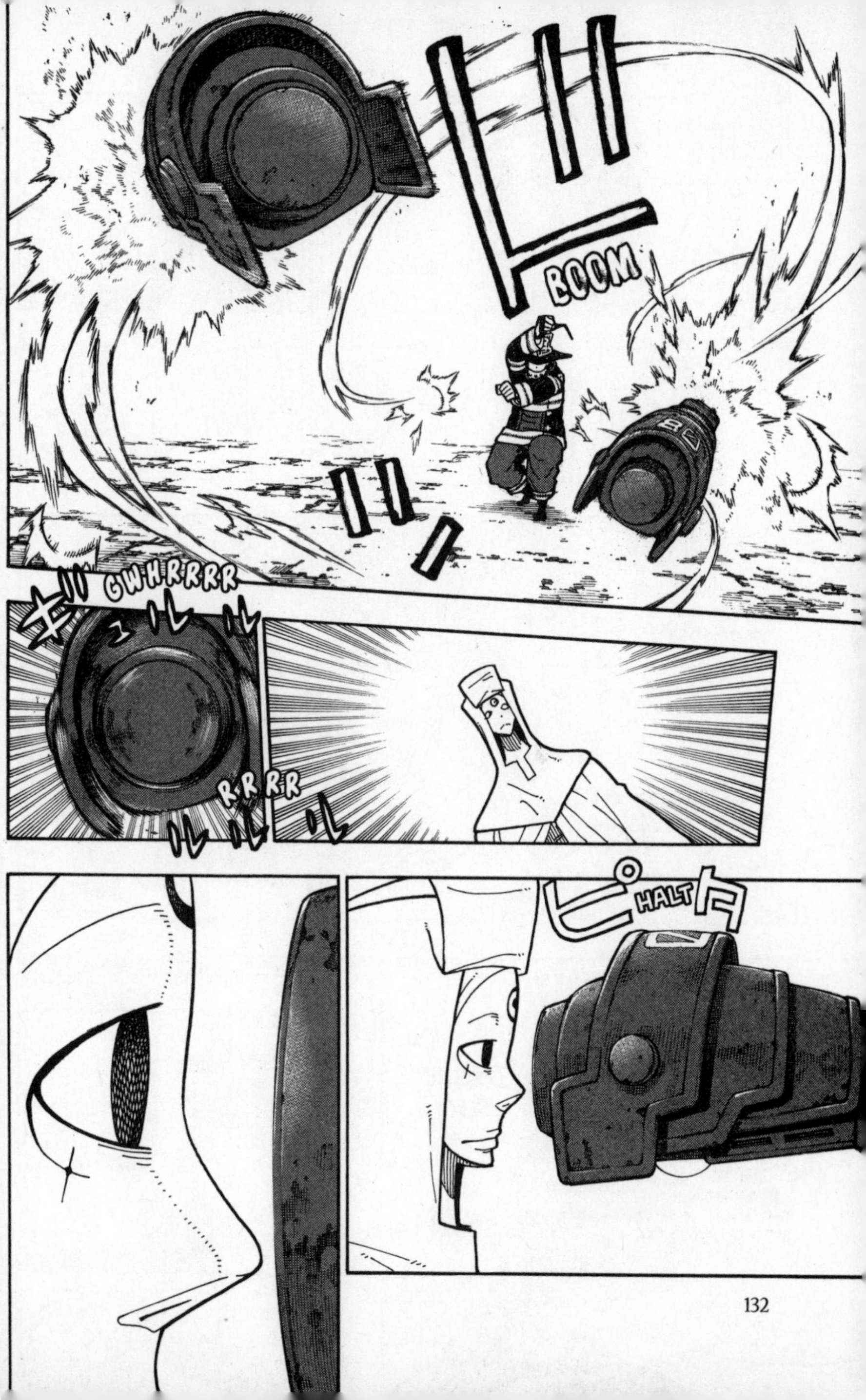
BOOM
GWHRRRR
RRRR
HALT

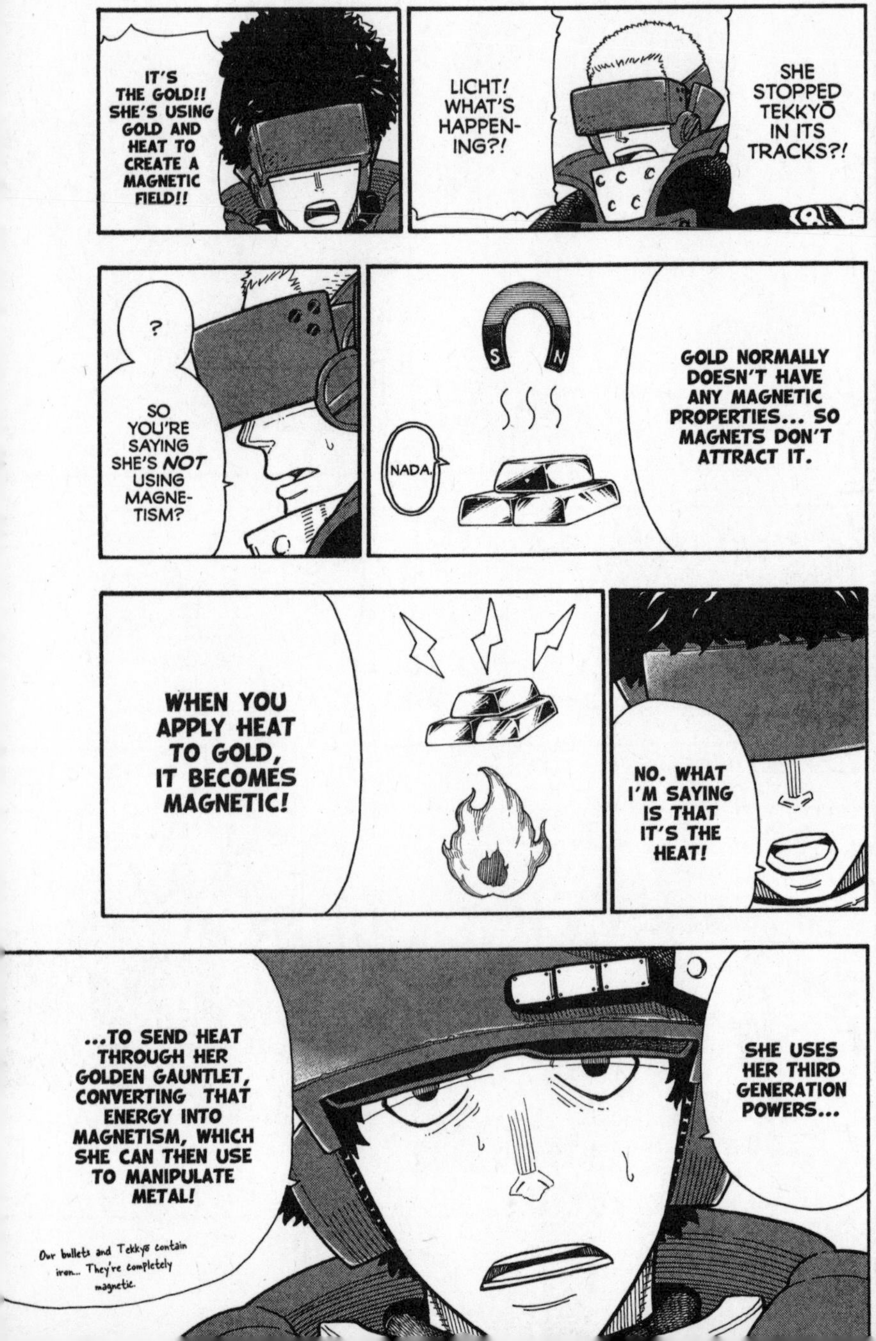
SHE STOPPED TEKKYŌ IN ITS TRACKS?!
LICHT! WHAT'S HAPPEN-ING?!
IT'S THE GOLD!! SHE'S USING GOLD AND HEAT TO CREATE A MAGNETIC FIELD!!
GOLD NORMALLY DOESN'T HAVE ANY MAGNETIC PROPERTIES... SO MAGNETS DON'T ATTRACT IT.
S
N
NADA.
?
SO YOU'RE SAYING SHE'S *NOT* USING MAGNE-TISM?
NO. WHAT I'M SAYING IS THAT IT'S THE HEAT!
WHEN YOU APPLY HEAT TO GOLD, IT BECOMES MAGNETIC!
SHE USES HER THIRD GENERATION POWERS...
...TO SEND HEAT THROUGH HER GOLDEN GAUNTLET, CONVERTING THAT ENERGY INTO MAGNETISM, WHICH SHE CAN THEN USE TO MANIPULATE METAL!
Our bullets and Tekkyō contain iron... They're completely magnetic.

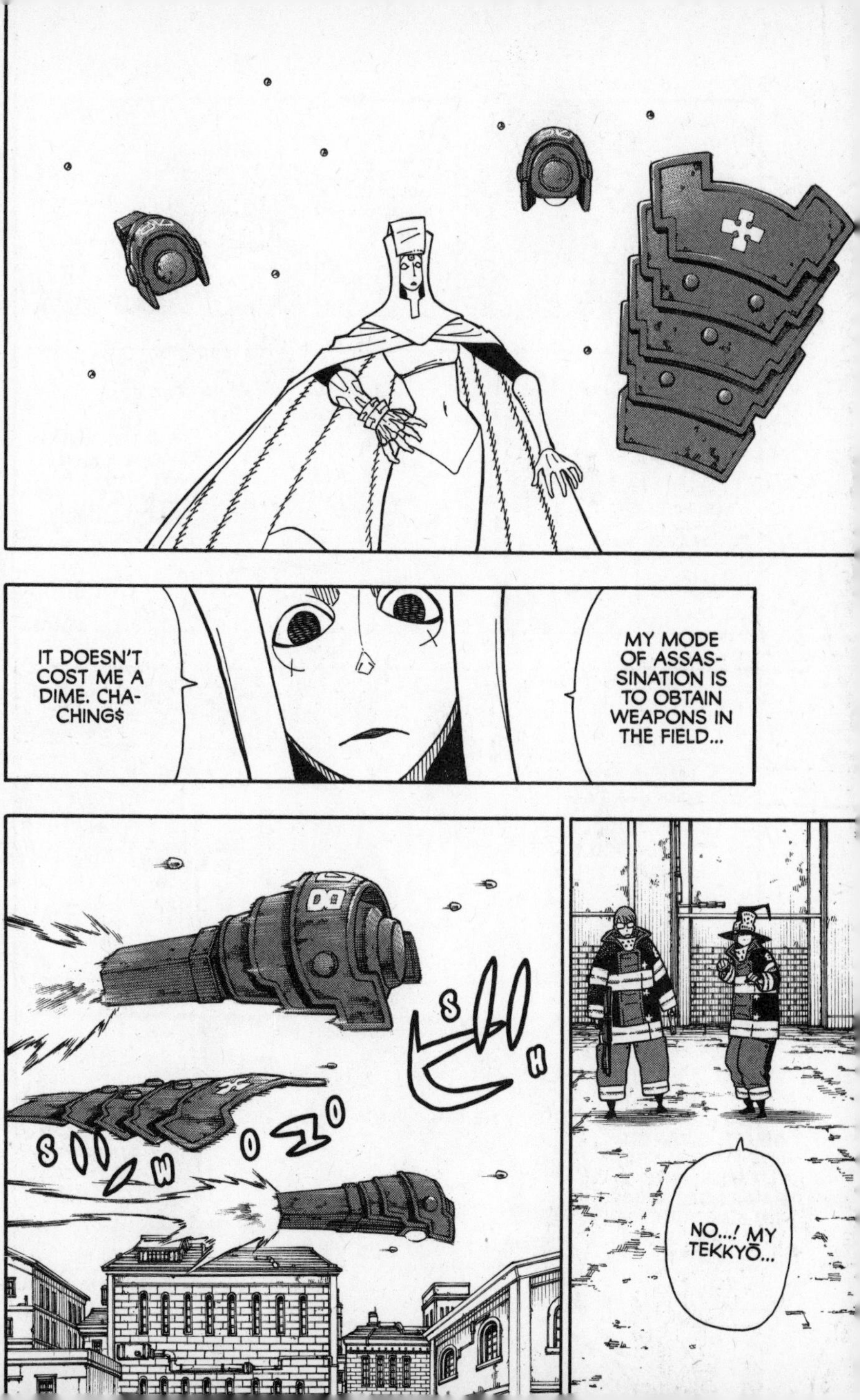
MY MODE OF ASSAS-SINATION IS TO OBTAIN WEAPONS IN THE FIELD...
IT DOESN'T COST ME A DIME. CHA-CHING$
NO...! MY TEKKYŌ...

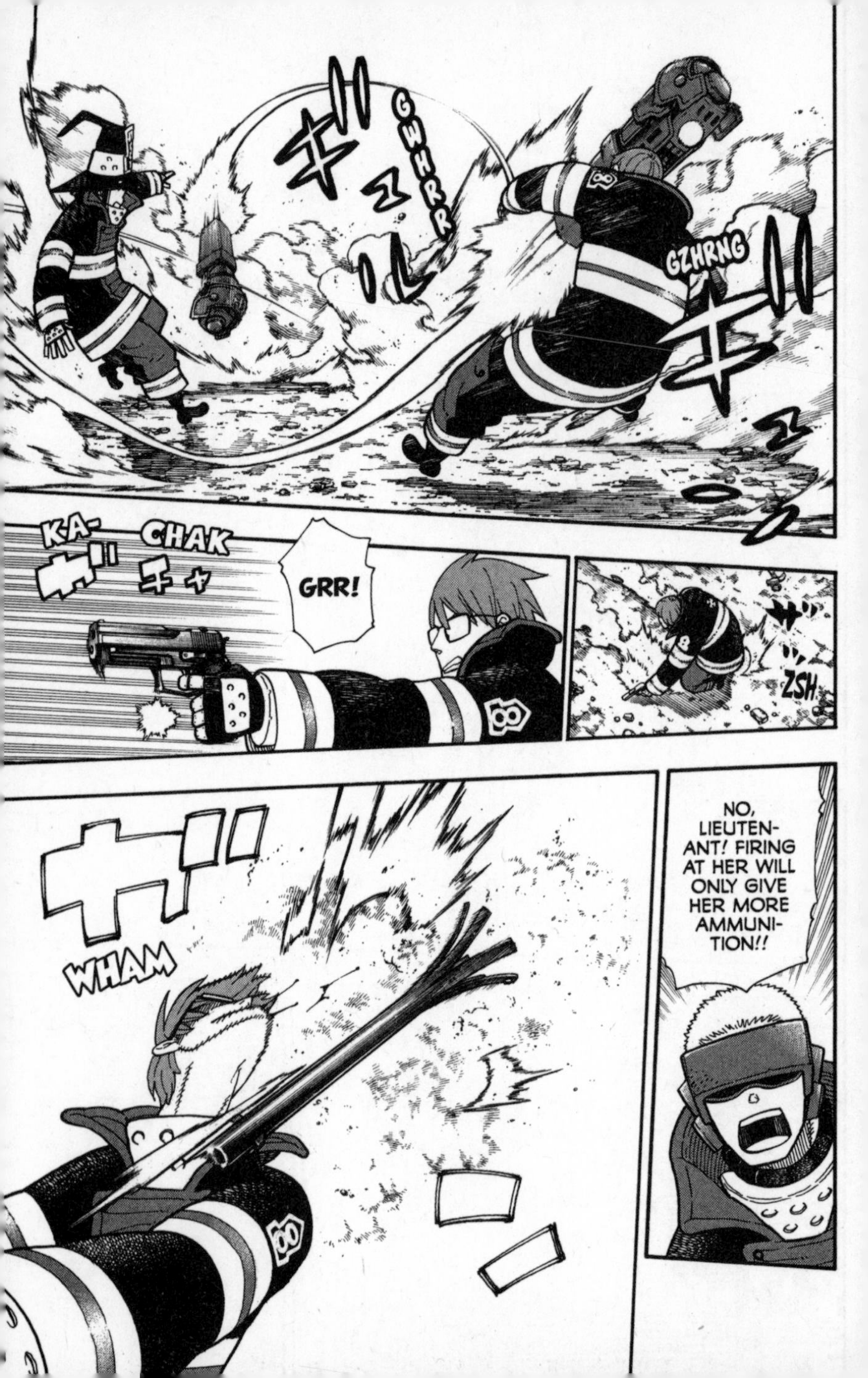
GZHRNG
GWHRR
ZSH
KA-CHAK
GRR!
NO, LIEUTEN-ANT! FIRING AT HER WILL ONLY GIVE HER MORE AMMUNI-TION!!
WHAM

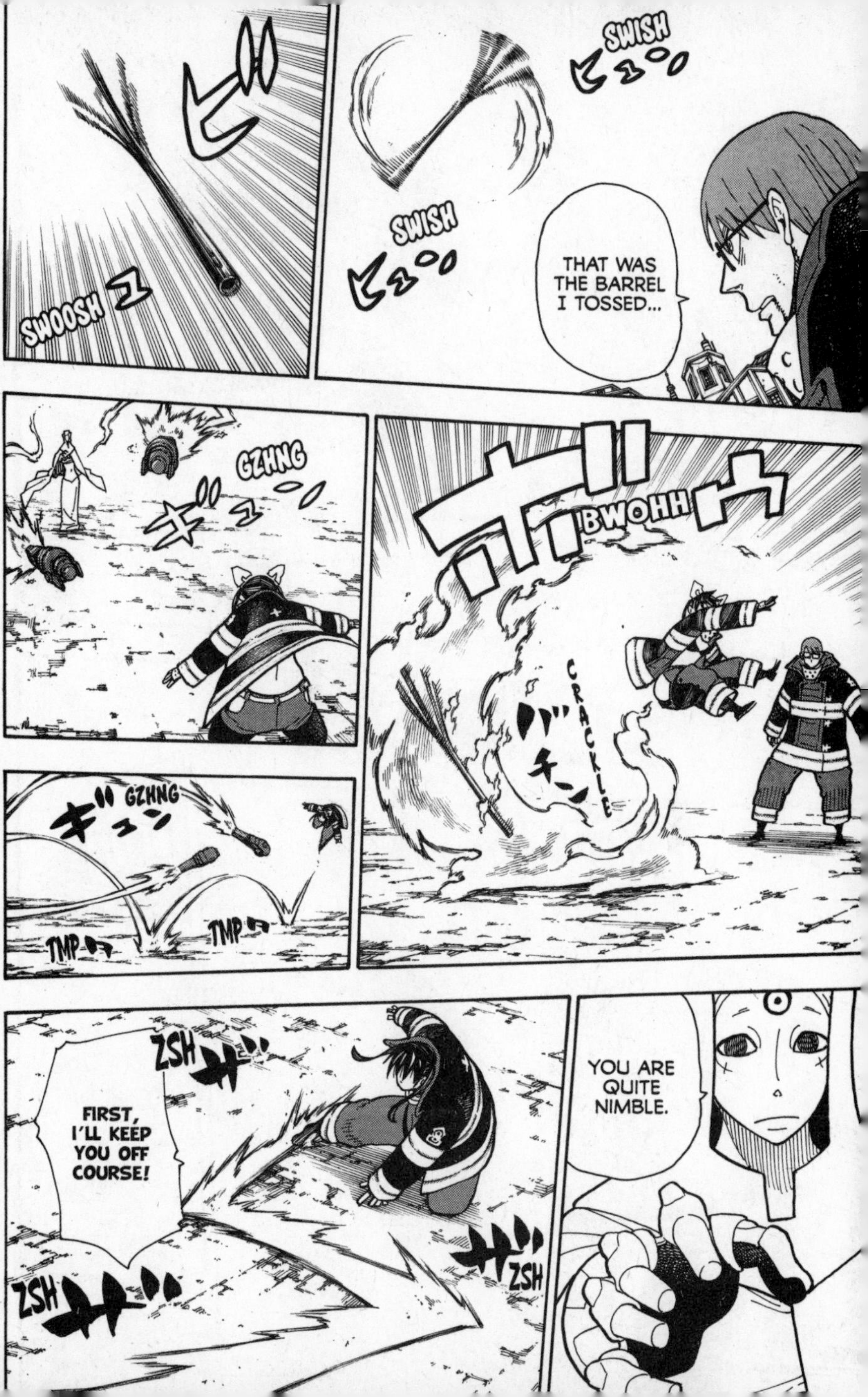
SWISH
SWISH
THAT WAS THE BARREL I TOSSED...
SWOOSH
BWOHH
CRACKLE
GZHNG
GZHNG
TMP
TMP
YOU ARE QUITE NIMBLE.
ZSH
FIRST, I'LL KEEP YOU OFF COURSE!
ZSH
ZSH

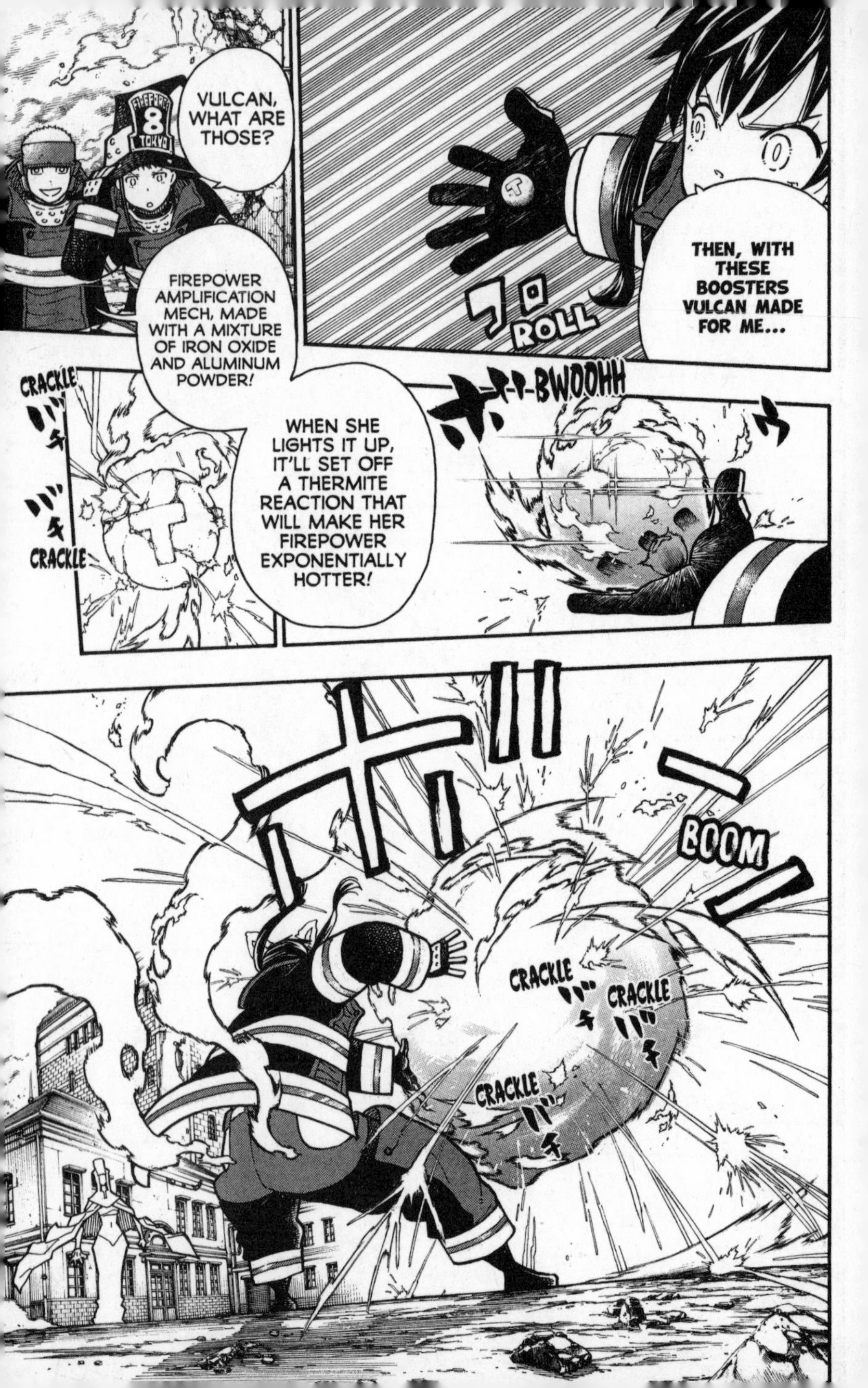
ROLL
THEN, WITH THESE BOOSTERS VULCAN MADE FOR ME...
VULCAN, WHAT ARE THOSE?
FIREPOWER AMPLIFICATION MECH, MADE WITH A MIXTURE OF IRON OXIDE AND ALUMINUM POWDER!
BWOOHH
WHEN SHE LIGHTS IT UP, IT'LL SET OFF A THERMITE REACTION THAT WILL MAKE HER FIREPOWER EXPONENTIALLY HOTTER!
CRACKLE
CRACKLE
BOOM
CRACKLE
CRACKLE
CRACKLE

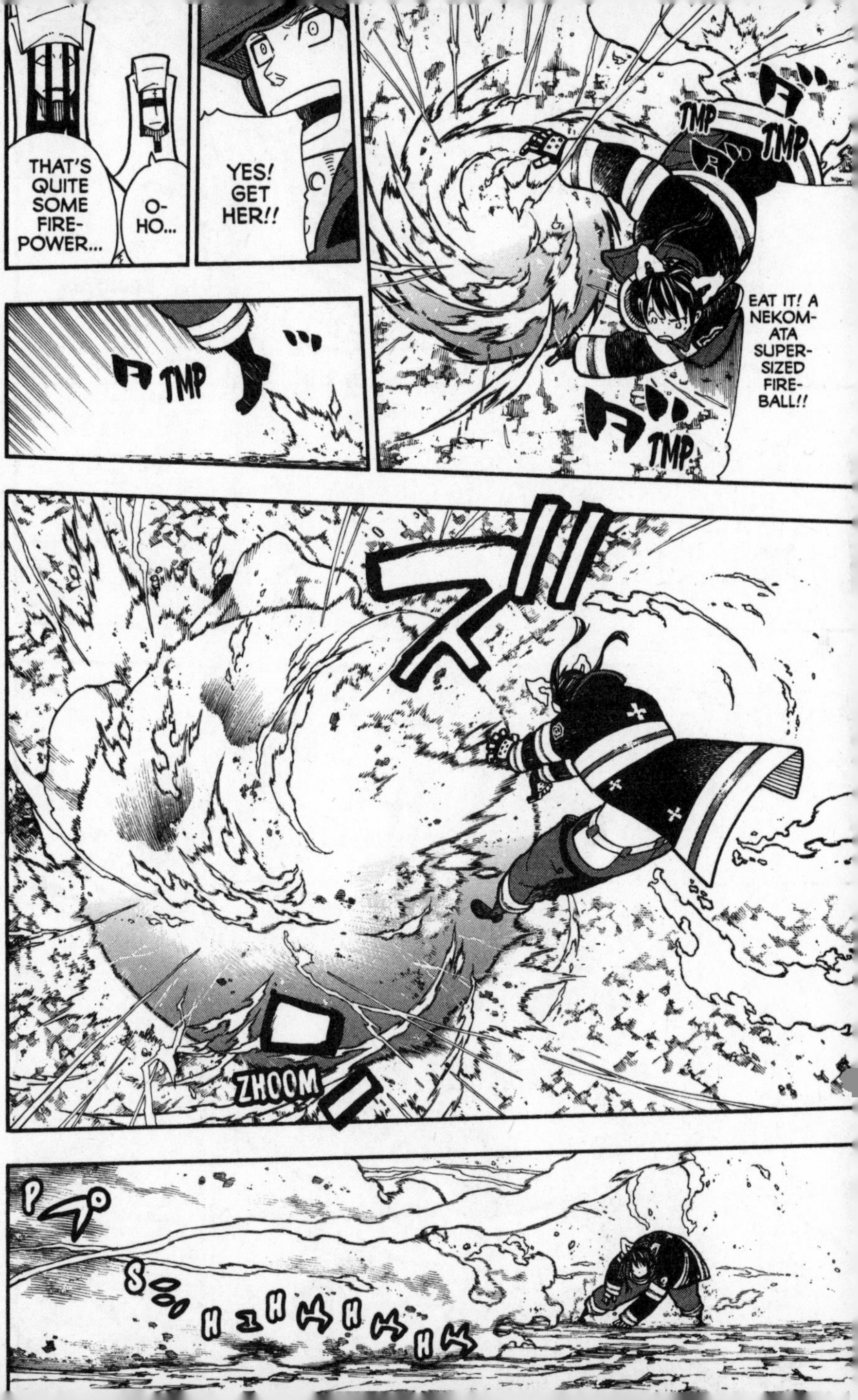
TMP
TMP
EAT IT! A NEKOMATA SUPER-SIZED FIRE-BALL!!
TMP
YES! GET HER!!
O-HO...
THAT'S QUITE SOME FIRE-POWER...
TMP
ZHOOM
P

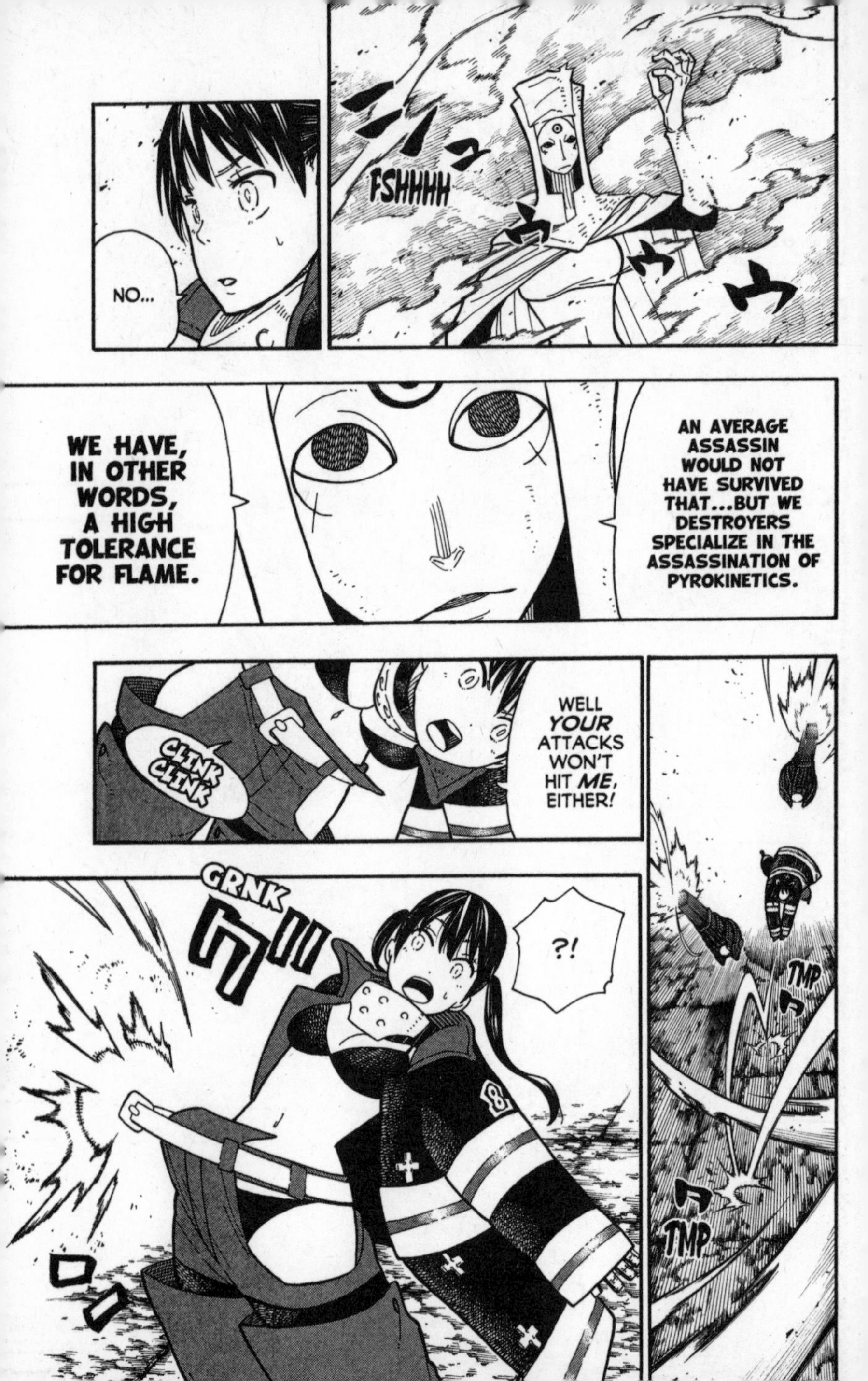
FSHHHH
NO...
AN AVERAGE ASSASSIN WOULD NOT HAVE SURVIVED THAT...BUT WE DESTROYERS SPECIALIZE IN THE ASSASSINATION OF PYROKINETICS.
WE HAVE, IN OTHER WORDS, A HIGH TOLERANCE FOR FLAME.
TMP
TMP
WELL *YOUR* ATTACKS WON'T HIT *ME*, EITHER!
CLINK CLINK
?!
GRNK

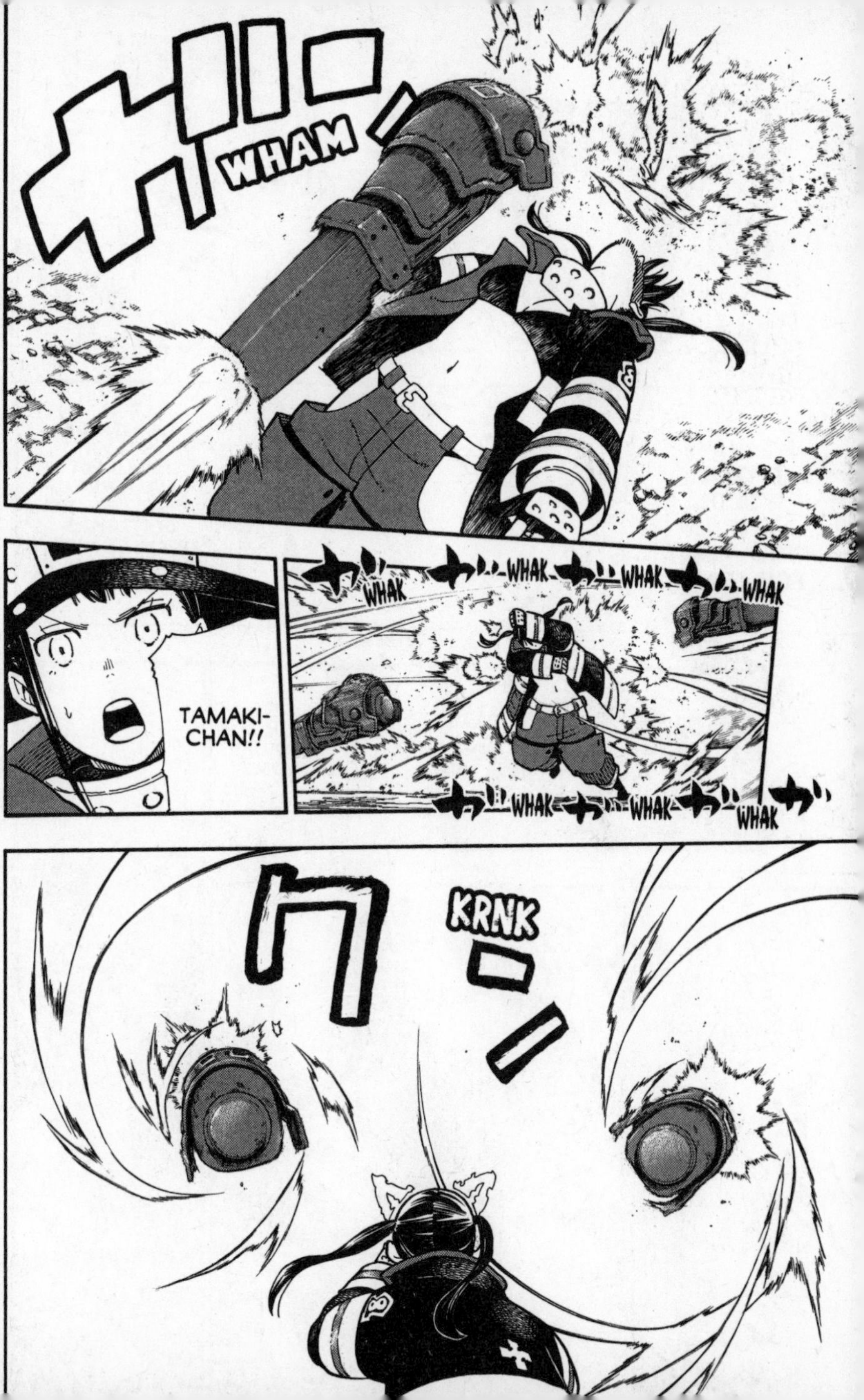
WHAM
WHAK
WHAK
WHAK
WHAK
WHAK
WHAK
WHAK
TAMAKI-CHAN!!
KRNK

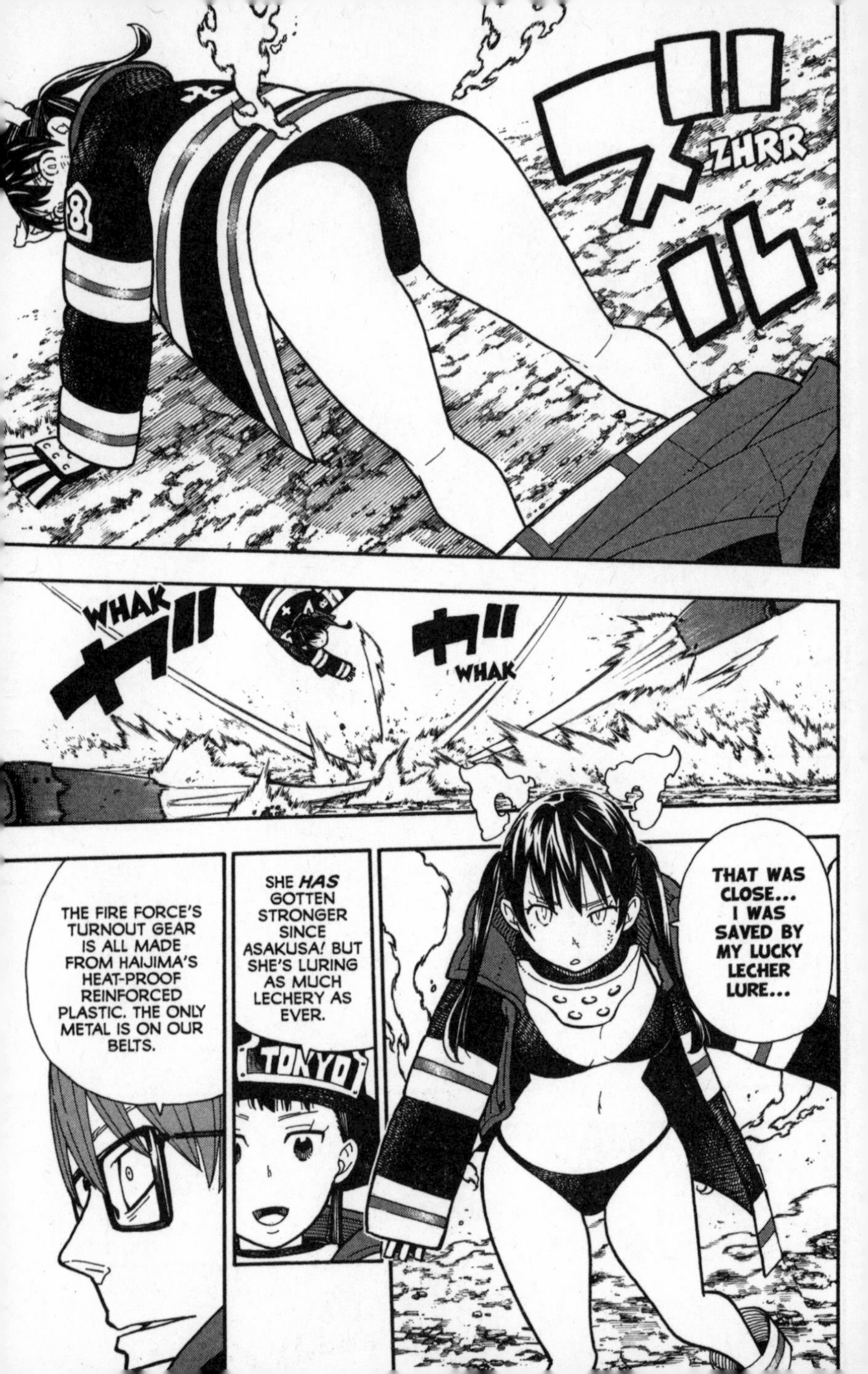
ZHRR
WHAK
WHAK
THAT WAS CLOSE... I WAS SAVED BY MY LUCKY LECHER LURE...
SHE *HAS* GOTTEN STRONGER SINCE ASAKUSA! BUT SHE'S LURING AS MUCH LECHERY AS EVER.
TOKYO
THE FIRE FORCE'S TURNOUT GEAR IS ALL MADE FROM HAIJIMA'S HEAT-PROOF REINFORCED PLASTIC. THE ONLY METAL IS ON OUR BELTS.

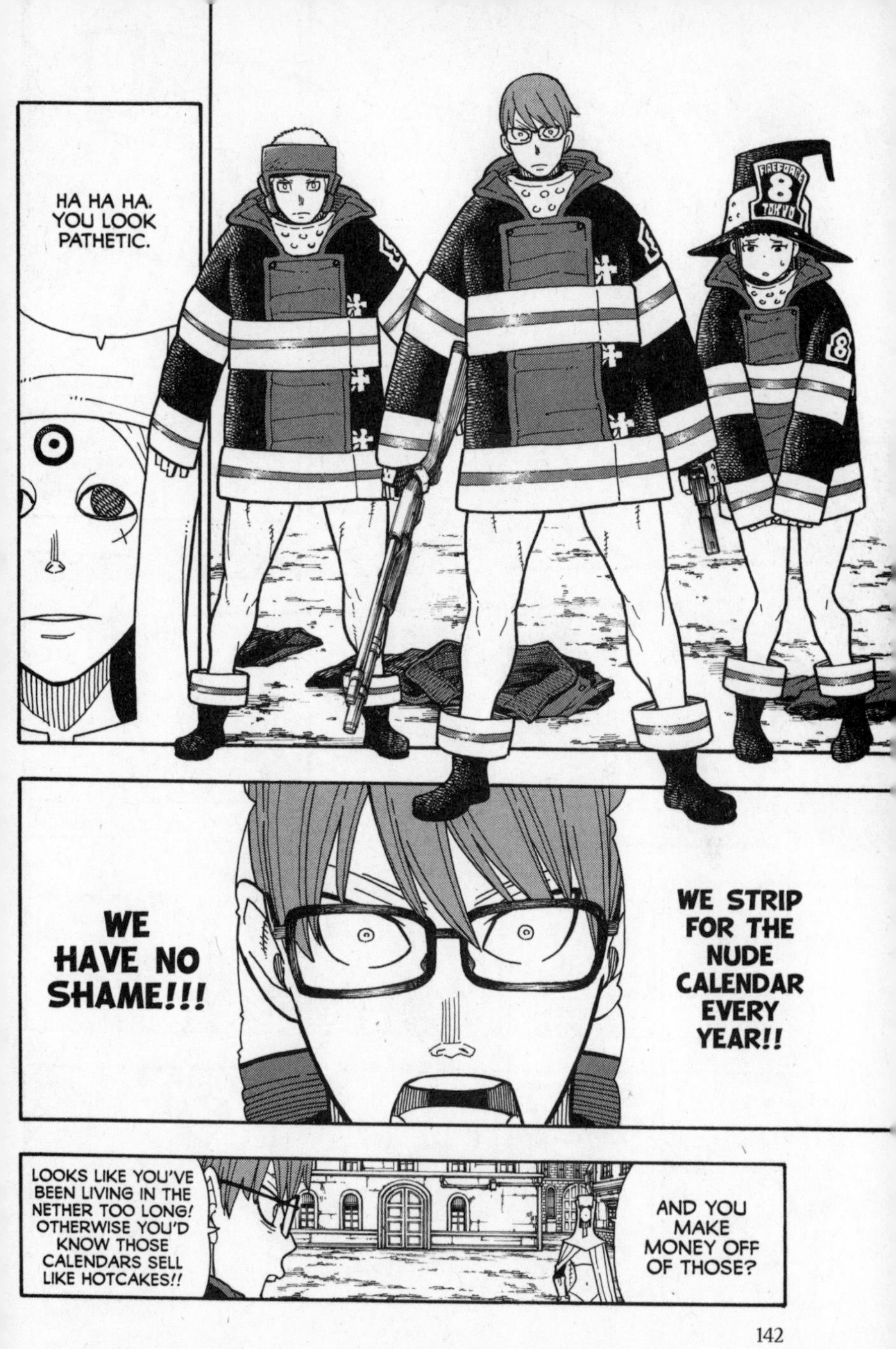
HA HA HA. YOU LOOK PATHETIC.
WE STRIP FOR THE NUDE CALENDAR EVERY YEAR!!
WE HAVE NO SHAME!!!
AND YOU MAKE MONEY OFF OF THOSE?
LOOKS LIKE YOU'VE BEEN LIVING IN THE NETHER TOO LONG! OTHERWISE YOU'D KNOW THOSE CALENDARS SELL LIKE HOTCAKES!!

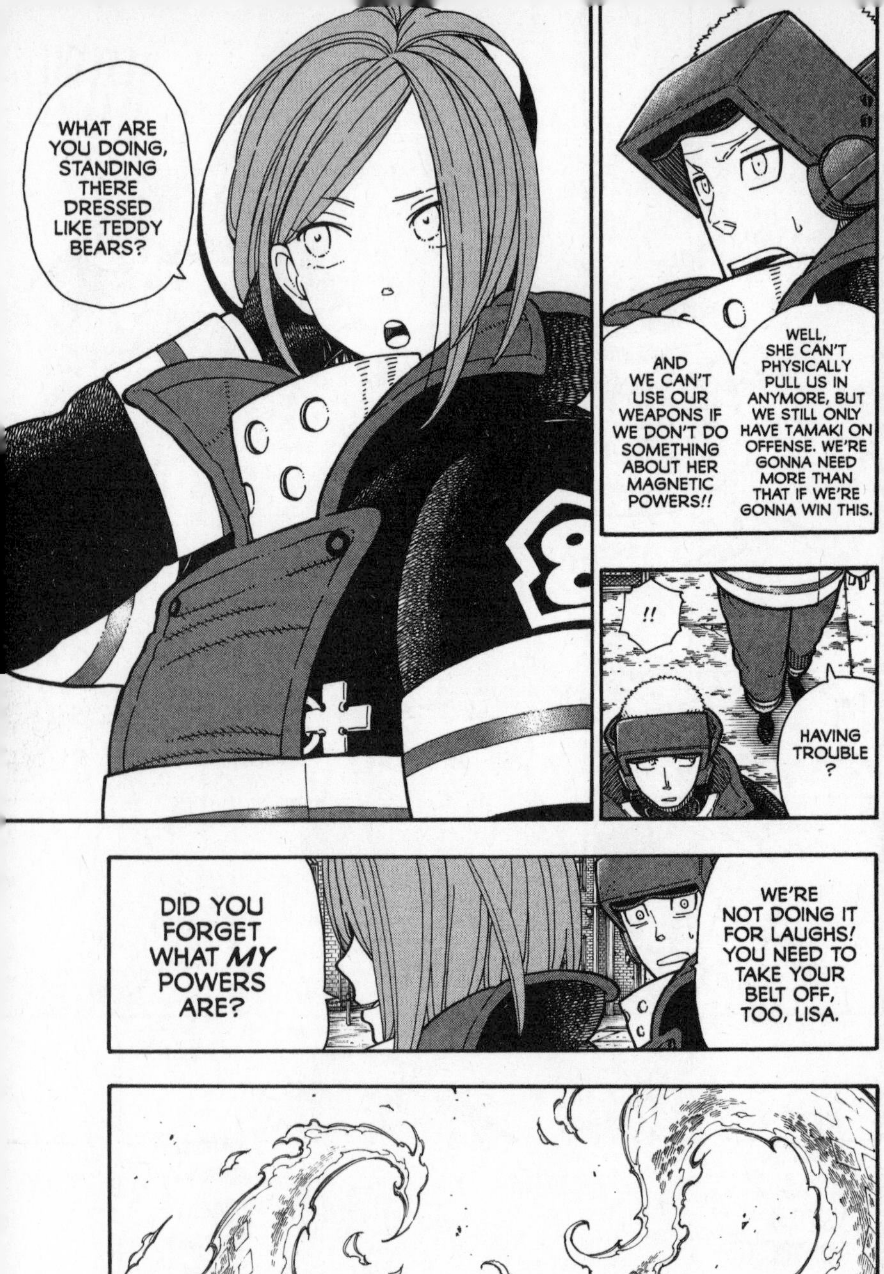
WELL, SHE CAN'T PHYSICALLY PULL US IN ANYMORE, BUT WE STILL ONLY HAVE TAMAKI ON OFFENSE. WE'RE GONNA NEED MORE THAN THAT IF WE'RE GONNA WIN THIS.
AND WE CAN'T USE OUR WEAPONS IF WE DON'T DO SOMETHING ABOUT HER MAGNETIC POWERS!!
HAVING TROUBLE?
!!
WHAT ARE YOU DOING, STANDING THERE DRESSED LIKE TEDDY BEARS?
WE'RE NOT DOING IT FOR LAUGHS! YOU NEED TO TAKE YOUR BELT OFF, TOO, LISA.
DID YOU FORGET WHAT *MY* POWERS ARE?

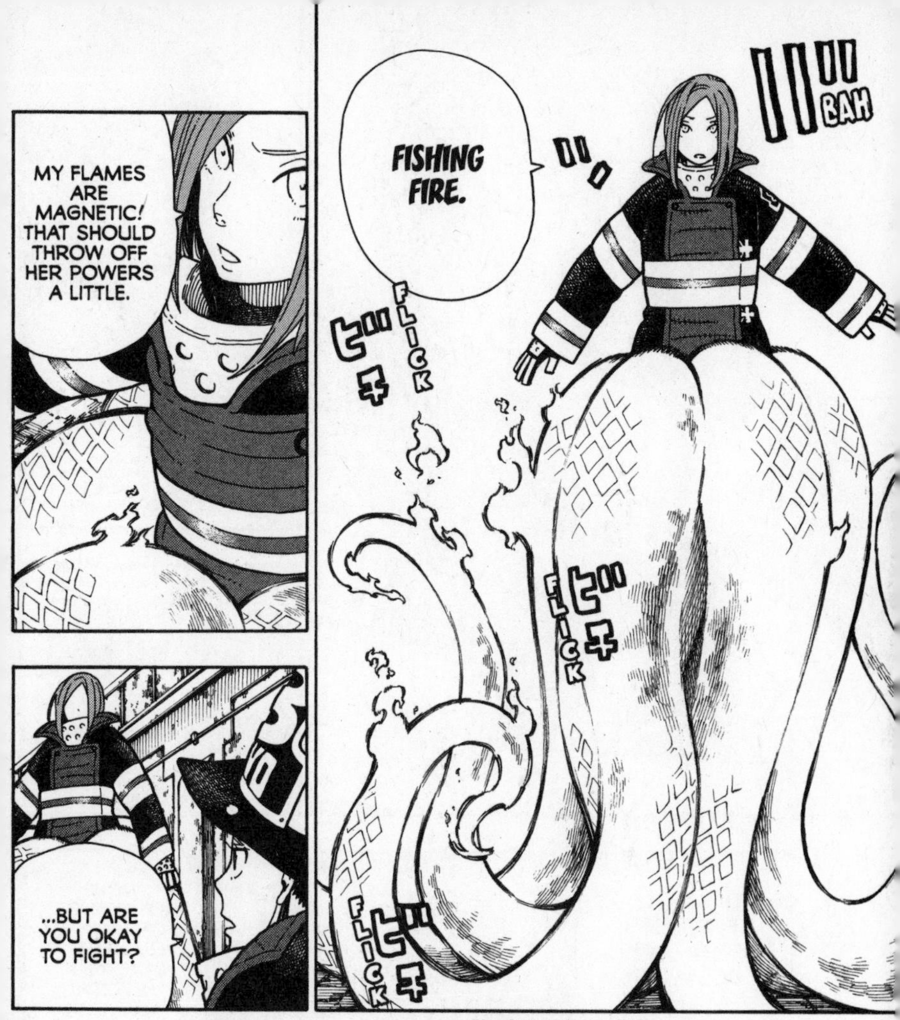
BAH
FISHING FIRE.
FLICK
FLICK
FLICK
MY FLAMES ARE MAGNETIC! THAT SHOULD THROW OFF HER POWERS A LITTLE.
...BUT ARE YOU OKAY TO FIGHT?

[Note: See translation notes Vol.7]

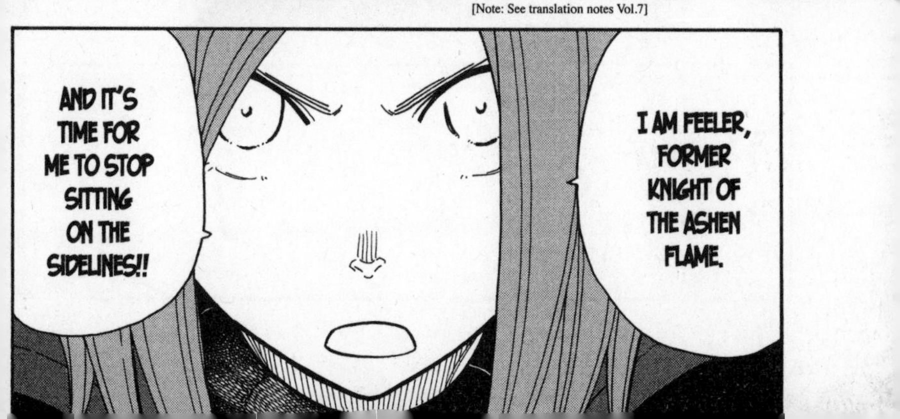
I AM FEELER, FORMER KNIGHT OF THE ASHEN FLAME.
AND IT'S TIME FOR ME TO STOP SITTING ON THE SIDELINES!!

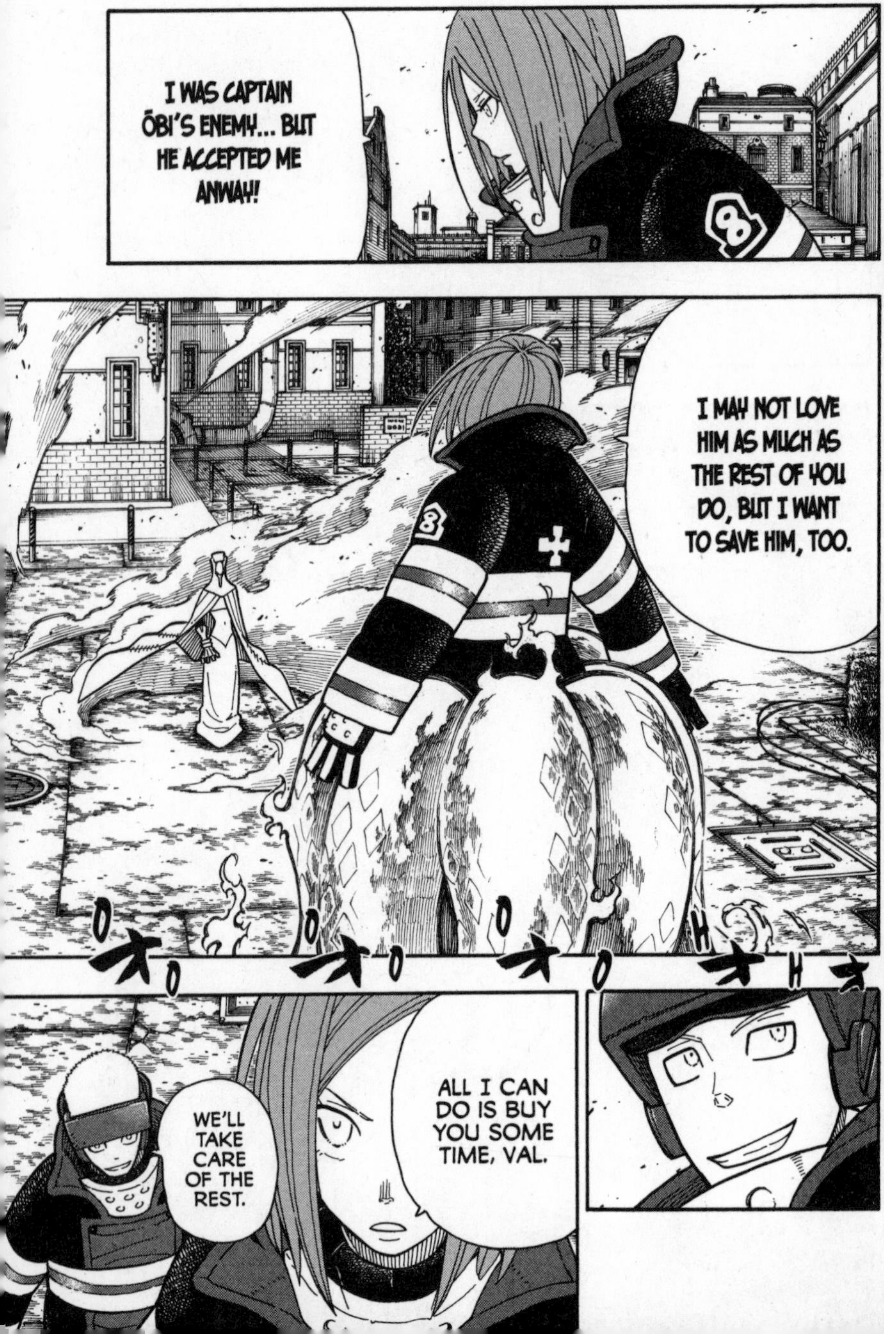
I WAS CAPTAIN ŌBI'S ENEMY... BUT HE ACCEPTED ME ANWAY!
I MAY NOT LOVE HIM AS MUCH AS THE REST OF YOU DO, BUT I WANT TO SAVE HIM, TOO.
OOOOOOHH
ALL I CAN DO IS BUY YOU SOME TIME, VAL.
WE'LL TAKE CARE OF THE REST.

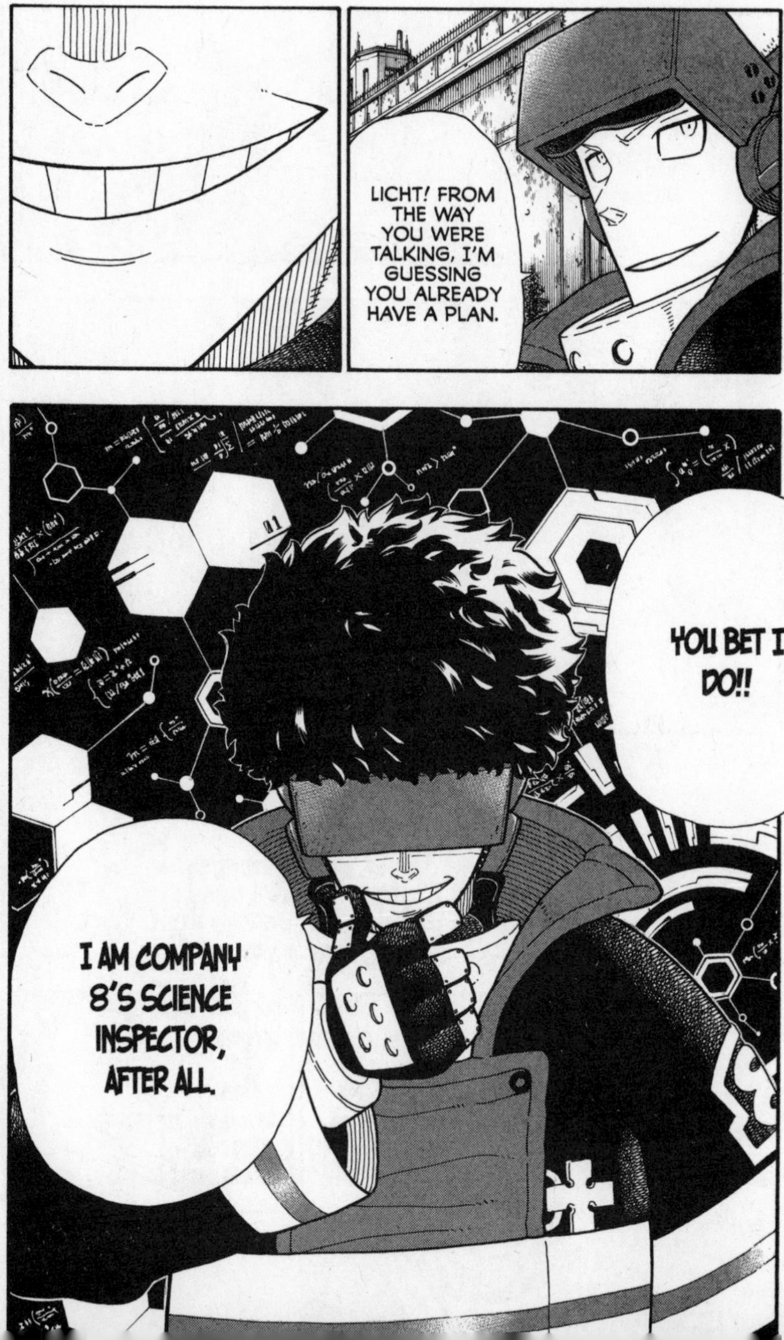
LICHT! FROM THE WAY YOU WERE TALKING, I'M GUESSING YOU ALREADY HAVE A PLAN.
YOU BET I DO!!
I AM COMPANY 8'S SCIENCE INSPECTOR, AFTER ALL.

Feeler

CHAPTER CLXXXV: BATTLE EXPERIMENT

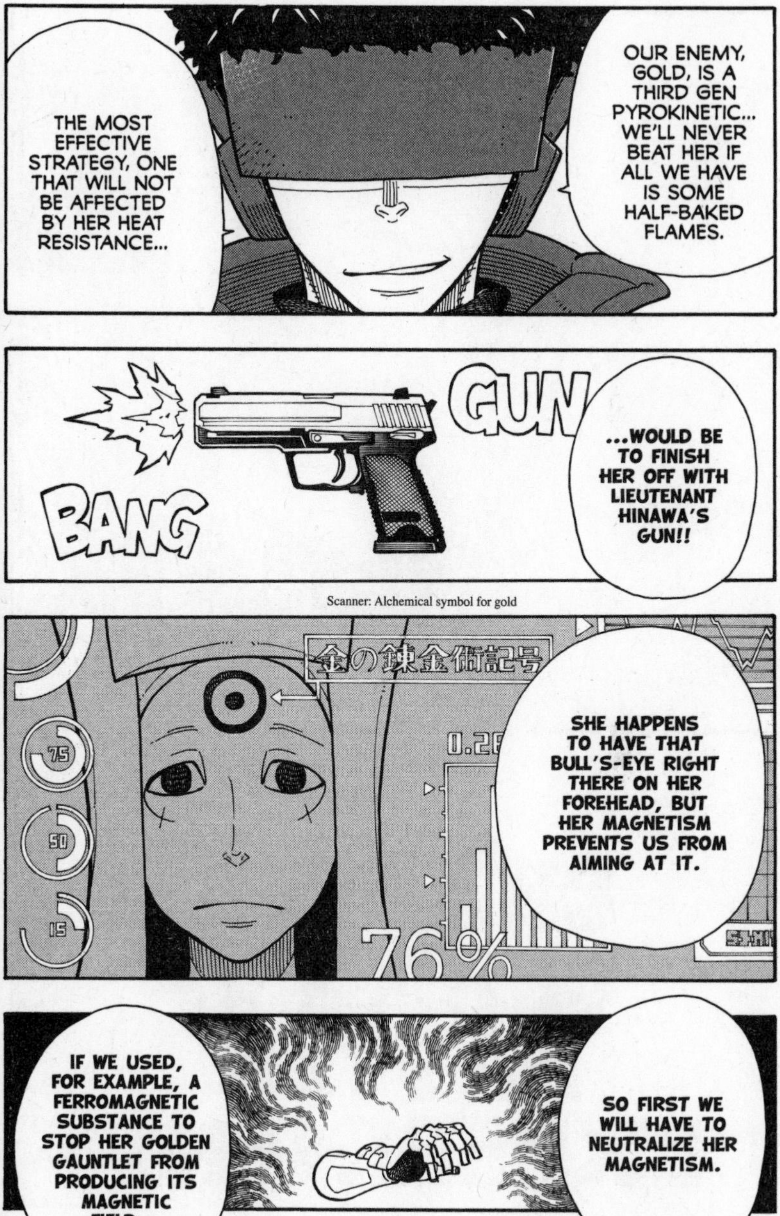
OUR ENEMY, GOLD, IS A THIRD GEN PYROKINETIC... WE'LL NEVER BEAT HER IF ALL WE HAVE IS SOME HALF-BAKED FLAMES.
THE MOST EFFECTIVE STRATEGY, ONE THAT WILL NOT BE AFFECTED BY HER HEAT RESISTANCE...
...WOULD BE TO FINISH HER OFF WITH LIEUTENANT HINAWA'S GUN!!
GUN
BANG
SHE HAPPENS TO HAVE THAT BULL'S-EYE RIGHT THERE ON HER FOREHEAD, BUT HER MAGNETISM PREVENTS US FROM AIMING AT IT.
金の錬金術記号
76%
SO FIRST WE WILL HAVE TO NEUTRALIZE HER MAGNETISM.
IF WE USED, FOR EXAMPLE, A FERROMAGNETIC SUBSTANCE TO STOP HER GOLDEN GAUNTLET FROM PRODUCING ITS MAGNETIC FIELD...

Scanner: Alchemical symbol for gold

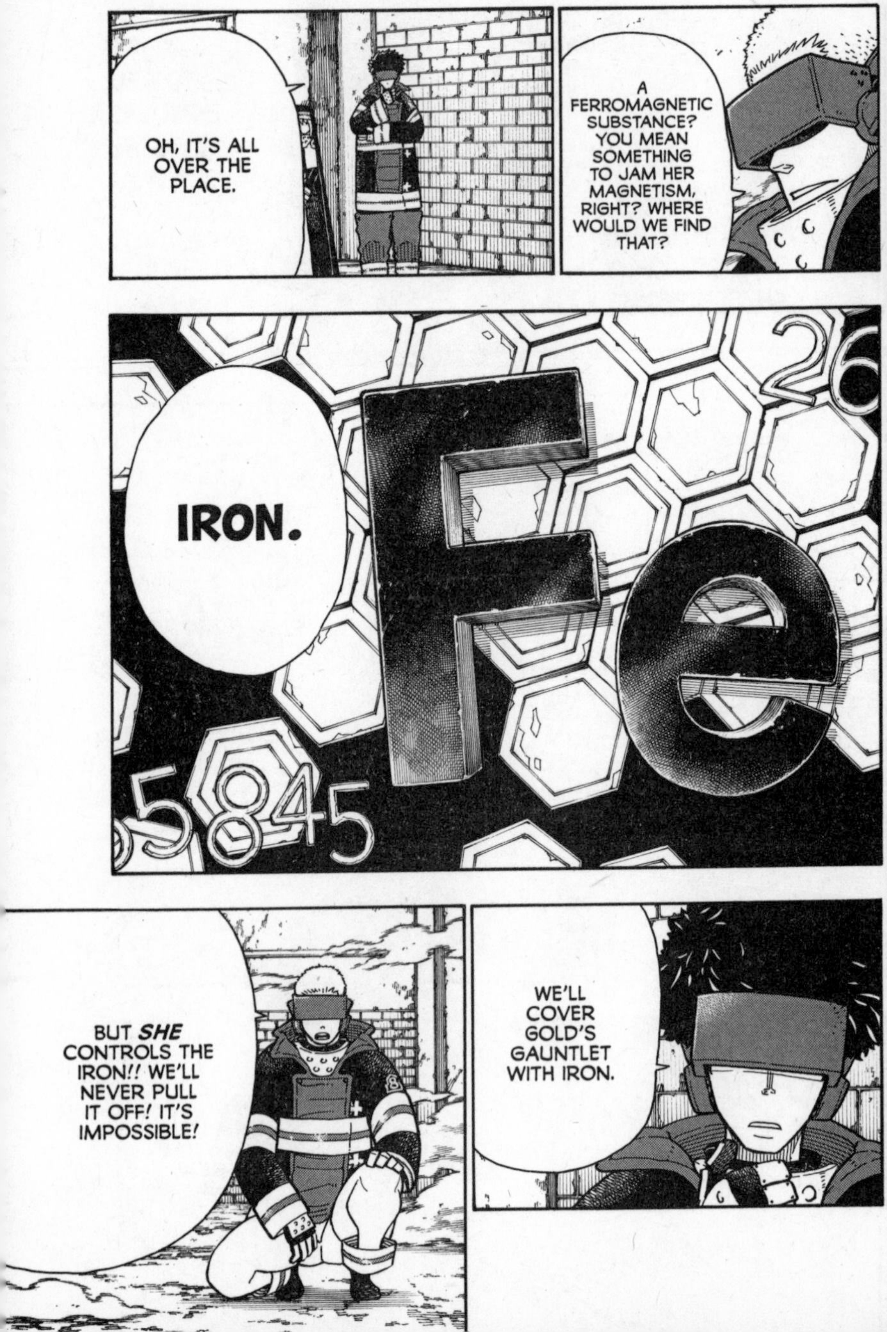
A FERROMAGNETIC SUBSTANCE? YOU MEAN SOMETHING TO JAM HER MAGNETISM, RIGHT? WHERE WOULD WE FIND THAT?
OH, IT'S ALL OVER THE PLACE.
IRON.
26
Fe
WE'LL COVER GOLD'S GAUNTLET WITH IRON.
BUT *SHE* CONTROLS THE IRON!! WE'LL NEVER PULL IT OFF! IT'S IMPOSSIBLE!

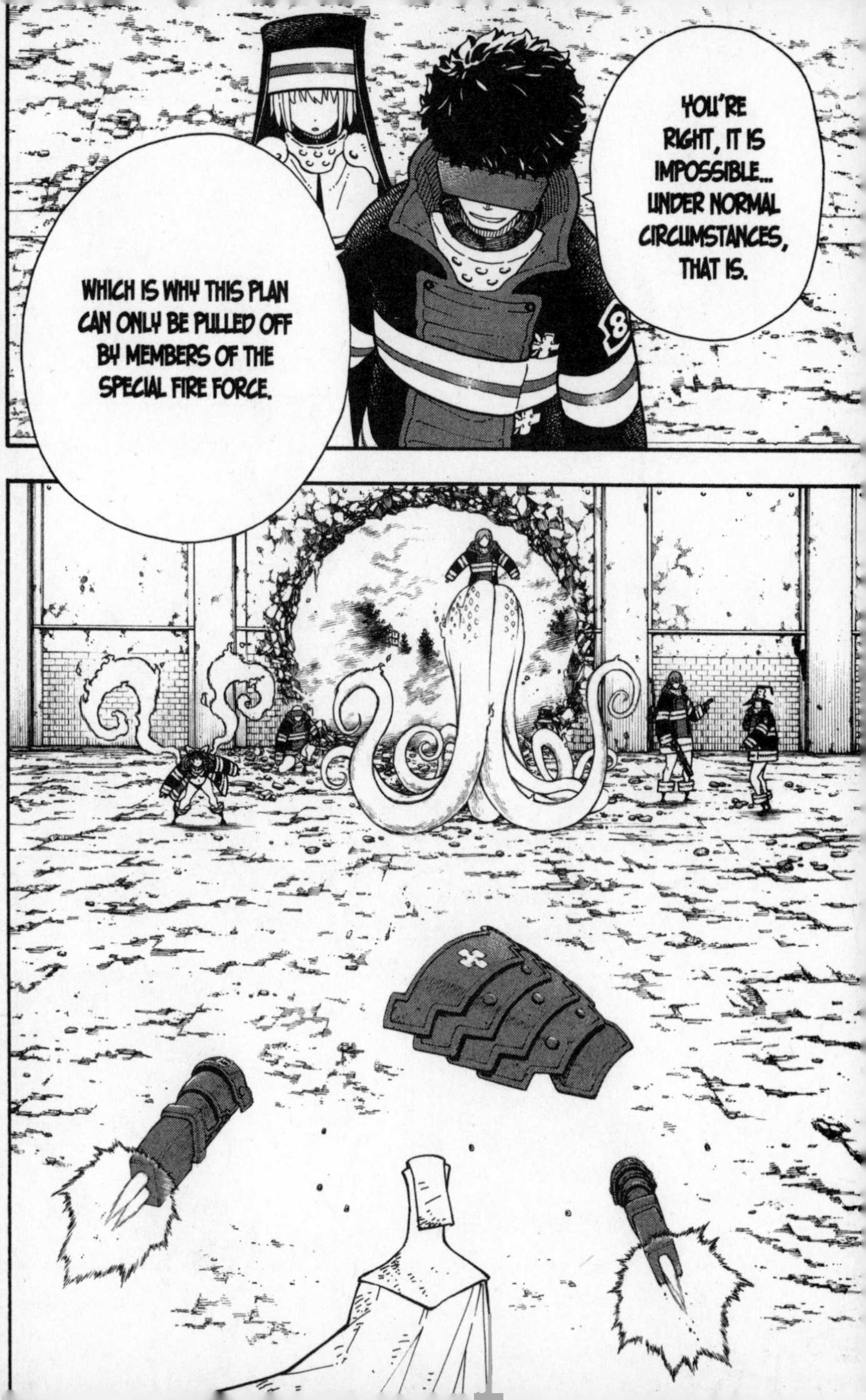
YOU'RE RIGHT, IT IS IMPOSSIBLE... UNDER NORMAL CIRCUMSTANCES, THAT IS.
WHICH IS WHY THIS PLAN CAN ONLY BE PULLED OFF BY MEMBERS OF THE SPECIAL FIRE FORCE.
8

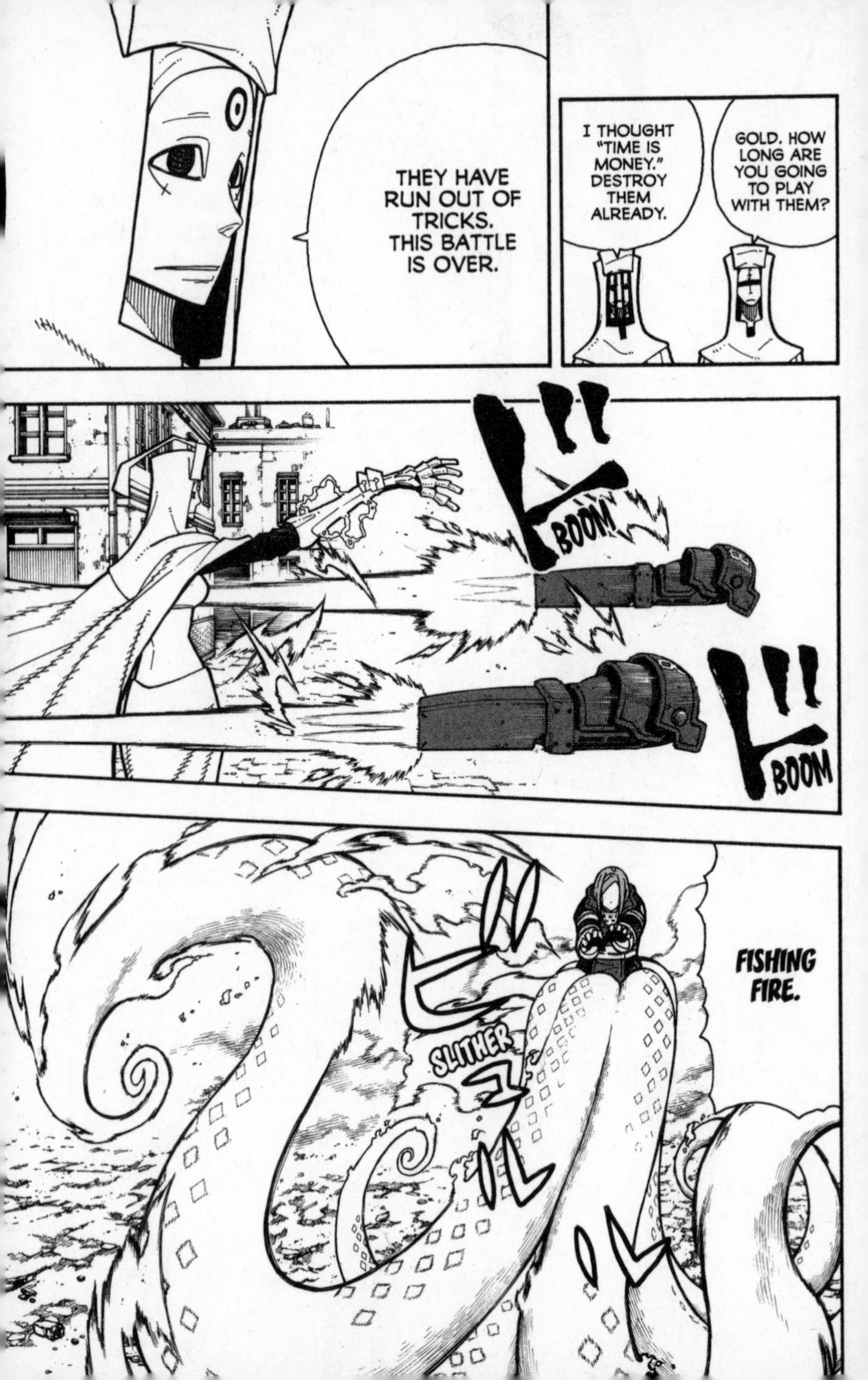
GOLD. HOW LONG ARE YOU GOING TO PLAY WITH THEM?
I THOUGHT "TIME IS MONEY." DESTROY THEM ALREADY.
THEY HAVE RUN OUT OF TRICKS. THIS BATTLE IS OVER.
BOOM
BOOM
FISHING FIRE.
SLITHER

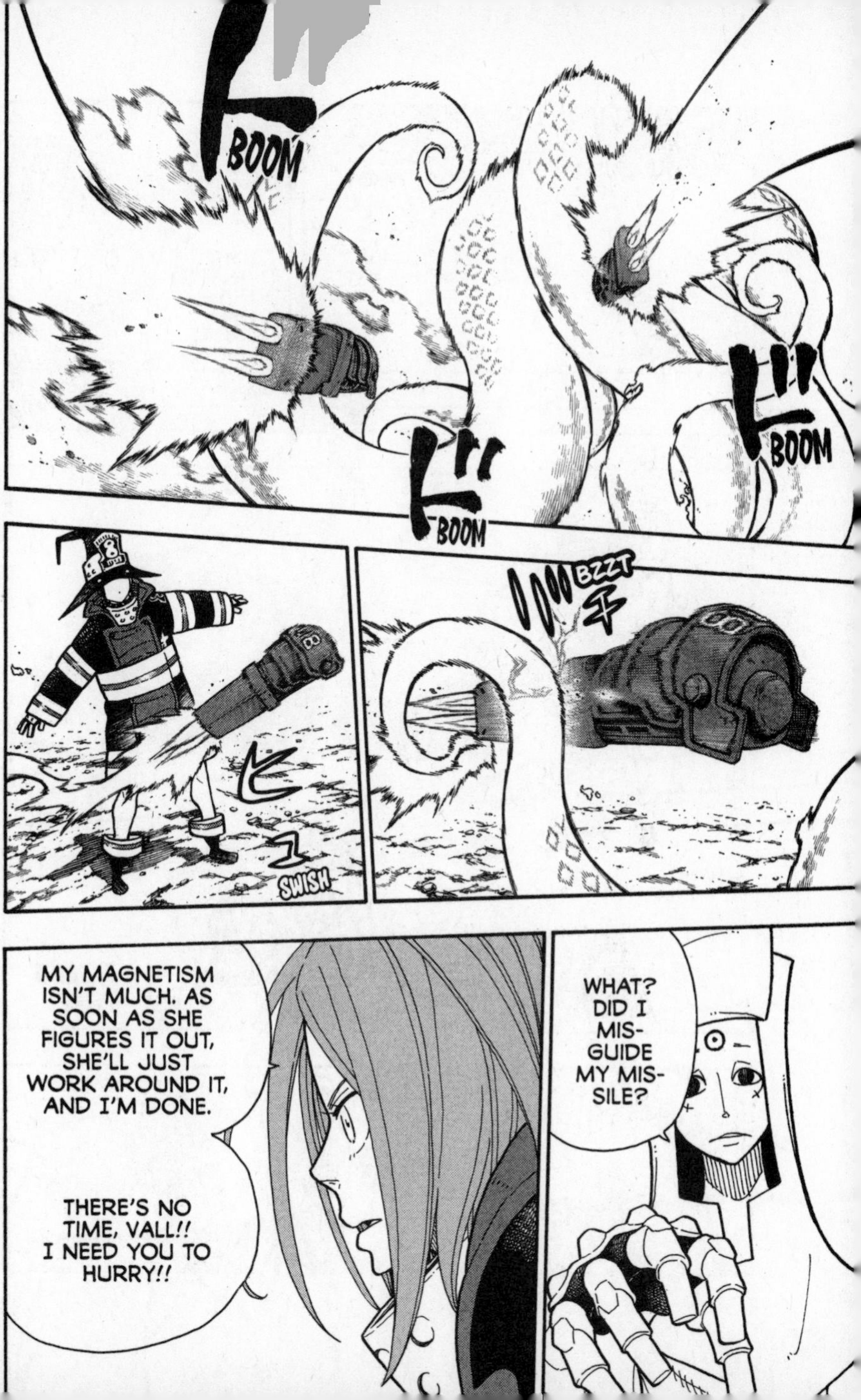
BOOM
BOOM
BOOM
BZZT
SWISH
WHAT? DID I MIS-GUIDE MY MIS-SILE?
MY MAGNETISM ISN'T MUCH. AS SOON AS SHE FIGURES IT OUT, SHE'LL JUST WORK AROUND IT, AND I'M DONE.
THERE'S NO TIME, VALL!! I NEED YOU TO HURRY!!

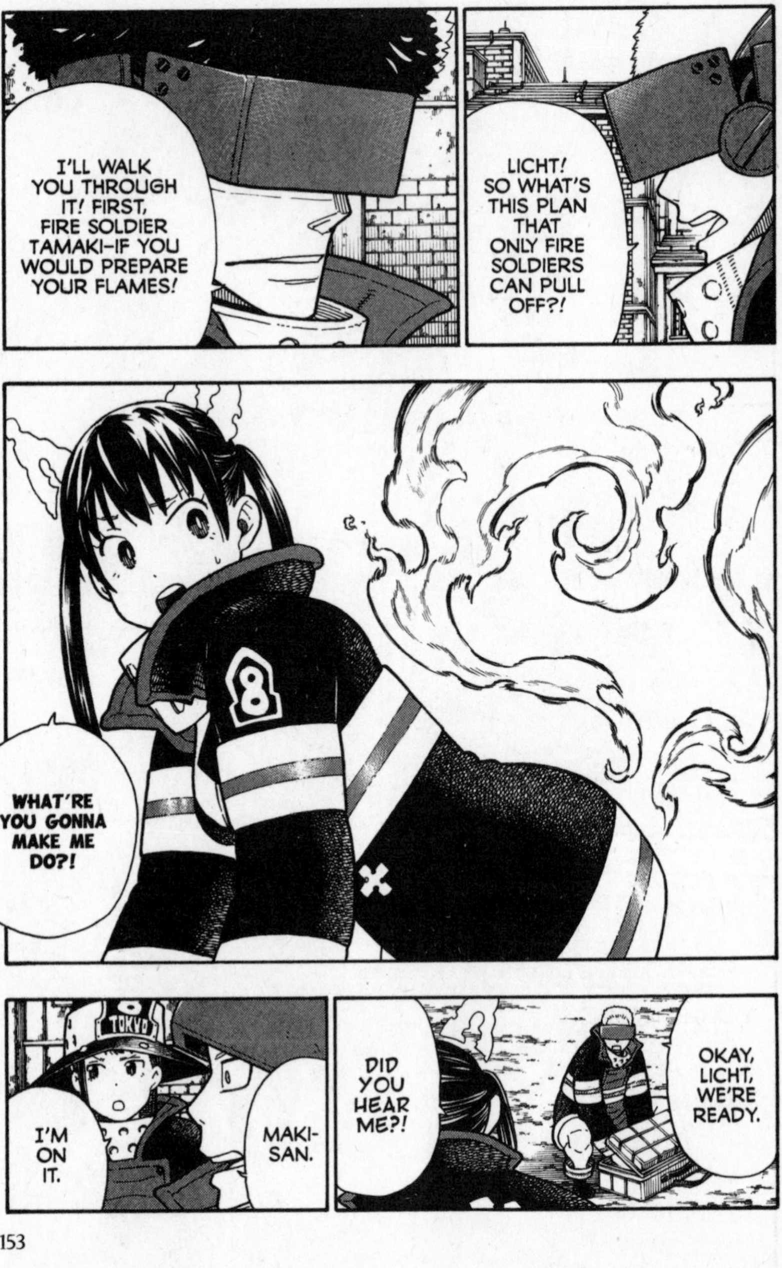
LICHT! SO WHAT'S THIS PLAN THAT ONLY FIRE SOLDIERS CAN PULL OFF?!
I'LL WALK YOU THROUGH IT! FIRST, FIRE SOLDIER TAMAKI–IF YOU WOULD PREPARE YOUR FLAMES!
WHAT'RE YOU GONNA MAKE ME DO?!
OKAY, LICHT, WE'RE READY.
DID YOU HEAR ME?!
MAKI-SAN.
I'M ON IT.

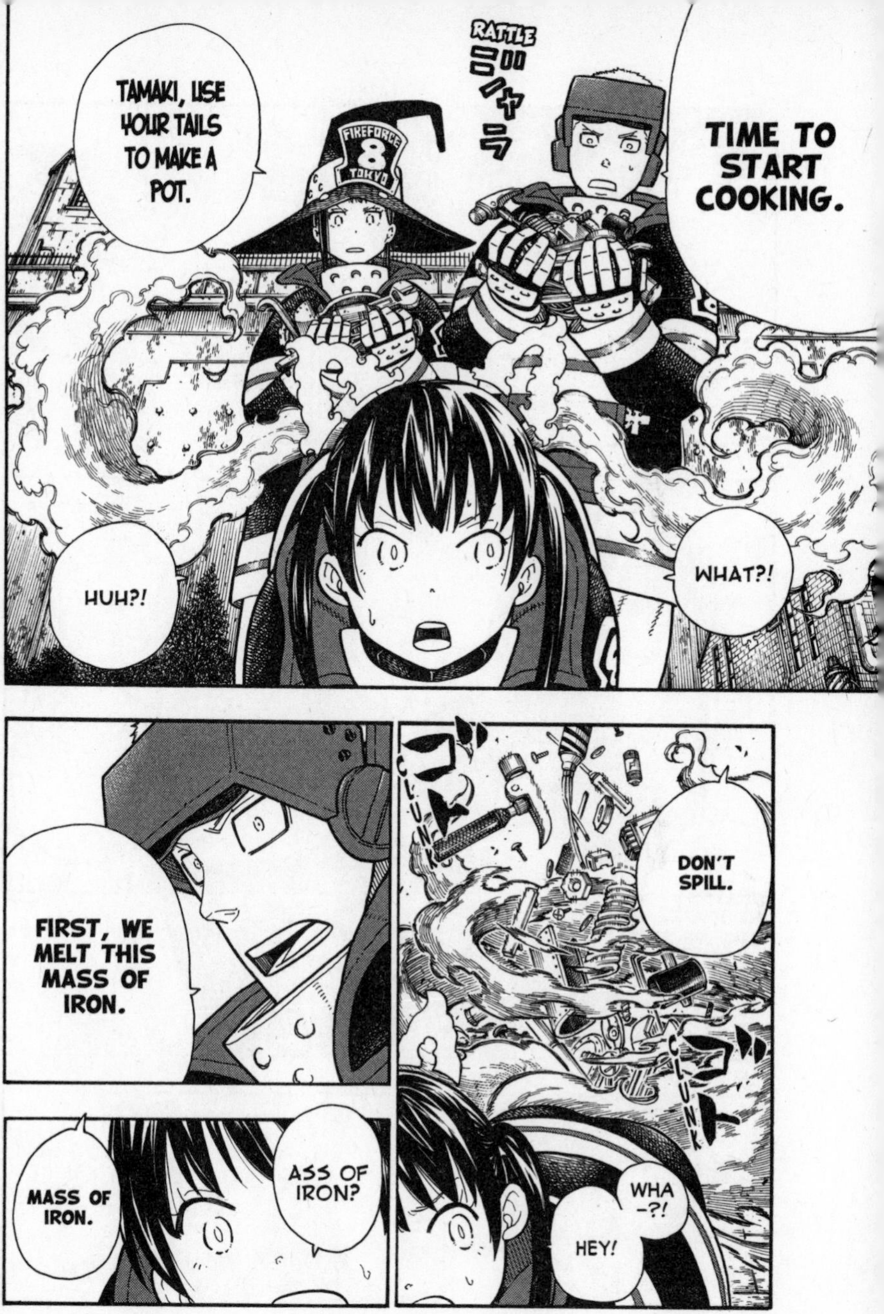
TIME TO START COOKING.
RATTLE
TAMAKI, USE YOUR TAILS TO MAKE A POT.
WHAT?!
HUH?!
DON'T SPILL.
CLUNK
CLUNK
WHA-?!
HEY!
FIRST, WE MELT THIS MASS OF IRON.
ASS OF IRON?
MASS OF IRON.

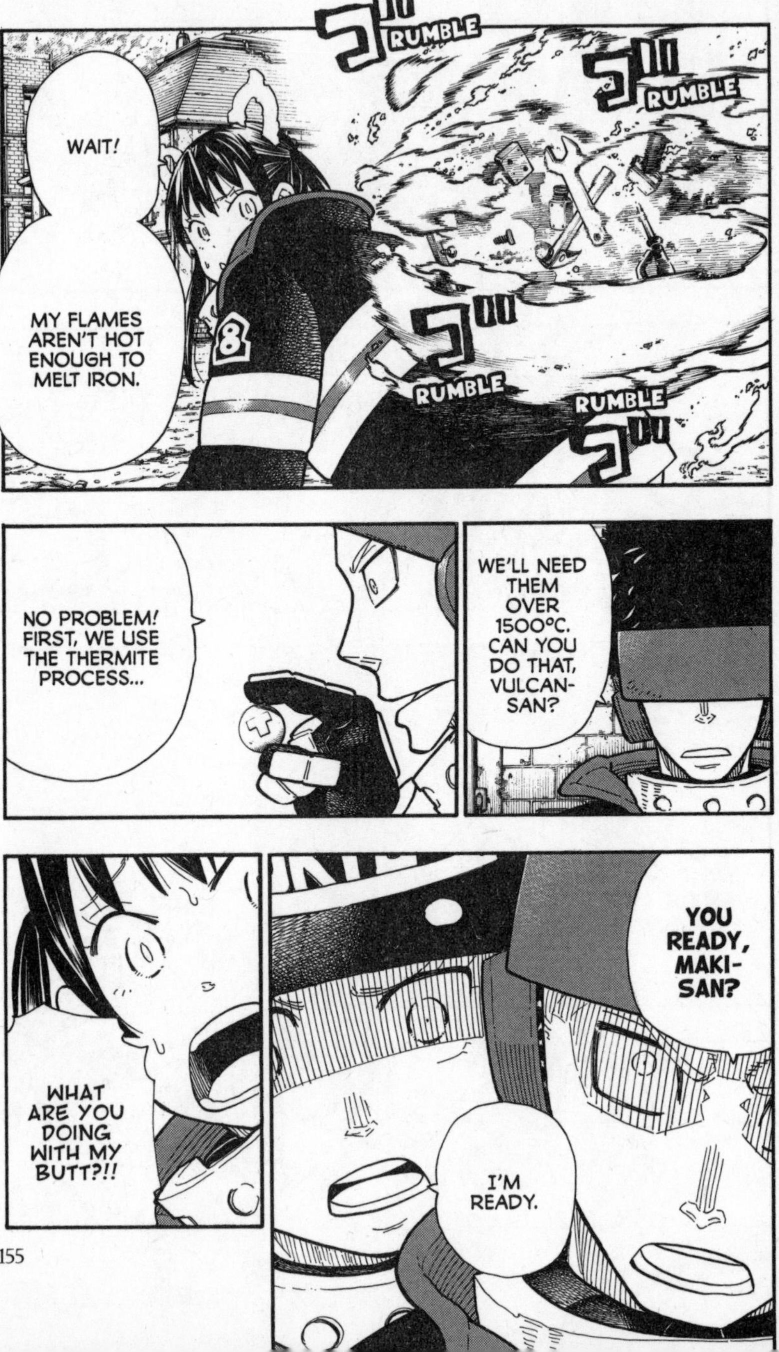
RUMBLE
RUMBLE
WAIT!
MY FLAMES AREN'T HOT ENOUGH TO MELT IRON.
RUMBLE
RUMBLE
WE'LL NEED THEM OVER 1500°C. CAN YOU DO THAT, VULCAN-SAN?
NO PROBLEM! FIRST, WE USE THE THERMITE PROCESS...
YOU READY, MAKI-SAN?
I'M READY.
WHAT ARE YOU DOING WITH MY BUTT?!!

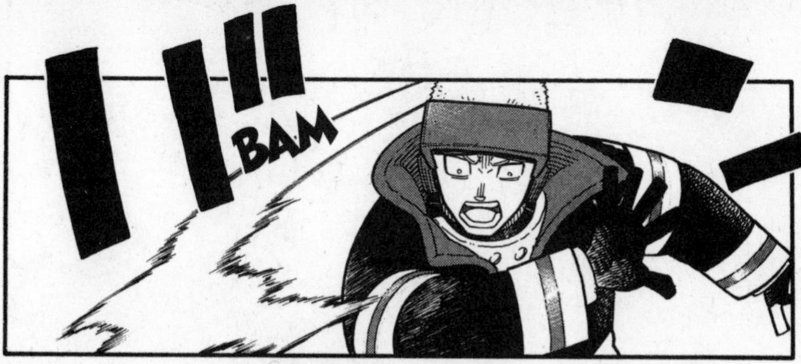
BAM
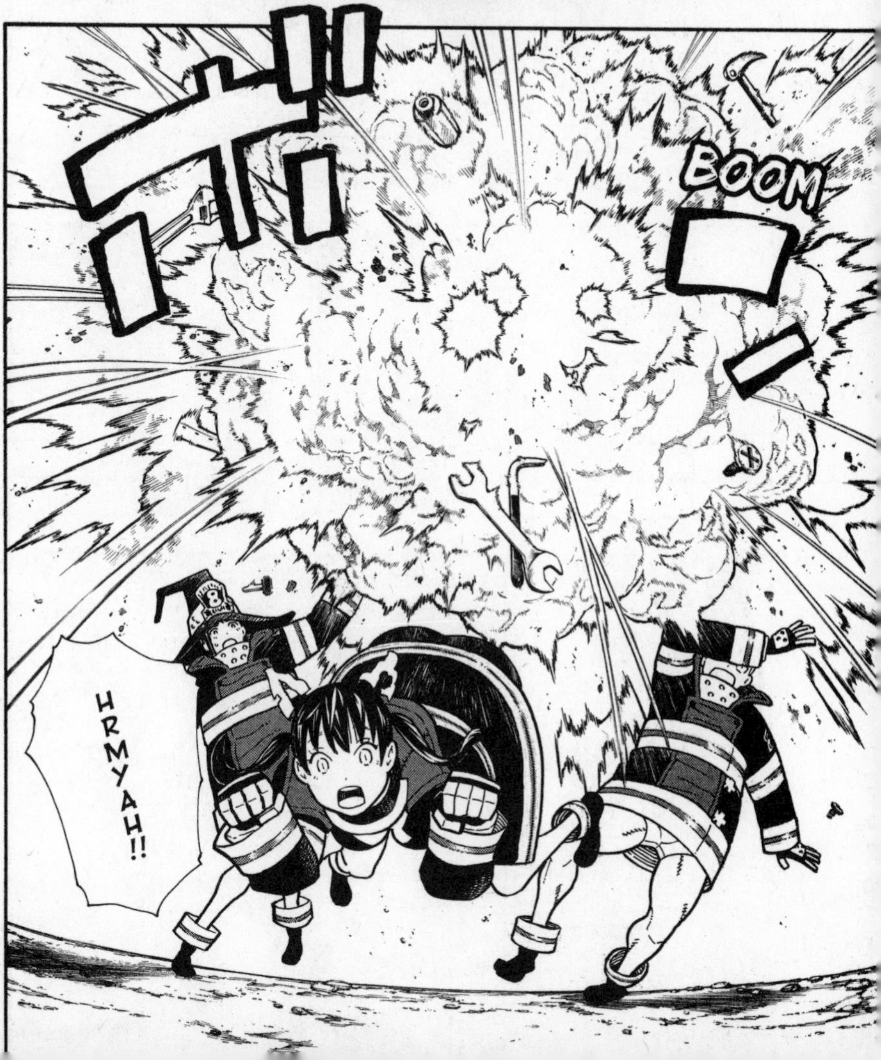
BOOM
HRMYAH!!

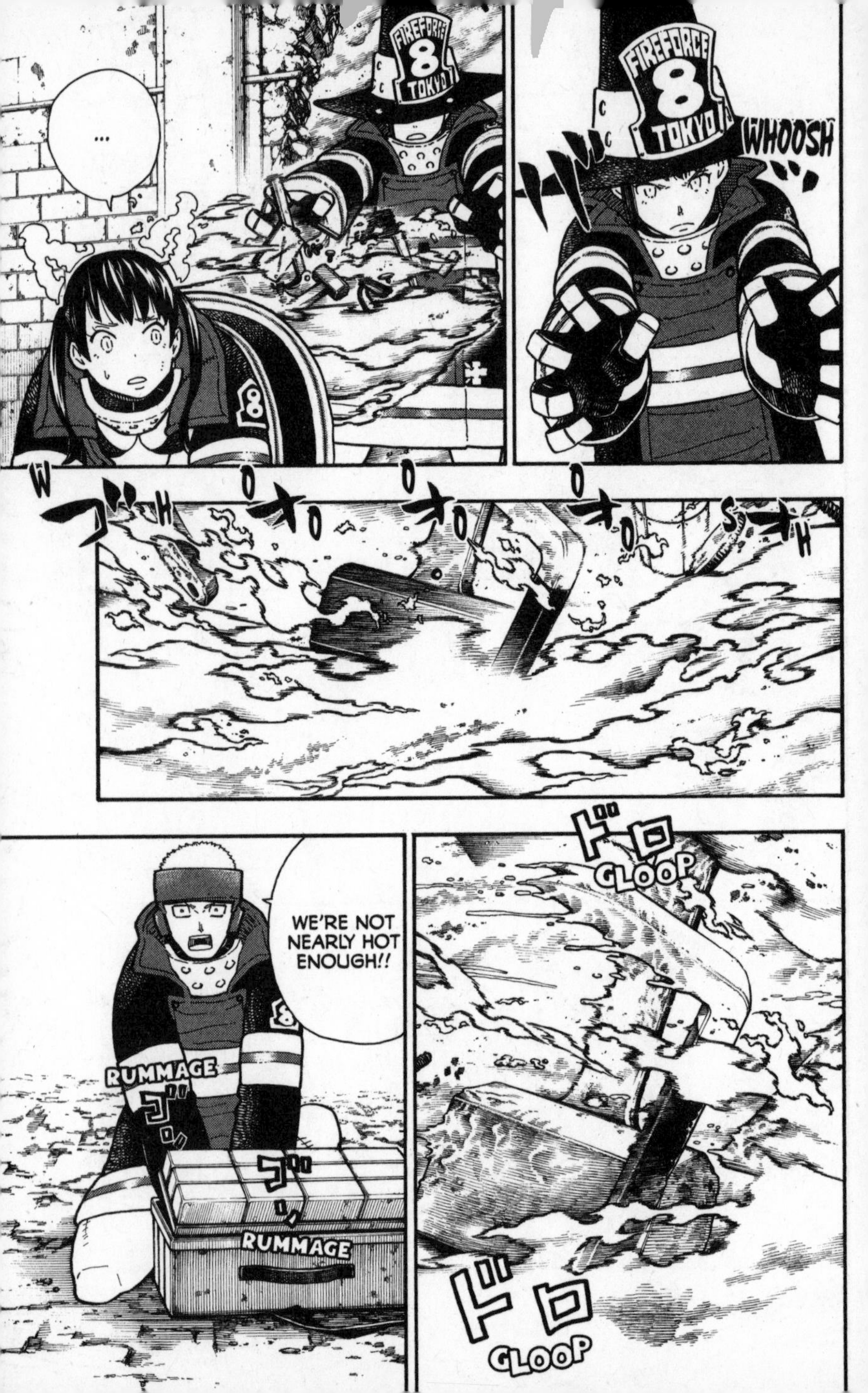

WHOOSH
...
WHOOOSH
ドロ
GLOOP
ドロ
GLOOP
WE'RE NOT NEARLY HOT ENOUGH!!
RUMMAGE
RUMMAGE

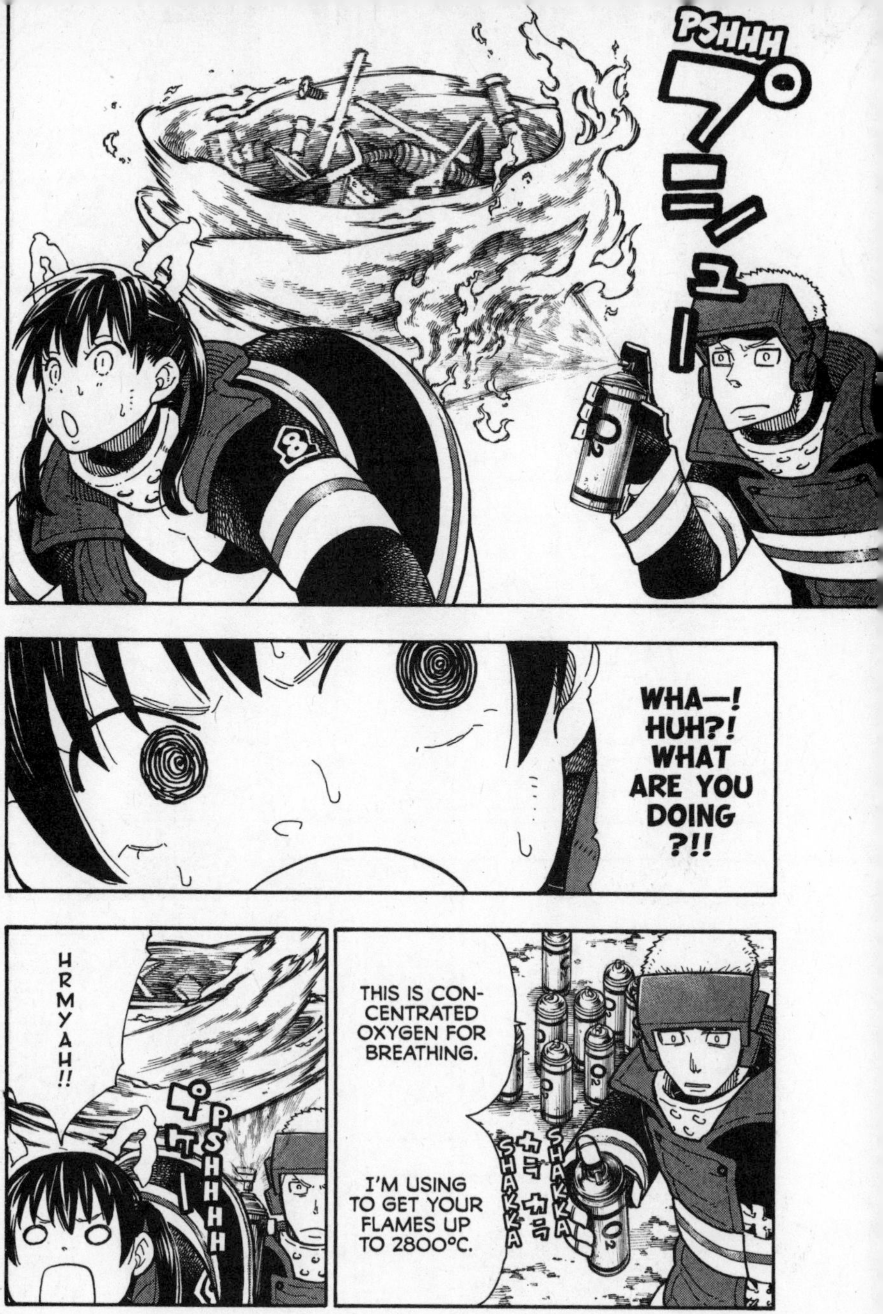
PSHHH
プシュー
WHA—! HUH?! WHAT ARE YOU DOING?!!
THIS IS CONCENTRATED OXYGEN FOR BREATHING.
I'M USING TO GET YOUR FLAMES UP TO 2800°C.
SHAKA SHAKA
HRMYAH!!
PSHHHH

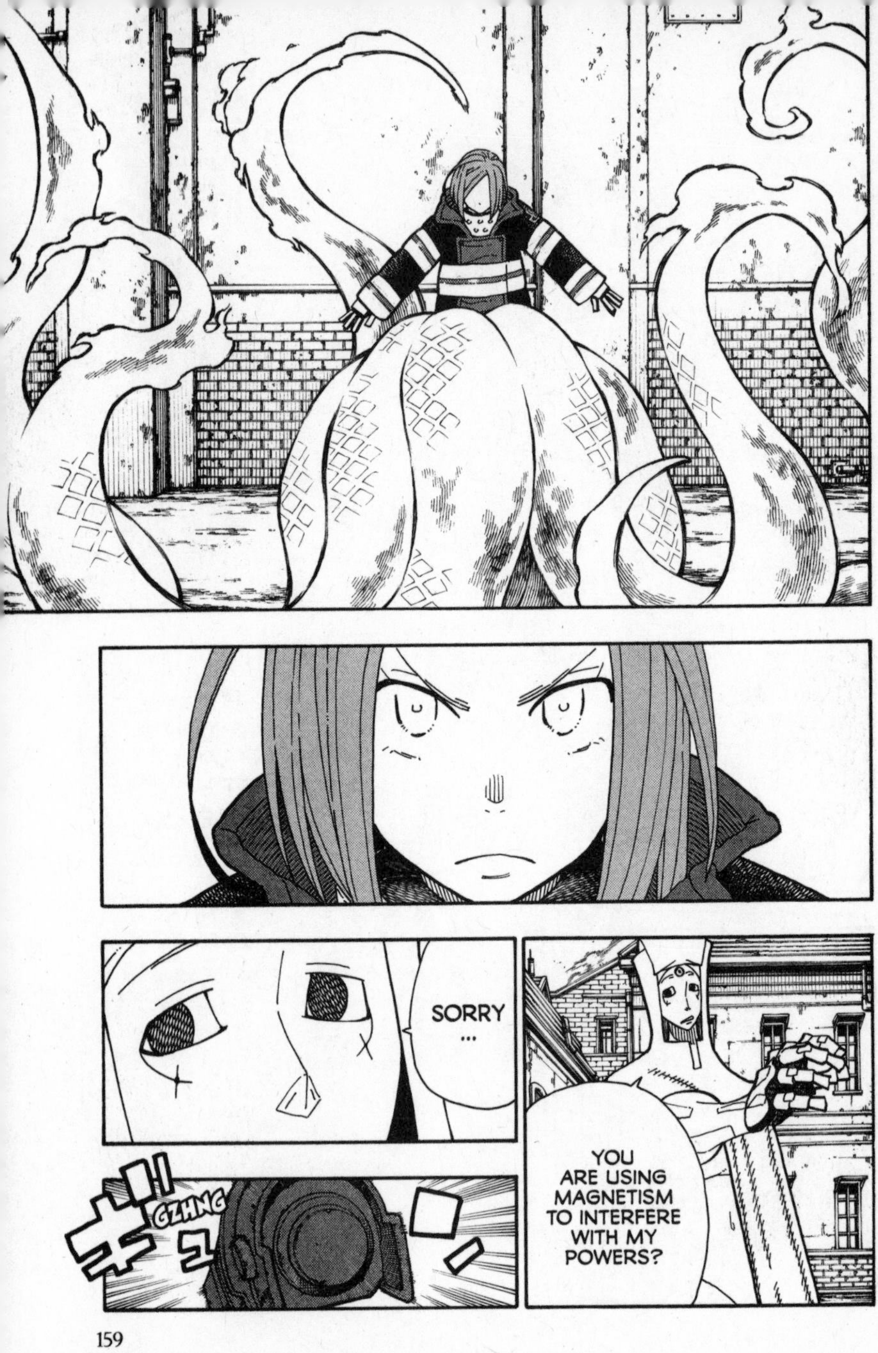
YOU ARE USING MAGNETISM TO INTERFERE WITH MY POWERS?
SORRY ...
GZHNG

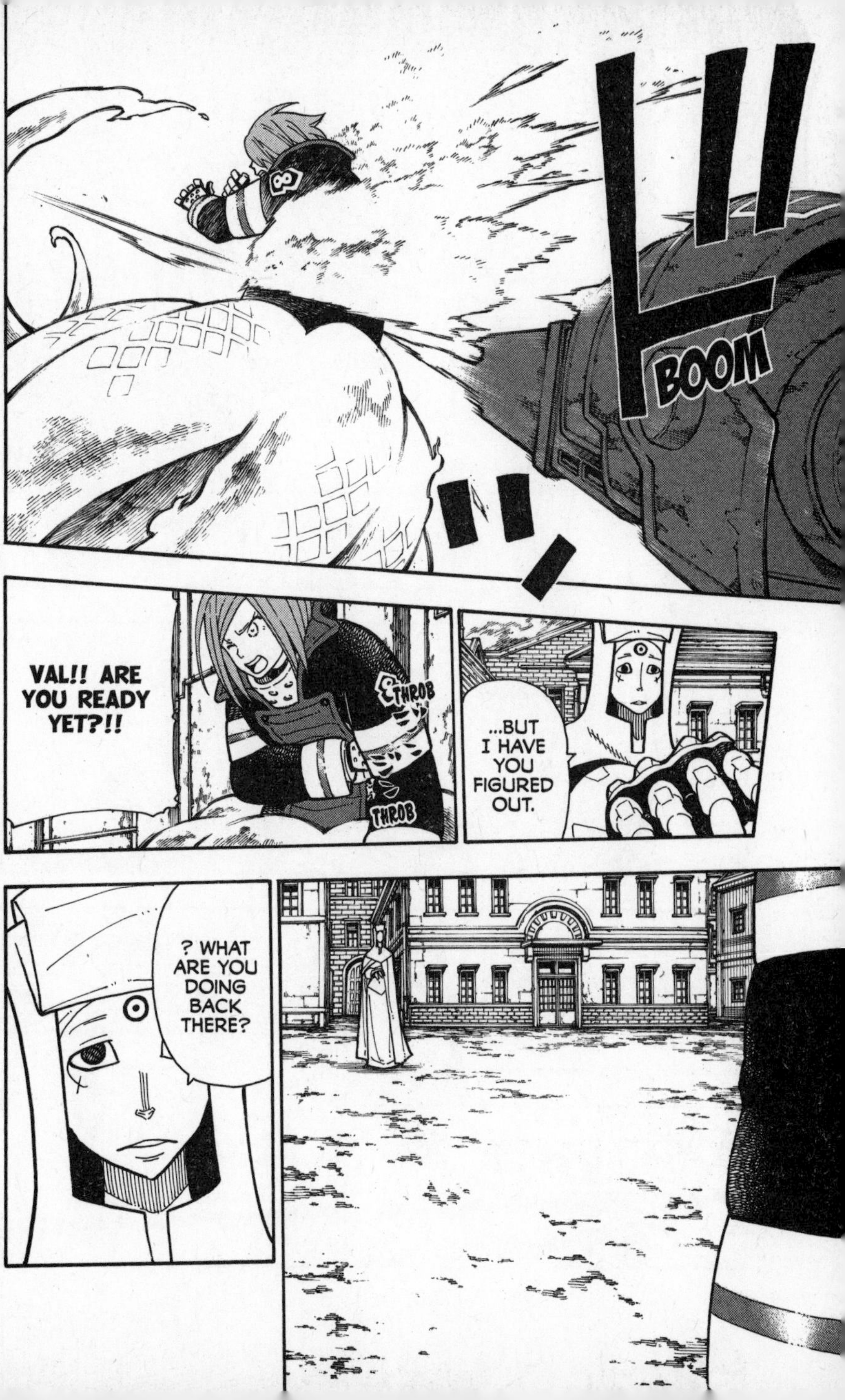
BOOM
...BUT I HAVE YOU FIGURED OUT.
VAL!! ARE YOU READY YET?!!
THROB
THROB
? WHAT ARE YOU DOING BACK THERE?

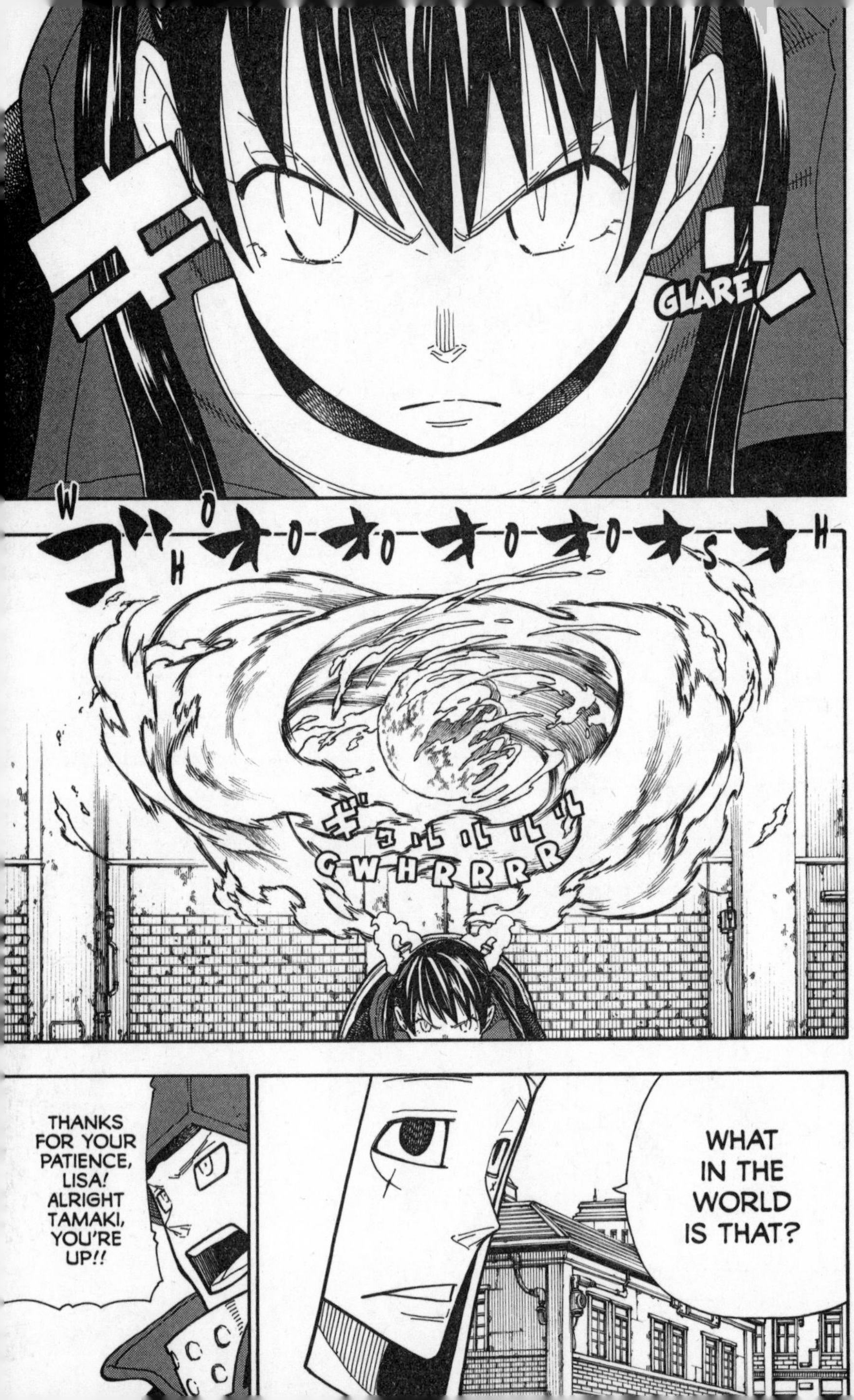
GLARE
WHOOOOOSH
GWHRRRR
WHAT IN THE WORLD IS THAT?
THANKS FOR YOUR PATIENCE, LISA! ALRIGHT TAMAKI, YOU'RE UP!!

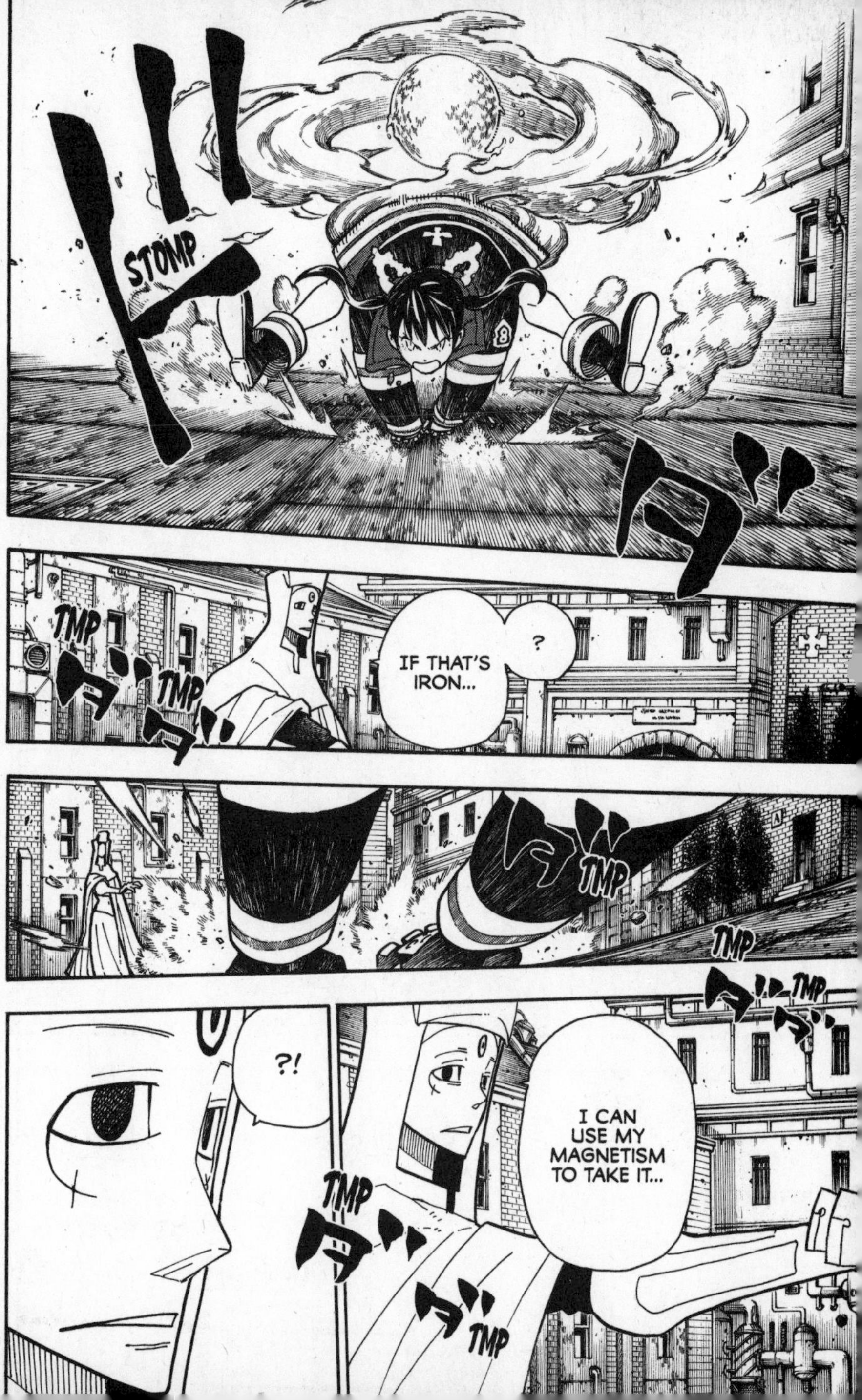
STOMP
?
IF THAT'S IRON...
TMP
TMP
TMP
TMP
TMP
TMP
I CAN USE MY MAGNETISM TO TAKE IT...
TMP
TMP
?!

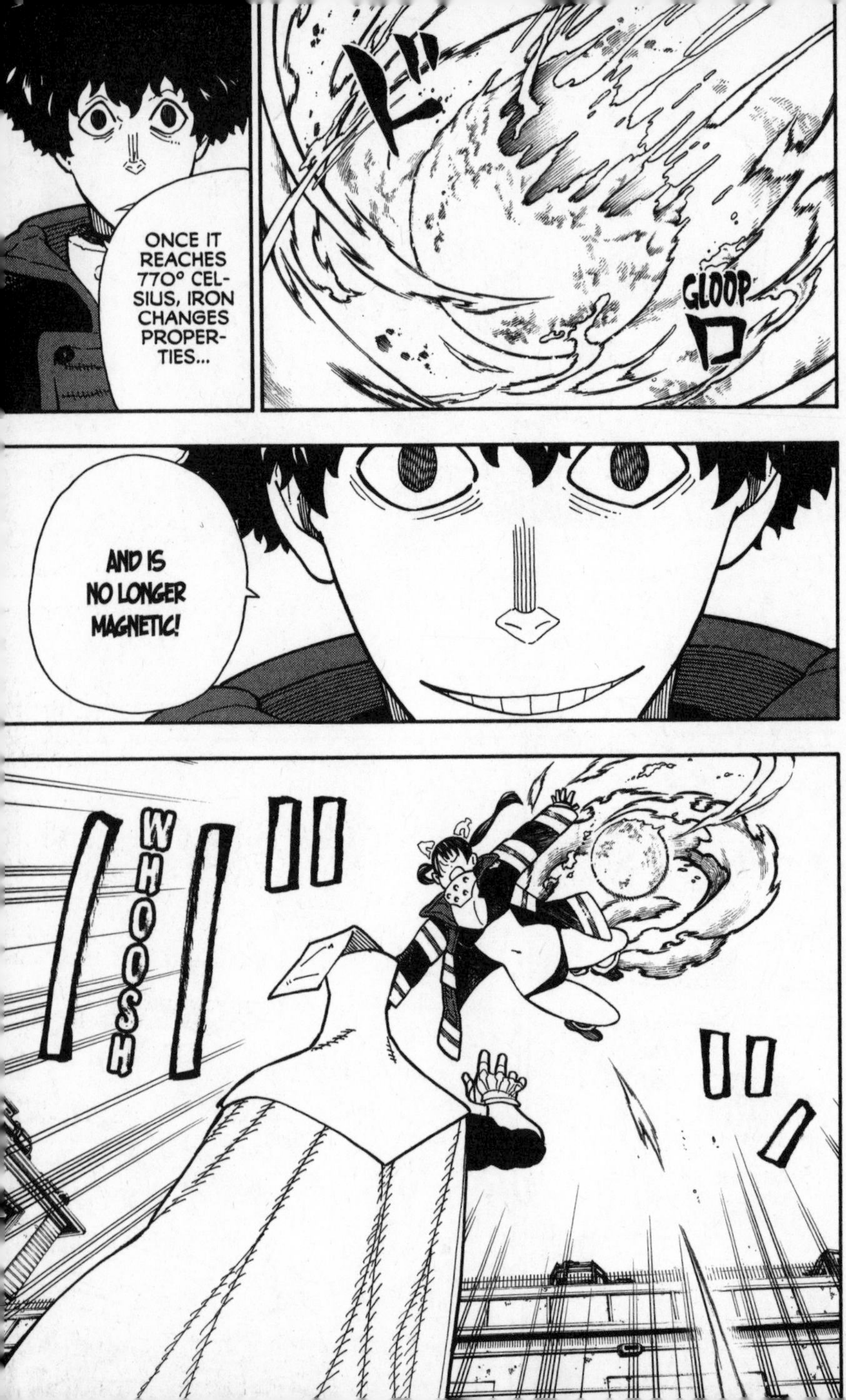
ド
GLOOP
ロ
ONCE IT REACHES 770° CELSIUS, IRON CHANGES PROPERTIES...
AND IS NO LONGER MAGNETIC!
WHOOSH

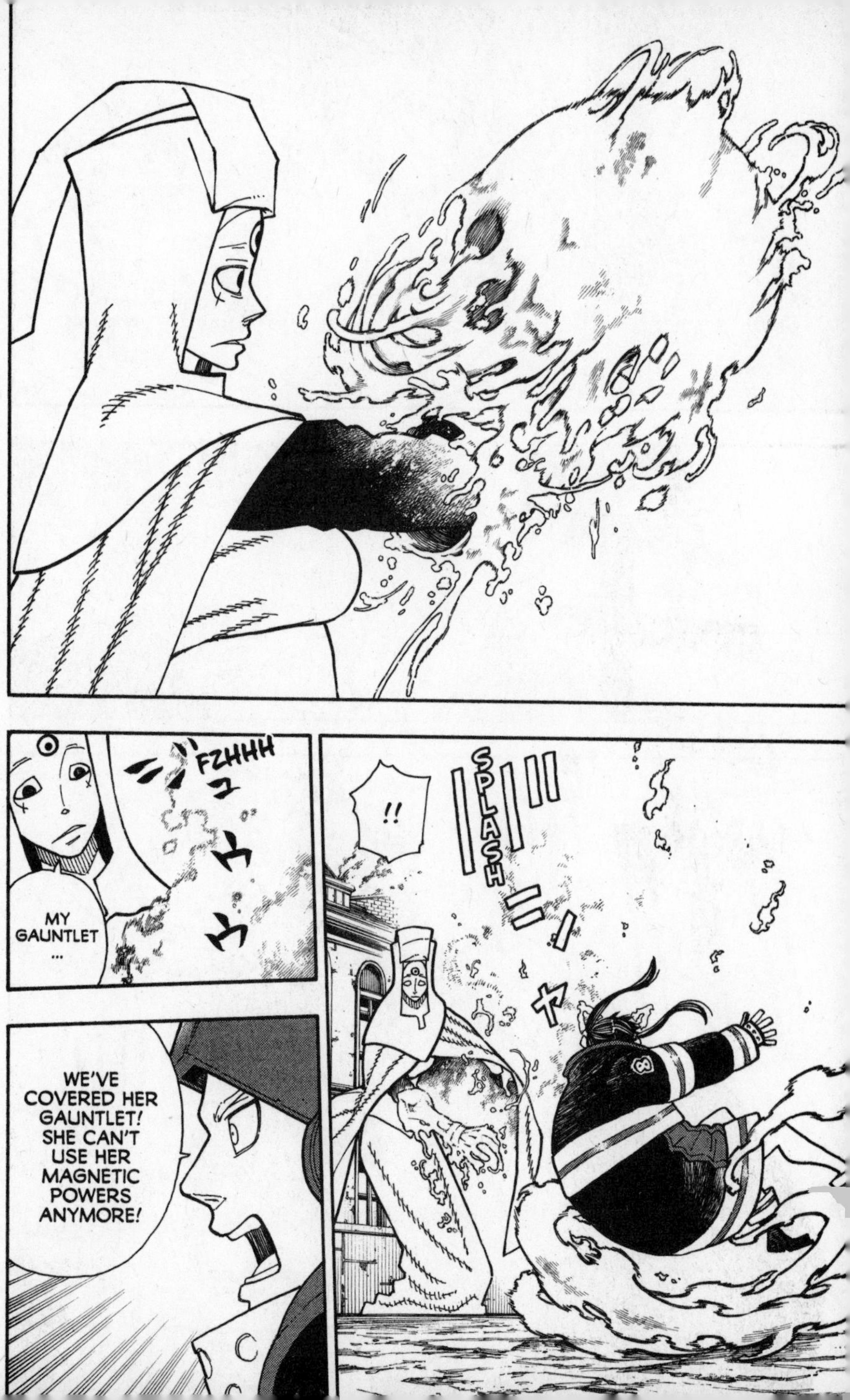
!!
SPLASH
FZHHH
MY GAUNTLET ...
WE'VE COVERED HER GAUNTLET! SHE CAN'T USE HER MAGNETIC POWERS ANYMORE!

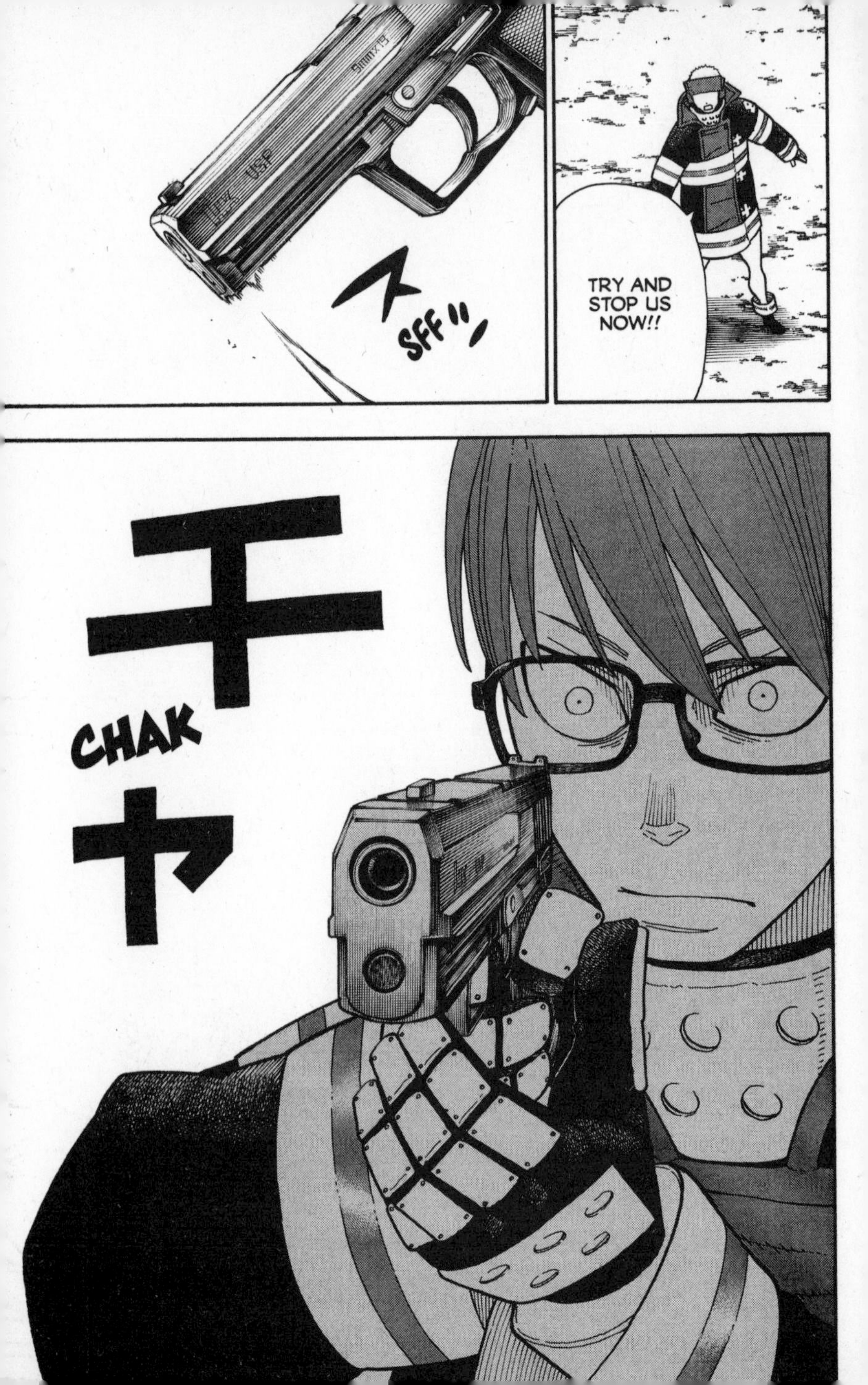
TRY AND STOP US NOW!!
ス
SFF
チャ
CHAK

FIRE FORCE

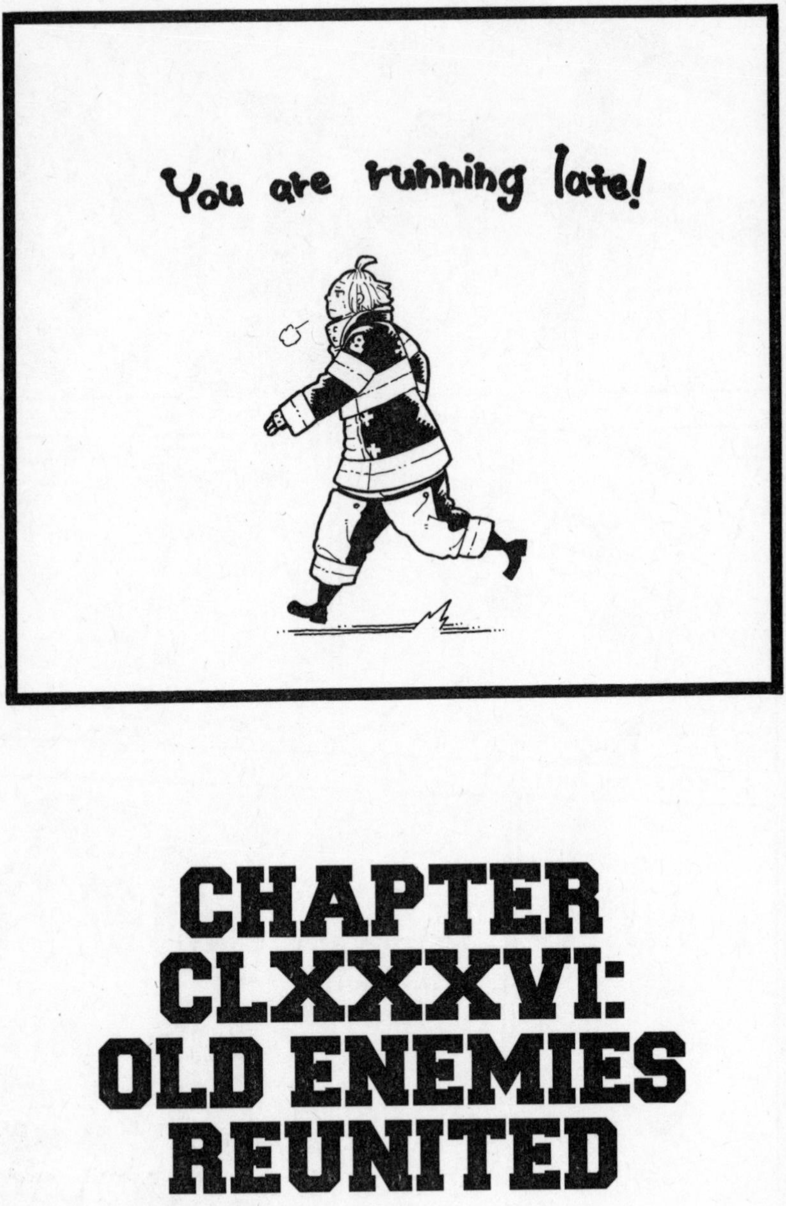
You are running late!

CHAPTER CLXXXVI: OLD ENEMIES REUNITED

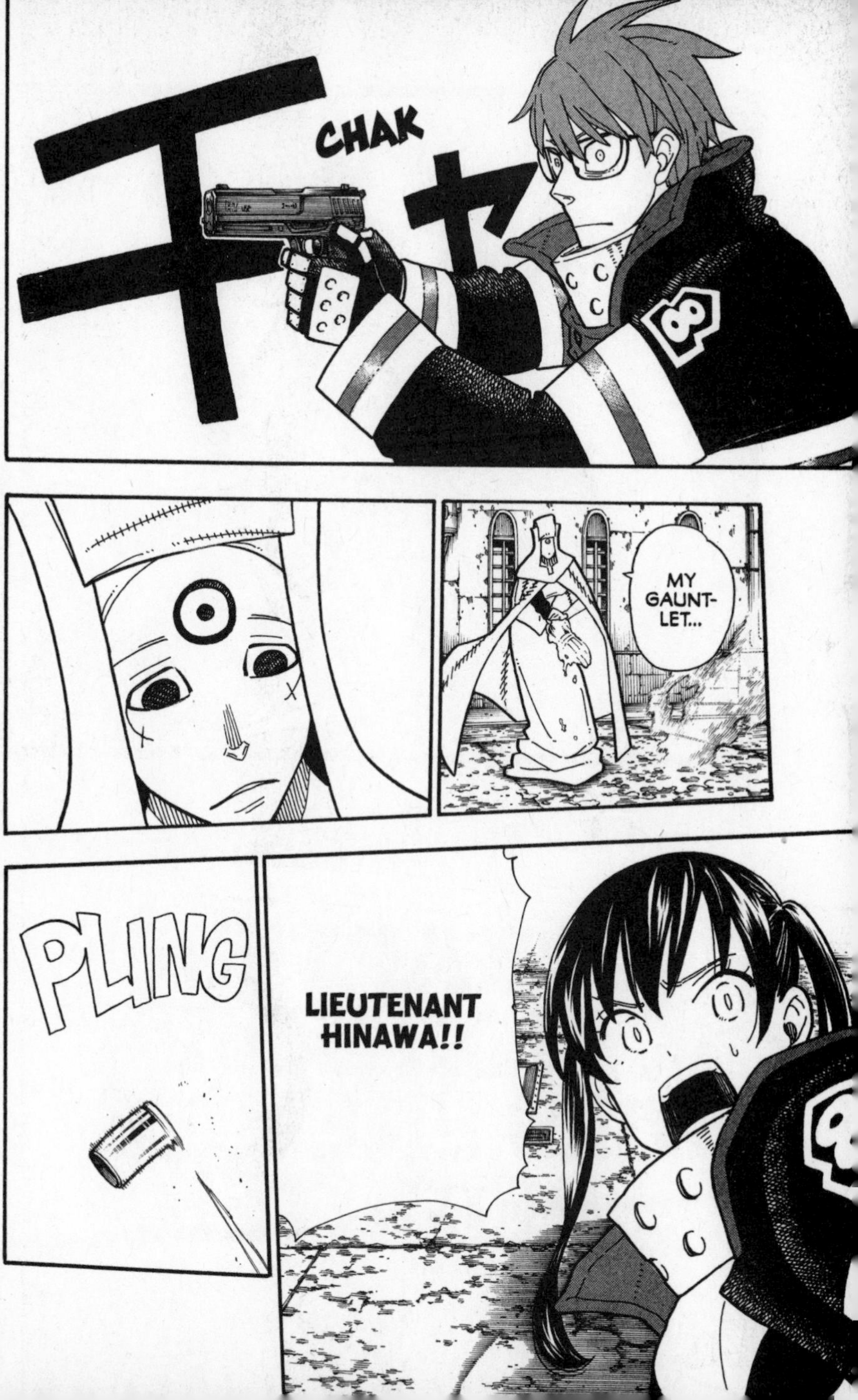
CHAK
MY GAUNT-LET...
LIEUTENANT HINAWA!!
PLING

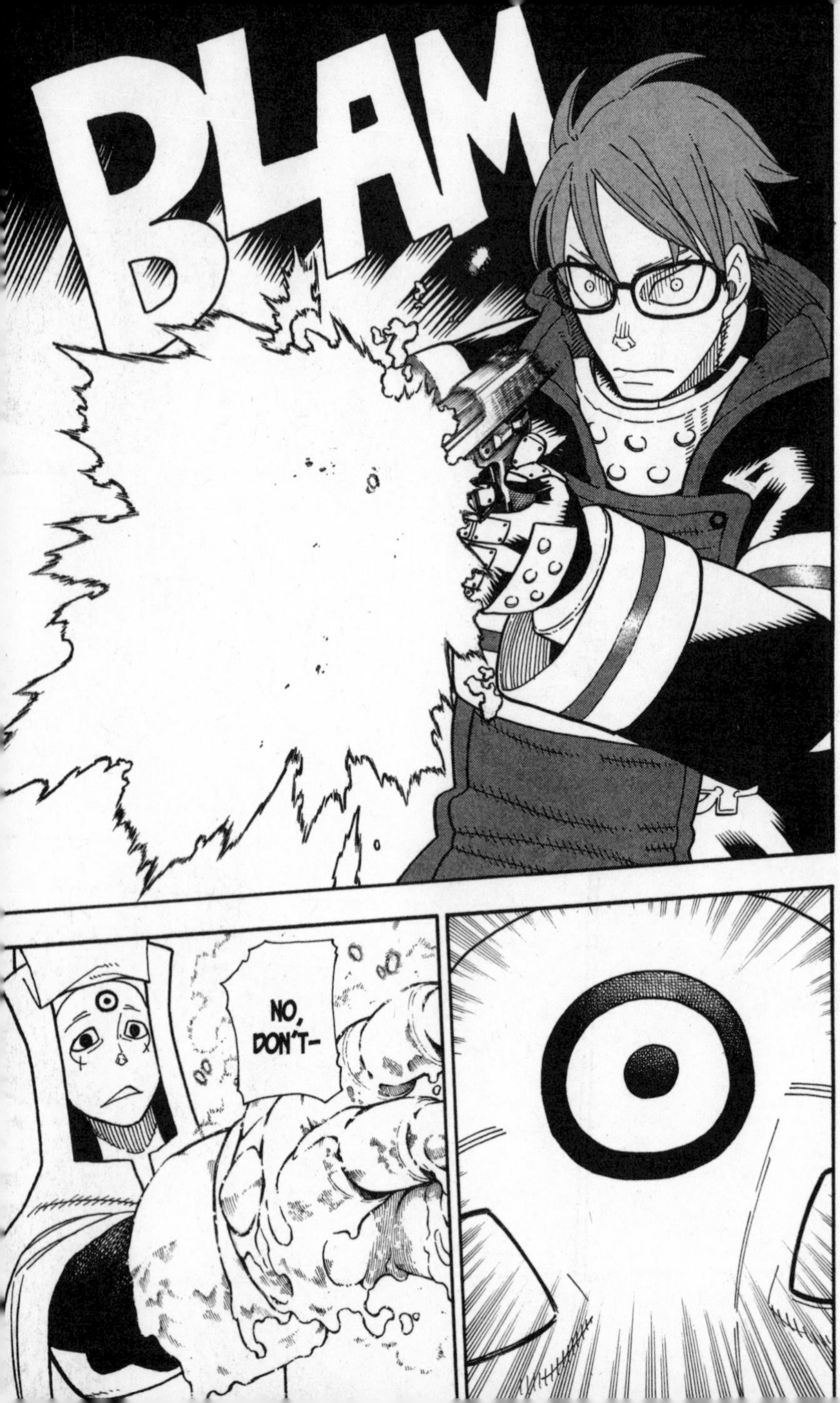
BLAM
NO, DON'T-

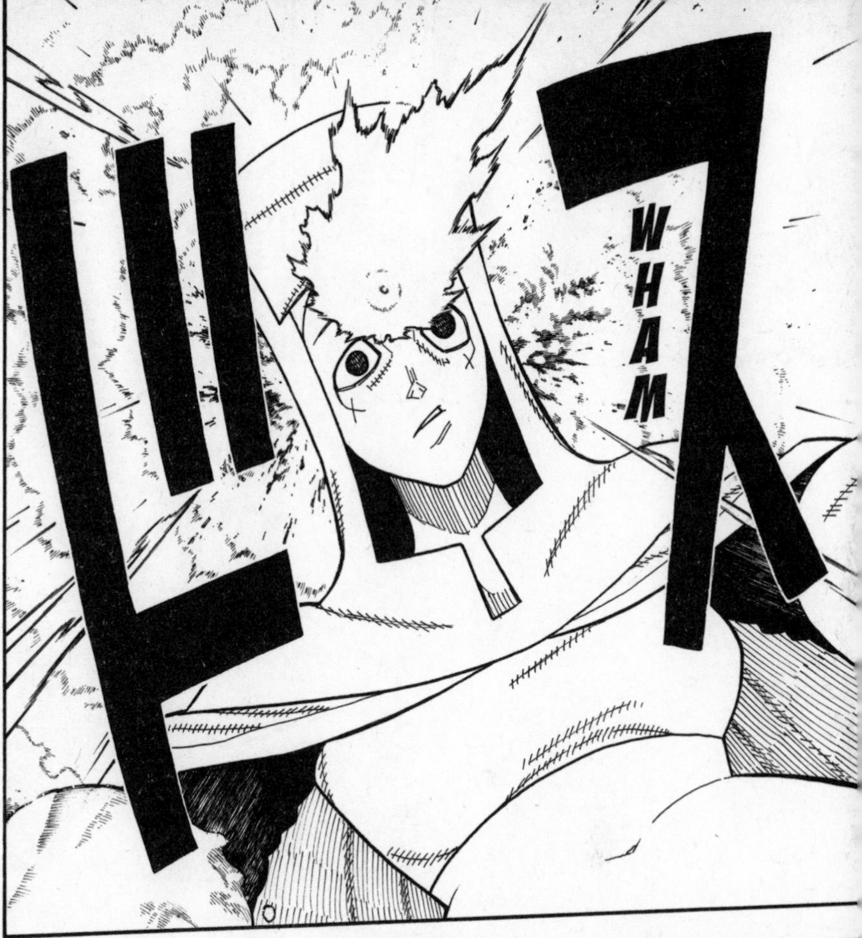
WHAM
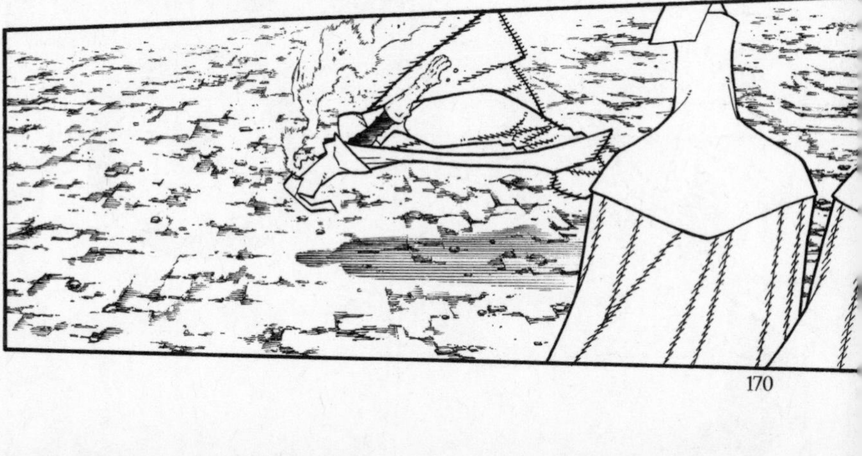

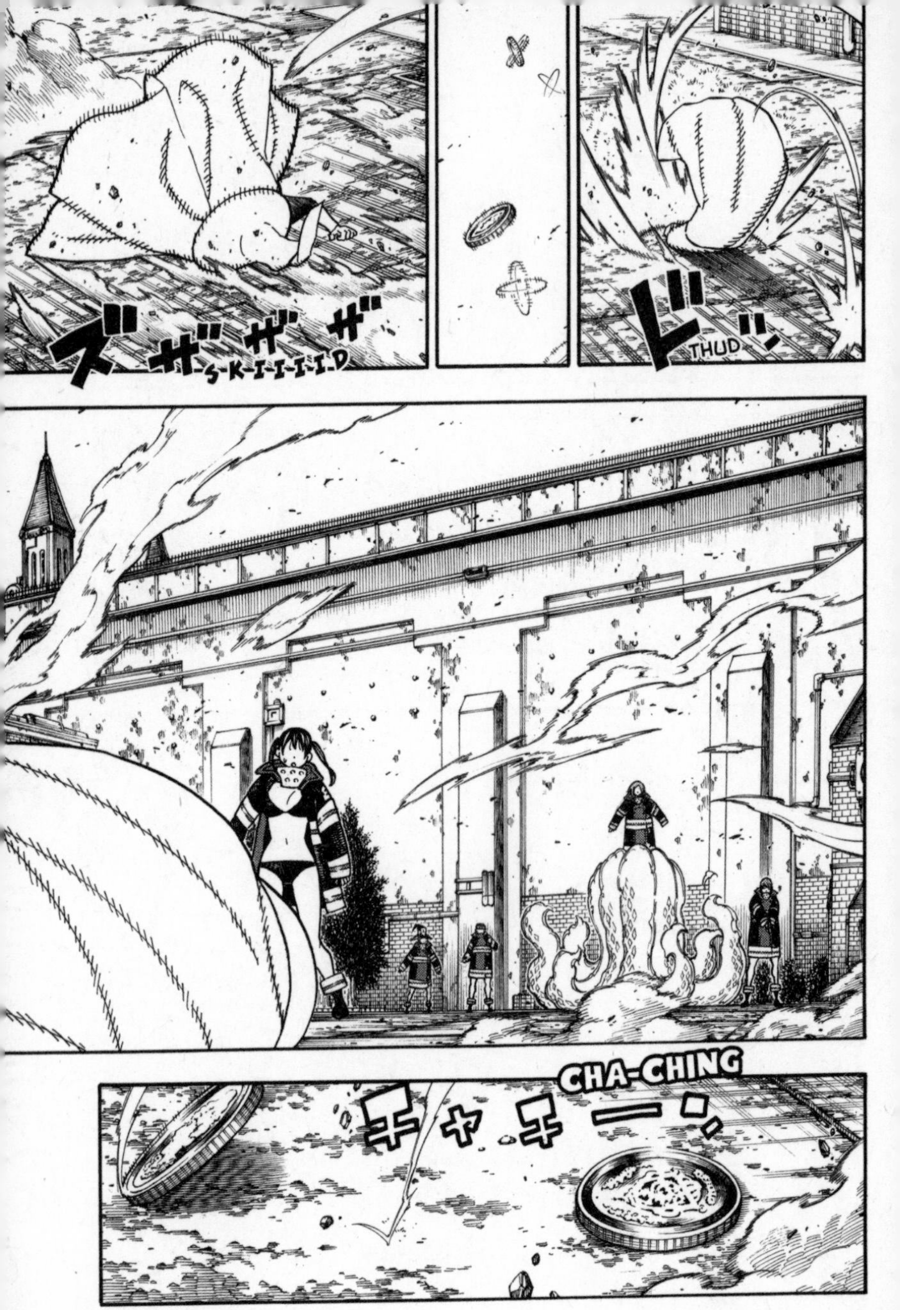
ドッ
THUD
ズザザザ
S-K-I-I-I-I-D
CHA-CHING
チャキー

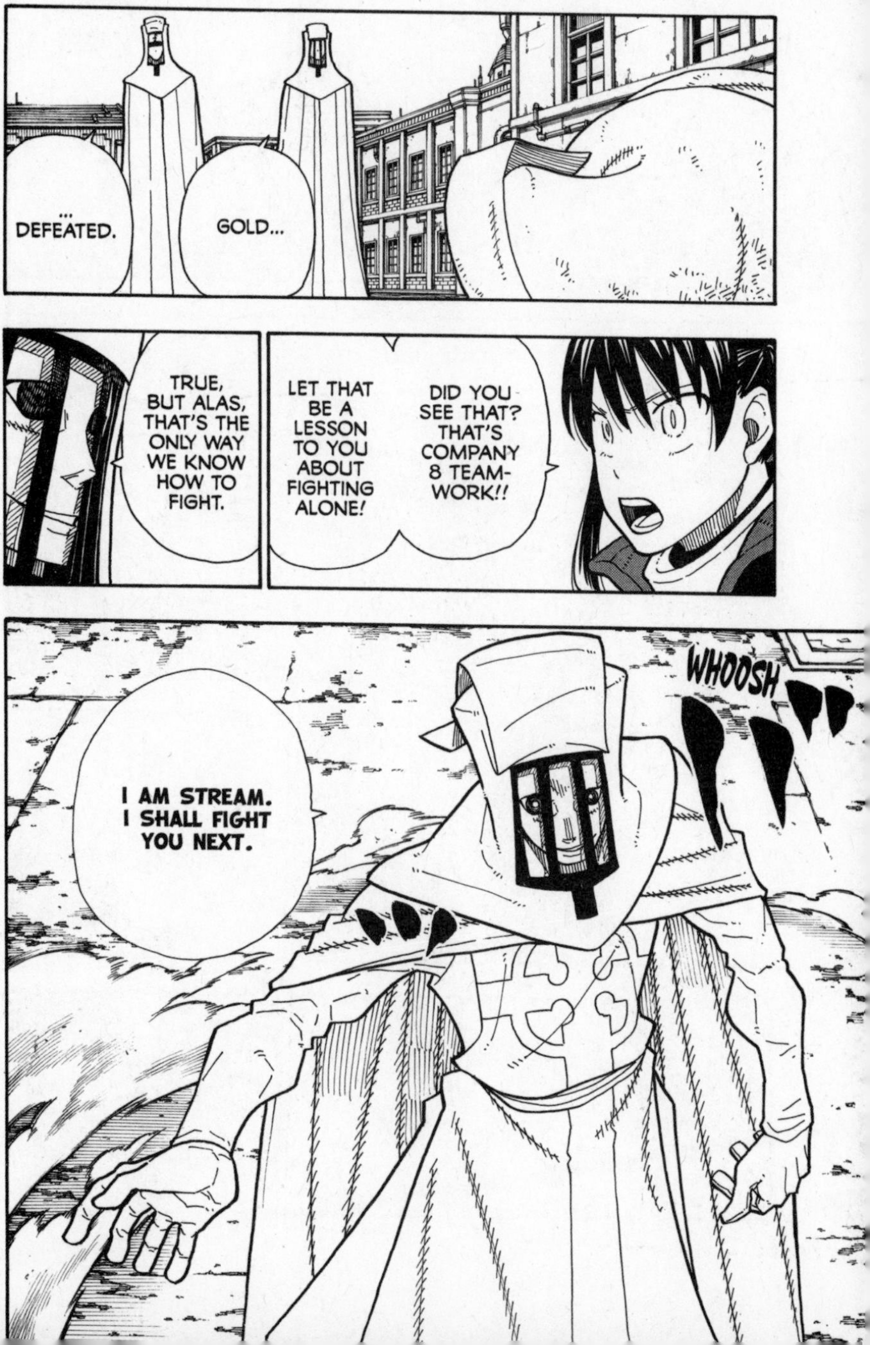
GOLD...
... DEFEATED.
DID YOU SEE THAT? THAT'S COMPANY 8 TEAM-WORK!!
LET THAT BE A LESSON TO YOU ABOUT FIGHTING ALONE!
TRUE, BUT ALAS, THAT'S THE ONLY WAY WE KNOW HOW TO FIGHT.
WHOOSH
I AM STREAM. I SHALL FIGHT YOU NEXT.

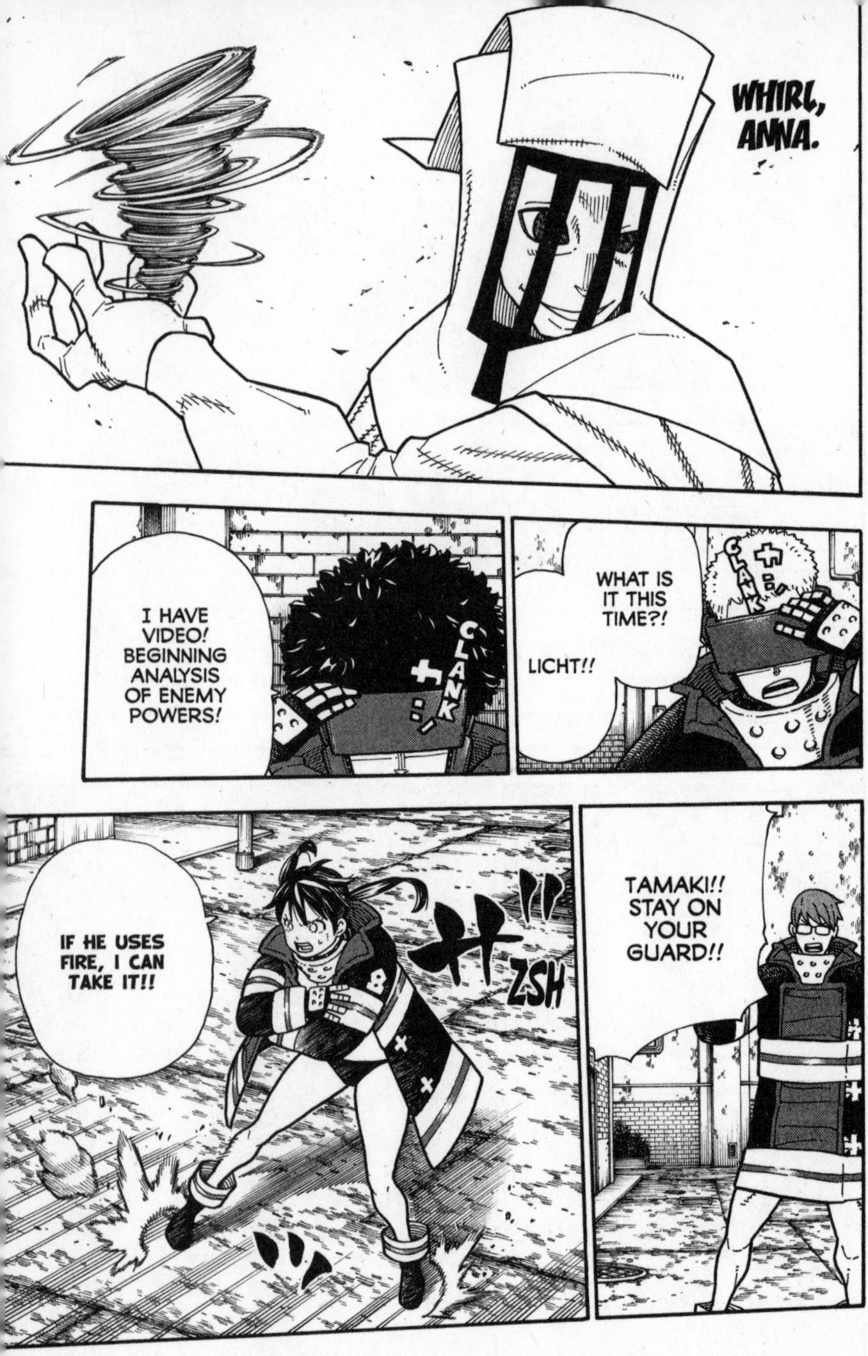
WHIRL, ANNA.
CLANK
WHAT IS IT THIS TIME?!
LICHT!!
CLANK
I HAVE VIDEO! BEGINNING ANALYSIS OF ENEMY POWERS!
TAMAKI!! STAY ON YOUR GUARD!!
ZSH
IF HE USES FIRE, I CAN TAKE IT!!

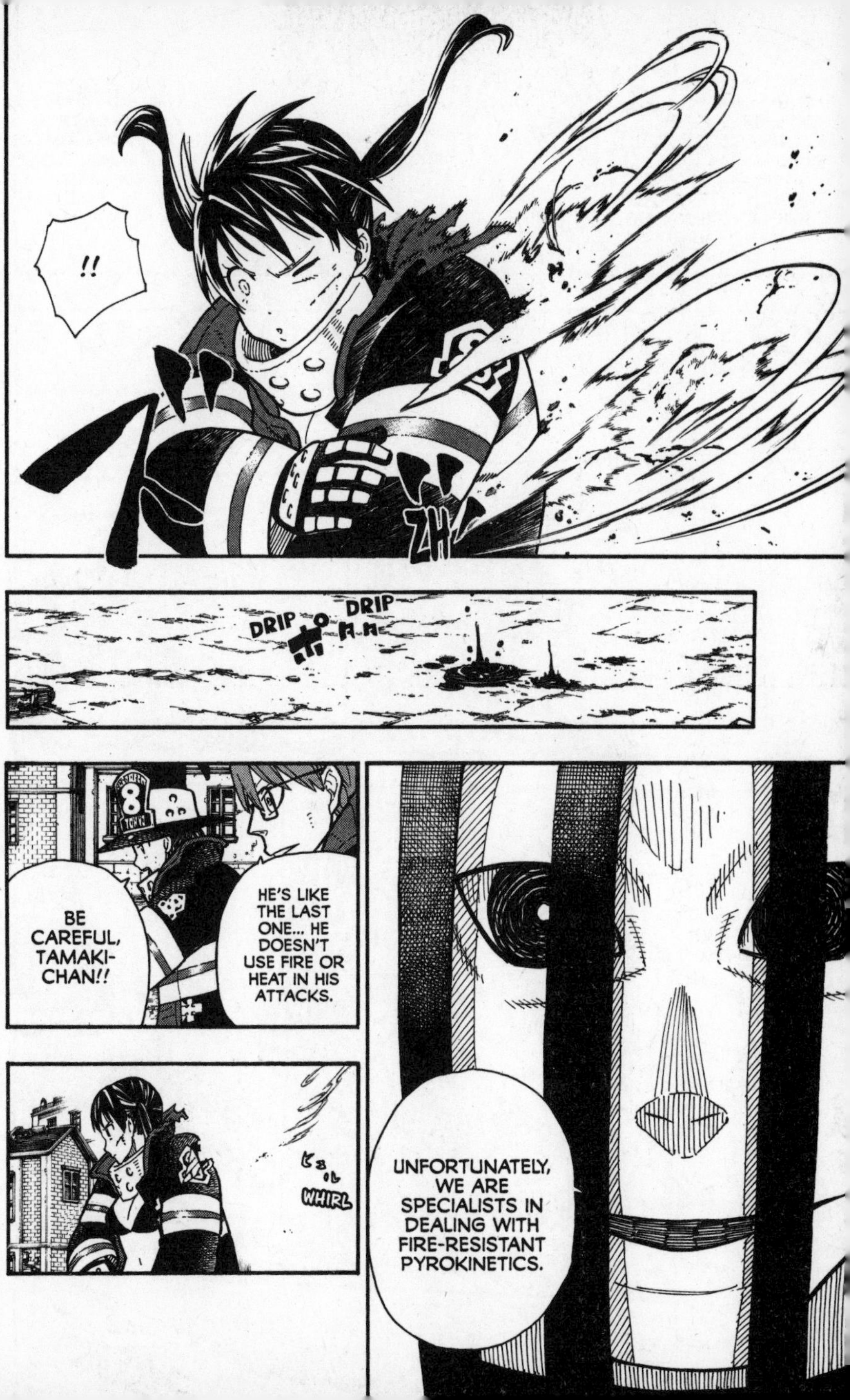
!!
ZH
DRIP DRIP
HE'S LIKE THE LAST ONE... HE DOESN'T USE FIRE OR HEAT IN HIS ATTACKS.
BE CAREFUL, TAMAKI-CHAN!!
UNFORTUNATELY, WE ARE SPECIALISTS IN DEALING WITH FIRE-RESISTANT PYROKINETICS.
WHIRL

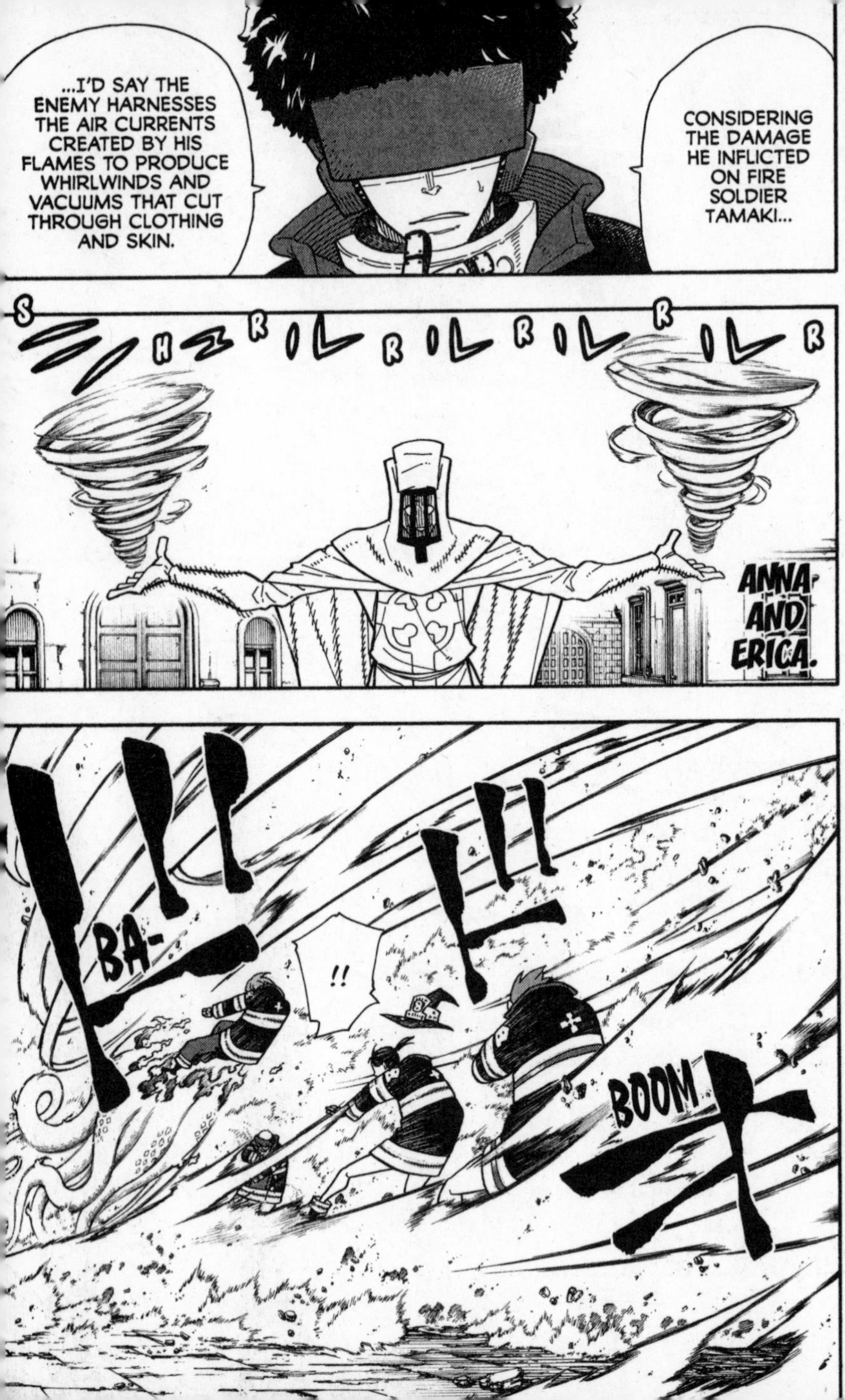
CONSIDERING THE DAMAGE HE INFLICTED ON FIRE SOLDIER TAMAKI...
...I'D SAY THE ENEMY HARNESSES THE AIR CURRENTS CREATED BY HIS FLAMES TO PRODUCE WHIRLWINDS AND VACUUMS THAT CUT THROUGH CLOTHING AND SKIN.
ANNA AND ERICA.
BOOM
!!
BA-

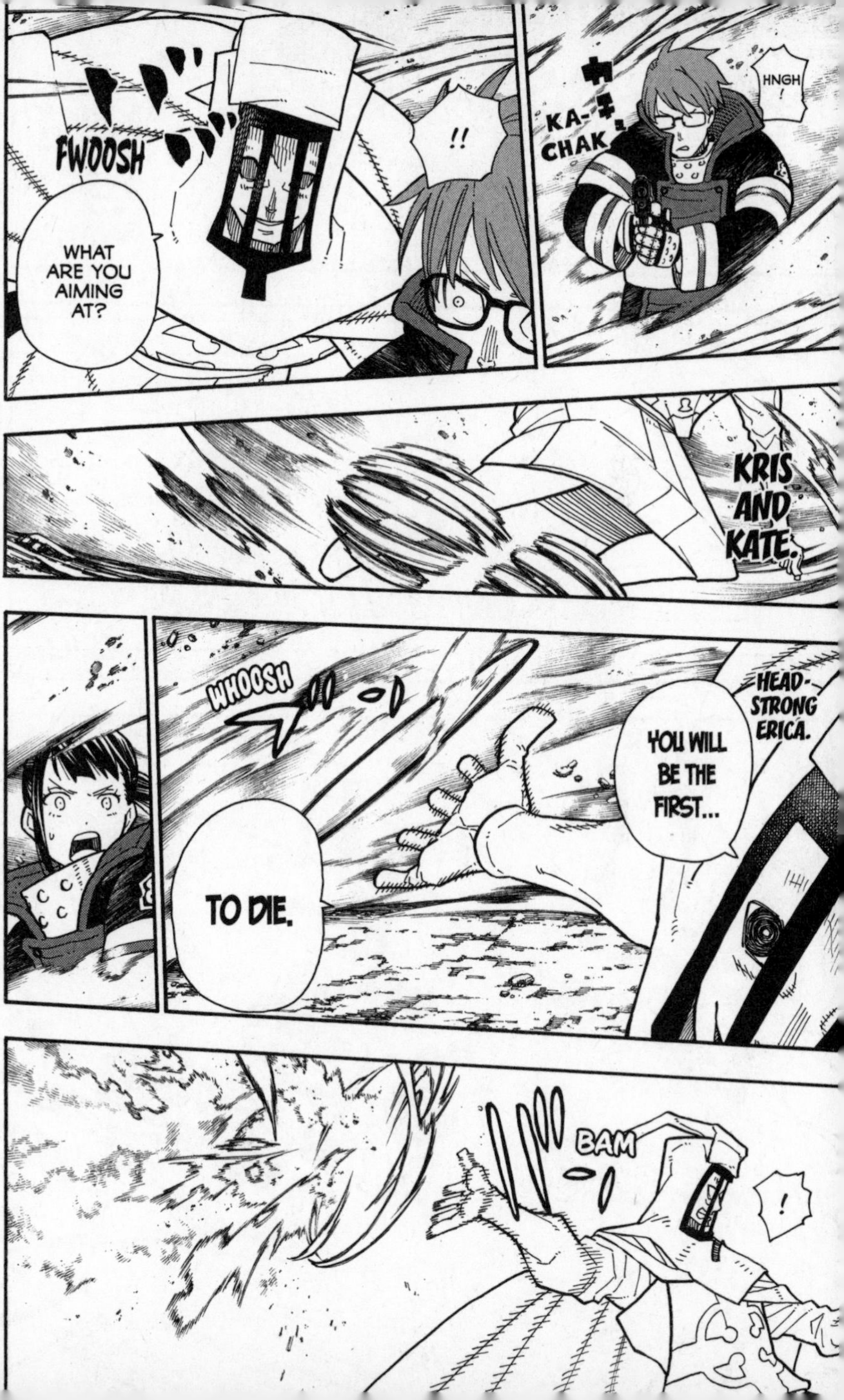
HNGH!
KA-CHAK
!!
FWOOSH
WHAT ARE YOU AIMING AT?
KRIS AND KATE.
HEAD-STRONG ERICA.
YOU WILL BE THE FIRST...
WHOOSH
TO DIE.
!
BAM

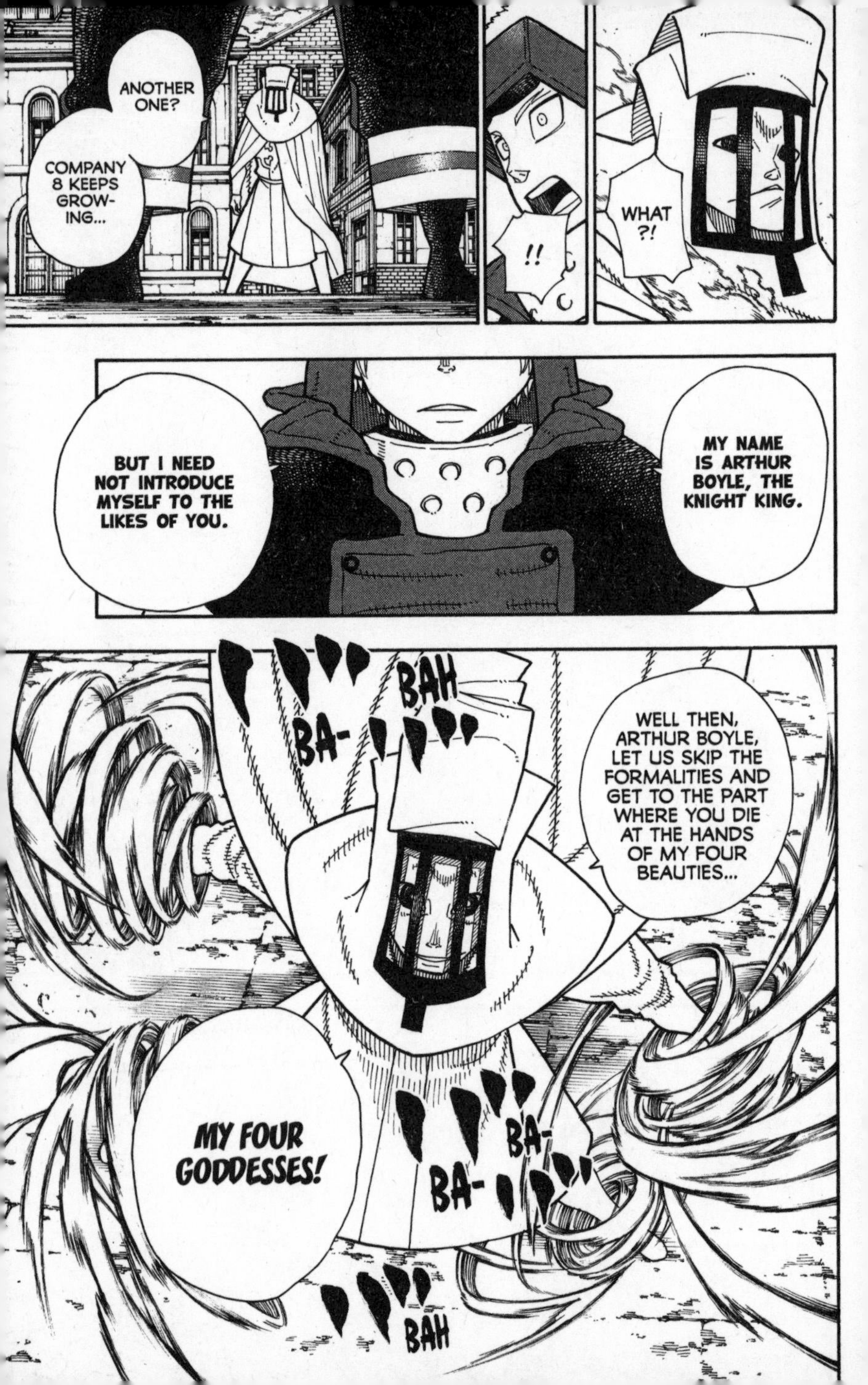
WHAT ?!
!!
ANOTHER ONE?
COMPANY 8 KEEPS GROWING...
MY NAME IS ARTHUR BOYLE, THE KNIGHT KING.
BUT I NEED NOT INTRODUCE MYSELF TO THE LIKES OF YOU.
BAH
BA-
WELL THEN, ARTHUR BOYLE, LET US SKIP THE FORMALITIES AND GET TO THE PART WHERE YOU DIE AT THE HANDS OF MY FOUR BEAUTIES...
MY FOUR GODDESSES!
BA-
BA-
BAH

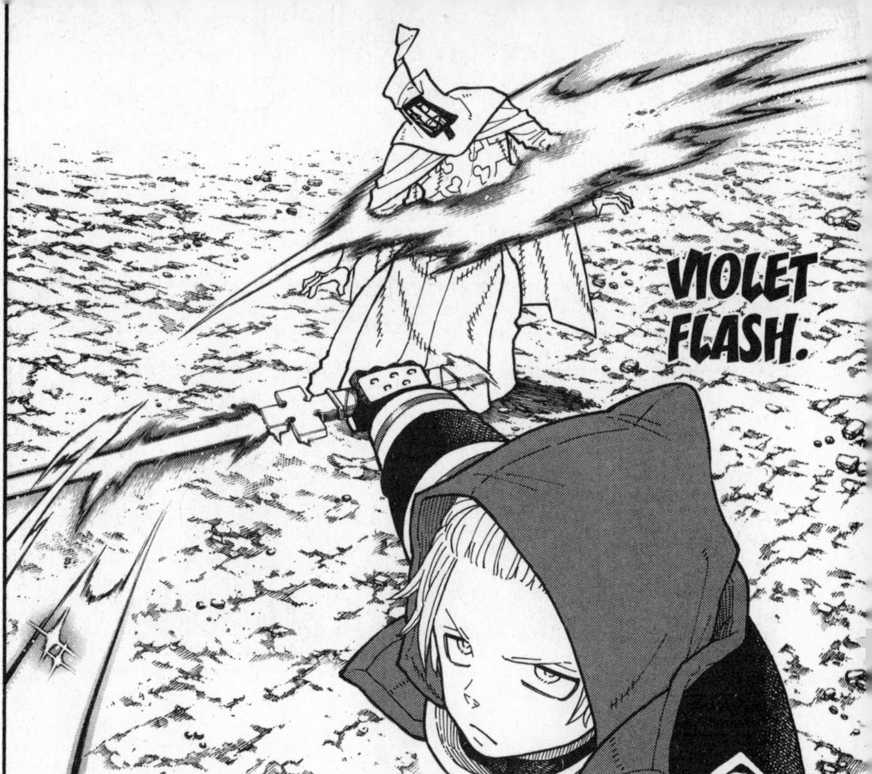
VIOLET FLASH.
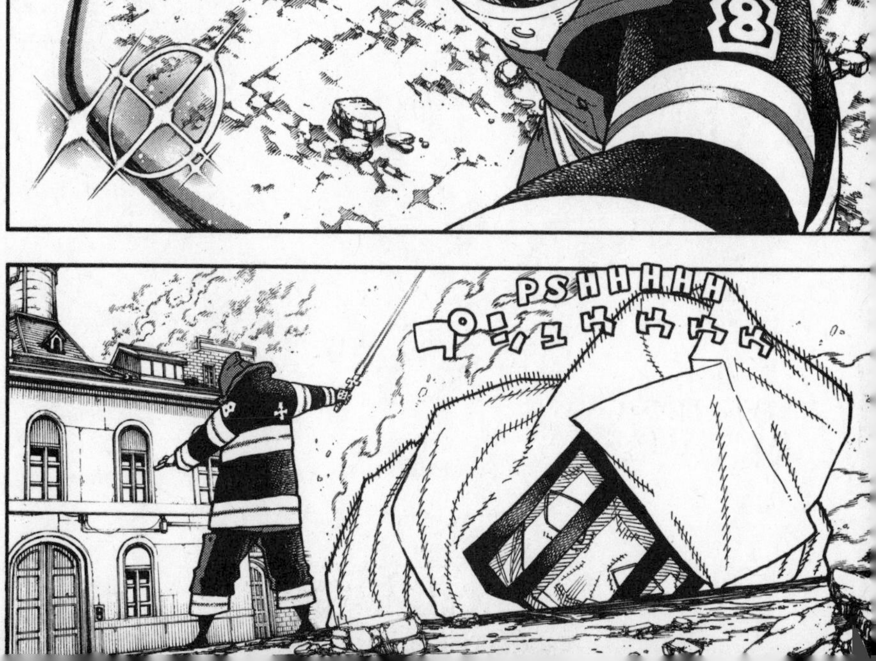
PSHHHHHH

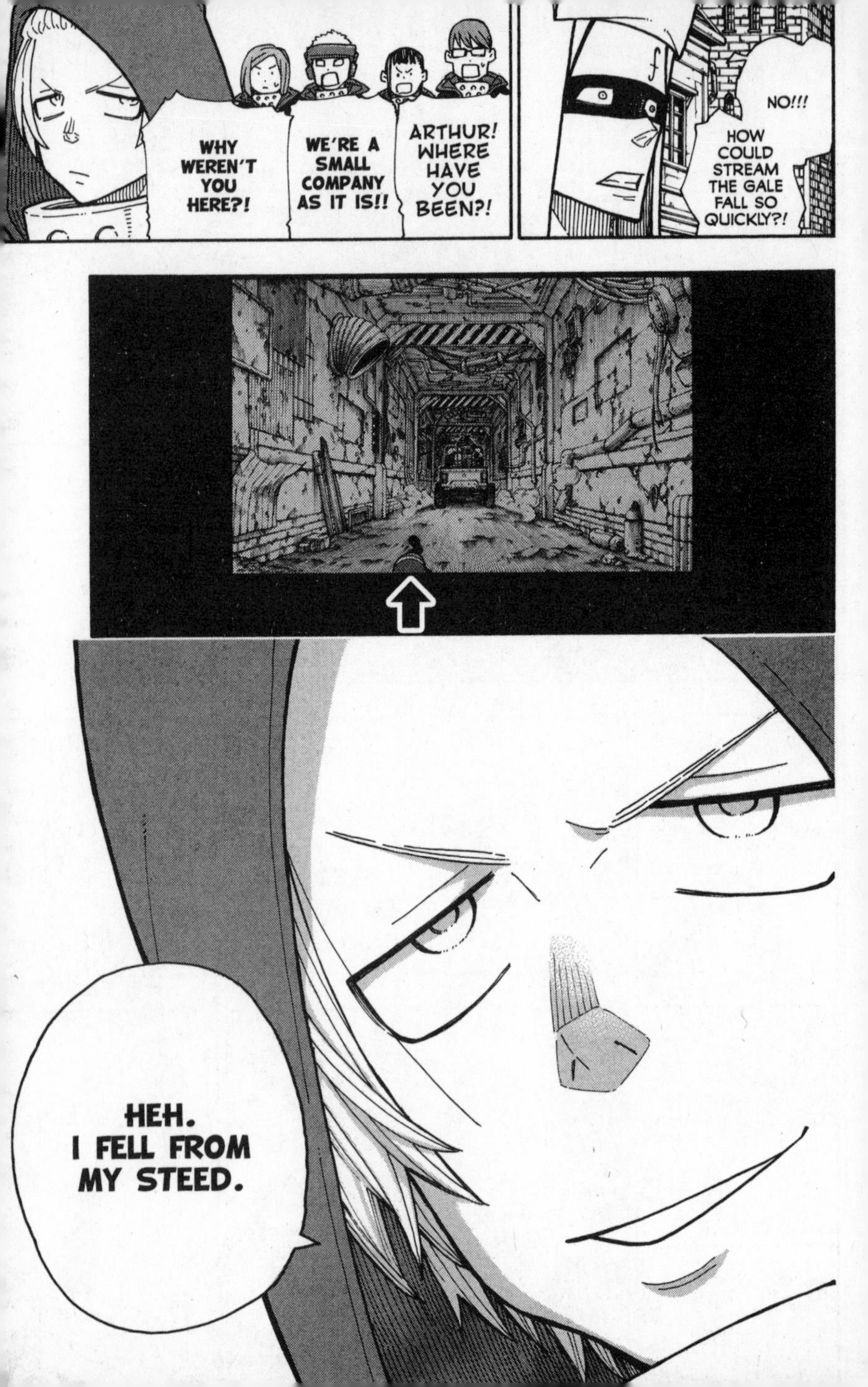
NO!!!
HOW COULD STREAM THE GALE FALL SO QUICKLY?!
ARTHUR! WHERE HAVE YOU BEEN?!
WE'RE A SMALL COMPANY AS IT IS!!
WHY WEREN'T YOU HERE?!
HEH. I FELL FROM MY STEED.

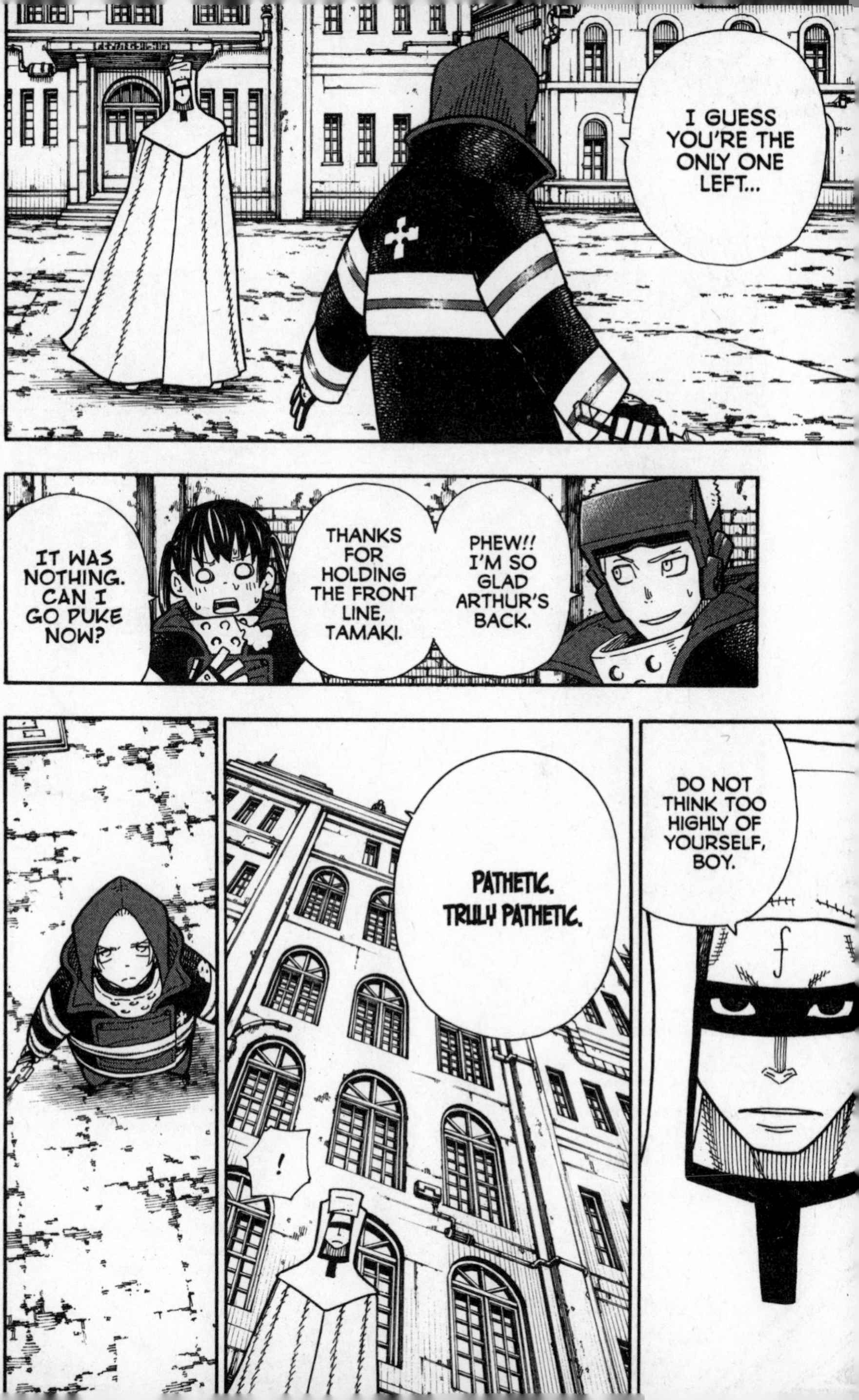
I GUESS YOU'RE THE ONLY ONE LEFT...
PHEW!! I'M SO GLAD ARTHUR'S BACK.
THANKS FOR HOLDING THE FRONT LINE, TAMAKI.
IT WAS NOTHING. CAN I GO PUKE NOW?
DO NOT THINK TOO HIGHLY OF YOURSELF, BOY.
PATHETIC. TRULY PATHETIC.
!

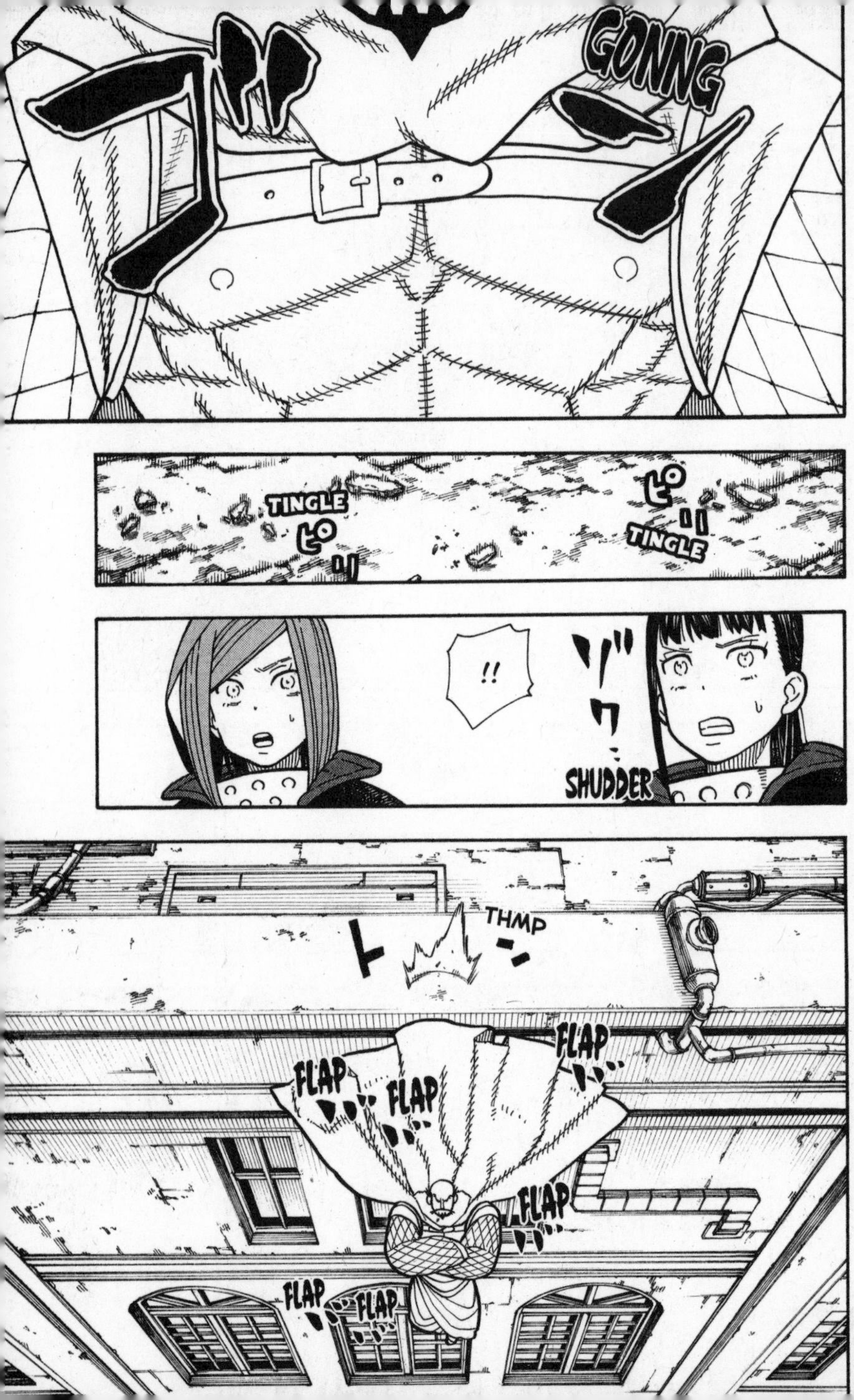

GONNG
ピリ
TINGLE
TINGLE
ピリ
SHUDDER
!!
THMP
FLAP
FLAP
FLAP
FLAP
FLAP
FLAP

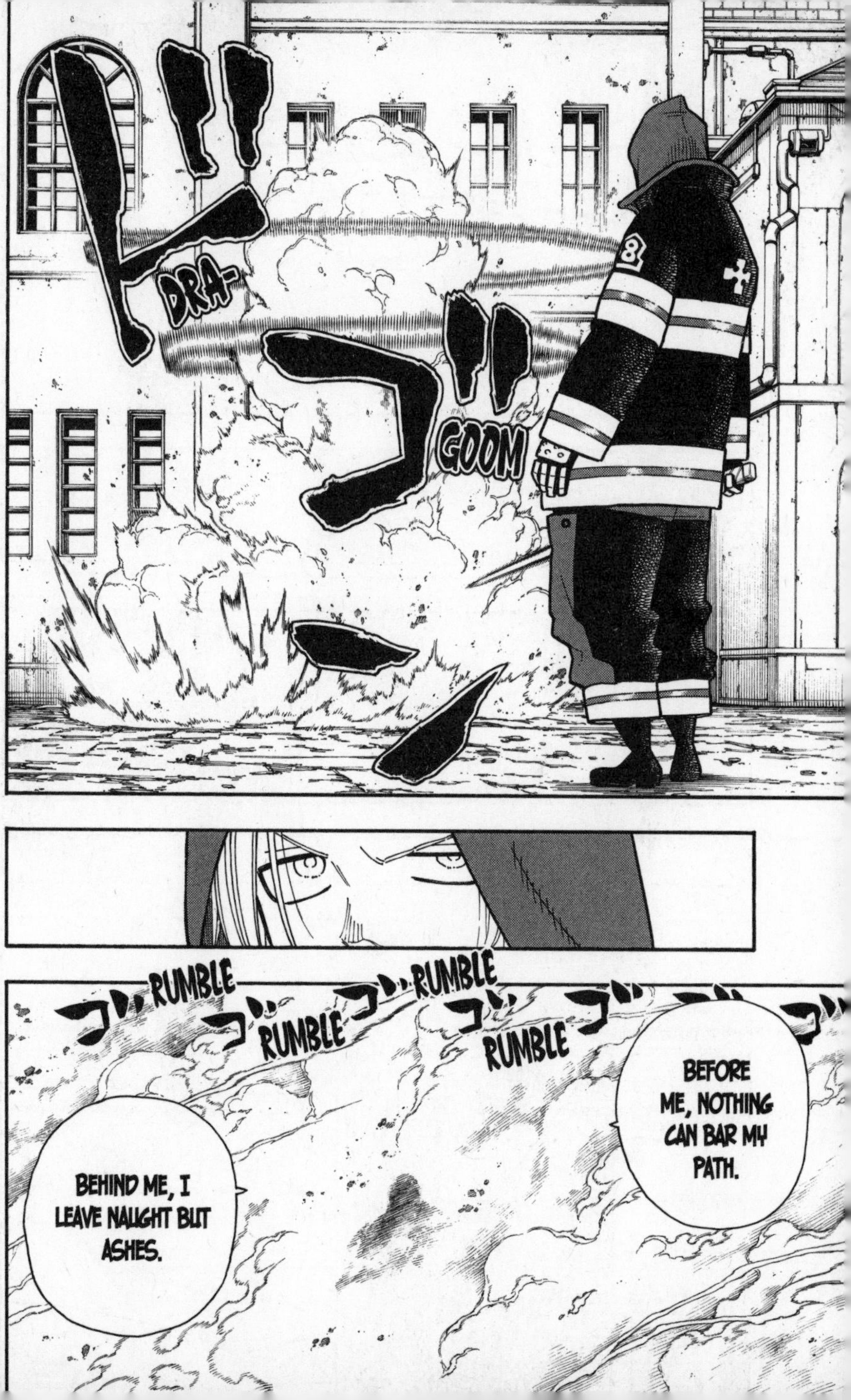
DRA-
GOOM
RUMBLE
RUMBLE
RUMBLE
RUMBLE
BEFORE ME, NOTHING CAN BAR MY PATH.
BEHIND ME, I LEAVE NAUGHT BUT ASHES.

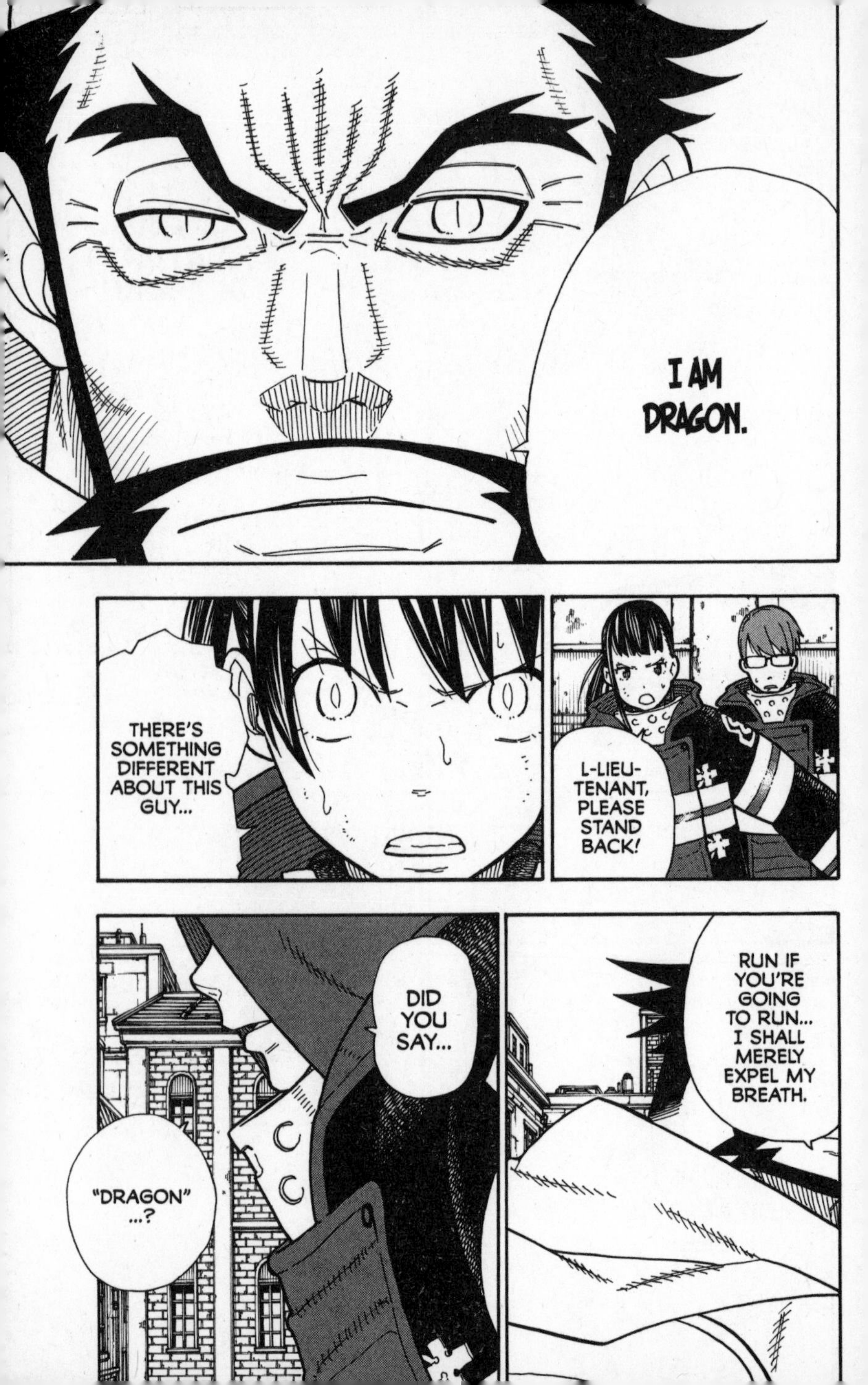
I AM DRAGON.
L-LIEU-TENANT, PLEASE STAND BACK!
THERE'S SOMETHING DIFFERENT ABOUT THIS GUY...
RUN IF YOU'RE GOING TO RUN... I SHALL MERELY EXPEL MY BREATH.
DID YOU SAY...
"DRAGON" ...?

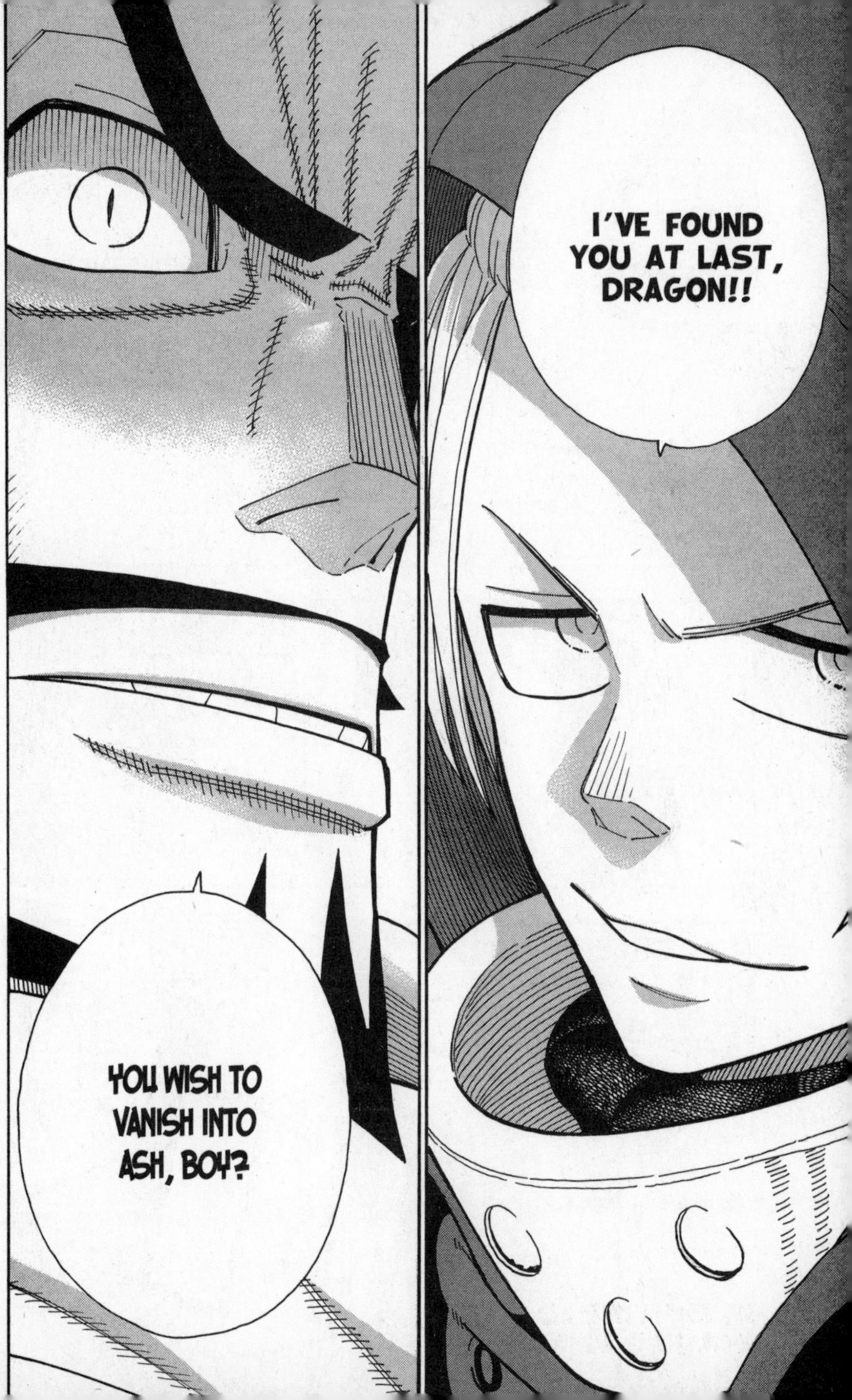
I'VE FOUND YOU AT LAST, DRAGON!!
YOU WISH TO VANISH INTO ASH, BOY?

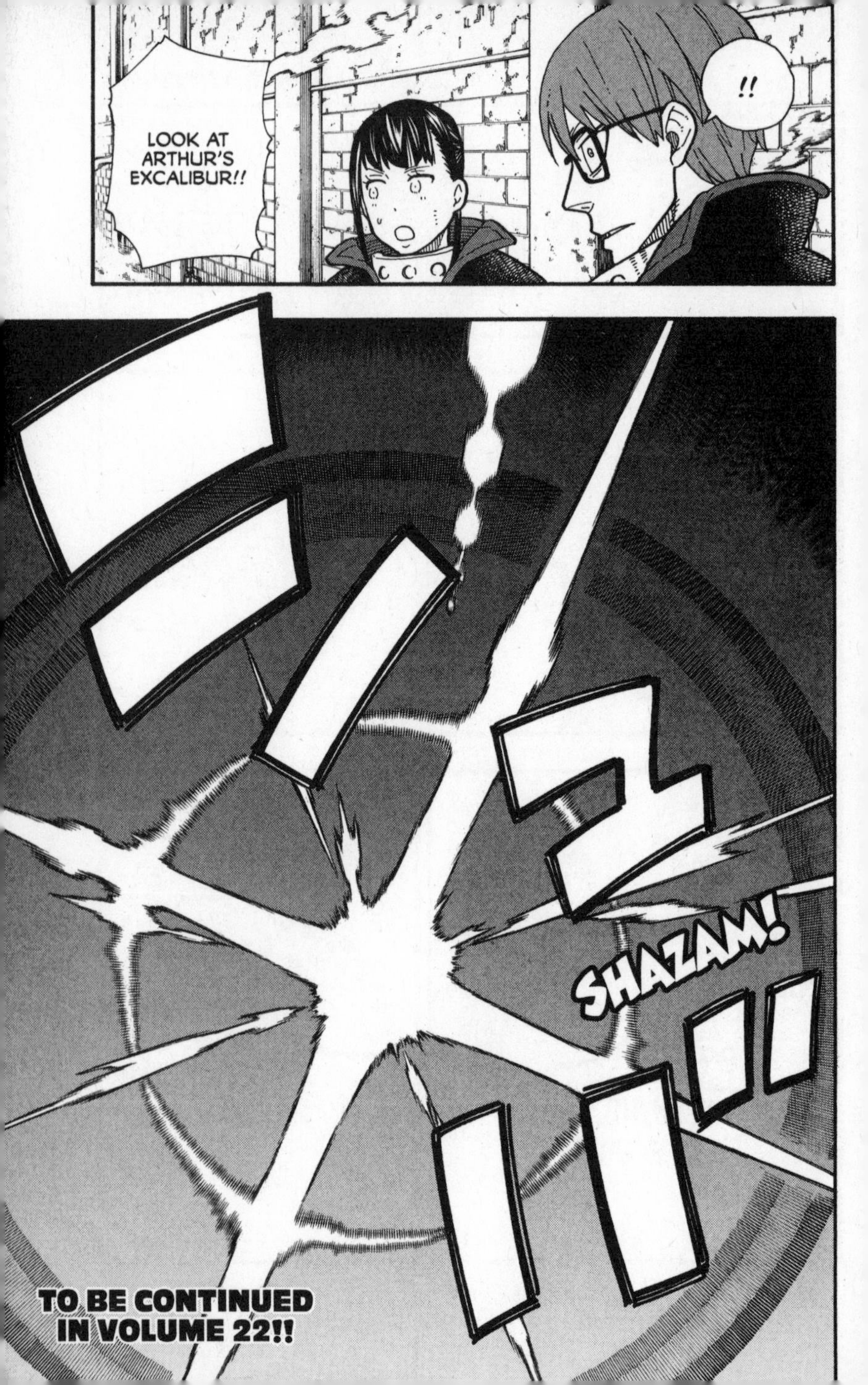
!!
LOOK AT ARTHUR'S EXCALIBUR!!
SHAZAM!
TO BE CONTINUED IN VOLUME 22!!

AFTERWORD MANGA ATSUSHIYA

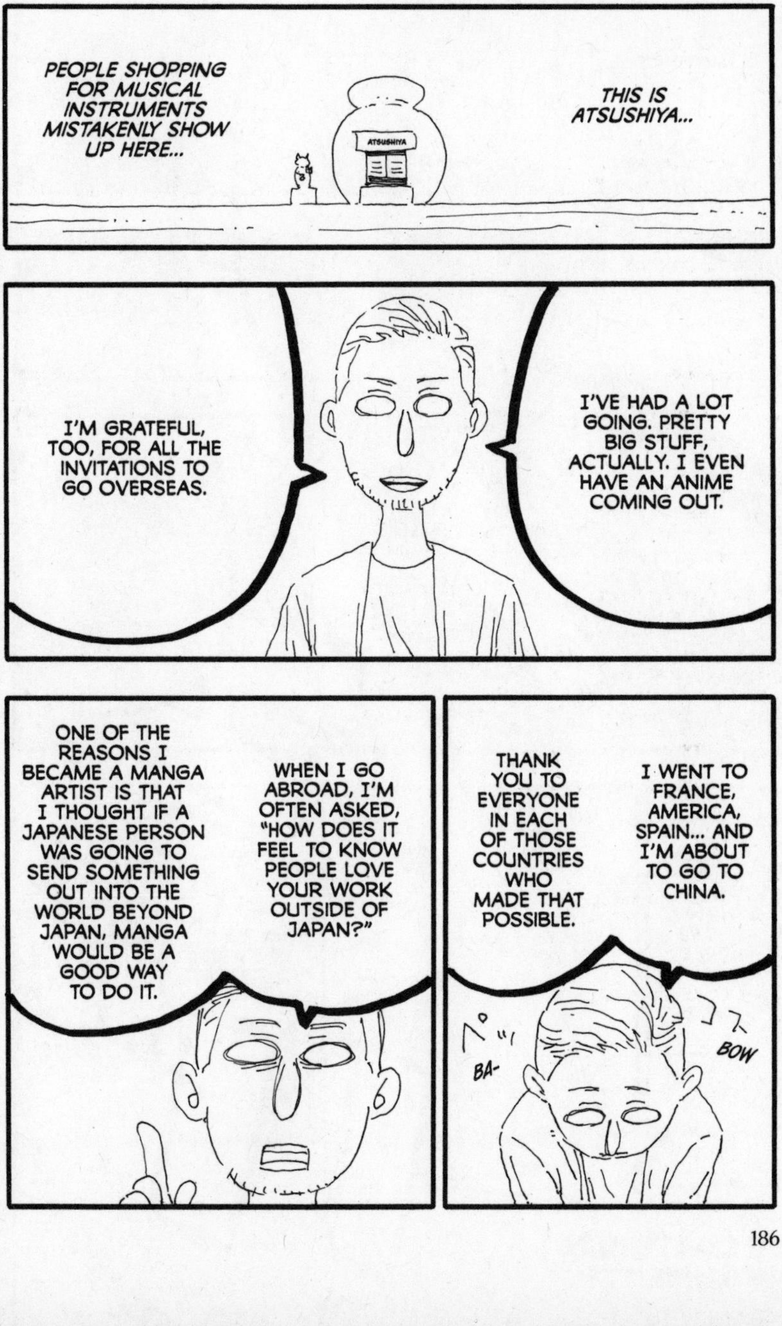
THIS IS ATSUSHIYA...
PEOPLE SHOPPING FOR MUSICAL INSTRUMENTS MISTAKENLY SHOW UP HERE...
ATSUSHIYA
I'VE HAD A LOT GOING. PRETTY BIG STUFF, ACTUALLY. I EVEN HAVE AN ANIME COMING OUT.
I'M GRATEFUL, TOO, FOR ALL THE INVITATIONS TO GO OVERSEAS.
I WENT TO FRANCE, AMERICA, SPAIN... AND I'M ABOUT TO GO TO CHINA.
THANK YOU TO EVERYONE IN EACH OF THOSE COUNTRIES WHO MADE THAT POSSIBLE.
BOW
BA-
WHEN I GO ABROAD, I'M OFTEN ASKED, "HOW DOES IT FEEL TO KNOW PEOPLE LOVE YOUR WORK OUTSIDE OF JAPAN?"
ONE OF THE REASONS I BECAME A MANGA ARTIST IS THAT I THOUGHT IF A JAPANESE PERSON WAS GOING TO SEND SOMETHING OUT INTO THE WORLD BEYOND JAPAN, MANGA WOULD BE A GOOD WAY TO DO IT.

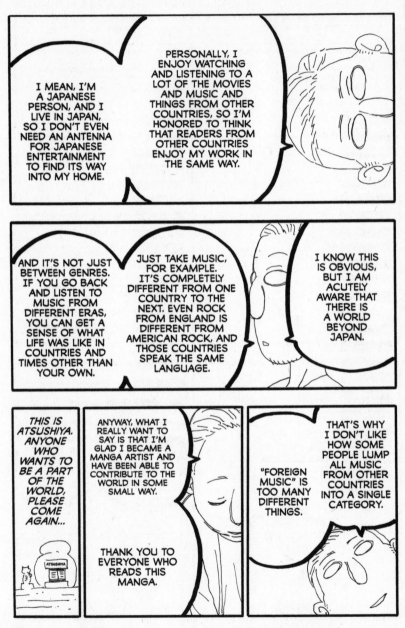

PERSONALLY, I ENJOY WATCHING AND LISTENING TO A LOT OF THE MOVIES AND MUSIC AND THINGS FROM OTHER COUNTRIES, SO I'M HONORED TO THINK THAT READERS FROM OTHER COUNTRIES ENJOY MY WORK IN THE SAME WAY.
I MEAN, I'M A JAPANESE PERSON, AND I LIVE IN JAPAN, SO I DON'T EVEN NEED AN ANTENNA FOR JAPANESE ENTERTAINMENT TO FIND ITS WAY INTO MY HOME.
I KNOW THIS IS OBVIOUS, BUT I AM ACUTELY AWARE THAT THERE IS A WORLD BEYOND JAPAN.
JUST TAKE MUSIC, FOR EXAMPLE. IT'S COMPLETELY DIFFERENT FROM ONE COUNTRY TO THE NEXT. EVEN ROCK FROM ENGLAND IS DIFFERENT FROM AMERICAN ROCK, AND THOSE COUNTRIES SPEAK THE SAME LANGUAGE.
AND IT'S NOT JUST BETWEEN GENRES. IF YOU GO BACK AND LISTEN TO MUSIC FROM DIFFERENT ERAS, YOU CAN GET A SENSE OF WHAT LIFE WAS LIKE IN COUNTRIES AND TIMES OTHER THAN YOUR OWN.
THAT'S WHY I DON'T LIKE HOW SOME PEOPLE LUMP ALL MUSIC FROM OTHER COUNTRIES INTO A SINGLE CATEGORY.
"FOREIGN MUSIC" IS TOO MANY DIFFERENT THINGS.
ANYWAY, WHAT I REALLY WANT TO SAY IS THAT I'M GLAD I BECAME A MANGA ARTIST AND HAVE BEEN ABLE TO CONTRIBUTE TO THE WORLD IN SOME SMALL WAY.
THANK YOU TO EVERYONE WHO READS THIS MANGA.
THIS IS ATSUSHIYA. ANYONE WHO WANTS TO BE A PART OF THE WORLD, PLEASE COME AGAIN...
ATSUSHIYA

ARROW

AFFILIATION: KNIGHTS OF THE ASHEN FLAME UNDER THE EVANGELIST
RANK: PILLAR BODYGUARD (GUARDIAN)
ABILITY: THIRD GENERATION PYROKINETIC

Attacks with a bow-and-arrow made of flames

Height	169cm [5'6.5"]
Weight	54kg [119lbs.]
Age	24
Birthday	December 20
Sign	Sagittarius
Bloodtype	A
Nickname	Arrow
Self-Proclaimed	N/A
Favorite Foods	None
Least Favorite Food	None
Favorite Music	None
Favorite Animal	None
Favorite Color	None
Favorite Type	None
Who She Respects	The Evangelist, Commander Shō
Who She Hates	No one
Who She's Afraid Of	No one
Hobbies	None
Daily Routine	To protect Commander Shō
Dream	None
Shoe Size	25.5cm [9]
Eyesight	1.5 [20/12.5]
Favorite Subject	None
Least Favorite Subject	None

ASSAULT

AFFILIATION: KNIGHTS OF THE ASHEN FLAME UNDER THE EVANGELIST
RANK: SPECIALIZED SLAUGHTER SOLDIER (EX-DESTROYER)
ABILITY: THIRD GENERATION PYROKINETIC

Attacks with large-scale missiles made of flame

Height	182cm [5'11.5"]
Weight	80kg [176.4lbs.]
Age	28
Birthday	May 5
Sign	Taurus
Bloodtype	A
Nickname	Bloody Fire Blast, Assassin of the Abyss, Perfect Soldier
Self-Proclaimed	I am I.
Favorite Foods	That thing at the cabaret club, that had a nice, salty flavor. What was it…?
Least Favorite Food	None
Favorite Music	That song I heard at the cabaret club that made my heart rise above all care. What was that feeling…?
Favorite Animal	Cats
Favorite Color	Black, yellow
Favorite Type	Someone with black hair, pigtails, bright yellow upturned eyes, and, well, she'd have to be petite and cute, with a boyish speech pattern.
Who He Respects	Lazy people; my own, untrained self
Who He Hates	Ne'er-do-wells who fight against the Empire, people who take over at a hotpot meal
Who He's Afraid Of	Who He's Afraid Of: My self when I cannot master my training.
Hobbies	Training. Improving myself.
Daily Routine	Undergoing all manner of training, preparing myself to easily accomplish any mission.
Dream	To see the world that exists when my training is complete.
Shoe Size	28.5cm [12.5]
Eyesight	1.5 [20/12.5]
Favorite Subject	Training
Least Favorite Subject	None

Translation Notes:
Six-legged gold, page 58

Gold the Destroyer is enjoying some golden wordplay. In the original Japanese, she starts by counting, and when she gets to "six," she switches the word for "six (*muttsu*)" with the word for "bug (*mushi*)." She then thinks of Ujikintoki, which is a flavor of shaved ice including green tea syrup and red bean topping, but more importantly, the *kin* in *kintoki* means "gold," and *uji* is a homonym with the word for "maggot." Ujikintoki reminds her of simple *azuki kintoki*, which is shaved ice with red beans but no green tea. Next she associates it with *kuri kintoki*, the chestnut variety of red bean shaved ice. This, in turn, reminds her of *kuri kinton*, or mashed sweet potatoes and chestnuts, a food eaten at New Year's representing wealth (the *kin*, once again, meaning "gold"). This reminds her of *uji kinton*, which is the green tea variety of this food, and brings us back to bugs.

FIVE GOLD.

SIX-LEGGED GOLD.

THE WORLD OF CLAMP!

Cardcaptor Sakura
Collector's Edition

Cardcaptor Sakura:
Clear Card

Magic Knight Rayearth
25th Anniversary Box Set

Chobits

TSUBASA Omnibus

TSUBASA WoRLD CHRoNiCLE

xxxHOLiC Omnibus

xxxHOLiC Rei

CLOVER Collector's Edition

KC/
KODANSHA
COMICS

burn, 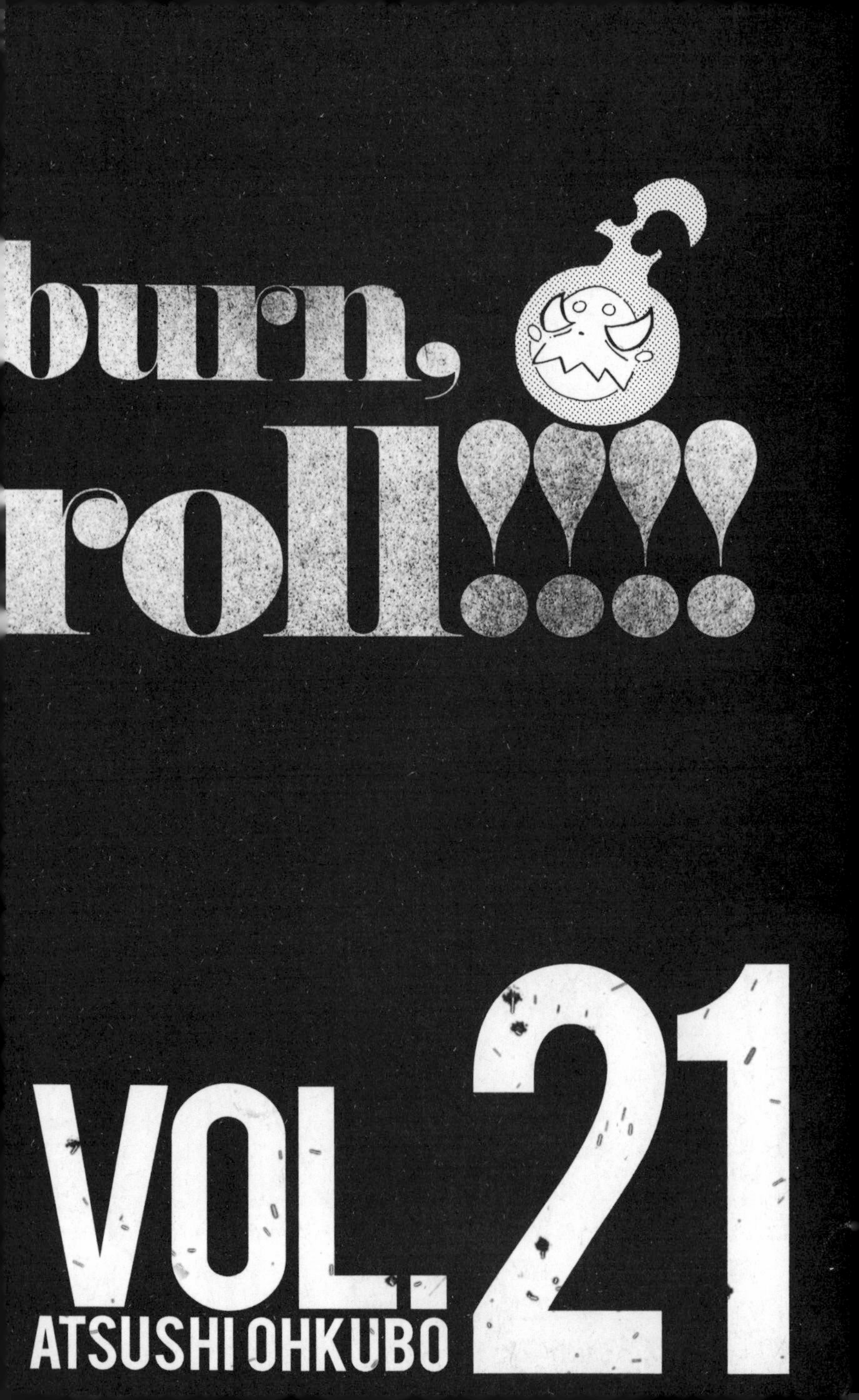

roll!!!!

VOL. 21

ATSUSHI OHKUBO